Women and European Politics

Women and European Politics

Contemporary Feminism and Public Policy

Joni Lovenduski

The University of Massachusetts Press
Amherst

First published in the United States of America
by the University of Massachusetts Press
Box 429
Amherst Ma 01004

Printed in Great Britain

Library of Congress Cataloging in Publication Data

Lovenduski, Joni.
Women and European politics.

Bibliography: p.
Includes index.
1. Women in politics—Europe.   2. Feminism—Europe.
3. Women in trade-unions—Europe.   I. Title.
HQ1236.5.E85L68 1985   305.4′2′094   85-16501
ISBN 0-87023-507-9
ISBN 0-87023-508-7 (pbk.)

For my parents

Contents

Defining Feminism; The Rights of Women: Antecedents; Legal and Socio-Economic Background; The Emergence and Development of European Feminism; The Rights of Women: Organisations; Britain; Germany; France; Russia and the USSR; The Nordic Countries; The Hapsburg Empire; Catholic Europe: Italy, Spain and Belgium; International Feminism; The Achievements of First-Wave Feminism

Feminism as a Social Movement; The Preoccupations of Feminism: Theory, Strategy and Tactics; Britain; The Netherlands, Denmark and Norway; Italy; France; Sweden; West Germany; Feminism and Political Change: Greece, Spain and Portugal; State Socialist Women's Movements; Second-Wave Feminism and the Political Mobilisation of Women

Political Participation; Political Interest; Political Ideology: Women's 'Conservatism'; Political Activism; Explaining Gender Differences in Political Activism; The Political Participation of European Women: Numerical versus Corporate Channels; Britain; Italy; France; West Germany; The Nordic States; Spain, Portugal and Greece; Women and Parties in State Socialist Systems; Political Parties and the Participation of Women

Women and Trade Unions in the European Liberal Democracies; Sweden; Italy; Britain; West European Unions; Women and Trade Unions under State Socialism; Business Associations; The Absence of Women from the Corporate Channel

List of Tables

Preface

A motivation for writing this book is my belief that discrimination on the grounds of sex is morally wrong and politically unwise. As a member of the sex which is discriminated against I hold these views strongly. I also believe that sex equality will come about only when women make use of the full array of political weapons available to them to achieve it; that is, political activity is essential to the struggle for women's liberation. It is as a political feminist that I have chosen my subject.

However, it is as an academic political scientist that I have written about it and as such I have made use of a wide variety of the analytical methods available to the discipline. Although mainly descriptive, this study makes use of the insights of the various schools of political analysis as and when they have seemed useful. I have aimed to outline the political roles of women in one particular geographical area and identify a number of themes which make them comprehensible both to specialist and non-specialist readers. I have been unable to identify one mode of political analysis which facilitates the achievement of that aim and as a result have no particular methodological insights to offer. My approach is essentially an eclectic one.

Although the second wave of feminism has brought in its wake a thriving women's studies discipline, sources for an inquiry of this kind are problematic. Data on women's political representation and participation are not systematically kept in many countries and are often not available to a foreign researcher when they are. And source material for the academic study of the women's movement has also posed difficulties. Basically, the academic investigation of a contemporary movement involves the use of press reports, movement documentation, interviews with participants and observers and academic accounts of these. The press cannot, by its very nature, provide either systematic or continuous coverage. The focus of journalism is on the newsworthy, and follow-up tends to be sporadic or non-existent, a syndrome which has the effect of distorting the movement activities and events. For example, readers of the British popular press during 1983 and 1984 would have had difficulty in avoiding an impression that there were no forms of feminist activity or groups in existence other than the peace women's camp at Greenham Common. The movement had ostensibly died. Yet in the London area alone numerous groups were advertising some forty or fifty different activities per month in the feminist press (see, for example, any issue of *Spare Rib* during 1983 or 1984).

Press distortion is a common problem in social science research, as is the presence of bias in participant documentation. As it happens, women's movement documentation is particularly difficult to use, reflecting as it does the great diversity of opinion which exists amongst feminists. In addition, there are difficulties with feminist academic sources. These arise from the fact that the women (and men) who have studied women's movements in different countries have varied in the sorts of academic training which they have had. Thus, the British movement is most often analysed by social scientists of one kind or another, whilst the French or Italian movements may be more likely to be described by those who have a background in the arts. Such differences lead to different emphases, and it is ultimately impossible to be certain that accounts have been standardised or otherwise rendered perfectly comparable. Readers should note, therefore, that what follows inevitably involves a considerable amount of interpretation and reconstruction.

The factual material which is included is, to the best of my knowledge, the most accurate and up-to-date available. For its provision I am grateful to numerous staff at the European London embassies who have often taken great pains to provide it. Also invaluable was participation with Jennifer Corcoran in the 1983 study funded by the EEC and led by Giovanna Zincone on the role of women in the decision-making arenas of France, West Germany, Italy and the United Kingdom, which is cited throughout the text. A further and extremely helpful source of information and insight has been Karen Beckwith of Oakland College, Michigan, who kindly made available to me her unpublished work on women in Italian politics. Elizabeth Meehan also allowed me to read some of her unpublished work. Mike Hopkins of the Loughborough University Library has been consistently helpful, as have the inter-library loan staff there. Judith Evans, Vicky Randall and Chris Wrigley have read and offered helpful advice on the various chapters as I have written them. Paul Byrne, Tony Burkett, Willy Paterson and John Whittaker have patiently read through and commented on the whole manuscript. They, as well as Edward Elgar, my editor, have been unfailingly supportive and encouraging. Patricia Swift has once again cheer-fully typed and retyped various version of the text. To all of them are due thanks, with the normal reservation of responsibility for errors to myself.

Joni Lovenduski
January 1985

List of Abbreviations

ADF	Allgemeine Deutsche Frauenvereine
ALRA	Abortion Law Reform Association
APEX	Association of Professional, Executive, Clerical and Computer Staff
ASTMS	Association of Scientific, Technical and Managerial Staffs
AUEW(TASS)	Amalgamated Union of Engineering Workers (Technical and Supervisory Section)
BDF	Bund Deutscher Frauenvereine
BIFU	Banking, Insurance and Finance Union
CBI	Confederation of British Industry
CDU	Christlich Demokratische Union Deutschlands
CGIL	Confederazione Italiana del Lavoro
CGT	Confederation General du Travail
CIF	Centro Italiano Feminile
CISL	Confederazione Italiani Sindacati dei Lavoratori
CLPD-WAC	Campaign for Labour Party Democracy Women's Action Committee
COHSE	Confederation of Health Service Employees
CREW	Centre for Research on European Women
CSU	Christlich Soziale Union in Bayern
DC	Democrazia Cristiana
DK	Dansk Kvindesamfund
DP	Proletarian Democrats
EC	European Commission
EEC	European Economic Communities
FDP	Frei Demokratische Partei
GMWU	General and Municipal Workers Union
IAW	International Alliance of Women
ICW	International Council of Women
ILO	International Labour Organisation
ILP	Independent Labour Party
LO	Confederation of Swedish Trade Unions

MLD	Movimento di Liberazione della Donna
MLF	Mouvement pour la Liberation des Femmes
MVM	Man-Vrouw-Maatschappij (men-women-society)
NAC	National Abortion Campaign
NALGO	National Association of Local Government Officers
NAPO	National Association of Probation Officers
NJACWER	National Joint Action Campaign for Women's Equal Rights
NOW	National Organisation of Women
NUM	National Union of Mineworkers
NUPE	National Union of Public Employees
NUSEC	National Union of Societies for Equal Citizenship
NUWSS	National Union of Women's Suffrage Societies
PCE	Partido Communisto de España
PCF	Parti Communiste Francais
PCI	Partito Communista Italiano
PLI	Partito Liberale Italiano
PRI	Partito Republicano Italiano
PS	Parti Socialiste
PSDI	Parti Socialdemocratica Italiano
PSI	Partito Socialista Italiano
PSOE	Partido Socialista Obrero Español
RPR	Rassemblement pour la République
SACO	Association of Salaried Employees and Civil Servants
SFIO	Parti Socialist (Section Francaise de l'Internationale Ouvriere)
SMs	Social Movements
SMOs	Social Movement Organisations
SPD	Socialdemokratische Partei Deutschlands
SPUC	Society for the Protection of the Unborn Child
TCO	Central Organisation of Salaried Employees
T&GWU	Transport and General Workers' Union
TUC	Trades Union Congress
UCD	Unión de Centro Democratico
UDF	Union pour la Democratie Française
UDI	l'Unione Donne Italiane
UIL	Unione Italiana del Lavoro

USDAW	Union of Shop Distributive and Allied Workers
WSPU	Women's Social and Political Union

1 Introduction

Amongst the more compelling reasons for embarking upon a study of women and European politics is that it has, until recently, been a neglected area of concern. Lately, the growth of women's studies has generated a variety of accounts of women's economic and social roles, but outside of the United States, women's political position has received relatively little attention. Indeed, detailed studies of women's political roles began to appear in the academic journals only during the 1970s. Prior to that, although gender differences in political matters did not go unnoticed, they were not really regarded as a legitimate concern for political scientists. The preoccupations of the discipline were such that, except in voting studies, it was sufficient to regard women's political marginality as an analytical constant which warranted little or no investigation. Only when women became noticeably more politically effective did they receive more systematic attention from scholars (Lovenduski, 1981b). Thus, the study of women in politics has been dictated more by events than by disciplinary imperatives. A consequence of this has been, as we shall see, the continued existence of important gaps in our knowledge both of women and of political life.

Gender differences in political behaviour are often imperfectly understood and left unexplained. Alternatively, they are exaggerated and explained in pejorative terms which stress the ways in which women fall short of men in the political world. It is arguable, of course, that the very act of scrutinising gender differences tends to lead to their exaggeration, because only a small proportion of either sex are politically active. That may be so but, just as differences in men's political roles reflect differences in their overall social and economic positions, so do those of women. And not only is women's political position a sensitive indicator of their overall status, it is also part of the means by which that status might be altered.

The political inequalities experienced by women are symptomatic of inequalities which pervade economic, social and domestic life. Alterations in any one of those spheres ought to be accompanied, therefore, by alterations in political roles. Such changes have been apparent throughout history but have been particularly evident in the twentieth century. Women have been mobilised into the workforces as a result of war or labour shortage, and have been expelled during peacetime or recession. Family patterns have been altered by changes in reproductive technology as well as by alterations in divorce laws and employment roles. Since the Second World War the two most important such changes have been the increasing entry of married women into paid employment and great improvements in both the techniques and availability of birth control. These developments have taken place against a background of increased access to education, longer life expectancies, better standards of health and child care and increased general prosperity.

Thus, whilst marriage and family production have remained popular with women, their significance has been altered by employment outside the home, by rising divorce rates and by decreasing family size. At the same time as families have become more dependent upon the earning powers of both spouses, women have become less dependent upon men. Successive cohorts of women have had higher rates of labour-force participation. State-regulated maternity benefits as well as smaller family size have meant that the fall in economic activity rates which accompanies childbearing has been compressed into a shorter and shorter period of time. Whilst motherhood remains an important and demanding role for women, it is no longer possible for policy-makers to regard it as their only role.

Many of the advances made by European women were made possible by the achievements of the first wave of feminists who fought for reforms in family, employment and educational provisions as well as for suffrage. Over the years since the movement first appeared (mainly in the last quarter of the nineteenth century), demands made by women for civil, social and human rights were gradually met. The general direction of change has been towards an improvement in, if not the amelioration of, women's position.

Such improvement is in part a reflection of the dynamics of a general social progress made possible by the widespread prosperity of the post Second World War years. But it is also due to the fact that European women have been mobilised to achieve political change. This has taken a number of forms. Women have organised both independently and in conjunction with pre-existing political groups. *Ad hoc* activities have been tried, as have traditional political practices. And altogether new forms of political organisation have been devised by women who have sometimes been convinced that the political system had little to offer, a challenge to which political institutions have had to respond. Where independent political organisation has not been possible, states have been required by both economic and demographic imperatives to take into account the changing nature of women's roles.

The results have been mixed. Beginning with their opposition to the suffragists, European men have resisted efforts by women to achieve political equality. Although concessions have slowly been made, the citadels of power have been jealously guarded by men. Once the franchise was won, it seemed that women were not prepared to object to male political prerogatives. Thus, in 1955 a United Nations report on the political role of women in Europe concluded that 'the political role of women is extremely small and grows still smaller as we approach the centre of political leadership ... noticeable in the structure of the State and its political organs ... it is also to be found in the government service, the political parties, the trade unions. . .etc. Nor are there any perceptible signs of improvement in this respect' (Duverger, 1955, 123). In the Europe of the 1950s, with its egalitarian liberal and socialist traditions, and a history of a widespread movement for suffrage, women were still marginal to the political system.

Nearly thirty years later, after a decade and a half of the intensive agitation for women's rights which characterised the second wave of feminism, political equality continues to evade women. A senior British politician and Member of the European Parliament, Barbara Castle, observed that when it came to political careers 'A few women, with a lot of luck, have achieved what they wanted. But women as a sex are still undervalued and under-used' (*The Guardian*, 2 October 1984).

By 1985 women had nowhere attained representation in political institutions which was equal to that of men. Rarely were they represented at leadership level in proportion to their presence in the relevant population. Some of this has been due to self-selection. Women have not invariably sought a leadership role in every sphere of activity in which they have been present, and where they have sought change, responses have been mixed. However, in contrast to earlier experiences, political institutions in the 1980s are slowly admitting more women. The number of women in the governing elites of most European systems is gradually increasing. Sex equality has become part of the agenda of most governments, and political forms are giving way to economic changes. Slowly the political circumstances of women are altering.

This book is essentially an account of the progress which has been made so far. Its concentration on Europe is partly a matter of personal interest and partly a response to the focus of most studies on the United States. The political experience of European women has received scant attention and few comparative accounts have appeared. It is a rich area for research. Europe illustrates the immense variety of cultural contexts in which women have sought and exercised political rights. Liberal democratic and state socialist societies contain class, religious, ethnic and regional configurations which make for a variety of political traditions, all of which have had their particular effects on women. A shared history of major events and common trends of economic development and social changes as well as specific efforts at international harmonisation are also to be observed. A better object for comparative study could not be found.

This volume is structured around what I believe to be the main themes of the political behaviour of European women. The next chapter is an account of the first wave of feminism across Europe, whilst the third chapter, on the second wave of feminism, concentrates largely on Western Europe. Chapters 4, 5 and 6 cover the behaviour, attitudes and representation of women in important political institutions, and the final chapter is an account of contemporary public policy on women.

Each chapter both explores themes and considers their manifestation in a number of countries. The single-country expositions have been selected as representatives of particular types of practice, or institutional or cultural effect. In each case, those examples for which the fullest information is available are presented first. Inevitably, full accounts of practices in each country are not available, and rather than exclude an interesting example on which the available information is incomplete, these too have been included, normally after the fuller accounts have been presented. Hence, readers will be aware of an information 'tail' within each chapter. As far as possible a comparison between the state socialist and liberal democratic systems has been sustained, but this has necessarily been a limited exercise constrained both by a relative lack of data on Eastern Europe and important structural differences between the two types of systems.

Space has been another constraint. The political position of European women is contingent upon their economic and social roles, and recognition of this is evident throughout the text. However, in what is a rather long book, detailed accounts of social and economic trends have been omitted. Where important trends and changes are mentioned, readers are referred to the substantial literature on these areas. The central concern of this study is the political roles of European women, and it is to these that we now turn.

2 The First Wave of European Feminism

Defining Feminism

In the intellectual and political climate of the nineteenth century, feminism was both a logical extension of the egalitarian tenets of liberal and socialist philosophies and a response to outdated constraints on women's lives. The first recorded expression of the idea that women were the political equals of men occurred during the French Revolution (1789), but it was only in the second half of the nineteenth century that emancipation and suffrage groups began to be formed. These grew and coalesced to become, by the end of the century, a widespread movement.

European feminism was pre-dated by its American counterpart, which had a considerable international influence. But distinctively European influences were apparent. Feminism was a political phenomenon which was grounded in particular circumstances. In each country in which a women's emancipation movement appeared, it soon adopted forms and sets of preoccupations and practices which reflected national political life. Patterns of class stratification, religious allegiance, legal arrangements and political divisions combined to produce a variety of forms and types of women's emancipation movement. International in some of its concerns and universal in some of its demands, the first wave of feminism was, like its 1970s successor, also culturally specific. In addition, feminist demands have tended to change over time, which, combined with the great variety of their manifestations, makes it difficult to construct a single comprehensive definition. Feminism is and has been both a set of ideas and a social movement. Although many of the concerns of the first wave of feminism were also central to the second wave, important differences in organisational form and style distinguish the two. In particular, the individual leaders and hierarchical structures which characterised the first wave of feminism were deliberately avoided by the influential radical feminists of the later movement. Whilst the history of the early struggles for women's rights is often a

6

history of a few prominent individuals, in the second wave informally structured social movements are a more obvious focus for
attention. Self-help groups and groups which provide services to
other women were, of course, very much a part of the repertoire of
both waves of feminism. But the consciousness-raising groups and
non-hierarchical organisations favoured by the later movement
were unknown to nineteenth-century women.

There is clearly a danger that a definition which highlights
feminism's later forms may exclude many of its early adherents.
That danger is avoided if we begin with a simple working definition of feminism, which is then elaborated as our discussion of
first-wave feminism progresses and further elaborated as we consider its second wave. In such a construction we might reasonably
apply the term 'feminist' to all those nineteenth- and twentieth-
century women who supported efforts to ameliorate the condition
of women through publicly organised activity to achieve reforms
of the political, economic and social institutions which discriminated against women.

This definition focuses on activists and subsumes socialist and
bourgeois feminism. It is therefore extremely convenient in an
account such as this, concerned as it is with nineteenth-century
European feminism as a background to women's role in contemporary politics. But differences between the first-wave feminists were important. It should be remembered that socialist
women, particularly in Germany, vehemently objected to the
label of feminist and wished to distinguish themselves from the
middle-class rights movement of the bourgeois women. Nineteenth-century socialist feminists saw the root of sexual oppression in private property and felt that their goals would be realised
only in the radical transformation involved in the construction of
socialism. Bourgeois feminists, on the other hand, envisaged
significant improvements in women's status without social revolution. Both worked for shorter-term goals of reform, but socialist
women felt that the inequality which working men suffered was
evidence that even a successful campaign to reform women's
status would not significantly improve their position. They saw the
exploitation of working-class women as caused by capitalism
rather than by men (Boxer and Quatert, 1978b).

The relations between socialist and bourgeois feminist organisations varied considerably. The degree and kind of contact which
took place between them was a function of the role of class
hostility in the politics of each country's socialism. Where and
when class politics played a less hostile role there were often quite

high levels of cooperation. Religious affiliations too were important, with perceived clericalism on the part of women often costing
feminists the support of male socialists. Although the churches
rarely became a specific focus of feminist agitation, religion was
responsible for a considerable amount of the variation in the
national contexts in which feminism operated. Feminists in countries which were mainly Protestant often adopted a different style
and priority order and were able to form different political alliances than feminists in countries which were mainly Roman
Catholic.

Although there was never a golden matriarchal age of the kind
envisaged by some nineteenth- and twentieth-century feminists,
there is evidence that, prior to the rise of Christianity in Europe, at
least some women enjoyed a considerable amount of autonomy.
Later Roman Law, for example, gave married women considerable freedom and independence. But as Christianity became
dominant, women were deprived of those freedoms as laws and
customs came to reflect the rather pathological attitudes of some
of the first Christian leaders towards sex. In the ascetic ideal of the
early Christian theorists, sexual activity was carnal, marriage a
reluctant concession to the flesh, and women were regarded as a
major vehicle of sin; they were Tertullian's 'devil's gateway'.

Whilst Christian misogyny was not the only or even the most
important cause of the subjection of women, it was one of its
important ideological underpinnings. More direct causes are to be
found in economic processes and political and legal systems. The
political invisibility of women before the nineteenth century is an
important clue to the nature of their oppression. The rare early
cases of women's active participation in politics have been
regarded by historians as disruptive. Bridenthal and Koonz (1977,
3–4) point out that many observers regarded the presence of
women in politics as a sign of social decay. The women who by
accident or design did engage in the political fray were viewed as
exceptions and attracted special scrutiny as a result. Politics,
conventionally defined, was regarded as unnatural practice for
women, and political and legal institutions expressly denied them
citizenship.

But when we define politics more broadly to encompass a range
of social activities, we find many historical examples of women's
involvement being regarded as normal. Thus, letters, diaries and
memoirs of upper-class women throughout history reveal intense
involvement by them in the affairs of their families, their property
and their class. It has been possible to trace a political role for

bourgeois and aristocratic women through first-hand reports as well as through church history, changes in property and family law and recorded political activity. Peasant and working-class women, on the other hand, have normally only become visible when they have protested. Our knowledge of the lives of ordinary women even as recently as one hundred years ago is limited, and extending it raises considerable problems of historical research. The history of these women is often a history of the inarticulate and illiterate seen through the eyes of the literate and articulate. It is a history of women who have left no accounts of their existence. And whilst insights may be gained from aggregate data on vital statistics, second-hand reports and cultural artifacts, these are no substitute for contemporary first-hand accounts (Branca, 1978, 14).

Class lines have always divided gender lines in such a way that ruling class women have normally been more privileged than both men and women of lower classes. Similarly, women of dominant racial or ethnic backgrounds have had rights not possessed by minority women (Stern, 1934). Class has not only divided women and had a determining effect on the ways in which their lives have been ordered, it has also affected what we are able to learn about the lives of our foremothers. Concepts of class as well as gender must therefore be invoked if we are to establish accurately the political role of women (Fox-Genovese, 1982, 13). They should not be regarded as an unstratified mass of individuals whose political roles depend only upon their sex, as the following account shows.

The Rights of Women: Antecedents

Between the sixteenth and eighteenth centuries women were occasionally politically engaged, but largely as a result of their family status. As individuals they had no public voice. Residues of feudal law and even the retention of feudalism in many places meant that a women might succeed to various positions upon the death of her husband or father. For example, women could become reigning queens. At a more general level certain local elected offices, such as church-warden, were open to women. Pre-nineteenth-century Englishwomen had the right to vote if they were otherwise qualified. Individual women performed bravely in the English Civil War and the wars of the Fronde in France, but these activities too are likely to have been a by-product of residual feudal responsibilities. The English Revolution's only mass radical movement (the Levellers) did not include women in their political programme, and the idea that women should have political rights equal to those of men was not yet taken seriously (Vann, 1977, 209–10).

Scrutiny of the work of the major eighteenth-century philosophers reveals no strong trend towards stands being taken over opportunities, rights and freedom for women. This was true despite the fact that the ideas on which the women's subjugation was based were ones which Enlightenment thinkers may have been expected to attack. The primary intellectual concern of Enlightenment thought was the discovery of the nature of humanity. Thus, a place could easily be found for arguments about the role and status of women. But the question, if taken up at all, was given only passing attention. In the *Encyclopedie* Jaucourt took up the issue of male authority in marriage, concluding that it resulted from civil rather than natural law. His argument was threefold: (1) reason points to the natural equality of all humanity; (2) a husband does not necessarily have more bodily strength, wisdom or intelligence than a wife, and (3) even biblical requirements for the obedience of women are grounded in positive law. A number of philosophers, of whom Condorcet was probably the most prominent, pursued Jaucourt's train of thought, arguing for the equality of women from the standpoint of natural law. But the major concerns of the Enlightenment were elsewhere and some, such as Rousseau, explicitly opposed women's rights (Keinbaum, 1977, 220).

If not overconcerned with the injustice of women position, Enlightenment philosophers did at least raise the issue. And once expressed, the idea of women's equality began to gain some momentum. A feminist voice could be heard in the *cahiers* or lists of grievances which heralded the French Revolution. These included demands for legal equality, for equal education, for marriage law reform, for the protection of female trades from male incursion and occasionally for political representation. As the revolutionary impetus grew, women joined and occasionally led protests, forming their own political clubs, writing their own newspapers as well as being found in the normal supportive roles. By and large these women were responding to the needs of their class and were never an autonomous force, but they were nonetheless cohesive groups formed on the basis of a shared women's interest. The French Revolution in this respect mobilised the highest level of women's organised activity yet seen. It generated the first examples of club activities, political assemblies and journalism on behalf of women's rights (Graham, 1977, 238).

From these twin origins of revolution and Enlightenment thought came the first significant theoretical tracts on women's rights. Olympe de Georges' *Declaration of the Rights of Women* appeared in 1791 and was followed by Mary Wollstonecraft's *A Vindication of the Rights of Women* (1792). Wollstonecraft's point was essentially that the principles of the French Revolution (liberty, equality and fraternity) ought also to include women. Olympe de Georges demanded similar rights to men for the women of the French Revolution. Whilst Wollstonecraft's work was mainly a tract on education, Olympe de Georges argued that women should have economic and political power in a new society. Under Robespierre the Revolutionary Assembly in 1793 prohibited the further existence of any women's organisations and declared illegal and punishable any gathering of more than five women. Olympe de Georges was arrested and guillotined. However, her ideas were taken up by early socialists and feminists such as George Sand and Flora Tristan.

Important too in the development of feminist thought was the rise of liberalism. The Enlightenment had assembled a battery of ideas and theories which could be used in the feminist cause, including the ideas of reason, progress, natural law, the fulfilment of the individual, the power of education, the social utility of freedom from restrictions and equality of rights. These, suggest Evans (1977, 21), combined with the phenomenon of women organising over women's rights, were important to the intellectual climate which permitted the emergence of the nineteenth-century feminist movement. But more was needed. The ingredient of the liberal Protestant belief that the individual was responsible for his or her own salvation was also necessary, hence the Reformation was a further, if sometimes unlikely, source of feminist ideas. Whilst some of the religious denominations which appeared during the Reformation continued in the Catholic view that women were sources of evil, others went to some lengths to demonstrate the falseness of that belief. Lutheran and Calvinist theorists regarded the sexes as equal (in matters of religion), although in practice men tended to dominate the Protestant churches. And some of the new religious sects allowed women to play quite a prominent part.

Thus, Enlightenment rationalism, and Protestant moral imperatives fused in the creed of liberalism to generate demands for women's rights. The major statement of this fusion is John

Stuart Mill's essay on *The Subjection of Women*, first published in 1869 and translated worldwide. Mill's is a cogent statement of the liberal basis for women's rights. Equality is conceived of as the absence of barriers to equality, and women's emancipation is seen as the removal of women's disabilities. This entailed the granting of equal citizenship to men and women, giving women access to employment, training and education and, importantly, the removal of the excessive authority which the law gave husbands over wives. Such a programme, if fulfilled, would allow women a full individual development as well as serving the requirements of the market economy. Mill's commitment to women's emancipation had limitations, however. The ascribed unequal status of women was untenable because ascribed status itself was untenable. His primary concern was women of the bourgeoisie (Jayawardena, 1983b, 84), and he accepted the traditional family roles of men and women. He regarded the family as an essential institution and was unable, as Okin (1977, 230) writes, to perceive the injustice in a situation in which men could have a career and economic independence and a family whilst women were obliged, at best, to choose between them.

Liberal formulations were the founding political theories of nineteenth-century feminism, but it was socialist movements which offered the strongest and most sustained political support to demands for women's rights. Socialists devised the first political theory to encompass the rights of women, and socialist political parties were the first to include women's rights in their programmes and to allow women at their meetings. In 1891 the Second International mandated that member parties advocate the equality of women. Working-class women were interested in obtaining political and legal rights, but they quickly became disillusioned with middle-class feminism. The inadequacies of liberal feminist theory to proletarian needs soon led proletarian women to socialism, which had a tradition of concern for women's emancipation dating to the theories of the French Utopian socialists of the early and mid-nineteenth centuries.

Also heir to Enlightenment philosophy, socialism provided a theoretical alternative to liberal feminism and socialist women's movements were as prominent in many European countries as were the bourgeois feminist groups in the rights movement which gained increasing currency at the end of the nineteenth century. The seminal work of socialist theory on women at that time was probably Bebel's *Women and Socialism*, which was published in 1879 before Engels' *Origin of the Family, Private Property and the*

State (1884) and was later revised to include some of Engels' work. First called *Women in the Past, Present and Future*, Bebel traced the history of women in Western civilisation from its early Christian past to its communist future. An unfocused book with a content ranging from illustrative tales about women in other societies to detailed statistics on German prostitution, it was widely read and well received by women of its day. Bebel held that capitalism, with its invasion of cash into all social relations, was responsible for the lovelessness of bourgeois marriage and for turning working-class girls increasingly to prostitution. His belief was that given the advent of socialism, women would be free to opt for the traditional roles which, under capitalism, were closed to working women. In his rather confused view the solution to the woman question lay in the fight for equal rights and would be a by-product of the achievement of a socialist transformation of society.

Engels' arguments were a little more coherent. His thesis (which he declared in his preface, would have been that of Marx had Marx lived to formulate it) was that an evolution in the form of relations between the sexes had paralleled the historical stages of society: 'Savagery' and 'Barbarism'. In 'Savagery' humans lived in tribes, held women in common and engaged in promiscuous sexual relations, and offspring were communally supported. 'Savagery' gave way with technological change to the pairing families of 'Barbarism' under which developed wealth and civilisation. The desire to accumulate property led to enforced monogamy for individual women to assure legitimate succession. The accompanying institution was prostitution. For Engels the development of private property was responsible for the subjection of women. This could only be rectified by transcending capitalist property relations. Thus, women's emancipation lay in their integration into social production and industrialisation, which, as an expander of places in social production, was a liberating force. Full emancipation of women could only be achieved when socialism was established. Both theories had their flaws and were remarkably unsophisticated by comparison to those which would be produced by socialist feminists in the 1970s. But the two books were tremendously influential, widely read by women of their day as well as by the male leaders of the socialist movement (Boxer and Quataert, 1978b, 11–12). Their central message was that the socialist movement must be more important to its women members than the movement for women's rights, a contention which was accepted by socialist women of the time.

Legal and Socio-Economic Background

Much of the struggle for women's rights was the concern of socialist and bourgeois feminists alike. In the early nineteenth century, European women, in common with most men, had few legal or civil rights. But from the late eighteenth to the mid-nineteenth centuries the barriers depriving serfs of various rights were gradually removed, enabling them to hold property, enter the professions and dispose of their own persons freely. Women were not included in this general liberalisation. Politically, they had no right to vote or to hold public office. In parts of Eastern and Central Europe, women were forbidden to join political organisations or to attend political meetings. Economic restrictions were severe. Women were barred from owning property, their inherited wealth was transferred to their husbands upon marriage, and they were prevented from engaging in a trade, running a business or joining a profession. Legally, women were not persons in most countries. They could not enter into contracts and were considered to be minor persons in the eyes of the law, subject to the powers of their fathers or husbands. Double standards also found legal expression whereby divorce, where it existed, was often relatively easier for husbands and more difficult if not impossible for wives. And finally, women were discriminated against in education. The new secondary school systems then being established were either exclusively for boys or made separate, inferior provision for girls. Gradually women came to feel the injustice of these restrictions and began to organise first over legal reform and then for educational and economic rights. Experience of trying to obtain rights in other areas soon led to a perception that political rights were essential to any strategy for women's emancipation. The experience of having to request rights from the men who controlled the political institutions was an early legacy of feminism, and the path from the first organisational efforts over property rights to the movement for women's suffrage was similar in most countries. But specific cultural features were also important and no country's experience of first-wave feminism was identical to that of any other. Whilst the objectives for which women were fighting were everywhere similar, the barriers which had to be overcome were often quite different. Hence, different tactics were used, different organisational forms were developed and the movements themselves had different levels of success.

Legal barriers were the first obstacles which had to be overcome. Closely intertwined with religious traditions, legal impediments to women's rights were formidable. But some systems were more tractable than others. Three legal traditions provide the frameworks in which European countries have made laws which affects women's status. These are Roman Law, English Common Law, and Customary, or Community Law. Roman Law is essentially private law, a means of the regulation of private relationships between individual citizens. By contrast, English Common Law is a system of public law, with private matters between citizens traditionally only of interest if they affect the Crown, other cases being left to equity or ecclesiastical courts. Accordingly, systems based upon Roman Law are more likely to intervene in family relations than is the case with the English system (Paulson, 1973, 43). In France, Roman Law was made more restrictive with the installation of the Code Napoleon after the revolution. An advanced and comprehensive legal system, the Code was particularly repressive of women's rights, and French women had been legally better off in the eighteenth century than they were in the nineteenth. Article 213 implanted the idea of a wife's subordination to her husband, Article 214 compelled her to live in his choice of domicile, Article 217 decreed that she could not dispose of her personal income without his permission and Article 267 that he kept the children in the event of divorce. In the case of adultery, a husband could be punished by the refusal of permission to marry his mistress, but the wife faced a prison sentence of between three months and two years (Article 298). Thus, Napoleon made the husband as much the dictator of the home as he himself was of France. The precise and detailed nature of the Code meant that it lacked flexibility and could be altered only with great difficulty (de Reincourt 1974, 311). It was to take French women some years before they were able to obtain the major legal reforms necessary to obviate the worst manifestations of the Code, much of which was still in operation at the end of the Second World War.

The third type of legal tradition is that in which law is based in the usages and practices of the community rather than of the courts as such. Found in the Scandinavian countries, the basis of law in such a system is custom. Women's rights advocates in those countries confronted a private law which operated within local habits of behaviour. Demands made by early Scandinavian feminists were for rights which neither custom nor public law yet granted all men, and logically, in order for the law to change, customs had first to be altered, presenting reform-minded women with substantial obstacles and tactical problems (Paulson, 1973, 94).

Systems based on Roman Law were to prove the most intractible over questions of women's emancipation, however, and these were also normally systems in which the predominant religion was Roman Catholic. Essentially, women enjoyed more legal rights and social freedom in the countries which were most influenced by the Reformation, especially its Calvinist variant. Vann (1977, 211–12) compares the USA, England, the Netherlands and Scandinavian countries with France and finds that in each case the Protestant countries were more liberal in their treatment of women. He also refers to the large number of feminist leaders who gained their first public experiences in participation in one or other of the Protestant sects, most significantly the Quakers in Britain and the USA.

Religious affiliations also influenced the strength and political complexion of a country's feminist movement. The Belgian and Dutch examples illustrate well the obstructive capacities of the Catholic Church. Both countries had constitutional parliamentary political systems dominated by the middle class at the end of the nineteenth century, providing what proved elsewhere to be virtually hothouse conditions for the emergence of a strong bourgeois feminist movement. But Protestant Holland developed such a movement, whilst Catholic Belgium did not. In France and Italy the intractable opposition of the Catholic Church to feminism led to a distinct anti-clerical element in the feminist movement, and in these two countries feminism was little stronger politically than it was in Belgium.

In religious and legal canon women's status resulted from their family roles. But these had altered significantly as a result of the industrial revolution—so significantly that it could be argued that women were stripped of their political power by the industrial revolution and feminism was the first manifestation of an inevitable movement to regain it. Accordingly, those scholars who have examined the role of women and politics in history have concentrated a considerable amount of their attention on women in the family. Their recurring perception has been that although formal political action has won major advances, women's lives have been more profoundly affected by structural changes in society. In pre-industrial society the common mode of political activity for women was involvement in the family strategy for social mobility. But the economic changes of the industrial revolution eroded women's family power as the family itself changed from a more or less self-sufficient production unit (outside of which survival was almost impossible) to a 'non-producing collectivity of consumers'. (Bridenthal 1977, 6–7). In the generation of adults alive when the Reformation began, almost all women were involved in the world of production, and all married women, so far as we know, were also involved in the world of reproduction as they had no means of controlling their fertility. Socialisation was not the exclusive concern of mothers, and parental responsibility was substantially shared with other relatives and the community at large. At that time the career of mother as we understand it today does not appear to have existed.

But once the industrial revolution was underway, women's position changed rapidly. The decline of domestic production and attendant changes in the structure of the family, rapid urbanisation, and so on, all had an effect. Although the nature of a woman's work in pre-modern society had been essentially bleak, it was productive and she reaped a power benefit as a result of the importance of her contribution. With the advent of industrial society and factory production, women's work role was diminished (Branca, 1978, 11). Conflict between two female roles was introduced by the separation of productive work from the home. A decline of women's work opportunities was initiated for married women in particular. These developments took place in three broad phases, varying in timing and strength from country to country, but everywhere following roughly the same pattern. From about the mid-eighteenth century onwards European society began to be transformed. A revolution occurred involving a sharp increase in population growth, the spread of commercial economic relationships and the industrialisation process itself. The mid-eighteenth century population explosion had placed immense burdens on women as mothers who gave birth more frequently and had more small children to care for. The sheer increase in the numbers of people forced the family to innovate to fulfil its support functions. Women's economic roles did not alter fundamentally but their work methods did. Men moved to support their families by working outside it, but women worked increasingly to supplement the family income, and did this mainly inside the home.

Until at least 1850 agricultural production maintained its hold; indeed, the introduction of labour intensive root crops, such as potatoes, increased the amount of agricultural work available to women. Domestic manufacturing followed agriculture as the second-largest employer, with its importance due at least in part to the fact that it demanded less of a transition for women than a movement to factory-based manufacturing employment (Branca, 1978, 25; Tilly and Scott, 1978, 14–15). The first phase of the industrial revolution was a transitional one characterised by the expansion of domestic manufacturing and the rapid development of the textile industry. As textiles came more and more to be factory produced, employment for married women declined (McBride, 1977, 283).

Two basic models were apparent in this phase. In the first model, which was to be found in Britain and Germany, domestic manufacturing began to give way to the factory system in the second half of the nineteenth century, initially in the cotton trade and later in the wool and linen trades. In England cotton manufacturing quickly gained over the entrenched rural production of wool and linen. Although at first rural and a heavy employer of married women, the industry soon moved to the factories and the cities. In Germany textile production was soon overwhelmed by the English competition, so that a brief increase in domestic manufacturing employment for women was soon reduced.

In the second model, a combination of a strong tradition of home working, adaptive rural workers and a vigorous export market (e.g. in French Silk) in cloth which was difficult to mechanise kept the domestic manufacturing system going for much longer. Indeed, in France, Belgium and northern Italy it was maintained until well into the twentieth century. In France as well, the take-off in population growth was modest by comparison to other countries, which enabled more people to stay in the countryside. Manufacturers were forced either to seek their workers there or do without. In all three countries the employment of women in agriculture remained high (Branca, 1978, 31). Elsewhere, however, the first phase ended by about the 1880s. During the second phase, which continued from about 1880 to the end of the Second World War, the structure of manufacturing changed towards heavy industry, concentrating increasingly on mining, metallurgy and machinery. At about this time there developed the notion that a single male wage ought to be sufficient for family support and that, concomitantly, women should retire from paid work upon marriage. In this system women were considered to have only a domestic role, broken, perhaps, by a temporary employment experience.

The third (and present) phase is the one which began at the end of the Second World War and has been characterised by married women re-entering the workforce in increasing and significant numbers in a diversity of occupations (McBride 1977, 283–4). Thus, from the beginning of the industrial revolution the economic role of the married woman was under pressure, except during periods of labour shortage (e.g. the two world wars). The pressure, however, differed for women of different classes. Whilst working-class women often became cheap labour for factory manufacturing, bourgeois women became isolated in their homes, kept occupied by the domestic science industry and the cult of the home which was prevalent in the nineteenth century.

In the 1850s a surplus of women over men led in Britain to about a quarter of the women between the ages of forty and forty-five being unmarried. Discussions of what to do about these 'surplus women' provoked for the first time widespread questioning of the idea that to be unmarried was to be surplus (Jayawardena, 1983b, 87). Middle-class women began involving themselves in charitable and social work leading eventually to the growth of women's careers in these areas as they came to be taken over by the state. Also evident were rises in the numbers of jobs in teaching and nursing, with teaching in particular getting a boost from new trends in providing education for girls. These new careers were important for middle-class women, as were those which became available in the white-collar clerical sector important to working-class women. Both required skills and were respectable, clean and afforded some opportunity for social contact. But until well into the 1940s both attracted mainly single women looking forward to leaving work upon marriage (Branca, 1978, 57; Tilly and Scott, 1978, 149–50).

For women, then, the industrial revolution was for the most part disadvantageous in that the fundamental change in the mode of production created more employment outside the home but only for a minority, or, more correctly, for young women. Technical progress opened up few 'masculine' trades to women who moved into mainly new areas of work. Women's wages rose as developments progressed but not to the level of men's. Such modifications did allow greater mobility and choice, but only for a minority of women. The more important feature of the revolution for women was the decline in the position of married women who were removed from the labour force (McDougall, 1977, 275; Tilly and Scott, 1978, 126). By the end of the period, middle-class women had relinquished their previous hold on family business finance, losing their knowledge of business and the professions, and working-class women had been deprived of family-based employment (Pope, 1977, 303).

Thus, one effect of the industrial revolution was to increase the extent to which women were dependent upon men. At a time when notions of equality and freedom became a part of the political discourse, women's position became more circumscribed. The evidence which exists suggests that the great religions and powerful states and other important institutions had already systemised and extended patterns of male dominance across most societies. The new work patterns brought in with the rise of industrial capitalism confirmed that dominance and, indeed, increased it. Thus, when feminism first emerged as an organised force, it was in a society in which women were at a political, social, economic and legal disadvantage. The European women's movement, as it developed through the nineteenth and early twentieth centuries, had to construct an agenda of reforms designed to redress economic as well as legal and cultural disadvantages. Indeed, it was to be some time after they first organised that feminists were to turn their attention to demands for political rights.

The Emergence and Development of European Feminism

If political rights were not the first objective of Europe's early feminists, political factors were, nevertheless, important in determining the shape and scope of their movements and campaigns. Political moderation, guaranteed civil liberties, the growth of middle-class liberalism and the increasing powers of legislative assemblies all favoured the development of large, active bourgeois feminist movements. These conditions obtained in Britain and the Nordic countries, which also featured Protestant cultures. In other areas such conditions were absent, notably in the Hapsburg Monarchy, the German Empire, Tsarist Russia and the European Catholic countries subject to laws grounded in the Napoleonic code. There the movement for women's emancipation developed differently, producing weak growths or, alternatively, large but divided movements (Evans, 1978, 91). Thus, the English movement, which was also the largest, was able to contain both bourgeois and socialist feminists. But bitter and acrimonious splits characterised many of the continental movements. Politically, liberals were the natural allies of women's rights; and feminists benefited significantly from the presence of strong liberal parties. Where liberal parties were weak or had not been formed and representative institutions themselves either did not exist or were underdeveloped, the initiative passed to the socialist women's movement.

Much of the division between socialist and bourgeois feminism was organisational. Differences tended to be largely tactical ones as both wings of the movement pursued broadly similar goals. The early feminists campaigned against women's abuse in prostitution, the sexual abuse of children, marital rape and for educational, employment and legal rights as well as for temperance observation and moral reform. Between them the nineteenth and early-twentieth-century feminists covered much of the ground that was to be retraced and elaborated by the second wave of feminism in the late 1960s and 1970s (see Jeffreys, 1982, Randall, 1982, Spender, 1983).

The Rights of Women: Organisations

Although the interests of first-wave feminism were wide ranging, their organisations reflected the narrower range of concerns on which it was possible to develop campaigns. The focus of the various associations changed as goals expanded. Evans (1977, 38) describes a characteristic progression from what he called 'moderate' or 'rights' feminism to 'radical' feminism concentrating on winning the vote. In his view feminism tended to widen its objectives over time. The progression had a logical order. The earliest organisations concentrated on amending double standards and obtaining legal rights, particularly for married women. Agitation over educational provision and employment rights soon followed, after which it was but a short step to the demand for women's suffrage. The goal of women's suffrage obtained increasing support from feminists during the period between the turn of the century and the outbreak of the First World War. As the war ended and many, but not all, countries extended the vote to women, new concerns of peace, welfare and sex equality at work came onto the feminist agenda. But without the unifying capability of the struggle for the vote, the movement in the inter-war years seemed dispersed and less powerful than it had been, surprising virtually all commentators when events gave it occasional prominence.

   The struggle for legal changes focused upon both property and family law. The progress which was made was especially important for married women and, in the case of property law, for middle-class women. Early agitation was over the acquisition of adult status by women and the protection of their property after marriage. In England, for example, women had no right of ownership. Some protection existed for French women, for whom marriage contracts could provide minimal protection, but French women too had little control over their own finances. Demand for reform of family law was manifested in the form of petition for divorce law reform as early as 1815. Laws were gradually altered, but it was well into the twentieth century before men and women began to be treated equally in divorce law, and divorce itself remained a relatively rare occurrence before about 1920. Italy did not get a divorce law until the 1970s, and other Catholic-dominated countries waited even longer. Eire, for example, still made no provision for divorce in 1985.

Perhaps the most widespread of all feminist preoccupations was the movement for educational opportunities for women. The issue was first raised at the end of the eighteenth century, with discussion extending throughout the nineteenth century and well into the twentieth century. Several positions were taken in these discussions, ranging from a conservative view that women were naturally intellectually inferior, to a wholly egalitarian view of the relative intellectual capacities of men and women. At the conservative end of the spectrum, thinkers like Proudhon reckoned that women had about one-third of the intellectual capability of men, and Rousseau argued that a domestic education alone was most suitable for women. Pseudo-scientists joined in with the view that any education was dangerous to women's reproductive functions, while phrenologists pointed to women's physically smaller brains as evidence of lesser ability. More moderate positions accepted that men and women had equal intellectual abilities but saw sex roles as immutable and requiring differing educations. Education was, however, an essential part of the new middle-class culture, and even where treated differently, women were not excluded. Gradually consensus that women's education should be improved emerged when the Taunton Commission in England called in 1864 for schools which provided girls with a sound basic education. In France the Ferry Law of 1882 capped a steady improvement in facilities for women (Tilly and Scott, 1978, 160). Differences remained, however, with girls in Catholic countries more likely than boys to have a religious education. In all countries girls were more likely to leave school after primary level. Nevertheless, changes were well underway and by 1900 women were almost as likely as men to be literate in countries like France and England. The spirit of reform touched all of the industrialising countries. By the end of the century women's education had become a feminist issue across Europe, with many feminists believing that education was the key to emancipation. Girls schools were established in London in the 1850s, and some of the Lycées were opened to French girls in the 1860s. Reforms in higher education soon followed (Branca, 1979, 174).

Access to education altered women's opportunities in significant ways. Primary education for girls was essential in their move from domestic service employment to shop or clerical work. Middle-class women were able to find respectable work outside the home, and the expansion of the educational sector itself opened new opportunities. The advent of the woman teacher affected concepts of education and school management, and teachers were amongst the earliest of the so-called women's occupations to unionise (Tilly and Scott, 1978, 189). Feminists in most countries soon became engaged in the struggle over the right to work, asserting that women had the right to enter the traditional male domains. Entry into the professions was fought for in Sweden, Norway, Britain, France, Russia and Italy and was won in most places, for most professions (except the clergy) by 1914 (Branca, 1978, 178).

Success in the struggle for women's rights to vote was more mixed, a reflection in part of the very different conditions under which it took place. Not all European women were without voting rights in the nineteenth century. In the aftermath of the revolutions of the 1830s and 1840s, a number of continental jurisdictions based suffrage on a combination of property ownership and class-membership qualifications, a practice designed to secure the positions of elites. These measures granted some women taxpayers the right to vote. Hence, Austria extended proxy votes in 1849 to women of the landed class in communes, and similar concessions were made in Brunswick in 1850, in Prussia and Westphalia in 1856 and Schleswig Holstein in 1867. Suffrage at municipal level was also occasionally granted in Anglo-American and Scandinavian countries. Within the framework of Victorian rhetoric, women's moral superiority to men entitled them to a special voice in matters of education, morals and charity, all best attended to at the level of the home or the community. Diplomacy, fiscal regulation and the stuff of national politics were, of course, reserved for men (Paulson, 1973, 95–7).

The demands of the feminists for full enfranchisement were political, as was opposition to them. They were not taken seriously by politicians. The most effective opposition to the women's suffrage movement was the prevailing ideology about the nature of women and their position in the idealised bourgeois family system. Aspects of this were internalised by feminists themselves, and a consequent emphasis upon not contravening relevant norms made for a subtle undermining of feminism itself (Billington, 1982, 672). At first women's claim for a vote assumed the equality of all, and therefore women emphasised their common humanity in order to claim their natural rights. But as the concept of equality came to lose meaning during an era of increasing social differentiation, women turned to arguments based upon expediency. Equality arguments had presupposed the independent individual and were necessarily humanistic and progressive. Arguments based on expediency, however, could be used both by radical feminists who felt that women had something different to offer and presented a new vision of society, or by conservative feminists who saw women as acting safely within existing parameters but as the reforming or philanthropic sex (Moore, 1982). Thus, women's suffrage was sought on more than one ideological basis, and potential existed for a variety of alliances between suffrage and other political organisations.

The battle for women's right to vote was considered by many European feminists to be their key struggle, and suffrage organisations eventually appeared throughout the Continent. But these fared quite differently and produced quite different levels of commitment and organisational forms in each national context. Nevertheless, in each country the suffrage movement was the high tide of the first wave of feminism, which gradually moved from primarily economic aims to primarily political ones eventually focusing on the vote. Once the vote was gained, the movement's aims became divided and contradictory, and it began to contract on all fronts, the promise of the suffrage left unfilled.

With hindsight it is evident that feminists had expected too much from the enfranchisement of women. The vote is, after all, an instrument capable of expressing only the most simple differences in political goals. Other political activities are more expressive and subtle and lead more certainly to political influence. But the struggle for the franchise was the opening salvo in women's battle for political equality with men, a battle which was led by feminists. It set the scene for later confrontations and conditioned later political developments amongst women. For these reasons the first-wave feminist movements and particularly the suffrage campaign in each country merit some examination if we are to understand properly women's role in contemporary European politics. Accordingly, the remainder of this chapter will consist of discussions of the different experiences which comprised the first wave of European feminism.

Britain

English feminism was primarily a liberal phenomenon deriving its formulation of problems, and its instrumental, pragmatic approach from mid-nineteenth-century liberalism and earlier reform movements. Its early demands were concerned more with the removal of restrictions rather than positive change or assistance for women. In campaigns over property rights and the removal of protective legislation women demanded full adult status. They asserted not the absolute equality of men and women but women's right to equality before the law. In general the movement combined a belief in the particular nature of women with liberal individualism to produce a characteristic bourgeois feminist mixture which fitted well with the prevailing domestic ideology and its somewhat contradictory tenet that women were subordinate to men but were their moral guides (Caine, 1982, 540).

England had what was probably the strongest of the European bourgeois feminist movements, and world-wide was certainly one of the largest and earliest, second only after the USA in its dates of formation (Evans, 1977, 68). Feminist ideas spread amongst English middle-class women as early as the 1840s, and sporadic efforts to improve the status of women occurred as early as the 1830s, when Owenites and Utopians were propagandising views which included equality for women. But there was no sign of an organised movement before the 1850s, when the Langham Place group first formed in London. The group gathered around Barbara Leigh Smith and Bessie Rayner Parkes, both women from radical Unitarian backgrounds. In 1856 Smith organised a committee to collect petition signatures favouring the passage of the Married Women's Property Bill then before Parliament. In 1858, in conjunction with Mrs Jameson, a noted feminist author, the group founded the *Englishwomen's Journal*. The Langham Place group was both a centre for discussion and activity and a focus for recruitment to the movement. Into its circle came Emily Davies, who led the campaign to open higher education to girls, and Elizabeth Garrett Anderson, the first British woman doctor. It was this group which in the 1860s began the suffrage campaign (Banks, 1981, 29–34).

Their first concern, however, had been to improve the position of married women in the law and to obtain other legal rights for women. Employment opportunities soon became a focus of activity, as did education (Randall, 1982, 140). In 1859 the group founded the Society for Promoting the Employment of Women, which operated an employment exchange and set in motion experimental placements of women in hitherto masculine occupations. In the drive for education for girls the main struggle eventually took place over access to higher education. Here issues of standards split the campaigners. Emily Davies was uncompromising in her position against special courses and education for girls, but others argued that special education and entrance examinations were tactically necessary given the relatively poorer education girls got at lower levels of the system (see Hollis, 1979, 154; Banks, 1981, 41).

English feminism had also a strong moral dimension with movements for moral reform centering around the removal of double standards, as well as temperance and purity campaigns. Josephine Butler's campaign to repeal the Contagious Diseases Acts was an important example of the movement's concern over both morals and double standards. The acts required prostitutes in garrison towns to subject themselves to compulsory physical examination and treatment for disease. This, for Butler, was tantamount to licensing sin. Opposition was mobilised in 1869 when Butler founded the Ladies National Association Against the Contagious Diseases Act. Kept separate from the suffrage and other struggles, as it cost the movement some respectability, this was essentially a campaign against double standards, but one which involved middle-class women in knowledge of the lives of prostitutes and of venereal disease. For women like Butler the campaign became central to the women's movement in that it involved most elements of women's oppression (Caine, 1982, 548–9).

The middle-class nature of British feminism did not prevent its proponents from making efforts to organise and assist working-class women. Emma Paterson's work in founding the Women's Protective and Provident League in 1879 was the first such attempt. Paterson saw protective legislation as an attempt to restrict the employment of women to the benefit of men (which it often was), and hence the League opposed it. Later its successor, The Women's Trade Union League, took similar positions. Such views antagonised male trade unionists and were unattractive to women workers, but Paterson had a point. Protective legislation did keep women out of many unpleasant work-places and situations, but it served to exclude women from many well-paid jobs in male-dominated industries. Little effort was made to improve the appalling conditions which obtained in many women-only industries. The view of Paterson was that protective legislation was no solution to women's work-place problems, which would be better resolved by the unionisation of women—a practice which would also prevent women from undercutting men in the labour market. The whole issue of protective legislation was a difficult one, pointing up the differences between middle-class feminists and working-class women throughout Europe. Its mishandling in England was merely one example of many instances in which middle-class women took initiatives on behalf of those whose lives they failed to understand.

Of all the campaigns begun in the nineteenth century, it was the suffrage movement which was the most important, not least because it united almost all feminists in the pursuit of a single goal. The women who first concerned themselves with the issue believed that they would be included in the suffrage extension of the 1832 Reform Bill. In the event, that bill specifically enfranchised 'male persons' and was thus the first to bar the women's vote in England. Organisational activity did not immediately follow, however. Early Chartists had included votes for women in their demands but soon dropped it in favour of male suffrage alone (Branca, 1978, 181–2). By 1851 Anne Knight had founded the Sheffield Association for Female Franchise, which succeeded in bringing the issue before the House of Lords. But the movement's real beginning was in Langham Place, where Barbara Bodichon (née Leigh Smith) played a leading role in bringing forward the issue by organising a petition to Parliament to be presented by John Stuart Mill (Banks, 1981, 119). Mill included women's political rights as part of his campaign platform when standing for election to the House of Commons and had publicised the issue via numerous articles and pamphlets (Branca, 1978, 182). His objective was that the Second Reform Bill should drop 'male' from the expression 'male person', thus enfranchising middle-class members of both sexes (de Reincourt, 1974, 315). The debate over the Second Reform Bill was the background for the foundation of Bodichon's London-based Women's Suffrage Committee and Lydia Becker's Manchester Women's Suffrage Committee in 1865. When demands to include women in the Second Reform Bill failed in 1867, these and other local groups federated into the National Society for Women's Suffrage. This new organisation was comprised mainly of women who knew each other from other (mainly feminist) campaigns and who had organisational experience. It was a movement led by politically experienced women and a direct development from earlier concerns over other feminist issues (Banks, 1981, 119). Under Lydia Becker's influence, the society pursued a strategy of drumming-up support from left Liberals to put private members bills on women's suffrage before Parliament. The organisation was successful in getting the issue debated almost annually between 1870 and 1901. A limited suffrage was sought which extended existing kinds of voting rights to women (Evans, 1977, 65). A few gains were made. In 1869 women ratepayers obtained the municipal suffrage, and in 1870 Jacob Bright introduced the first women's suffrage bill to get a second reading in Parliament (Branca, 1978, 182). But the Conservative Party was strongly opposed to the issue; even when a bill got past a Conservative minority in the Commons, it fell foul of their large majority in the House of Lords. And Liberal support was not all that reliable. When it came to tacking women's vote onto the Reform Bills of 1867 and 1884, many Liberals were reluctant to do so, fearing that women's inclusion would lose the reform. In addition, the women's suffrage movement itself was split during the 1870s, kept going mainly because of the support it seemed to be obtaining in the House of Commons. Hence, during the twenty years after 1867 the suffrage movement made only minimal gains. Other feminist causes were more successful, however. Educational and professional opportunities improved; women were admitted to Oxford and Cambridge; and in 1876 women gained the right to register as physicians. Teaching, nursing and other professions expanded, providing more opportunities for women, and the same years saw the launching of the moral-reform movement, thus widening the feminist net (Evans, 1977, 66). Such changes provided the foundation for the spread of support for women's suffrage, which by the turn of the century generated a mass movement. Women had begun to work through the political parties for the vote. The Conservative Primrose League and the Women's Liberal Federation were formed by the early 1890s. In 1897 another women's suffrage bill got a second reading, once again raising hopes. Feminists centralised their efforts to organise huge petitions in its support by uniting in the National Union of Women's Suffrage Societies (NUWSS) presided over by Millicent Fawcett. The bill failed.

Closely linked to the Liberal Party at first, the feminists gradually became disenchanted by the unreliable nature of Liberal support and began to gravitate toward the Labour movement. The Independent Labour Party (ILP) was feminist from its inception, and other socialist groups soon began to support women's suffrage. Whilst many Liberals had been reluctant to support the women's vote, fearing that, once enfranchised, women would vote Conservative, Labour had no such objections. This was because Labour support for women's votes was support tied to universal suffrage for women and men, a position which had hardened by 1907, when it became party policy. By this time disillusionment with both the Labour and Liberal parties had spread amongst feminists, and the initiative passed to the militant suffragettes led by Emmeline Pankhurst (Banks, 1981, 125).

Emmeline Pankhurst had organised the Women's Social and Political Union (WSPU) as a single-issue organisation whose sole goal was obtaining votes for women. Her supporters were prepared to use more militant tactics than Fawcett's moderate suffragists. Called suffragettes, members of the WSPU soon were using violent means to draw attention to their cause, a development unique in the history of the European women's movement. They attracted considerable publicity as the women chained themselves to buildings, attacked government figures and burned railway stations. Extremely active, they set fire to 107 buildings during the first 7 months of 1914. Imprisoned, the women resorted to hunger strikes, resulting in forced feeding which horrified public opinion (Branca, 1978, 183). Until 1906 the WSPU was a tiny provincial group financially dependent on ILP support. By 1907 it had broken with the Labour movement and engaged in a brief flirtation with the Tories, changing its aims from universal to limited suffrage. Thus, from 1907 onwards the WSPU had the same aims as the moderate members of Fawcett's NUWSS. Differences were over tactics. Banks believes that the activities of both groups made little difference as male Labour and Liberal activists were not prepared to support limited suffrage, and the Tories, although not in principle opposed to women's voting rights, contained numerous virulently anti-feminist members (1981, 126–7).

Liberal pragmatism and willingness to support many bourgeois feminist demands meant that the emergence of socialist feminism in England did not really occur until quite late on in the movement's development. This accorded with a rather late polarisation of politics along class lines in England, which itself may have been due to the Liberal capacity for class collaboration. The Labour Party, although Marxist influenced, was less so than its continental counterparts and was more gradualist as well. Its women's section, established in 1906, was also cautious and gradualist. By 1910 it had 5,000 members and, like the party itself, a mainly middle-class leadership. Because of Labour Party links with the constitutional suffragists, the Women's Labour League was, according to Evans (1977, 176), at least as feminist as it was socialist, at any rate until the vote was gained.

Women's suffrage was first obtained on a limited basis in 1981 in an Act which introduced adult suffrage for men but restricted it to women over thirty who were local electors or university graduates or the wives of local electors. Age rather than property restrictions allayed fears of a women-managed nation but also reduced the chance that the enfranchisement of women would assist only the Conservatives. The 1918 Act was celebrated as a victory by feminists and seen as the beginning of a step-by-step progression to full political equality for women (Banks, 1981, 129). The movement continued to be active until women were granted the vote on the same terms as men in 1928, after which it has popularly been deemed to have disintegrated.

In fact the British Equal Rights movement continued to be active, but the issues over which it was concerned were less spectacular and also less unifying than the suffrage cause had been. Although detailed exposition of the work of English first-wave feminists after 1928 is beyond the scope of this book, it is nonetheless worth pointing out that women continued to be active over such matters as birth control, equal pay, divorce and various aspects of welfare provision as well as involving themselves in the international peace movement. Much of this activity took place in the trade unions which were to emerge as an important locus of activity in the second wave of British feminism (see Banks, 1981; Evans, 1977; Wilson, 1980; Spender, 1983).

It is true, however, that the movement for women's political rights and representation subsided once the vote was won. Organisations continued to exist, but membership and activism fell off. The National Union of Women's Suffrage Societies was renamed the National Union of Societies for Equal Citizenship (NUSEC), which, along with the Women's Freedom League and the Six Point Group, acted to ensure that women's rights issues were kept before Parliament. The fact that women had not yet achieved full suffrage kept them fairly active during the 1920s, when several feminist groups worked together on national and international issues. The 1919 Sex Disqualification (Removal) Act gave women access to the professions and may be seen as paving the way for other changes in the 1920s, so that by 1928 much of the programme of first-wave feminism had been achieved (Banks, 1981, 163–4). The fight for equal pay and the removal of marriage bars continued, but the infusion of feminism with welfare politics does not appear to have produced a particularly sparkling mixture. The

Second World War interrupted feminist activity, after which activists concerned themselves almost exclusively with the construction of the welfare state. That state was built along lines which assumed a woman's dependence upon her husband, and whilst this was challenged by numerous feminists at the time, their voice went unheard until the second-wave movement emerged in strength (Wilson, 1977, 154).

In Britain, as elsewhere, the impact of the vote itself was disappointing, with women MPs few in number and women's voting patterns not significantly different from men's. Although evidence can be produced to demonstrate that the men who passed many of the post-war reforms which expanded women's rights believed that there was a distinctive women's vote, there is little systematic evidence that such a vote existed.

Germany

German feminism was as much influenced by its temporal and national setting as it was by the mainstream of feminist ideas. Its history is significantly different from that of the English movement and in common with other continental women's movements featured a bitter split between socialist and bourgeois feminists. The split was particularly acrimonious, reflecting a highly polarised society. Many of the characteristics of the nineteenth-century German feminist movement were a response to the authoritarian nature of the Second Reich, which lasted from 1871 until the end of the First World War. Important too was the revolution of 1848, in which woman had been active and which led to the passage of the Preussiche Vereinsgesetz (Prussian Association Law) in 1851, a combination law which forbade women from belonging to political groups or from organising politically. The law was repealed only in 1908, hence it was in effect for most of the history of first-wave German feminism and was of considerable importance in its organisational development.

The first recorded agitation for women's rights was by Louise Otto-Peters, who during the revolutionary period around 1848 demanded political equality between women and men, arguing that women should be able to earn an independent income as the only way of avoiding marriage. Otto-Peters founded the first German women's journal called *Frauen Zeitung* in 1849, the programme of which included demands for the full array of economic and political rights for women (Mies 1983, 123). *Frauen-*

Zeitung was produced in Saxony between 1849 and 1850 and moved to Thuringia where it appeared until 1852. Various women's educational associations also appeared around 1848, but fell foul of the Association Law under which the local police were given the power to determine what comprised a political association (Gerhard, 198, 562).

Only in 1865 did the first signs of an organised movement appear when Louse Otto-Peters founded the General German Woman's Association (Allgemeine Deutsche Frauenverein or ADF). Its aims were modest and directed at improvements in education and property rights. Across-the-board-equality goals were eschewed in the hope of avoiding shutdown by the police. Caution was thus an early hallmark of the German feminist movement, a tendency encouraged by the retreat of Liberalism between 1865 and 1870 (Evans, 1977, 105). However, the ADF appears to have pursued more radical objectives in non-Prussian areas of the German Empire where the Association Laws did not obtain. In the industrial areas of Saxony the organisation was based on principles of self help and political autonomy. There the ADF was involved in campaigns over equal pay, educational improvement, the vote and the peace movement. Sympathetic to the Social Democrats, the ADF nevertheless opposed the social democratic view that it was only the position of working-class women which was unequal (which its proponents intended to alter by excluding women from industrial work altogether). Bourgeois feminists held the view that, even in conditions of low pay, working was better than not working because it at least excluded women from domestic slavery (Kawan and Weber, 1981, 424). Cooperation between feminists and the political left was, however, unusual as the major effect of the political ban was a conservative dogmatism and hesitancy on the part of the bourgeois feminist movement.

In 1984 the ADF tried to bring under its aegis the various women's philanthropic societies founded since its inception by establishing of the Federation of German Women's Associations (Bund Deutscher Frauenveriene or BDF). In the BDF, women favouring the moderate line were in the majority. The BDF concentrated on the educational preparation of women for the professions, with the needs of the state and community its overriding concerns. It remained aloof from the struggle for political rights (Gerhard, 1982, 563). By 1902, however, the moderates' grip on the Federation had relaxed as membership swelled to the 70,000 mark and many of its original leaders retired or died. The leadership passed to more radical women, including Maria Stritt, Minna

Cauer, Anita Augsburg and Lida Gustava Hetman. Under their influence the BDF mounted a campaign against the 1896 Civil Code, largely because it had done nothing to improve the lot of middle-class women. At the same time the moral-reform issue became important as Josephine Butler's work in England became known and attracted increasing support. The Federation converted to the Abolitionist cause in 1902.

Apart from their activities in the BDF, the more radical of its leaders also founded a number of separate organisations. In 1902 Augsburg, Hetman and Stritt founded the German Union for Women's Suffrage in Hamburg, where the political ban on women did not obtain (Evans, 1977, 107). In 1899 a movement against the state regulation of prostitution was also begun in Hamburg, and Helene Stocker's Bund für Mütterschutz was also established. These and other organisations were united in the union of Progressive Women's Associations (Verband fortschrittlicher Frauenvereine), which campaigned for their aims. the leaders belonged to each other's associations and campaigned for each other's causes. Their ideology was at root one of liberal individualism, which in Wilhelmine Germany had radical implications and was disliked by the conservative bourgeois women who had founded the feminist movement. That old guard felt that any kind of attack on the state reeked of Social Democracy and that such rights as women could obtain should be won via service in welfare organisations rather than fought for by political means. This view was shared by the rather unprepossessing German Liberals. The moderate women opposed sexual freedom and felt that universal suffrage would lead to anarchy (Evans, 1980, 358). Although the BDF began to support women's suffrage after 1902, it took until 1908 and the lifting of the Association Laws before the bourgeois feminist movement gave widespread support for votes for women. From that time on it grew rapidly, despite splits into a number of hostile factions.

The limited concerns of German bourgeois feminism left a considerable amount of political ground clear for the development of the socialist women's movement attached to the SPD (Sozialdemokratische Partei Deutschlands). In particular, some feminist activists were attracted to socialism as a result of their disillusionment with the conservatism of the bourgeois movement. And its narrowly middle-class perspective meant that the BDF failed absolutely to organise working-class women, leaving a clear field for socialist women's organisations. There were, however, significant obstacles to the formation of an effective socialist women's movement. The Association Laws, combined with a political ban on the Social Democrats between 1879 and 1890, made the organisation of working women extremely difficult. Proletarian anti-feminism characterised the attitude of the organised male working class, only a minority of which believed in women's right to work (Mies, 1983, 128). During the ban on the SPD, associations of working women, which had strong feminist overtones, sprang up in the major German cities. Attempts were made to unify these organisations in the Association of Women and Girls of Germany, a group centred in Hamburg. The trade unions opposed the Association, and by 1892 Social Democratic trade unions were admitting women as members, taking much of the steam out of the association, which, supported neither by parties nor unions soon collapsed. But its existence did show the Social Democrats that the organisations of working-class women would have to be part of their work. As a result the SPD took the lead amongst European socialist parties in the organisation of women, devising a form of association which could at the same time express and take account of the needs of working women and prevent the spread of bourgeois ideas amongst them. The socialist women's organisation needed to attract women without arousing the suspicions and fears of socialist men, who were deeply opposed to elements of separatism which might threaten the unity of the movement. Socialist women were required to prioritise the class struggle and envisage their sexual oppression as secondary to the economic oppression of the class system.

All of this was perceived by Clara Zetkin, to whom is due most of the credit for the formation of the successful German socialist women's movement (Evans, 1977, 160). No creative theoretician, Zetkin was nonetheless clear and succinct in the views she set out at the Social Democratic Party Congress at Gotha in 1896 and which comprised her theory of women's emancipation. There were three main contentions in Zetkin's argument: (1) women's struggle for emancipation is identical with the struggle of the proletariat against capitalism; (2) nevertheless, women need special protection at work; (3) improvements in working women's conditions would enable them to make more effective revolutionaries, i.e. they would then participate more actively in the class struggle. Proletarian women should not fight against men but against the capitalist class together with men (Mies, 1983, 140–3). Zetkin also emphasised women's roles as wife and mother and took care that socialist agitation did not alienate women from these roles.

Zetkin was able to benefit from the political ban on women's participation by setting up an organisation for socialist women which was separate from the party proper. Merely recruiting women directly into the party as the French socialists were to do, would in Germany have led to the party's being banned by the police. Thus, the German party financed a separate women's section which recruited women into the socialist movement. The toleration of party men was maintained by ruthlessly crushing all bourgeois feminist tendencies which appeared within the section. The movement placed class before sex interests and refused cooperation across class lines. Male suspicions were thus effectively dealt with. After women's political participation was legalised in 1908 and the party decreed that all women should become direct socialist members of their local party unit, separate women's conferences were retained and these enabled women to form an homogeneous block within the SPD.

Women delegates to SPD conferences voted in blocs largely as a result of Zetkin's tactics. Zetkin herself moved increasingly to the left of the SPD, the leadership of which took the opportunity to replace her with the more moderate Luise Zeitz after the Association Law was lifted in 1908. Zeitz was an excellent recruiter, and the movement had nearly 175,000 members by 1914 when the BDF numbered 250,000 (Evans, 1980, 557, 370). Socialist agitators took active part in the unionisation of women workers recruiting 216,000 by the outbreak of the First World War. The circulation of the women's socialist journal, *Die Gleicheit*, which Zetkin continued to edit, was 124,000 by the outbreak of war. Hence, a large and impressive organisation of socialist women was formed, probably the largest in the world (Evans, 1977, 163).

The concerns of the socialist women's movement in Germany were often similar to those of the bourgeois feminists. Socialist women took up such liberal causes as equal education, equal pay, equal entry into the professions and the establishment of workplace crèches. They favoured the availability of contraception and ran educational courses for women. But their stands on women's issues were not always positive. In local legislatures the demand for the vote was sometimes dropped in favour of votes for men only. Open discussion of contraception and abortion was discouraged, and Evans (1977, 164) cites evidence that sexist behaviour was frequently used to keep women out of party decision-taking bodies and that women party-congress participants were often subject to ridicule. The socialist women's movement was consciously aimed at recruiting the wives of male members, and it geared some of its activities to housewives, running campaigns over food prices, and so on. Its membership numbered more housewives than women workers and was supportive of a family-based socialist subculture.

Our account so far attributes the split in the German women's movement more to the stress of the leaders of the Social Democratic Party on unity than to major differences in objectives. In fact, the division was more complicated than that. Many of the more radical bourgeois feminists leaned toward cooperation with the SPD. Not only did the two movements have similar aims but also both represented disenfranchised groups. Although all adult males had the vote, the government was neither responsible to nor elected by the Reichstag. Heated debates took place amongst the bourgeois feminists over the issue of cooperating with the socialists, notably over the question of admitting SPD organisations to the BDF. Radicals generally favoured this strategy but were defeated by the old guard who were able to argue that admission of socialists might give rise to prosecution under the Association Law. After 1902, when the BDF had come round to support for universal suffrage, cooperation became more of a possibility and did occur in some areas. But bourgeois feminists were aware that the commitment of Social Democratic women's organisations to universal suffrage was merely programmatic, that it was neglected in practice. And, of course, at that time the SPD women's movement was not particularly interested in cooperation either. Up until 1906 Zetkin's prime aim was to prevent her organisation from being absorbed by the BDF or abolished by male socialists. This involved dissociation from bourgeois feminism in every possible way. Her views were not accepted without opposition, and joint meetings between organised bourgeois and socialist women took place in a number of cities from 1898 onwards. Ultimately, however, Zetkin prevailed.

The struggle for women's suffrage in Germany was a struggle between bourgeois feminists and socialist women as well as between women and the state. Whilst it was unjustified to accuse, as Zetkin did, German bourgeois feminists of class egoism and of wishing to improve their own position at the expense of women workers, irreconcilable class differences did exist. These manifested themselves in discussions over working conditions for domestic employees and more generally in the liberal individualism of the bourgeois women. Radical bourgeois feminists opposed the upper-class stranglehold on German political and economic institutions, but they failed to perceive the gap between middle and working-class women. Women's suffrage, which was granted only after the revolutionary upheavals which generated the ill-fated Weimar Republic, was an issue which carried a different meaning for the different groups of women. After the ban on participation was lifted, the balance of bourgeois feminism shifted back to the right. Thus, by 1914 only the minority German Suffrage League supported universal suffrage. Both the BDF and the Alliance supported a property franchise (Evans, 1977, 112). Dominance by the right wing continued through the war, and the German bourgeois feminists did not campaign for women's rights during the Weimar Republic. Its radical pacifist wing virtually disappeared, and what was left of the BDF was eventually incorporated into the Third Reich, merging with the National Socialist Women's Organisation in 1933 (Kawan and Weber, 1981, 425) after the Federation had supported the Nazis in the 1933 elections. Needless to say, the women in the socialist movement suffered the same fate as their male counterparts and the German women's movement disappeared until after the Second World War, its ideas lost altogether to a generation of women. In its day, however, it had been an impressive organisation, the socialist wing in particular a model emulated by other countries. The important innovation of German socialist feminists was a separation between the women's sections and the rest of the movement which enabled women's issues to be developed and women to have groups in which they felt comfortable and in which they could learn to speak in public and think for themselves. The socialist movement benefited in that women could be recruited directly into the section where they were converted to socialist as well as feminist ideas.

France

The absence of combination laws and a long-standing socialist and feminist intellectual tradition were features of the French political climate of the late nineteenth century which would lead us to expect to find at least as thriving a socialist women's movement as existed in Germany. In fact, neither bourgeois nor socialist first-wave feminism in France ever amounted to mass organisations. Yet French women were amongst the earliest to claim their rights.

During the political ferment of 1789–93, women in Paris and major provincial cities began to organise themselves in struggles for equal rights. Women's political clubs were formed, and in 1791

Etta Palm spoke before the Assembly in favour of equal rights in education, politics, law and employment, and tried to form a national movement of women's clubs. At about the same time, Marie Gouze, known as Olympe de Georges, drafted her *Declaration of the Rights of Women*, modeled on the basic document of the French Revolution, the *Declaration of the Rights of Man and Citizen*. But feminism generated by the French revolution was short-lived, with Olympe de Georges executed as a royalist in 1793 and the women's political clubs dissolved at Jacobin instigation (Evans, 1977, 16). In its earliest manifestation French feminism was a marginal phenomenon, episodic and involving a few prominent individuals who had relatively few supporters, a syndrome which was to become characteristic of the French women's movement.

Nevertheless, the 1789 revolution launched a long series of campaigns to extend political rights, and the logic of this for those interested in women's rights was unavoidable. Women activists participated in the revolutions of 1830, 1848 and in the Paris Commune of 1870. In the early part of the nineteenth century the Saint-Simonians and George Sand stressed possibilities for women's emancipation in marriage and urged improvements in women's education. The Fourierist Considérat in 1848 proposed a resolution to bestow equal political rights on women but were defeated by the constitutional committee of the French Assembly. A similar motion by Pierre Leroux in 1851 met the same fate (Stern, 1934).

By 1869, when Mill's essay was published, a continuous, distinctive movement had not yet come into being. In 1866 Maria Deraismes had joined with former communard Paule Mink and Louise Michel in the foundation of the first feminist group in France, the Society for the Demand for Women Rights (Société pour la Revendication des Droit des Femmes). This group was short-lived, but by 1870 Deraismes was able to establish the Association pour les Droits des Femmes (Women's Rights Association) which in 1881 became La Société pour l'Amelioration du Sort de la Femme et la Revendication de ses Droits (Society for the Improvement of Women's Lot and the Demand of their Rights) which lasted well into the twentieth century and became one of the main pillars of French feminism. The other main pillar was the group created by Deraismes in conjunction with her sometime collaborator Leon Richer in 1870, the Ligue Française pour les Droits des Femmes. Richer, a staunch republican was reluctant to support women's suffrage whilst, as he perceived it,

French women were still in the yoke of the church. Under his leadership the league avoided the suffrage issue and became one of the most active Third Republic feminist groups (Sowerwine, 1982, 5–7).

The suffrage was a problematic issue both for bourgeois and socialist feminists in France, not least because of the early opposition of the Catholic church to the Third Republic. Although feminist leaders were themselves republicans, such allegiances were not widespread amongst French women in general. Organised French feminism contained an important anti-clerical strand. It had, after all, begun with the attempt to replace the Catholic monarchy with a rationalistic, republican form of government. But the religious propensities of the majority of French-women were such that most feminists emphasised reform of educational institutions and of women's legal status. They were reluctant to support women's political participation until improvement in educational opportunities decreased the likelihood of church loyalty making women a source of reaction. Not all French feminist leaders felt this way, but a large number did and an early reluctance to demand the suffrage was a distinctive element of French feminism (Boxer, 1982, 533).

This is not to say that no suffrage groups were formed, however. When her small radical group was prevented from discussing the suffrage issue at the 1883 national feminist congress, Hubertine Auclert established La Société le Suffrage des Femmes (Women's Suffrage Society), which aimed to secure full equality before the law as well as access to the professions, equal pay, easier divorce and the vote. The society was small, self-divided and faced an enormous problem in convincing republicans that women, once enfranchised, would not simply vote for monarchism and Catholicism.

It was not a success. Auclert's deputy (Maria Martin) closed down the society's journal, *La Citoyenne*, in 1891 and refounded it as *Le Journal des Femmes*, which lasted until 1911. She also aided Eugenie Potonie-Pierre in the establishment of Solidarité des Femmes (Women's Solidarity), manouevring Auclert out of power. The suffrage movement meanwhile reformed in the shape of l'Union Française pour le Suffrage des Femmes (French Union for Women's Suffrage) led by Protestant Radical Party members and eventually attracting about 300 members. Established women's rights groups affiliated to the French Union, which by 1913 could claim 10,000 members if all of the members of all of its affiliated groups were counted (Evans, 1977, 133). Support came mainly from a few Protestant and left-wing liberal intellectuals, with the mass of politicians unwilling to approve the enfranchisement of a group whose voting behaviour was likely to strengthen clericalism, thus endangering the republic (Bidelman, 1976, 106). Whilst there was undoubtedly some basis for their fears, Evans (1977, 134) reminds us that the cry that the republic was in danger was a Third Republican politician's regular excuse for postponing reforms.

But French politicians could afford to be ambivalent over questions of women's rights. The majority of French women showed little interest in the feminist movement which, with its opposition to protective legislation and rejection of motherhood as the natural vocation of women, proved unattractive to majority feminine opinion. Thus, whilst numerous groups and journals came into existence and competed for support, French bourgeois feminism remained 'less a movement than a mosaic of leaders' (Boxer, 1982, 553), a characteristic which was to return to haunt second-wave feminists of the 1970s (see Ch. 3 below).

Moreover, it could be argued that it is surprising that there was any first-wave feminist movement at all in France, if the rise of bourgeois feminism is explained, as it often is, by the rise of the middle class. Paulson (1973, 49–51) writes that the limited extent of economic change in France between 1815 and 1848 produced only slight modification of the social structure, placing explanations of events based on the triumph of the middle classes in grave doubt. More significant to the understanding of the peculiar nature of French feminism in Paulson's view is the equally peculiar nature of the French family, which gave considerable psychic reward to women for their conformity to an undoubtedly downtrodden role.

Despite its weaknesses, by the turn of the century French bourgeois feminism was embarking upon a decade of successful minor reforms with considerable progress being made in ameliorating the legal and economic differences between French men and women, preoccupations which perhaps reflected the very large numbers of French women in paid employment. At the beginning of the nineteenth century more than four million French women worked outside their homes in non-agricultural labour, comprising more than one-third of the workforce. But by the 1860s, artisans whose work was being threatened by factory production began to call for women's exclusion from employment, an opposition which was an important element in the early adoption by French socialists of demands for equal pay. Socialist men also favoured protective legislation, but women were divided on the issue. Educated bourgeois women hoping to enter the newly accessible professions wished to have rights and supported freedom of employment, opposing protective legislation of all kinds. Such aspirations provided a basis for at least a measure of support for some bourgeois feminist positions.

Conditions for working-class women, however, were such that almost no basis of support for feminism existed. Most working-class women were employed in sectors little affected by industrialisation (or protective legislation) and of the large numbers of women at work in 1860 only about 27 per cent were employed in manufacturing. Neither the persistence of the small-scale family enterprise nor the family-reinforced church dominance of working women's lives was particularly conducive to the development of a feminist consciousness (Boxer, 1982, 556–7). Proletarianisation led to the emergence of the family-wage economy, in which each member of the family was forced to bring in a wage to contribute to the family budget simply in order for the family to survive. Between 1850 and 1920 the domestic mode of production was generally supplanted by the industrial mode, but in France more than elsewhere, an intermediate form of production persisted (Sowerwine, 1982, 10). Such economic ambiguities combined with proletarian anti-feminism and a fragmented socialist movement to ensure that French socialist feminism was no more successful than its bourgeois counterpart, and bore almost no resemblance to the large German movement. In France the alliance between socialism and feminism was little more than a confused association of leaders without followers.

French socialists were formally committed to women's suffrage from the mid-1880s onwards but never took any effective action over their commitment. The labour movement was hostile or indifferent to feminism, committed to the family wage and suspicious of women workers (Evans, 1977, 174). The French Left drew upon a mixed theoretical tradition, which included both the misogyny of Proudhon, who believed that only the roles of housewife or prostitute were suitable for women, and the utopian socialists who supported variants of women's emancipation. The works of Bebel and Engels were also important, but Sowerwine (1982) makes the point that these were improperly understood by a leadership who were not particularly theoretically able and contained no-one who could read German. Poor translations and a lack of access to theoretical writings tended to reduce most leadership statements on women to little more than reiteration of support for their emancipation. But even if properly understood, the writings of the Marxist theoreticians had little to offer on how, tactically, to go about organising socialist women on questions of women's emancipation. No formulation that women were dually exploited under capitalism existed. It is tempting, therefore, to regard the writings of Bebel and Engels as important only insofar as they signalled the appropriateness of a concern over women's rights to male socialists (Sowerwine, 1982, 17).

From 1879 onwards women were permitted to join French socialist parties, but relatively few did so, becoming at most 3 per cent of the memberships by the turn of the century. The hostility of French male socialists to separate women's sections was a considerable obstacle, opening the way for organisation amongst working women by bourgeois feminists. In the mid-1870s the working-class movement was largely unstructured. Thus, when faced with the hostility of most of the feminist groups to the suffrage, Hubertine Auclert was able to place notices of her group's meetings in the main socialist newspaper, *Le Proletaire*. Auclert attended the 1879 Marseilles Socialist Congress, where the majority came out for the complete civil and legal equality of the sexes. But the alliance formed there soon foundered on the conservatism of Auclert's middle-class supporters and Louise Leonie Camusat's short-lived l'Union des Femmes, founded in the Socialist Party, became France's first organised group of socialist women in 1880. Camusat's group was responsible for generating the processes whereby all of the many current of the French Left came to include women's rights in their programmes of minimum demands. Schisms on the Left meant that, until unification in 1905, a plethora of socialist groups existed, each usually with its leading women. But great resistance to the importation of bourgeois feminism into the party prevented the establishment of a separate women's organisation and French socialist women were admitted to parties only on the same terms as men. The creation of the International Secretariat of Socialist Women at Stuttgart in 1907 implied that there should be women's sections within each party, but in France only the most forlorn effort was made to comply. After 1905 the newly united Parti Socialist (Section Française de l'Internationale Ouvriere), the SFIO, was unwilling to agree to the establishment of a separate women's organisation. It adhered to that decision until the collapse of the Third Republic in 1940 and its post-war successors continued with it. A direct result of this policy was that women never joined the French socialist parties in the proportions or numbers that were experienced in other European countries.

The problems, as identified by Madeline Pelletier, one of the French socialist women's outstanding leaders, were twofold. First, women were unlikely to be attracted to direct membership in party sections whose main preoccupation was with electoral problems and strategies. These were less than interesting to women who could not vote. Second, socialist male opposition to women's suffrage persisted and was most evident at local level. The fear that women would bring clericalism to the voting booth persisted after the formation of the SFIO in 1905, when commitment to women's suffrage was made at a general programmatic level (where it remained). Women's suffrage never became a practical objective for the socialist movement, rarely appearing in the individual programmes of its candidates (Sowerwine, 1982, 109).

Clearly, economic and demographic differences, most notably the comparative rates of economic change, account for differences between the French and German socialist women's movements, but organisational factors too are important. Hostility to bourgeois feminism was also prevalent in the German movement, but the Prussian Association Law prevented the SPD from recruiting women members directly. Separate organisations were a legal necessity until 1908. In France no such legal pressure existed and socialist leaders, including such women leaders as Louise Saumoneau, resisted a separate organisation for women. In so doing they failed to make their movement attractive to working women, who had no opportunity to acquire the feminist ability to articulate their disadvantaged position and their sisterhood with women. The policy of integration led to the subordination of women's demands to those of the party and the functioning of its women's movement as a sort of auxiliary rather than as a movement in its own right. This produced a vicious circle whereby a male organisation essentially devoted to electoral politics (a men-only activity) recruited a few women. So long as women did not have the vote, they did not interest the party and the party did not interest them. As the party did not recruit women, it had no female clientele to satisfy and they therefore did not prioritise matters to do with women's emancipation. Thus, the French socialist women's movement never gained a mass following, reaching a membership of only about 1,000 in 1914, when the party numbered 90,000 and over half of those were the wives or daughters of male members (Evans, 1977, 174).

Efforts to ally socialist and bourgeois feminism in France occurred regularly, and although many individuals worked in both movements, as in Germany, organisational unification efforts were doomed to failure. Class differences proved insurmountable, with even the suffrage issue providing no substantial basis for unity. Its first manifestations amongst the earliest, the French women's suffrage movement, was one of the latest to win the vote. Only after the First World War did the movement grow to any size when the Union claimed to have 100,000 members by 1929 (Branca, 1978, 181). Their crusade went unheeded until 1944, when de Gaulle enfranchised women by edict. The socialists, who did more for the suffrage movement than other parties, did very little, and French women were enfranchised in a process which left them indebted to no political party.

Russia and the USSR

The example of first-wave feminist organisation provided by Tsarist Russia differs again from the models provided by England, Germany and France and is in many respects unique. There, economic backwardness combined with an extremely repressive state. The political climate was one in which, throughout many of the years when feminist issues were significant, most political reform organisations, however modest their aims, were revolutionary. And when revolution finally and inevitably occurred, a whole new range of issues were raised for feminists.

The 1861 emancipation of the Russian serfs generated excitement throughout the society, one by-product of which was a nascent women's movement dedicated at first to the spread of education as an essential precondition of women's independence (Engel, 1978, 51). But active pressure for women's rights tended to remain limited, as lobbying for economic rights in the still largely feudal society was irrelevant and legal political activity was impossible. Whilst the Chaikovskii circle of the 1860s was the first in Russia in which women played an independent role, it was to be some considerable time before a feminist movement developed. In order to survive, the feminists had to stay outside general politics, a situation which could be changed only by revolution. Such logic meant that activist women quickly moved into revolutionary politics, where concern over political action soon took precedence over women's rights. Women were active in the People's Will and played important parts in the assassination missions of populist and other terrorist groups. Sofia Perovskaya carried out the People's Will death sentence on the Tsar in 1881, becoming the first woman to be executed for a political crime in

Russia. Women continued to take part in terrorist movements throughout the last years of the nineteenth century, many of them turning up later as members of the Social Revolutionaries. But the existence of politically active women does not of itself comprise a feminist movement which only developed after industrialisation began to take-off in the 1890s and especially after the 1905 revolution led to the manhood suffrage and the possibility of a certain, if limited, amount of room for political manoeuvre.

Russian feminists after 1905 began to concern themselves with political issues, and a multi-faceted movement which included amongst its concerns suffragism and various elements of social feminism, emerged. The Union for Women's Equality appeared in 1905, to be succeeded by the All-Russian League for Women's Equality, both with classic bourgeois feminist programmes (Lapidus, 1978, 27). In general, the movement was led by the new women professionals, containing a particularly large number of doctors. Liberal in its orientations, Russian bourgeois feminism was nonetheless concerned with the rights of peasant and working women (Stites, 1980, 23). The 1908 All-Russian Conference of Feminists attracted 1,045 delegates (including Kollantai), of whom 45 were workers and 1 was a peasant (Rosenthal, 1978).

Amongst the Russian Social Democrats the emancipation of women was a goal to be resisted, but as the party started losing women to bourgeois feminism after 1905, individual socialist women began to press for a socialist women's organisation. Until that time, Krupskaya's publication of *The Woman Worker* in 1899 had been the only sign of Russian Marxist interest in the woman question. The movement got underway when Alexandra Kollantai began to interest herself in the struggle of proletarian women. Her *The Social Bases of the Woman Question*, first published in 1909, is one of the most emphatic Marxist critiques of the bourgeois feminist movement and makes clear the class basis of socialist feminism. Police action forced her into exile, and the embryonic organisation she formed disintegrated. In 1914 a group of Bolshevik women in Moscow, including Krupskaya and Inessa Armand, made arrangements for the celebration of International Woman's Day in 1914 and in the same year launched a journal, *Rabotnitsa*, aimed at working women. Police soon clamped down on these efforts, which were revived when Bolshevik women began organising amongst women of the urban poor during the war years (Stites, 1980, 26).

Women in the Russian Social Democratic movement had considerable difficulty in obtaining male support for activities amongst women. They tended to be less middle class than women in the other left-wing parties and were disadvantaged by the fact that prestige in the Social Democratic movement tended to be acquired via the production of theoretical writings, something women's relatively inferior education left them ill equipped to do. A network of women's clubs was eventually created, but it proved impossible to get a mass movement going and women tended to be less prominent amongst the Bolsheviks than the anarchist Socialist Revolutionaries (Evans, 1977, 182).

Thus, prior to 1917, Marxist women leaders, who were fiercely dedicated to the emancipation of women workers, had to struggle on two fronts. They had ideologically to confront what they saw as the errors of the bourgeois feminists, and practically to battle against the indifference or even hostility to women in the Marxist movement (Glickman, 1978, 81). In such circumstances, agitation was carried on mainly by bourgeois feminists who focused their activities on lobbying the liberal Constitutional Democrats (Cadets) to support the issues in the Duma (legislature). The Duma did pass a bill to enfranchise women in 1912, but the Cabinet turned it down (the Duma's functions were purely advisory), and it never became law. Symbolic rewards were obtained, however, and in 1913 the Duma declared International Woman's Day to be a public holiday (Rosenthal, 1977, 375). By the outbreak of war in 1914, all the major parties were committed to women's political, legal and economic equality, although disagreements on the means by which to achieve it were endemic.

The war forced women into the factories, and by 1917 they were 43 per cent of the industrial workforce. The high casualty rates meant that many women were family heads coping on low wages with high inflation, shortages and rationing. When the Tsarist collapse finally came, it began with demonstrations by Petrograd women on International Woman's Day in 1917. The women were protesting against poor living conditions and the recently reduced bread ration. Joined by male workers and students, the protest soon escalated into the first of the 1917 revolutions (Hough and Fainsod, 1979, 40).

Women were actively engaged in events throughout the revolutionary period and their participation in the Civil War was even greater. Bolshevik victory in the Civil War ensured that theirs was the only one of the women's movements to remain, and women's issues thereafter became the responsibility of the Zhenotdel or Party Women's Bureau (Stites, 1980, 27), which was perhaps the first example of the syndrome which came to be termed 'state feminism'.

The Zhenotdel was established as a result of concern over the low proportions of women in the party at the behest of Bolshevik women interested in putting some of the socialist ideas on women's rights into practice. Established at the instigation of the All-Russian Conference of Proletariat and Peasant Women in 1918, the Zhenotdel was led by Inessa Armand. Its tasks centred around the education and recruitment of women; the Zhenotdel organised women as shop stewards, set up factory arbitration committees and combated tendencies to fire women first. Politically, it sponsored women as deputies to local soviets and pressed motions on women's rights at party congresses. In addition, its activists worked for the maximum inclusion of women in literacy drives and encouraged the establishment of communal institutions for child care and food provision. Its relationship with the party was an uncomfortable one, however, and its task was made difficult by the fact that it had no powers of enforcement. During the 1920s the Zhenotdel's position became increasingly difficult and it was finally abolished by Stalin who assigned its duties to commissions attached to the local and regional boards of party executives (Lovenduski, 1981a, 289).

Revolution brought Russian women the vote, and the Zhenotdel brought them what was perhaps the first attempt to administer women's rights programmes in a systematic way. It is difficult to determine whether Zhenotdel action brought what were clearly improvements in women's working conditions in the Soviet Union or whether these came because they were necessary to entice women into an underpopulated labour force. The political circumstances in which it emerged were both complex and unique, making for difficulties in assessing its impact or applying its methods elsewhere. But the Zhenotdel's very existence arose from a recognition that equality before the law was itself insufficient to ensure women's emancipation (Lapidus, 1976, 304), a perception that forms the core of Western feminist sex-equality policy demands today (see Ch. 7 below).

The Nordic Countries

Both the liberal democratic regime in Britain and the autocratic Second Reich hosted strong first-wave feminist movements, whilst those which emerged in the analogous French and Russian systems were small and unconfident. Indeed, it was to take French-women until well into the twentieth century to obtain political rights. These examples suggest that explanation for variations in the first wave of feminism and its effects is likely to be found in a complex variety of factors, that reference to political institutions alone will only deepen the puzzle. Economic and cultural factors must also be considered, as must attitudes and belief systems. Cultural factors, particularly religious beliefs and feelings of nationalism, were also very important factors in the political emergence of women.

Examination of feminist movements in the Protestant cultures of the Nordic political systems reveals important similarities both amongst the five states and between them and England. For Evans (1977, 70) the only European countries where conditions remotely resembled those which obtained in England were the Nordic countries of Denmark, Sweden, Iceland, Norway and Finland. In each of these states a predominantly Protestant culture combined with some form of constitutional power. Three other important influences also favoured feminist support. In all five countries the widening of the political nation under pressure from liberal reform movements to include new population groups led to demand for women also to be included. This was also true of Britain and the USA. Where manhood suffrage was extended, the idea that it should further be extended to women easily took hold. Second, each country also featured entrenched resistance to feminism in the shape of conservative or aristocratic elites or autocratic, non-elected governments or both. Third, the role played by nationalism in getting rid of such governments and in underpinning manhood-suffrage extension also favoured feminism (Evans, 1977, 91).

In Sweden the movement was divided along class lines with considerable debate taking place over whether women should press initially for inclusion in a limited property suffrage or join with working-class men in the struggle for universal suffrage (Register, 1982, 603). Eventually, the Swedish women's movement came to work politically for the defeat of the conservatives in the light of their intransigence over the issue of the vote. This worked so well that by 1909 women had obtained the right to stand for municipal office. And the liberal-dominated Riksdag, returned in 1911, soon produced an official government suffrage bill which passed the lower chamber but fell in the second. Liberal downfall in 1914 meant that suffrage enactment was postponed and the rising Social Democrats won feminist attachments away from the liberals.

In Sweden as in other Scandinavian countries the emergence of feminism as an organised movement in the 1870s postdated many of the economic and legal reforms which had occupied feminists elsewhere. Early organisations were involved in campaigns to extend these reforms, but they quickly turned their attention to the suffrage issue, winning eligibility for school board and poor-law board places as early as 1889. The Fredrika Bremer Society was formed in 1902. Led by Anna Whitlock the group had 13,000 members in 187 local associations by 1914. This success was in some measure due to a background of increasingly bitter national crises over manhood-suffrage extension, the rapid pace of industrial change and the growth of both the Social Democrats and the Liberal Union Party, which united the middle classes behind the suffrage issue. Gradually the Liberals became the largest Riksdag party, overtaking the Conservatives in 1905 (Evans, 1977, 71–3). Generally, the Swedish situation was similar to the British in that political dualism prevailed, keeping the suffrage movement united by giving it an obvious party focus.

In Denmark the campaign for women's vote was never as militant as the English campaign and never gained a mass following. Several organisations were involved, the largest of which was *Dansk Kvindesamfund* (DK—Danish Women's Association) founded by Fredrik and Mathilde Najer in 1871. Primarily concerned with legal and educational reforms, the Danish Women's Association hesitated before demanding votes for women, for fear of damaging its respectability (Dahlerup, 1978, 142). But when electoral reform was raised in an 1898 parliamentary bill and made no mention of women, members of the DK left the organisation and joined with other feminist groups, including the Danish Women's Suffrage Society, to form the Danish Women's Association's Suffrage Federation, which continued to work closely with the DK. A moderate, slow-moving body, the Federation, which was connected to the Liberal Party was accused of holding back the struggle for the vote by feminists associated with the left-wing Reform Liberal Party. These critics left to form their own society, the National League for Women's Suffrage. The National League campaigned for voting rights at all levels whilst the Federation concentrated on the municipal suffrage. By the turn of the century progress had begun to be more rapid as the Reform Liberals and the Social Democrats gained strength, coming to power in alliance in 1913. Until that year continuous debates on suffrage extension provided a background against which the membership of the suffrage organisations grew rapidly. By 1910 the National League had 11,000 members in 160 branches and the Federation had

12,200 in 144 branches. The total population of women at that time was 1.5 million. By 1906 even the DK had come to work for suffrage at both levels. Municipal suffrage was won in 1908 but efforts to get national suffrage fell in the upper house in 1913, to be passed during the war in 1915. Danish women gained the vote gradually in a struggle involving mainly middle-class women. Social Democrat women did organise and some members refused to work with bourgeois feminists, but no sharp split developed along the lines of the German movement (Dahlerup, 1978, 142).

In both Sweden and Denmark the women's suffrage struggle was closely related to prolonged constitutional battles and political realignments involving both Liberals and Social Democrats. Universal suffrage figured large as an issue in these events, supplying a milieu in which feminists became identified with the struggle for the vote to an extent which Evans (1977, 81) believes was unparalleled elsewhere. These two countries thus differed from the other Nordic countries, where the Conservatives were less strong and less able to obstruct Liberal constitutionalism.

In Norway, Finland and Iceland, nationalism was the dominant middle-class ideology, something with which the Conservatives never came to terms. All three countries had been dominated by foreign powers throughout the nineteenth century. In Norway, left-wing Liberals had managed to secure parliamentary government from the Swedish Crown by 1884 in a struggle which mobilised women who became politicised in the process. The early feminist movement there was based in the middle class, which had won an array of rights similar to those of Swedish and Danish women by 1884, when the Norwegian Association for the promotion of Women's Interest was founded. A strong literary feminism, most notable in the works of Ibsen, had had a considerable influence on attitudes. After a period of moderation by feminists, a suffrage movement was founded in 1895 as the national Women's Suffrage Association led by Gina Krog. A municipal property-based suffrage was achieved by 1901, and independence in 1905 was followed a few years later by full women's suffrage. Finland and Iceland had similar patterns of rewarding women mobilised in nationalist movements (Evans, 1977, 84, 90) with Finnish women enfranchised in 1906, the first example of women obtaining a national suffrage.

Nordic feminism was gradualist and on the whole moderate, successful both at mobilising proportionately large numbers of women and at gaining its objectives. Nordic women obtained voting rights in national elections before most other women. In common with the English movement, splits between bourgeois and socialist feminists were not debilitating and women were able to prioritise feminist goals.

The Hapsburg Empire

Other priorities exercised feminists in the Hapsburg Empire, where divisions over both class and nationalism had a marked influence on the political emergence of women. Attitudes too played a role, with fear of women's conservatism proving a major obstacle in the struggle for voting rights.

The best developed and largest of the feminist movements in the empire were to be found in Austria. Whilst the Austrian socialist women's movement was eventually to prove one of the most advanced on social issues of any in Europe (Lafleur, 1978, 245), Hapsburg Austria was not promising ground for bourgeois feminism. It was overwhelmingly Catholic, constitutionally authoritarian and hosted little in the way of a nationalist movement. In addition, Austria, like Prussia, had combination laws which prevented women from joining or forming political associations. There was, however, a limited property franchise under which certain propertied women had the right to vote in both the German and Hapsburg Empires, which, it so happened, gave quite a number of Hapsburg Empire women the vote. The franchise carried little weight and women were not allowed to stand for office, but they did resist the diminution of their rights as the removal of property qualifications from the franchise gradually disenfranchised women. Bourgeois feminist groups, however, kept mainly within both the letter and spirit of the law and avoided political organisation. Thus, Auguste Fickert's General Austrian Women's Association, founded in April 1893, adopted a programme which was predominantly comprised of non-political points amongst which it managed to conceal one or two political demands, including that for the vote. But its suffrage aims were limited to the protection of existing rights, and the idea of women's suffrage only gained a hold in the women's movement after universal manhood suffrage was granted in 1906–7 (Evans, 1977, 94–5).

The bourgeois women's movement was small, apolitical and of limited significance, differentiated largely by varying degrees of conservatism and possessed of a Catholic women's organisation supporting protective legislation and proselytising the sanctity of women in the home. The Christian Social Party, the pan-German Nationalists and the Liberals opposed the extension of the suffrage to women. Hence, although the socialist commitment to women tended to be mainly programmatic, it was a significant improvement over what other parties offered women. Socialist women leaders held that their task in such a situation was to defend not only socialist but liberal positions on women's rights and thus advance suffrage and equality demands as well as acting to improve the conditions of working women. Throughout the 1890s and the early years of the twentieth century, the Austrian socialist women's movement was minute, its most publicised achievement being the reprimand it received from Clara Zetkin at the 1907 Stuttgart Congress of Second International women for dropping the demand for women's suffrage in the 1906 Austrian campaign for universal manhood suffrage. Stung, the party expanded its women's organisations and introduced *Vertrauenspersonen*, who were women cadres responsible for recruiting women into the party. The tactic proved effective and by 1910 women's socialist party membership had reached 15,000 (Lafleur, 1978, 234). The major obstacle on the Left to the extension of women's suffrage in Austria was, as in all European Catholic countries, a fear that, once enfranchised, women would vote Conservative. When the vote was finally obtained in the wake of the First World War, Austrian women were more likely than men to vote for non-socialist parties, but the difference was not large.

Led by Adelheid Popp, the Austrian socialist women's movement came into its own in the post-war period, keeping alive the association of socialist feminism with radical emancipatory ideas. Confronted by the twin adversaries of Catholic society and traditional conservatism, its identity was a distinctive one which proved attractive to large numbers of women. By 1925 the movement had 165,000 members and comprised 29.7 per cent of Social Democratic membership. The women were able to obtain party support on a range of issues including contraception and abortion and were by every measure a successful feminist political group. But the post-war economy was particularly hard on women, and by the late 1920s and early 1930s socialist women had become preoccupied with economic crisis, unemployment and the rise of fascism. Whilst bourgeois feminists eschewed party politics and concentrated their energies on the international peace movement socialist women argued that peace required the defeat of fascism, for which the socialist feminist continued to struggle. When the party was destroyed in 1934, the women's movement went too, its legacy the proof that feminist and socialist ideas could be compatible. Its success no doubt reflected the polarised nature of Austrian public life, in which clerical conservatism and socialist anti-clericalism were reflected in parallel subcultures which had little contact. Certainly, the Austrian movement was in many respects an exceptional one, according readily with none of the models apparent in other countries.

The fate of feminism in the remainder of the Hapsburg Empire is more easily understood, however. Although economic development by the late nineteenth and early twentieth century was such that a middle class was emerging as Vienna, Prague and Budapest became industrial cities and Protestantism had engaged sectors of each of the populations, feminism was not a hardy growth. Racial conflicts and government authoritarianism, according to Evans (1977, 102), distorted feminism throughout the Empire. Whilst in Austria, as we have seen, there was no development of a radical bourgeois suffrage movement, in Hungary, radicals and moderates in the bourgeois feminist movement were separated along ethnic lines. Bohemian feminism was late, nationalistic to an almost perverse degree and unable to obtain political party support. The Empire was a hotbed of nationalist activity in the years preceding the outbreak of war, and it proved impossible for women of either socialist or bourgeois feminist persuasion to cooperate across ethnic lines (see Bohachevsky-Chomiak, 1980; Jancar, 1981). Women obtained the vote only after the Hapsburg Empire was overthrown and the various nationalities rearranged into their own states. Of the successor states, only Yugoslavia failed to enfranchise women. Evans (1977) argues that the vote was granted to women only after their conservative tendencies had been appreciated by male elites and that fear of revolution and the desire to achieve electoral stability were the major motivating factors in such decisions. Whilst this argument is not valid for some of the European countries under consideration, it works well for many of the Hapsburg successor states, most of which faced chronic instability in the immediate post-war period.

Catholic Europe: Italy, Spain and Belgium

In Italy, Spain and Belgium, Catholicism was a major influence on feminist development. Despite an appreciable proportion of women in employment by the end of the nineteenth century and a relatively high level of industrial development, Belgian feminism was a relatively feeble variant with both the bourgeois and socialist branches timid in the extreme. In Italy late unification and economic backwardness meant that organised feminism did not really gain a hold until the 1890s, and then only in the considerably more developed northern part of the country. The economically orientated Society for Women's Work was founded in 1898, and a similar group, the Association for Women (Associazione per la Donna) was founded to press for women's rights in education, in particular to secularise women's education. The National Council of Women was founded in 1903 and a suffrage movement quickly appeared influenced by the liberalisation of politics and the granting of universal manhood-suffrage in the Giolitti era. The National Committee for Women's Suffrage was founded in 1905, obtaining some socialist and liberal support. The first women's suffrage congress in Italy was held in Rome in 1908. But the suffrage movement failed to win over parties of the centre and right, which were mindful of the Catholic leanings of the mass of Italian women. The Catholic church itself created a widely supported women's organisation, which attracted widespread membership (Evans, 1977, 137; Springer, 1981, 20–21). In the Italian Socialist Party (PSI) feminism fared little better as feminist issues were seen by the leadership as divisive (LaVigna, 1978, 171) and PSI interest in women was confined to their economic roles. The Socialist Party did support women's emancipation at programmatic level, however, and Anna Kuliscioff and others founded a Union of Women Socialists in 1915. After the foundation of the Italian Communist Party the Left took more of an interest in the women question. From 1921 onwards the weekly communist paper *l'Ordino Nuovo* carried a regular *Tribune della Donne*, which took up such questions as contraception and abortion. But after 1925 the movement had to go underground or into exile (Slaughter, 1981, 186). Although socialist and communist women were extremely active during the resistance (see Camet, 1981), there was little opportunity to develop socialist feminism after Mussolini came to power. All the major bourgeois feminist groups supported Mussolini, seduced by his promises to reform various elements of their status. Dissolution rather than reform was their reward.

In Spain, where women were particularly oppressed, even by the standards of the late nineteenth century, the middle-class women's movement was so poorly established that the regime could not be persuaded to allow an international feminist conference to meet there in 1919. The Catholic Church-backed 1881 Civil

Code discriminated against women in inheritance matters and contained a series of measures designed to restrict the autonomy of married women. Feminist groups, whilst political from the outset in demanding the suffrage, were unable to overcome such well-constructed and reinforced cultural resistance to their aims and remained small groups of individuals clustered around a few leaders. Women did begin to be active in the political parties during the 1920s, but the socialists were unwilling to organise party women's movements, and influence was limited to that which could be obtained within the relatively weak women's labour movement. The Communist Party and Socialist Party contained prominent women members and women were active on both sides of the fighting in the Civil War. But when Franco's forces emerged victorious to impose a right-wing authoritarian regime, the conventions and laws restricting women began to be enforced once more, and the opportunity to develop feminist organisations disappeared for almost forty years.

In Spain, then, the rise of fascism cost at least two generations of women's movement experience and recruitment. In central Europe the price was at least one generation, and in all of Europe a further generation was lost as a result of the loss of impetus caused by the Second World War itself. By the time these various mid-twentieth century horrors had resolved themselves, the surviving original feminists were elderly women and their organisations, if they still existed at all, were feeble reminders of what they once had been.

International Feminism

An important feature of both wings of the first-wave movement had been the capacity to set up and maintain credible international organisations. At a time when many women seemed willing to regard themselves as unfit for politics until someone suggested otherwise, such organisations aided the spread of ideas about women's emancipation across national boundaries. They were invaluable to women beginning new national groups in countries where the movement developed late or slowly.

In political terms the most important organisations were the International Council of Women (ICW), the International Women's Suffrage Alliance, later to become the International Alliance of Women (IAW), and the Socialist Women's International. The ICW was founded by American feminists in 1888, inspired by the model of the highly successful World Women's Temperance Union established in 1884. It was a federation of National Councils of Women, which by its 1899 London Congress existed in Germany, Sweden, Great Britain, Ireland, Denmark and Holland as well as various non-European states. The London Congress also included delegates from Italy, Austria, Russia, Switzerland and Norway, all countries whose councils had not completed organising their work. And observers came from France and Belgium. The organisational programme covered the range of women's emancipation issues with the exception of the suffrage. Its goal was to represent all women and the ICW adhered to principles of unanimity, refusing to take up the suffrage issue.

By 1902 such a position was no longer tenable and Carrie Chapman Catt led an initiative to found an international group devoted exclusively to the suffrage issue. The IAW thus came into being at the 1904 meeting of the ICW. In each country its aims were to get the vote for women on whatever terms men obtained it. The IAW was particularly helpful in aiding women attempting to form national groups and was eventually successful in persuading the ICW to adopt the demand for the women's vote. With peace and internationalism amongst their concerns, the two organisations strongly supported the League of Nations, devoting many of their efforts to its promotion. At national level both also became involved in the establishment of the various welfare programmes, with the welfare of working women becoming a particular concern. To this day various National Councils of Women remain important women's pressure groups in many European countries (Hurwitz, 1977, *passim*; Evans, 1977, Appendix).

The Socialist Women's International was a somewhat less unambiguously feminist group, founded by Clara Zetkin in conjunction with the Second International in 1907 at its Stuttgart Conference. An international organisation of socialist women, it attracted delegates from England, France, Germany, Hungary, Austria, Bohemia, Norway, Belgium, the Netherlands, Switzerland, Italy, Sweden and Russia. Some were genuinely delegates from socialist women's movements, others were there as individuals. As was the Second International itself, the Women's International was dominated by the Germans, with Clara Zetkin's theories inspiring most of its pre-war resolutions. Accordingly, its two operating principles were support for women's suffrage and no cooperation with bourgeois feminists (Evans, 1977, 1968). After the First World War, when Zetkin left the Second International to join the new Communist Party of Germany, the

Women's International was revived by the Austrian Socialists under the leadership of Adelheid Popp, after which it became a genuine international women's movement encompassing more than 900,000 women by 1925 (Lafleur, 1978, 223). Prior to that it had remained a poorly resourced offshoot of the Second International, mainly the instrument of Clara Zetkin.

The importance of international feminism to the emergence of national women's movements is difficult to assess in the current state of research on the topic. Such evidence as is available suggests that its existence was an important inspiration to many national groups and that it sustained the work of many feminists who otherwise would have been isolated. It is thus curious that no equivalent organisational structures have emerged to support feminists in the last quarter of the twentieth century.

The Achievements of First-Wave Feminism

Historically, women's rights demands have tended to accompany demands for the extension of human rights. Indeed, political participation has, until fairly recently, been almost exclusively an elite prerogative, with gender differences only becoming conspicuous as the franchise spread and modern participatory structures such as political parties appeared. Women have organised to press their case during periods of change and have been much in evidence during revolutionary upheavals. But, although their participation tends to have been welcomed when harnessed with the struggles to extend the rights for men of one or other class, women have found that at victory their enthusiasm is rechannelled from disruptive to stabilising activities, consigning them once more to surrogate roles (Bridenthal, 1977, 4). Thus, the history of women's emancipation has been a history of false starts and broken promises, of organisational activity followed by atomisation, followed by regrouping to resume the struggle.

Sustained organisation, independent of kin networks, by women only really began in the nineteenth century in what was from its inception a middle-class movement. Beginning with religious and charitable causes, feminists moved to what were primarily economic aims, coming only later to political goals which eventually focused on gaining the vote. Whilst some working-class women did become organised, both bourgeois and socialist women's movements were led by middle-class women. Class differences between leadership and followers are not unusual in modern

politics, even in working-class movements. More fundamental
were the differences in class orientation which separated bourgeois and socialist feminism. However, there is no evidence to
suggest that enfranchisement for women would have come sooner
had the movement been unified.

As has been mentioned, perhaps the most important obstacle to
women's suffrage was men's perception of what women would do
if they got the vote. This was most apparent amongst socialists and
on the liberal Left, where, especially in Catholic countries, a
perception of feminine conservatism impeded support for
women's suffrage. Everywhere men gave women the vote when it
was to their advantage to do so. Liberal and socialist parties came
to power, often in coalition and usually after bitter and protracted
constitutional struggles. Frequently, the enfranchisement of
women was part of an effort to stabilise or legitimise the system
which emerged. In Europe, feminists were most successful where
they were able to attach themselves to a rising nationalist or liberal
cause. In countries where they were able to ally themselves only
with minor political currents, male politicians were less willing to
hand over the franchise (Evans, 1980, 375).

In most of Europe, women first gained the right to vote in the
aftermath of the First World War, at a time of upheaval and
dislocation which was shortly to be followed by major economic
depression and another world war. Women's arrival at political
citizenship occurred when most of the important political structures and institutions were in place. The upheavals of the next
thirty years ensured that women's participation had little effect on
those structures and institutions. Such alterations as occurred,
occurred for other reasons. The movements' apparent loss of
steam after the vote was won is, at least in part a product of the
circumstances which followed victory.

In the 1920s and 1930s in Europe, gender did not prove to be
sufficiently cohesive a bond to sustain a political movement. As
enfranchisement removed what incentive there had been for
cooperation between bourgeois and socialist feminists, other political priorities became predominant. For many socialist women,
feminism was a stage on the route to a more revolutionary politics
(a traffic which was notably sparse in the other direction). For
bourgeois women, feminism became an increasingly narrowly
defined concern as the radicalisation of politics in the era after the
Bolshevik Revolution led some of them to adopt increasingly
conservative positions. Bourgeois feminism appeared in some
respects to be ideologically blind as many of its remaining adher-

ents bargained with rising fascist movements, which upon attaining power immediately dissolved or incorporated the women's organisations. Radical bourgeois feminists, like their socialist counterparts, were often imprisoned by the newly dominant right, their movements ended as the war years began. Others were active in resistance movements, emerging as important members of post-war political parties.

Internal factors, too, hastened the decline of first-wave feminism. In countries where it was not actively suppressed, a growing conservatism made feminism unattractive to younger women who simply did not join, responding to the more urgent political demands of the time. In addition, the active recruitment of women by political parties meant that many politically orientated women took advantage of opportunities afforded by party work. But perhaps the most disappointing result of the suffragist victory was the fact that no women's vote emerged in that women did not use newly acquired political muscle to place more women in the gladiatorial arenas of politics. Many suffragists simply assumed that women voters would demand and vote for women candidates. Essentially liberals, they believed that the withdrawal of obstacles to political leadership would be sufficient to ensure that women would become political leaders at least in proportion to their numbers in the population. Their hopes proved to be without foundation.

However, a number of policy changes did occur as a result of the consciousness of male legislators that there were now women voters to be considered. New measures in health, education and welfare policy in the 1940s and 1950s, as well as abortion liberalisation, equal rights and equal pay legislation in the 1960s and 1970s, and consideration of positive action and positive discrimination by policy-makers in the 1980s, all remind us that the women's vote should not be written off just because only a few women have become political leaders. This does not mean, however, that the promise of political feminism has been fulfilled. One of the arguments faced by the suffragists was that women's needs were taken into account in the political choices made by their husbands and fathers. The idea that women should decide and act for themselves was at the very heart of the suffrage struggle, as was the view that society would benefit from the special insights and characteristics women would bring to political office. Whilst many of the suffragists came to acknowledge that they may have overestimated the power of the women's vote in an ever-widening franchise, they did not intend that women should remain in the shadows of political life. In struggling for the removal of formal barriers to women's political equality with men, early activists, where they were successful, accomplished only the first stage of what is likely to prove a long and laborious process. The first wave of European feminism declined with much of its political programme achieved at statutory level but unrealised in practice.

3 The New Movement for Women's Liberation: Second-Wave Feminism

Many of the organisations of the first-wave of feminism continued their work without interruption and were still in existence in the 1980s. Others resumed their activities after the Second World War and became important pressure groups representing women's interests. But from the late 1920s until the end of the 1960s the women's movement appeared to be a spent political force. Without the common goal of the suffrage, the energies of feminism were dispersed across a number of activities. Separate organisations pursued special concerns, and feminism was widely presumed to have had its day. This was not because the movement's work had been completed, however. Although the impact of the first wave of feminism remained evident in all of the countries which experienced it, at the end of the 1960s no country could boast that its women had achieved either political, social or economic equality with men.

When the first signs of a feminist resurgence appeared in the 1960s, they did so after almost forty years of political quiescence by women, a quiescence which was mistakenly interpreted as an indicator of satisfaction. The rennaissance of feminism began in a number of countries during the 1960s and was a force to be reckoned with by the 1970s. The strength of the new movement, dubbed the 'women's liberation movement', and the speed of its growth took almost all observers by surprise. The wide range of activities and the sheer scale of the feminist critique indicated a considerable dissatisfaction among women. Both these factors suggest that a precondition for a women's liberation movement is the full array of political rights guaranteed by a liberal democratic political structure. In Europe this is borne out by differences between the state socialist and liberal democratic systems. Whilst the position and therefore the potential grievances of women in East and West Europe bear marked similarities, only in the liberal democracies were women's demands articulated in the form of an active and creative mass movement. The differences between the two systems would appear to be fundamental to feminism, which has no independent form in the state socialist systems. Although these have women's organisations which for some time have had what are undoubtedly feminist goals, they are not really analogous to the spontaneously formed women's groups found in the West. Rather, they are akin to the various affiliated and independent traditional women's right groups which are often well integrated into the presure-group systems of the liberal democracies.

A relative freedom of manoeuvre and association permitted a great variety of new feminist organisations to appear in Western Europe in the 1970s. These did not aim to displace pre-existing women's groups, rather they sought to create new modes of organisation through which women's political, social and cultural energies could be creatively released. The second-wave of feminism appeared after a number of established women's groups were already in place. Thus, from the outset the new women's movement had two wings, and it is important, if not always easy, to distinguish between them. Organisation is perhaps their most important distinguishing feature. Women's rights groups have tended to be organised along traditional hierarchical lines with formal structures and clearly stated objectives. Women's liberation groups, which are often called 'autonomous feminist' groups, have avoided formal organisational structures, political affiliations and hierarchy. But objectives of the rights and liberation groups often differ only in emphasis and there is even some overlap of organisational forms.

The two types of organisation might best be seen as a continuum, at one end of which women's rights groups work hard to become respected and influential pressure groups, whilst at the other, women's liberation groups have favoured more radical methods of direct action. Both types of group play a role in women's movement politics, with the relative significance of each varying somewhat by country in liberal democratic Europe. In state socialist Europe only the 'rights' type of group is to be found.

Although new rights groups have appeared during the last twenty years, their form is one which was inherited from first-wave feminism. Indeed, differences between the two types of women's group may be seen in part as a reflection of differences in the political environments of first- and second-wave feminism. The structure of the rights groups parallels the structures of the organisations which they have aimed to influence. The autonomous feminists are, as we shall see below, more concerned to create alternatives than achieving influence. They are not pressure groups in the traditional sense of the term.

Autonomous feminism is very much a product of its time and place. It could not have existed at the time of the first-wave movement. It would not have been legal. This difference in the legal status of the two waves of feminism is an important one. Briefly, the women's liberation movement has had resources of basic civil and political rights whilst those involved in the first-wave of feminism did not. Indeed, it was civil and political rights which they were trying to obtain. Paradoxically, the second-wave movement stems in part from the disappointment many women felt about the benefits those political rights could bring them and in part from an imaginative use of those rights. In many countries several decades of formal political equality had failed to alter a situation in which women had little political influence. A motivating force behind the new women's movement was anger that this should be the case, and that anger often led to a rejection of the formal political arena with its legal political institutions and towards a search for alternative political modes. The new women's movement has wherever it has occurred involved elements of self-education, of consciousness-raising and the building of its own institutions within patriarchal (male-dominated) society.

Neither the women's rights organisations nor the women's liberation groups have limited their objectives to legislative or administrative change; both have aimed also to change norms, values and attitudes. Dahlerup and Gulli (1983, 19) make the point that both parts of the movement are marginal to the political system, but the women's liberation wing is rather more so. Taking several issues in Norway and Denmark as their examples, they illustrate that the women's liberation groups have been most engaged in raising issues whilst the rights organisations have followed them through the decision-making process, using conventional pressure group tactics such as resolutions, lobbies, meetings, and so on.

The distinction between the two types of group may also be characterised as involving the consistency of willingness to work within the system. Such work is the *raison d'etre* of rights groups, but only an occasional tactic for the others. In short, then, the movement differs over strategies but is often found to be united over tactics and cooperation between its two wings in countries where both exist.

Contemporary feminism, like its first-wave counterpart, is a complex of organisations, initiatives and ideas. At grass roots level numerous women engage in a range of activities which are loosely linked into a widespread social movement. At the level of thought, a rich body of theory has been developed into several distinctive feminist philosophies. Clearly, an appreciation of its forms and its preoccupations is essential to the understanding of the politics of second-wave feminism. Thus, before embarking upon a discussion of the experiences of feminism in the different European countries, we must first consider both its characteristics as a movement and its theoretical preoccupations.

Feminism as a Social Movement

When attempting to generalise about first or second-wave feminism, scholars most often turn to the concept of a social movement for a means of organising their material (Freeman, 1975; Bouchier, 1979, 1983; Banks, 1981; Randall, 1982). There is now quite a literature on social movements, and numerous definitions may be cited. Blumer (1951, 199) refers to a 'collective enterprise to establish a new order of life'. Heberle (1951, 6) regards a social movement as 'a collective attempt to reach a visualised goal, especially a change in social institutions . . .[the] main criterion is that it aims to bring about a fundamental change in the social order'. King (1956, 27) discusses 'a group venture extending beyond a local community or a single event involving a systematic effort to inaugurate changes in thought behaviour and social relationships'. Killian (1964) points to the common elements of collective action for social change in all of these definitions, any one of which might make a starting point for an analysis of the European women's movement. Other American scholars make similarly useful contributions. Noting that in the USA (as in Europe) second-wave feminism coincided with other protest movements, Jo Freeman (1983a, 196) suggests that the reason many different movements appear during the same historical period is probably because the resources one movement generates may be used for and by cognate movements. Hence, student and New Left organisation in Europe generated several other movements, as did the United States civil rights movement.

Dahlerup and Gulli (1983, 9) define a social movement as a deliberate collective activity to promote social change with a minimal degree of organisation and having as its main resource the commitment and the active participation of members or activists. They add that social movements persist over time and have several component parts. Finally, they assert that social movements are definitionally unfinished and represent interests which have not been incorporated into the normal decision-making processes.

Jo Freeman (1983a, 192, 199–200) makes rather more of movement resources, dividing these into categories of *tangible*, including money, space and publicity; *specialised*, including expertise, network access, decision-maker access, status in group and polity; and *unspecialised*, including time and commitment of members. Freeman uses resource categories and the constraints on them as factors capable of distinguishing between what she calls the younger and older branches of the US movement, a distinction broadly similar to the one made above between rights and liberation branches of the European movement. Constraints on resource use are values, past experiences, constituencies, reference groups, expectations and relations with target groups. All of these are self-explanatory except reference groups, which Freeman sees as a standard against which people compare themselves in order to judge behaviour and attitudes. These standards differ for rights group and liberation group women. The latter emphasise their radicalism and fear cooption, whilst the former tend to think in terms of effectiveness. Differing frames of reference translate into a different relationship with the political system. Liberation group women are concerned to 'live' equality and see institutional structures as barriers, whilst rights group women regard structures and institutions as a help. They often had experience (via parties, trades unions, and pressure groups) in working the system, and where it could be worked they preferred to do that (Freeman, 1983a, 200).

Social movement literature also provides us with the notion of a social movement organisation. Social movements (SMs) may consist of various social movement organisations (SMOs) with loose links and boundaries between the organisational core and the movement at large. Thus, for example, many movements have no membership but only activists. Movements themselves often have no boundaries but shade off into other organisations. Dahlerup and Gulli (1983, 12) point out that the women's movement has been a manifest expression of such organisational fluidity in that during its ten to fifteen-year history a continuous proliferation of groups, organisations and projects has taken place at the same time as old and new core groups were declining. Commentators often see this fluidity as fragmentation and therefore a weakness of social movements. Dahlerup and Gulli argue that in the case of the women's movement it should be seen as a specialisation and therefore a strength (see p.96 below).

Social movement organisations may consist of two types, which might usefully be labelled formal and informal SMOs. Formal SMOs are centralised, hierarchical and have a well-developed division of labour. Informal SMOs are decentralised, segmented, reticulate, have no real centre and only a simple division of labour. Strategically, formal SMOs are better suited to short-range goals which involve institutional change in structures whose organisational survival is not the dominant concern. Informal SMOs are better for achieving personal changes in orientation and attitude via recruitment and conversation in structures in which organisational survival is itself a goal. Formal SMOs devote minimal resources to group maintenance. Informal SMOs, with their emphasis on changing people, devote major resources to group maintenance. Both are capable of long-term health and survival, provided neither pursues strategies whch are inappropriate to their organisational form (Freeman, 1983a, 204). In practice, rights groups tend to be comprised of formal SMOs and liberation groups of informal SMOs. Hence, the first-wave feminist movement was largely characterised by formal SMOs, contrasting sharply with the diversity of structures to be found in the second.

It is because women are marginal to the political system and women's causes are seen as peripheral that it has been necessary for feminists to opt for social movement forms. These, if strong enough, help women to gain access at particular points of the political system. Access, once achieved, immediately raises problems of incorporation or cooption for many feminists who are loathe to accept the values of the hierarchical political system. In addition, the focus of part of the movement on broadly conceived life-style issues is not conducive to the development of negotiable goals. The ultimate point of a feminist women's movement must be change in the way politics and the role of the state is conceptualised. That this is a qualitative change may be concealed by the fact that states will make incremental changes in what are apparently the right directions. If the state is to respond to feminist demands, its problem is one of maintaining an economic focus while adding goals of human development to traditional state concerns.

The Preoccupations of Feminism: Theory, Strategy and Tactics

Feminist theory has two related aims: understanding the nature of the oppression of women and devising strategies by which to end that oppression. The potential for disagreement and division is large, and it is perhaps surprising that the movement has been able to unite over so many issues.

As in the first-wave movement, particular texts had an influence on feminist theory. These included Simone de Beauvoir's *The Second Sex*, (1949), Betty Friedan's *The Feminine Mystique* (1963), Germaine Greer's *The Female Eunuch* (1970), Shulamith Firestone's *The Dialectics of Sex* (1971) and Kate Millet's *Sexual Politics* (1972). Probably the most important of these was Simone de Beauvoir's book, which first appeared in 1949 but gained influence only slowly until the movement for women's liberation itself began to grow rapidly in the 1960s. Betty Friedan's book is often credited with being the spark which touched off second wave feminism in the USA after its publication in 1963. All of the texts were influential, however, and read (in translation if necessary) throughout the movement. They raised the questions and explored the themes which became the common issues of women's liberation.

There is, in fact, no single feminist theory as such, but there are feminist theories within a number of philosophical traditions, and there are some common elements to the various theoretical · strands. Notable amongst those common elements is the perception that women's issues are political issues (the personal is political) and that to be a feminist is to define those issues as the focus of one's political energies. An important concept used by almost all feminists is that of 'sexism', meaning the unequal treatment of women simply because of their sex. 'Sisterhood' is also a widely used term, referring to the solidarity of all women both within and outside the movement. Sharing these concerns are liberal, socialist and radical feminists, each of whom brings a different theoretical and strategic perspective to a fundamentally feminist stance.

Liberal feminists hold that progressive reforms will lead ultimately to equality for women. They emphasise nurture-based views of women's oppression and see socialisation at various points rather than direct male obstruction as responsible for women's disadvantaged status. They have goals which are emancipatory rather than liberatory and are the most conservative wing of the movement. Their demands are, however, seen as radical by powerholders and are widely resisted (Bouchier, 1983, 66).

Socialist feminism draws on a long tradition of concern by socialist theorists with the 'woman question'. Its theory is continuously developing but has several identifiable core elements and preoccupations. Reflected in this thought are the various tactical differences which exist between Fabian, Trotskyist, Leninist, Maoist, humanist and libertarian Marxist socialism as well as differences between socialist and social democratic strands. In practice, socialist feminism shades into liberalism to its right and radical feminism to its left, but its distinguishing feature is the importance it ascribes to the politics of class division, although this is today more ambiguous than it was at the turn of the century (see Ch. 2 above). Another key idea of socialist feminism is Engels' view that bourgeois marriage reproduces in microcosm the conflicts and contradictions of bourgeois society. Engels felt that exploitation of women by men was a product of capitalist economic arrangements. It would end when capitalism ended. Marxist feminists today are not convinced of this and regard women as dually oppressed by both capitalism and men. Socialist feminists are socialists, but they believe that existing socialist groups have demonstrated a lack of interest in women's need to confront male as well as capitalist oppression. They thus find it necessary for women to have separate organisations, at least in the short term. Marxist feminists have constructed complex theories based on ideas of wage-labour ideology and the family to demonstrate how capitalism benefits from the exploitation of working-class women both at work and in the home. According to such theories, the exploitation of women differs from that of men in three ways: women are a reserve army of labour who receive low wages, have no prospects and lack security, they perform unpaid work in the family and are superexploited as consumers and sex objects (Bouchier 1983, 69). The main purpose of the family is to enable the performance of unremunerated work in the home, which although not part of the market economy is essential to capitalism. The reasons for capitalism's dependence on the family are that it is the site of a hidden subsidy, that it breeds and trains new workers, and that it is a free support system for the production of commodities. Socialist feminists also place great stress on the sexual and personal constraints of family life, with writers such as Barrett and McIntosh (1982) demonstrating the manner in which the nuclear family exhalts individualist values at the expense of more politically dangerous social ones.

Preoccupation with the ideological apparatus of the feminine mystique has also characterised the theories of socialist feminists who have tried to show how and for whose benefit that mystique has come into being. Beginning with the mythologies surrounding the roles of housewife and mother, socialist feminists have also attempted to look at the consumer aspects of ideology, in the form of the notion of the ideal home (Figes, 1972; Mitchell, 1966, 1971, 1974; O'Brien 1981). It is difficult to summarise socialist feminist writing on ideology as the theories are complex and the language used to explain them is often obscure. A central notion is the fetishism of the home and the role this plays in binding the woman more tightly to the family, the better to serve capitalist purposes. Empirical accounts of the role of ideology are rather more accessible, concentrating on accounts of women's experience and the realisation that the problems of individual women were neither unique nor a product of personal inadequacy but a widespread phenomenon with a system-based explanation (see Rowbotham, 1973; Levine, 1982).

Radical feminism occupies some of the same terrain as socialist feminism, and some radical feminists think of themselves as feminist socialists, a term which suggests similar views but different emphases. The tactics and preferred organisational forms of radical feminism are distinctive and it is the radical feminists who have kept the vision of a feminist utopia alive. Radical feminism is unambiguous in its location of the sources of women's oppression, which it sees as first and foremost the fault of men. Not a fully developed or complete body of thought, radical feminism has been consistently innovative and its theories have changed over time. They may be seen as grouped around four main themes. The most influential of these is the concept of 'patriarchy'. Now used by most feminists, the term 'patriarchy' points to the fact that male dominance is the oldest form of dominance and for radical feminists signifies the primacy of sex over class divisions. It is patriarchal (literally, father-led) culture which defines biological femininity as inferior. Like their socialist counterparts, radical feminist theorists stress the role of the family in the oppression of women. The family is the basic source of male power. It is there that the exploitation of women by men is institutionalised. Motherhood roles, too, are also widely considered to be a confidence trick, but many feminists dispute this, arguing that motherhood outside the boundaries of the nuclear family need not be an oppressive experience. Sexuality is the third theme, and possibly the most important preoccupation of radical feminism. It is sexuality which makes men the 'intimate' enemy. There is a range of radical views on this question. At a minimum, calls are made for an end to the double standard, to monogamy and to compulsory sex in marriage. In the late 1970s there was a swing away from advocating androgyny as a way to liberation towards a celebration of womanhood, paving the way for greater acceptance of the maximalist view that celibacy or lesbianism offer the only theoretically consistent sexual possibilities for committed feminists. Maximalist views are not widely held but their existence sites a parameter and points up certain contradictions in their position to those women who do not agree. The fourth theme is more loosely defined and might be called 'women's studies'. Radical feminists are committed to rescuing knowledge about women and are especially committed to historical excavations of the origins of patriarchy (Bouchier, 1983, 78–80).

The three political tendencies of feminism do not include all of its concerns, nor are they as readily distinguishable as Bouchier's account might suggest. They are, however, present wherever a second-wave feminist movement has emerged, with particular mix and form of each varying fairly predictably by national culture. Banks (1981) traces three strands of equal rights, evangelical and socialist feminism in the first-wave of feminism to the liberal, radical and socialist forms of the contemporary movement, arguing that each appeals to a different sort of woman. Whichever terms are employed, it is important to remember that all strands of feminist thought are essentially radical in their assertion of women's equality and their challenge of the dominant evaluation of women as less than human and the definition of humanity itself as something which is essentially male. Feminism, argues Miles (1981, *passim*) affirms a specific-value framework which signifies a shift in women's political activism from a pressure-group nature to a whole alternative politics. Such a view implies that involvement in the feminist movement will itself have a profound effect on the nature of a group or organisation choosing such a course.

Certainly, the tactics of second-wave feminist politics have involved radical activities, and new kinds of political action. Feminists have pursued traditional political activities of all kinds but have also established, for example, women's health centres and refuges, rape counselling services, abortion services, research and publishing cooperatives and, most recently, peace camps and their networks of support groups. In general, strategic choices have not parallcled divisions in the movement, and virtually all modes of political activism have been attempted. There has, however, been an implicit tactical division of labour between the tendencies. The main liberal strategies have been legal and legislative action, coalition building with established political groups, single-issue campaigns, service delivery and influencing public opinion. Socialist feminists have participated in reform campaigns, practised labour movement entrism, developed critiques of capitalist culture and produced theories of revolutionary change. Radical feminists have concentrated on the establishment of a small group-based counter-culture, set up consciousness-raising groups and established alternative structures such as all-female communes, business ventures, and so on. All of the tendencies have had some experience of most of the available activities, and all agreed early to accept arguments for separate women's political activities, at least in the short term. Organisational separatism has attracted a considerable amount of male hostility in most countries. But drawing upon the experiences of the first-wave movement, feminists are convinced that, in the short term at least, women will only develop the skills required to fight their oppression in the absence of their oppressors. Whilst some radicals would extend their preference for separatism to all areas of life, most feminists regard separatism as a strategic and tactical expedient rather than a long-term goal. Hostility to men is not so total nor so widespread as many of the women's liberation movement's critics suggest. And as Bouchier (1983, 53) points out, critics of feminism's exclusion of men should recall that when the women's movement first re-emerged, its early proponents began by asking (in vain) over and over again for a dialogue with men which would simply treat women's issues with the same seriousness as they did issues affecting men.

Apart from separatism, the other important feature of new feminist organisation has been the widespread eschewal of organisational hierarchy and role specialisation. This has been combined with an avoidance of leaders and spokespersons and a preference at national level for rudimentary umbrella or coordinating groups. This pattern has its advantages, especially in the mobilisation of women new to political activism. Members do develop quickly and skills are shared by all. These small 'structureless' groups are, in their ideal form, what Rowbotham (1979) calls 'prefigurative' in that they are a form of participatory egalitarian democracy keeping faith with liberatory goals. But as Freeman (1975) has argued, such forms do not of themselves prevent the formation of elites who may in fact have particular advantages in a loosely structured and informal organisation. And even when elites do not emerge, the form is ill-suited to the pursuit of many goals, leading to duplication of effort, overload of key personnel and problems with maintaining continuity. Freeman refers also to what she calls the tyranny of structurelessness, which may lead to a stifling conformity in which display of obvious and useful skill differences is regarded as competitive and even anti-feminist. This results in

difficulties in making rapid responses to events. More importantly, in virtually every country under discussion in this volume
the women's liberation movement is taken less seriously than it
might be because of ineffective national coordination.

Vicky Randall (1982, 164–5) reminds us that the argument
might be made that feminism produces the structure it needs. But,
like all social movements, feminism has multiple goals, and goals
of self-realisation may require an organisation ill-suited to the
goals of political change. These contradictions are not particularly
apparent for the long periods during which numerous small groups
are working at their particular project in a congenial atmosphere,
but they become important when the movement is under threat or
when it wants to bring about a concrete and immediate change.

The variety and range of 'national' feminisms to be found in
Europe is wide. Each movement is a distinctive one which,
although influenced by women's liberation politics elsewhere
(especially the USA), could have assumed its particular form only
in its country of origin. Strong feminist movements emerged in
Britain, Italy, Holland, Finland, Denmark and Norway during the
early 1970s at the same time as weaker forms appeared in West
Germany, France, Sweden and Belgium. In the new liberal democracies of Spain and Portugal, feminism emerged later and developed more slowly, but both had identifiable autonomous feminist
movements by the end of the 1970s. In almost all cases the first
signs of new women's liberation movements appeared on the Left,
where many of its early proponents had received their political
training in the student politics of the 1960s. Their feminist activities signalled an interest in a cause which was to take them far from
the socialist mainstream into new modes of thought and action.
These, whilst often repeated in a number of countries, also
reflected the political environments in which they were set. Cultural and institutional as well as ideological and organisational
factors, then, produced variations in second-wave feminism. The
remainder of this chapter will illustrate these points, examining in
detail the various European feminisms of the 1970s and 1980s.

Britain

First-wave British feminism was never really extinguished but was
replaced during the 1930s by what Banks (1981) calls 'welfare
feminism' and what Wilson calls 'reasonable feminism', at a time

when many women were active in the peace movement and others in the birth control movement. As the birth control movement became more successful, so it became more respectable, and channels for feminist activism appeared to evaporate. For the first two decades after the Second World War, women in Britain, as in the USA, tended to accept domestic seclusion as desirable if not always possible. With the exception of a few organisations such as the Six-Point Group and the Women's Freedom League, demands for the political liberation of women had ceased to be made (Wilson, 1980, 187). At official level, when the government found it necessary to consult women, it contacted traditional groups such as the Women's Institute or the Townswoman's Guilds or representatives of the women's organisations of the political parties, the unions, and the churches. Such groups made representations in the realm of women's rights but were far from radical in their outlook before the re-emergence of feminism at the end of the 1960s.

The origins of the second wave of British feminism are numerous. Certainly, considerable inspiration was drawn from the experience of United States women, but there were many indigenous British beginnings as well. Wilson (1980, 184) identifies the Women's Peace Groups' commemoration of fifty years of suffrage in 1968 as a catalyst. Randall (1982, 152) points to a growth of militancy amongst working-class women and to experiences gained by women activists in the Vietnam Solidarity Campaign, the rise of the student Left and the revitalised Marxist parties of the 1960s. Coote and Campbell (1982, 17) pinpoint the publication of Juliet Mitchell's essay 'The Longest Revolution' in the *New Left Review* in 1966 as marking the beginning of a long process of reinstating the 'woman question' onto the political agenda of the Left. This was followed in 1969 by the publication of Sheila Rowbotham's pamphlet *Women's Liberation and the New Politics* in which the author linked housework responsibilities with unequal rights at work and made a powerful case for the necessity of understanding the subjugation of women in British society. Both writers were expressing ideas whose time had come. The first consciousness-raising groups had appeared in London by 1968.

Theoretical developments were paralleled by a mood of labour militancy in which women concerned about equal pay began to take action at the end of the 1960s. Most famous was the strike by women sewing machinists at the Ford motor factory at Dagenham in 1968, which was an equal-pay strike. The women demanded regrading from an unskilled (predominantly female) to a semi-skilled (predominantly male) classification. The strike became a media event and the furore which followed involved the women being entertained to tea by a personally sympathetic Employment Secretary (Barbara Castle). The dispute was never satisfactorily settled. The women were conceded 95 per cent of the male rate but failed to obtain regrading to semi-skilled status, and the matter was once again at issue in December 1984. The 1968 strike, despite its limitations, became a source of inspiration for other women, and shortly thereafter the trade unionist National Joint Action Campaign for Women's Equal Rights (NJACWER) was founded. Throughout the same period preparations were being made for the passage of the Equal Pay Act of 1970, activity which was important in establishing the beginnings of feminist networks. During that time rights-groups women established a pattern of activism which was to provide a base for the campaign which led to the passage of the 1975 Sex Discrimination Act. Such events both caught and helped to set a mood. Coote and Campbell write of the recollections of a Bristol woman who in trying to organise transport and a group to attend a NJACWER demonstration in London, failed to organise the excursion but found that the group she had contacted began to meet on a regular basis as a result. Formed in May 1969, this was the first Bristol women's liberation group.

Another important catalyst was a direct United States import. It was the circulation in Britain of Anne Koedt's paper 'The Myth of the Vaginal Orgasm' which indicated to many women that some of their personal problems were shared and focused a dissatisfaction with prevailing sexual exploitation, even where the essay did not tally with women's personal experiences. Coote and Campbell see the response to Koedt's paper as an antidote to the permissive 1960s, which in practice had led to expectations that women be more sexually available to men who were to acknowledge less responsibility for their sexual activities. British culture in the 1960s had also been characterised by new or revived kinds of liberatory thinking and thus supplied both the modes of thought and the contradictions which nurtured a feminist resurgence. Set squarely within such modes of thought was Germaine Greer's immensely popular book *The Female Eunuch*, published in 1970. Greer was widely read, quoted and misquoted, and in receipt of considerable media attention. Containing strong and interesting views on sex and sexuality, her book provided a (nearly) home-grown discussion departure point for British women. Also influential was Shulamith Firestone's *The Dialectic of Sex*, which argued that women were an oppressed class, a notion which horrified the traditional Marxist theorists of the British Left. From the start, then, the emergence of the second wave of British feminism was rooted in socialist organisations and ideas about sexuality, marking a tension between two strands of thought which were to be present for at least fifteen years. That tension was to characterise most of the other European movements as well.

Organising British feminism was something which began almost by accident, when a group of women attending a Ruskin College (Oxford) History Workshop objected to the absence there of any discussion of women's history. In response they decided to organise what became the first national Women's Liberation Conference at Ruskin College in 1970. Three hundred people were expected, but 600 turned up, including representatives of the various New Left groups, from NJACWER and from suffrage organisations and from such newer organisations as the Women's Liberation Workshop. Attenders reported a deep sense of disillusion with traditional forms of political activity, which many felt had little if anything to offer those struggling for sex equality. The conference agreed to set up a National Women's Coordinating Committee based on a structure of small autonomous groups in the localities or of special interests. Each group had equal status, and activity would be loosely coordinated through national meetings to which each group could send two delegates. It is from this point that the women's liberation movement in Britain developed into an autonomous political movement. Women's marches were held in London and Liverpool on International Women's Day in March 1971, by which time the four original basic demands had been worked out and were carrried on banners. These were equal pay now, equal education and job opportunities, free contraception and abortion on demand and free twenty-four-hour nurseries. The names of women who wished to meet again were collected and the London march alone resulted in fifty new women's groups being formed. National conferences continued to be held until 1978 by which time three further demands had been added to the original four: financial and legal independence, a woman's right to define her own sexuality and freedom from intimidation or use of violence or sexual coercion, regardless of marital status and an end to all laws, assumptions and institutions which perpetuate male violence and aggression towards women (Coote and Campbell 1982, 26). The seventh demand caused some considerable discussion at what was to be the last national conference in 1978.

The 1978 conference was dominated by a split between the two divergent strands of British feminism, often referred to as the radical and socialist wings of the movement. In common with their counterparts elsewhere, British radical feminists see the fight for liberation as being essentially against men and are deeply suspicious of any attempt to link feminist to other struggles. In their view, women are an oppressed class and what is essential is the formulation of a pro-woman line. Radical feminists are divided over their aims. One possible goal is to destroy masculinity as a social construct and thus transform men into human beings with whom harmonious relations may be held once they no longer possess the power to dominate women. Alternatively, biological distinctions might be better avoided by establishing ways of living and reproducing which are independent of men. Some British radical feminists might properly be labelled 'revolutionary feminists' in that they take extreme separatist positions involving the repudiation of heterosexual relations and of male children. Most stop short of such extremes, however. Radical feminists also eschew the male-constructed political system and argue that there is no evidence that change through the political system can alter the way that men treat women (Coote and Campbell, 1982, 29).

Coote and Campbell remind us that although second-wave feminism had socialist roots, the development of socialist feminism as a distinct political current began as a response to the challenge of radical feminism. Many newly convinced feminists were not prepared to abandon associations with left-wing politics, and indeed, a characteristic distinguishing the British from the American movement is the strength of the organised Left. Britain, with a mass-based Labour Party and a trade union movement which constitutes an enormous working-class assembly has always been more responsive to socialist ideas than the USA. British socialist feminists held that women's oppression should be understood in a framework which gave weight to economic forces and Marxian notions of class conflict. They rejected separatism as a way of life but conceded that there was a need for separate women's assemblies in the short term. They were particularly concerned to draw as many women as possible into the movement and were especially keen to attract working-class women. They were also concerned to enlist male support. Socialist feminists in Britain did not eschew existing political arrangements but saw the need to fight both in and against male-dominated power relationships. For them 'the women's liberation movement is not a sanctuary from male supremacy, but a means of combative engagement with it' (Coote and Campbell 1982, 31–5).

Both strands of the liberation movement in Britain have normally been cabable of working together, and it is more common to find a tactical unity than not. Both have come to agree that men should be excluded from most feminist gatherings. Socialist feminists initially experienced problems with the issues but agreed to women-only organisations after learning with horror that the presence of men made some women feel excluded, after which they were inclined to follow the dictates of sisterly solidarity.

Organisationally, the British movement is a series of small groups often based in local women's centres and linked in loose networks which bring supporters together for various national campaigns. There has been from the outset a link between the new feminism and the trade union movement, with Trades Councils frequently taking a lead in making pro-women union policy proposals. Early campaigns included efforts to prevent the Heath government from abolishing family allowances (paid to the mother) in favour of tax credits (paid to the family breadwinner, usually the father) in 1973. Activity also took place at elite level (notably on the part of a few Labour Party women over pension rights and the passage of the Sex Discrimination Act, which established the Equal Opportunities Commission in 1975). Workplace campaigns included an extensive effort to unionise night cleaners in the major cities, and equal rights at work activities were common in the early 1970s. In early 1974 a conference was organised by the National Council for Civil Liberties of women's group members and trades unionists at TUC headquarters. Shortly thereafter the London Trades Council issued a ten-point charter for working women which had been drawn up by its Communist Party members. A widespread campaign by a network of working women's charter groups was soon organised around the ten points, which included equal pay and opportunity, eighteen weeks paid maternity leave, a minimum wage, increased family allowances, an end to social security and tax discrimination, and so on. Eventually the demands were accepted by the TUC, which revised its own working woman's charter to included most of them in 1975.[1]

Apart from the consciousness-raising movement, which continued throughout the decade, four campaigns were particularly prominent in the development of British feminism during the 1970s. Their importance is evident both from the large numbers of women (and sometimes men) involved in them and their prominent position on an agenda which was also taken up by rights group women. These were the campaigns over child care, the women's aid movement, the various women against violence activities and the campaign for abortion on demand (Coote and Campbell, 1982, Randall, 1982).

The child care campaign was perhaps the most disappointing. Child care was an early major concern of the British women's movement. Efforts included setting up nurseries on a self-help basis with a range of fund-raising efforts, including attempts to obtain state grants. Children's community centres were set up which were run as full-time parent-controlled non-sexist nurseries. But such schemes foundered on the shoals of government cuts in funding. Policy success was of the posturing variety, with many influential bodies officially recognising the importance of child care but few prepared to prioritise the issue. Child care is extremely expensive and it has been difficult to persuade successive British governments to provide the funding. Provision actually contracted at a rapid rate after the mid-1970s. Whilst the campaign continues, its members have been understandably demoralised at its lack of more than symbolic success.

More visible and extremely successful has been the women's aid movement. One woman, Erin Pizzey, set up the first refuge for battered wives in 1972. She is a skilled publicist and was able both to attract attention to her centre and to alert the public to the prevalence of domestic violence against women. Pizzey proved to have a talent for attracting funds from the government, from charitable trusts and from other donors. In the wake of her activity, women throughout Britain formed groups with a view to setting up refuges. Twenty-seven groups were represented at a national conference in 1974. By 1975, 111 such groups were represented, 28 of which had already established refuges and 83 of which were at the planning stage. By 1980 the movement consisted of 99 groups which had established 200 refuges throughout the country.[2] Unusually, the Women's Aid Movement has a national organisation, the Women's Aid Federation, to which almost all of the groups belong (Bouchier, 1983, 141–2). The Federation has its own headquarters, a non-hierarchical structure and explicitly feminist objectives. Its aims include the demands of the women's liberation movement as well as insistence on the autonomy of each group, open-door policies for all refuges and the right of women in each refuge to self-determination. The campaign attracted support from across the women's movement bore parliamentary fruit with the Domestic Violence Act of 1976, whereby women could get a court injunction to restrain a violent husband or cohabitee. Women's Aid also widened the constituency of the movement in that its management involved numerous women in the provision of services and fund-raising as well as the women it assisted. Its success in policy terms by comparison to that of the child care movement may be attributable to the fact that Women's Aid required significantly less in the way of resources.

Activities of the campaigns against violence to women began with another initiative to provide services. This was the opening of the first rape crisis centre in North London in 1976. The need for counselling services for those who had been sexually assaulted was identified following widespread women's movement discussion of the issue of rape. The North London centre opened with the aid of grants from two charitable trusts and from the Department of the Environment. Run by a feminist collective it was widely copied and by 1981 sixteen centres had appeared in various parts of the country, along with rape crisis (telephone) lines. This campaign too had a parliamentary dimension in the 1976 passage of the Sexual Offences (Amendment) Act, which improved the privacy safeguards available for rape victims during trials. The chief aim of rape crisis centres was, however, to provide a woman-centred basis of support for women who had been victims of assault by men. The issue has continued to draw women into activity. 'Reclaim the night marches' have been widely supported, as have various protests against foolish and frivolous statements by members of the judiciary during rape trials, which seemed to be particularly prevalent during the early part of the 1980s (Pattullo, 1983, 16–22). Further impetus in this area has come from the organisation of the Women Against Violence Against Women as a result of the series of brutal murders in the North of England by the 'Yorkshire Ripper' (Coote and Campbell, 1982, 204).

The abortion movement has been the only other women's campaign (besides Women's Aid) to generate a national organisation in Britain. The National Abortion Campaign should be seen as part of the feminist movement and of the birth control movement and may thus trace its roots right back to the earliest of the nineteenth-century feminist groups. Its activities illustrate many of the characteristic strengths and weaknesses of the British women's movement and are worth outlining in some detail. The National Abortion Campaign (NAC) is a single-issue group launched during 1975 with the immediate aim of defending the 1967 Abortion Act. It was and is a specifically feminist group, containing both socialist and radical feminists. Organisationally, NAC is a non-hierarchical series of local groups which are linked for mutual support and for planning national campaigns. Policy at national level is made by annual conferences and six-weekly planning meetings open to all members but probably mainly attended by members of London NAC. NAC itself favours 'a woman's right to choose', with abortion on demand up to term. With its roots in the feminist movement, NAC has avoided organisational hierarchy and centralism. It has operated as a proselytising group which organised demonstrations, local pickets of MPs surgeries, day schools and conferences. Marsh and Chambers (1981, 46–49) consider that NAC grew every time an amending bill was introduced in Parliament, so that by 1979 it had around 350 affiliated local groups.

NAC's socialist members had been mainly drawn from the International Marxist Group, which had considerable experience of trade union politics. While their tactics, especially the inclusion of males, were resented by radical feminist NAC members, successful efforts to recruit trade union members and to forge links with individual unions were the foundation of its success. Skills at parliamentary lobbying were gained during campaigns to defeat restrictive amendments to the 1967 Act, and by the end of the 1970s NAC was maintaining a set of Westminster contacts and, along with the Abortion Law Reform Association (ALRA), attending occasional meetings with the Department of Health and Social Security. If not a well-established pressure group, it was certainly a force to be reckoned with.

More significant for this study was NAC's mobilisation of the feminist network in the labour movement. This began at local level where members who were in trade unions were encouraged to pass resolutions through branches which supported the 1967 Act, called for abortion on request and for affiliation to NAC. Motions were also put forward to go to union national conferences, to the TUC annual congress and to Labour Party conferences. Progress was patchy, but NAC was able to make full use of women's movement networks. Women in the National Union of Public Employees (NUPE) and the National Association of Local Government Officers (NALGO) were particularly helpful, as were women in official trade union positions. NAC activists looked first to union women's officers and to researchers working on women. These first contacts developed into networks of feminists who were at that time beginning to become organised within the union movement (Coote and Campbell, 1982, Ch. 5). Initial contacts were developed by various NAC and Labour Abortion Rights Campaign sponsored conferences and 'fringe' meetings of NAC at Labour Party and union annual conferences. These led to further contacts, who took issues back to their branches, where they often proposed support and affiliation resolutions. Thus, NALGO and NAPO (National Association of Probation Officers) officials first contacted NAC as a result of the issue being raised in their unions.

The women's movement and experience gained in battles over equal pay in the unions had left residual networks of women with the skills and the confidence to tackle the abortion issue in the Labour movement (see Meehan, 1985). Local NAC groups also looked to area unions and Trades Councils as a place to organise. They wrote to individual union branches and Trades Councils in their area asking for support and donations and inviting trade union delegates to come along to local NAC meetings or local campaign arrangements committees. Success varied, with some unions very reluctant to take up the issue. The large male-dominated unions in particular were reluctant to affiliate nation-ally, but at branch level, sections of both the National Union of Mineworkers and the building workers unions became affiliated. Gradually, networks were extended and strengthened until local union affiliations were sufficient to provide NAC with both funds and an organisational base upon which to operate. The Corrie Bill provided considerable impetus to local groups,[3] whilst national affiliations were still percolating up through the union hierarchies from branch level in 1983. Both the National Association of Probation Officers and the Confederation of Health Service Employees affiliated at national level for the first time in 1983. Normally success in obtaining union support depended upon the presence of women activists at the relevant meetings, although considerable support was forthcoming from the male Left.

'Abortion on request' had been taken regularly to the TUC (Trades Union Congress) Women's Conference and later to the TUC Annual Congress, where it was passed in 1975. In 1978 the Congress pledged to support a march in the event of another restrictive bill. In 1979 the pledge was fulfilled. NAC's most publicised success was the official TUC demonstration against the Corrie Bill on 31 October 1979.

Involving an estimated 100,000 marchers, it is widely believed to be Britain's largest ever pro-abortion rights march and was the largest trade union demonstration ever held on a cause outside the normal collective bargaining ambit.

The most important point which emerges from our description of NAC's activities is the existence and range of the feminist network in Britain and its capacity for mobilisation if a women's issue is believed to be at stake. Whilst prudent assessment would stress that it has been better placed to defend the abortion status quo than it has apparently been to correct women's disadvantaged position in the labour market, the network's potential must nevertheless be acknowledged.

During the 1970s the British movement also saw the formation of women's health centres and publishing collectives, and women organised within the professions as well as within the political parties and the unions. Women's publishing imprints became well established, and a small but significant women's studies movement got under way. Universities and polytechnics became continuing centres for the organisation of student feminists, and many specialist groups became particularly influential. Women in the Media, for example, have been credited with a quiet revolution in the way important women's magazines address their readers, leading perhaps to another impetus in a gradual revolutuion in public attitudes.

New developments amongst rights groups in the 1980s included the establishment of the '300 Group' which aimed to get 300 women elected to parliament. This all-party group cooperated with more traditional organisations such as the National Federation of Women's Institutes. One important joint initiative was a series of workshops on how to get elected to local councils held during 1984. As elsewhere, considerable effort was put into the development of a feminist theory, with many women taking up the work of Gramsci, Althusser and Lacan, transforming their philosophies more or less successfully to suit feminist purposes.

From about 1975 onwards a radicalisation of the British movement was apparent, which led it to new preoccupations but also to splits and dispersals of early groups. An apparent movement decline at the end of the 1970s has been characterised as the inevitable outcome of the process of decentralisation and a tendency to split (Bouchier, 1983). An alternative view is that the British movement had always been characterised by numerous small groups, and what changed through the years after 1975 was their preferred form of activity. As confidence was gained, groups turned from consciousness raising to the various fields of feminist practice. Typically, these included work in the areas of education, aid or service delivery of various kinds, cultural activities and work in established institutions such as parties, trades unions and the administration. These areas are sites of relatively permanent feminist activity and involve women from rights and liberation movement backgrounds. There is also an evident continuation of life-style feminism to be found in such phenomena as the women's peace camps at Greenham Common and elsewhere. The Greenham Common protest had generated a national network of women's support groups by the end of 1984, and the peace women's movement was said to involve tens of thousands of women across the UK by the end of 1984 (Huws, 1985, 6).

David Bouchier estimates that about 10,000 British women were regularly active and involved in the women's movement in 1983, in about 300 groups of all types, with a periphery of another 20,000 who were occasionally or marginally active. Within those numbers were a core of about 2,000 each, of radical and socialist feminists who in effect devoted their whole lives to the movement. Then, as now, activity tended to concentrate in urban areas, but communications were sufficient to ensure that dispersal did not lead to isolation. A large number of cultural groups exist particularly in music and the theatre (Bouchier, 1983, 177–7). At the same time feminist concerns have become more acceptable and many of the more traditional women's groups have shown support for feminist goals. Thus, its boundaries tended to change as the movement has developed, and the loosely structured organisational forms preferred since the early 1970s are proving to have a flexibility unmatched by other types of organisation. Although social movements typically become more centralised as they become better established, the British women's movement has become more dispersed but at the same time more encompassing.

The Netherlands, Denmark and Norway

During the 1970s the women's movement in Holland and some of the Nordic countries developed in a similar manner to that in Britain. Each drew on American experience but was also a product of indigenous influence, including various organisations which had been in existence since the nineteenth-century movement for women's suffrage. Thus, in Holland important organisational influences included the Dutch Federation of Countrywomen and the Dutch Federation of Housewives, which were politically neutral but nevertheless affected by the new women's liberation movement. More influential were such groups as the Union for Women's Interests (Vereniging voor Vrouwenbelangen), a residue of first-wave feminism which had kept up the struggle for women's rights during the 1950s and 1960s. Mainly comprised of professional women, it had contacts amongst the

Liberal Party and was one of the first established groups to perceive abortion as a women's issue. The abortion issue was also instrumental in mobilising women's groups in the various political parties and the Vrouwenbond NVV, which is an organisation of the wives of trades unionists attached to the socialist Dutch Federation of Trades Unions (Outshoorn, 1983, 10).

New feminism in the Netherlands began with the formation of MVM (Man-Vrouw-Maatschappij: literally, 'men-women-society'), which had been founded by professional men and women and is comparable to the United States National Organisation of Women (NOW), although it never attained the size of NOW. Essentially a rights group, MVM aimed to be a women's lobby participating in the pressure group system and up to 1975 was a major source of expertise on women's issues. Indeed, many of its leaders were coopted onto government status of women committees. This cooption left a void in the MVM leadership and may have been partly responsible for the group's decline in the late 1970s (Outshoorn, 1983, 10).

When the new women's movement first surfaced at the end of the 1960s, its demands were for sexual freedom, free abortion and contraception, but in the absence of a concept of patriarchy to explain women's oppression, these demands worked against women. It was difficult to connect sexual liberation and women's economic vulnerability, hence early writings tended to stress how emancipation would make women a more attractive proposition to potential husbands and employers (de Vries, 1981, 392).

Dutch new feminism really took off with the rise of Dolle Mina in 1970.[4] Dolle Mina was good at generating publicity and its name became synonymous with liberated women. The group attracted a wide following, but it had organisational difficulties largely because it lacked leadership. Originally, Dolle Mina included men, but they tended to drift off when consciousness-raising techniques became important and men were excluded from many meetings. As consciousness-raising became widespread from about 1972 onwards, large numbers of groups appeared. Radical and socialist feminist wings became evident in the movement, ranging from absolute separatist radical feminists at one end of a continuum to socialist feminists who see the women's liberation movement mainly as a recruiting forum at the other (de Vries, 1981, 396). The radical feminists tendency stressed women's centres and worked in a series of single-issue campaigns, each with its own group (e.g. health, rape, battering). The only issue over which all groups worked together under one organisational umbrella was abortion (Outshoorn, 1983, 11–12). The movement has led to the revival of feminism in all sorts of women's organisations, especially amongst women in the political parties and the trades unions, where feminists became firmly entrenched. Feminists also became well established in many sectors of society such as education and the social services.

In both Norway and Denmark the first new feminist organisations appeared a little later than in Holland. The New Feminists in Norway and the Redstockings in Denmark both began in 1970 contemporaneously with Dolle Mina. Both had decentralised diffuse structures and both devoted a large part of their energies to consciousness-raising activities. By 1972 both had produced countervailing socialist feminist groups. Like Holland, both Norway and Denmark had pre-existing feminist movements which fought for married women's rights and which remained active throughout the post-suffrage decades (Dahlerup and Gulli, 1983). The presence of such groups gives newly emerging women's liberation groups the advantage of having to engage established political institutions only on specific issues. As a result, the disadvantages of the preferred small group structure were not serious ones, and women's movement organisations were able to develop at their own pace and were afforded the luxury of regular splits and continuous fragmentation. The long-term result has been that, as in Britain, well-established feminist networks have emerged in many important institutions.

The four areas of feminist practice found in Britain also characterised the Nordic and Dutch movements. The wish to extend the women's movement to poor and working-class Dutch women has resulted in a vast network of feminist adult education groups, in addition to the outgrowth of women's studies at universities. A groundswell of interest in improving educational qualifications amongst working-class women and ordinary housewives was reflected in the growth of high schools for adults known as open schools or 'Mothers Mavos' because mainly women take advantage of the opportunities they afford. 'Mothers Mavos' are not feminist institutions, but many of their teachers are feminists and many courses have a considerable feminist content. Women's studies courses in Dutch universities face the expected problems of ghettoisation, but there has been a well-organised struggle to get specific women's studies teachers and lecturers established within and outside disciplinary boundaries. These are rooted in numerous staff and student groups and have been reasonably successful in, for example, getting feminist scientists established in women's studies posts (de Vries, 1981, 399). Educational provision of this kind raises considerable problems for feminists, especially those who eschew contact with the state in any form. State funding clearly means state control over at least some elements of the curriculum, and the churches in particular have wished to affect input into popular women's courses. Moreover, state funding for such initiatives has tended to dry up during times of recession, and alternative finance is difficult to obtain.

Aid or self-help has taken the same form in most feminist movements and the three under consideration are not exceptions. Projects involving service delivery have been common, aimed at assisting women and including therapy groups, refuges for battered women, rape crisis centres and support groups of various kinds. Campaigns around single issues have been a major component of practice, and these have most often been over issues which have involved all parts of the movement, including rights groups. The major mobilising issue in all three countries has probably been abortion rights, which turned up on political agendas throughout Western Europe during the 1960s and 1970s.

Cultural work too is well developed and includes theatre groups, festivals, bookstores, publishers, newsletters, theoretical magazines and women's cafés and other centres. There are also often feminist inputs into the mass media, so that what feminism has to offer is consumed by numerous women who avail themselves of its cultural manifestations. In Holland in particular, considerable energy is put into creating agreeable and comfortable places where women meet, in the belief that there is no need to wait until after the revolution to learn that society might be different.

Apart from campaigns, political practice also involves entrism into major political organisations, either converting existing women's groups to feminist views or establishing feminist networks there. In the Netherlands, entrenched proletarian antifeminism is an obstacle faced by the large numbers of women organising as feminists in the political parties, the unions and a number of left-wing campaigns. The largest of these is the Red Women group in the Labour Party. There is also an appreciable feminist presence in the Dutch Federation of Trades Unions (de Vries, 1981, 400). In Denmark, party women's sections are rather weak, with several having been disbanded during the early 1970s. However, beginning with parties of the Left, feminists have organised in all of the parties, and Norway too has feminist influenced women's sections within its parties (Dahlerup and

Gulli, 1983, 13). Such practices do not occur without resistance, both from within the women's movement, which fears cooption and dilution of its aims, and from within the political parties, which perceive such efforts to organise internally as threats to organisational unity. But in welfare states, where so many of the necessities of life are filtered through state agencies, it is difficult for the women's movement to avoid traditional approaches to the policy agenda. Political party and union work in practice involves all the dangers its opponents fear; issues tend to get defined as women's rather than party concerns and receive lower priority; demands have to be translated into terms which male politicians can understand and hence become diluted. Moreover, women are forced to participate in the very large hierarchical structures that the movement has attempted to displace (de Vries, 1981, 402). Thus, the continuing prevalence of small groups linked in loose campaigns and communications networks is not just a mainstay of feminist practice, it is also an important counterweight to some of the realities of political effectiveness. At the beginning of the 1980s feminists were coming to terms with problems of how to maintain movement priorities, some of which were organisational. They were also learning how best to affect structures which threatened to overwhelm their preferred series of small autonomous groups. Dislike of established institutions remained a major characteristic of movement activists. In Holland such dislike led to the repudiation of parliamentary work by the abortion coalition (WVE), which in turn led to many party women leaving WVE ranks. In the Dutch movement a generation gap is apparent between older women (first-generation second-wave feminists), who will work within the system, and a rising second generation, which will not (Outshoorn, 1983; de Vries, 1981), raising interesting questions about the long-term socialisation capacities of organised feminism.

Italy

Italian feminism contrasts sharply with the movement elsewhere and its strengths appear to derive from rather different sources. Immediately after the Second World War, Italian women gained a brief high political visibility with the formation of the UDI and the CIF in 1945 and important speeches on the political role of women by Pope Pius XII and Palmiro Toliatti. The UDI (l'Unione Donne Italiane, or Union of Italian Women) initially contained a majority of communist and socialist members, a trend which encouraged the Catholic-based Christian Democrats to establish the CIF (Centro Italiano Feminile). Both were organisations designed to help deliver the women's vote, which was granted in the 1946 constitution. The UDI was also a rights group which exercised itself particularly over the problems of working women. The CIF essentially sought to support women's traditional political roles and was (and remains) home and motherhood centred. That initial organisational flurry was short-lived and proved a high point which was followed by the increasing alienation of Italian women. The Communist Party (PCI), which dominated the UDI, was exercised first by the Cold War and later by the need to come to terms with Catholic sections of society if it was ever to have a share in government. Neither preoccupation favoured the formulation of policy on women, which could be seen as undermining the family. Over its first two decades, the UDI tended to become more dependent upon the PCI, and women's matters became subsumed in family policy. But the Christian Democrats over the same period found themselves gradually losing touch with a secularising society. Neither the Left or the Right seemed capable of, or interested in, mobilising women in the 1950s or early 1960s. Difficulties in recruiting women were shown in the decline of Catholic Action membership from a total of 1,895,000 to 630,000, with the party suffering proportionately (Ergas, 1982, 257).

The next significant mobilisation of Italian women was the one which became the women's liberation movement. Developments began in the late 1960s within and as a response to the student movement of that time. Components of a new conception of politics were the stock in trade of many student groups which were anti-authoritarian in their ideologies and liberatory in their goals. Against this background, women soon became aware of the contradiction of masculine dominance of the Left. Their dissatisfaction led to the elaboration of several important feminist principles involving a radical critique of patriarchal structures and of the Marxist tradition. A feminist politics emerged with four characteristic components: first, autonomy from established organisations and ideologies; second was separatism from men, the better to interpret women's history and culture; third, rigid hierarchical structures were rejected and the new organisational forms were created, notably small groups of equal memberships and without patterns of delegation (*piccoli gruppi*); finally, consciousness raising was practised in these groups in order to develop a new understanding of one's life, the lives of other women and the position of women in society. On such understandings would be based the newly political personal (Eckman, 1978, 4). Whilst radical feminism played a large part in the Italian women's movement, its influence on Italian feminist theory appears to have been less pronounced than in Britain or in the Netherlands, perhaps because of a stronger tradition of Marxist politics and a greater national valuation of the significance of theory in Italy. Generally, the discourse of the Italian feminists asserted the link between class and sex domination. They pointed out the consumeristic exploitation of women as housewives and sexual objects, the imperialism and chauvinism of male values, the authoritarianism of male-female relations in what Marten (1984, 7) refers to as an 'insistent accentuation of the "anti-capitalistic" nature of the movement and their aims'.

The early publications of feminist works were translations of English and American tracts, but by 1972 women in various groups were producing their own theoretical formulations. At first only two groups were particularly coherently organised. The Movimento di Liberazione della Donna (MLD), which was associated with the Radical Party and which worked in the areas of educational opportunity, divorce, abortion, non-sexist education and other 'rights' activities. Lotta Feminista, the other organisation, was concerned with the campaign for wages for housework and was especially active in northern Italy. In addition, most of the ultra-left groups spawned feminist collectives which eventually were to prove to be staging posts for left-wing women on their way to mainstream feminism. But the majority of the movement was comprised of small, informal local groups with mainly consciousness-raising goals. National-level problems were occasionally considered as well. EFFE, a monthly magazine along similar lines to that of the British *Spare Rib*, appeared in 1971 and soon reached a circulation of around 50,000 (Colombo, 1981, 465). Various campaigns were waged, the most important of which were those over divorce, abortion and, most recently, rape. An extra dimension was added to these campaigns in Italy, where for many individuals they were closely associated with many other aspects of a long-overdue secularisation process. Ill advisedly, political Catholicism campaigned for a referendum to abolish divorce in 1974. Its defeat on May 12 of that year was seen as a watershed for Christian Democratic politics, and it also became clear that many women had voted against abolition of the divorce bill, which had only been approved by the legislature in 1970 and came into effect at the end of 1973. Colombo (1981, 465) makes the point that the referendum on divorce demonstrated that feminism was in touch with prevailing trends and was speaking to realities of contemporary society. Even if, at its theoretical frontiers, it was in advance of what most women were willing to accept, there was a substantial audience ready to receive the message. In 1975 began the formation of feminist groups in the trade unions and the establishment of the *coordinamenti* and the feminist 150-hour courses (see Ch 5 below). But the breakthrough issue was abortion, which provided the impetus for the development of a widespread movement (Marten, 1984, 7).

The abortion campaign effected the consolidation of the Italian women's liberation movement in that it led to the creation of areas of solidarity and processes of interaction with the political system. Collectives and consciousness-raising groups had generated closeknit women's networks, which became mobilisable when a political valence was attributed to sexual oppression. And the issue brought many new women into the movement, both as individuals and as members of established groups such as the UDI, which were prepared to take an independent feminist line on the abortion question. Abortion law reform emerged as a locus for joint action between the various feminist groups and important organisations of the New Left and the Radical Party, which opened a campaign calling for a referendum to abrogate the fascist law. Within the women's movement itself the abortion campaign activated all the various groups and involved numerous initiatives. Some groups practised abortion by the Karman method and others organised charter flights to London, where abortion laws were more liberal, or trips to an illegal abortion centre in Florence. Service delivery alone involved contact with hundreds of women each month, and the movement grew continuously during the campaign. Women of all political persuasions were exercised by the abortion issue and the campaign benefited from badly handled opposition to demands for liberalisation. It seemed to many women that the male political system was denying a woman's demand that had already aroused widespread political support. Party proposals from the PCI were restrictive, tepid and led the UDI to put forward its own proposals. Once the referendum was won, the ensuing confrontations as new laws were proposed to fill the void left by the repeal of the old one increased the cohesion of the women's movement and the processes of female identification around it which favoured recruitment. The effect was to strengthen considerably the women's liberation movement after 1975, with collective mushrooming, health centres proliferating and a national demonstration called in Rome on 6 December 1975. Feminism had become a presence which could be ignored neither by the media nor by the major political parties. Attempts by the Christian Democrats to block abortion reform in 1976 led to another nationwide demonstration, this time with the UDI and the various women's sections or commissions of the Republican, Socialist and Communist parties participating in conjunction with the autonomous feminist groups. As Ergas (1982, 268) aptly suggests, the movement had shifted from a defensive oppositional to a propositional phase. But this was itself a turning point, and once the question of producing an acceptable law took over, feminist groups had to give way to rights groups, a concession which signified a transformation in the nature of Italian feminism. A new phase was beginning during which rights issues became a priority as the recession deepened and what had previously been demands for liberation were transformed by the political system into questions of rights.

The methods of consciousness raising and the small group structure has served the Italian women's movement well while its major goals were the recruitment of previously apolitical women and people-changing on an individual level. Such a structure was also well suited to the construction of new theory and the development of women's studies. But it was less sure in its strategies and effects when it had to deal with the formal political environment. In the institutional arena the new feelings of confidence and political efficacy generated by women's participation in small groups were obvious benefits. Indeed, the feminist challenge to conventional political actors lay in its influence over the previously or normally apolitical. But as feminism gained strength and became more certain of its demands, political parties on the Left attempted to incorporate it, usually by paying more attention to women's issues. Suspicious of such institutions, feminists resisted this but were still left with the problem of what to do about voting for women candidates in elections or consultations over the content of various new laws affecting women's status which were passed during the 1970s[5]. A general instruction to vote Left in the elections of 1976 manifested itself in an increase of women's votes for the PCI but did not ameliorate feminist qualms about cooption by the male-dominated political parties. Collaboration with the state raised the same questions of principle in Italy as elsewhere (Eckman, 1978, 23) but were exacerbated by the pattern of institutional change and dispersal which characterised the Italian state during the 1970s.

Following the protests of the 1960s, and especially the series of strikes and demonstrations of the 'Hot Autumn' of 1969, the formerly highly centralised Italian state underwent a complex process of institution-building involving the inauguration of many new forms of representation and self-government. New structures ranged from school-system management to neighbourhood community management and underwent a quantum increase in the years between 1975 and 1977. These new institutions had little decision-making power and their establishment in fact coincided with a period during which the executive was expanding its powers vis-à-vis the rest of the political system, making something of a nonsense of the decentralisation process (de Santis and Zincone, 1983). However, they did provide an increased scope for political participation and broke down social movement anti-partisanship as party resources became an advantage for groups attempting to colonise such structures. The New Left, which had formerly targeted the centralised government, was now having to contend with a new range of political institutions. The process was one in which patterns of political confrontation, which had accounted for much of the New Left's success, gave way to forms of scrutinised political bargaining (Ergas, 1982, 269). In short, the state outflanked the Left. The new organisations included space for women as regional and municipal governments established *consulte feminile*, via which women's associations were consulted on matters concerning women. Ergas writes that the weakened New Left changed the environment surrounding the feminist movement, which, without recognisable organisational forms, systems of accountability or concentrated organisational numbers, now found it almost impossible to participate in the new structures. Ironically, the passage of a liberalised abortion law also undermined the movement as it removed much of the market for self-help service delivery mechanisms and concluded the campaigns around which it had grown.

Colombo (1981), Ergas (1982) and Eckman (1978) all mention the change in concentration by the Italian movement from rights issues to life-style issues, at the end of the abortion campaign. But the vacuum left by the abortion campaign was at the beginning of the 1980s filled by a national feminist campaign to alter the law on rape. A protracted parliamentary wrangle over the new law on violence against women (see p.269 below) meant that the issue was still on the agenda at the beginning of 1985. Hence, Italian feminism benefited from a series of national issues capable of giving thematic unity to the movement as a whole. The new preoccupation with life-style issues did not result in such a pronounced dispersal of the movement in Italy as occurred in Britain. But in other respects developments have been similar. Networks have been built in the unions and the parties and these continue to expand as sex equality issues are addressed in new contexts (Ergas, 1982, 272).

Important to understanding the change in emphasis in the Italian movement are the attitudes of the second-generation feminists and changes in many of the traditional women's organisations. Whilst the first generation of second-wave feminists have tended to retreat into their private lives or chosen to work in small groups on special issues, younger feminists have shown a preference for attempting to win change by working within established structures. At the same time, the attitude to feminism of many of the political forces and mass organisations of women has changed. The UDI in particular, but also the women's groups of the political parties, have shown a capacity both to confront feminist themes and to harbour feminist values. As a result, the PCI in March 1979 heard an announcement by leader Berlinguer that more attention would be paid to the feminist cause, which led to widespread party discussion of issues of women's oppression, of both the economic and sexual varieties. The UDI at its eleventh congress in 1982 voted for a radical restructuring to reflect the spirit of 1980s feminism in the form of its hundreds of local groups, a decision which has involved breaking its formal links with the PCI.

An argument could therefore be made that, far from being coopted, Italian feminism has affected a significant colonisation of the adjoining political terrain. What remains to be seen is whether in its more institutionalised manifestations the movement is able to maintain links with the many groups which continue to emerge amongst Italian women. These are the roots of the drive for liberation in Italy; they are important both as the source of radical initiatives which give the women's movement its vitality and as the site of changing attitudes which give it numerical strength.

Second-wave feminism, in the countries discussed so far, had left-wing roots, mainly middle-class proponents and a set of ideas whose time had come. In each case the mobilising capacity of the movement was enhanced by various campaigns which enabled the formation of alliances with other groups and with traditional women's organisations. This has facilitated an efficient division of labour between liberation and rights groups. The abortion campaigns were notable in this regard and in that they led to support of the woman's movement from working-class and lower-middle-class women. The result of a decade of campaigns was in each case a widespread, if insufficient, change of attitudes and the emplacement of established feminist networks ready for future campaigns and other kinds of political work.

But in other European liberal democracies the movement under ostensibly similar conditions was neither so widespread nor so successful. The examples which follow suggest a two-step explanation for this: in some countries important initiatives for many changes came from outside the feminist movement and even pre-dated its emergence. Hence, important alliances which elsewhere had given a coherence to the movement by connecting rights and liberation wings were not made. The locus of initiative rather than being near the centre or mainstream of a broad church women's movement, remained outside its boundaries. That this was the case may not have been so much due to the skills of initiators wishing to preempt movement successes as it was to the closed nature of the feminist groups themselves.

France

Such an explanation seems to account for the relatively limited mobilisation capacity of feminism in France, where distinguishing features have been a tendency towards intellectualism, bitter internal struggles and a certain elitism. Like their Italian counterparts, the parties of the French Left established women's organisations during the wartime resistance movements. These emerged as women's rights organisations in the post-war period and were seen as vote organisers when the franchise was extended to French women in 1944. Women's groups in the socialist Party and Communist Party were important in the movement to obtain legal and political rights in the immediate post-war era but then declined in importance. The 1960s were years of steady reformist activities but also years of increasing activism and radicalism amongst youth, generated by the Algerian war and rebellion and, towards the end of the decade, the student movement.

The increasing influence of existential Marxism encouraged the making of connections between political and cultural life which were an intellectual source of the Mouvement pour la Liberation des Femmes or MLF, (Marks and de Courtivron, 1980, 29–30). New feminist groups first appeared amidst the student revolt of 1968. From the outset French feminism had a heavily intellectual flavour to it, and it may have appeared inaccessible to many French women (Sauter-Bailliet, 1981, 410). In addition, psycho-analytic theory, influential internationally, was more at the centre of debate amongst French feminists, hence radical, reformist and Marxist categorizations do not fit so readily. Various authors distinguish different numbers of tendencies. Randall (1982, 157) identifies five distinct components in the array of small groups which emerged in France during the 1970s. First is radical femin-ism, beginning with the Feministes Revolutionnaires, who, with Simone de Beauvoir as a rallying force, saw the roots of women's oppression in the structure of patriarchy. Prone to spectacular actions, this group organised the Manifesto of the 343, in which several prominent women announced that they had had abortions in order to embarrass the French judiciary, who then had to decide whether to prosecute or to let the law fall into disrepute by ignoring the announcement. The tactic was widely copied abroad. They were also responsible for laying a wreath to his wife on the tomb of the unknown soldier at the Arc de Triomphe (Sauter-Bailliet, 1981, 412). The official press reacted to the wreath as though it were a sacrilege, which, as Marks and de Coutivron (1980, 31) point out, it was. Located in the centre of Paris, the tomb is one of the most important: 'signs of a French, and by extension, of a victorious, universal male order. It is the shrine of shrines that glorifies war and the cult of the dead'. The second tendency is that of socialist feminism, involving groups such as the Cercle Dimitriev, formed in 1972, which has sought to combine women's struggles with its anti-capitalist politics. Cercle Dimitriev has opposed what it sees as the MLF's lack of strategy, and created precinct committees to popularise the struggle and to support isolated women. Central to its concerns has been to retain the idea of the political Left. Les Petroleuses also fits into this category, but is more committed to class-struggle politics and to revolutionary communism than is the Cercle Dimitriev (Sauter-Bailliet, 1982, 411). (Dimitriev was the name of the founder of the Union des Femmes during the Paris Commune and Petroleuses ('arsonists') was the name given to women in 1871 who mounted the barri-cades, to be ruthlessly put down. They were alleged to have set fire to several parts of the town.) The third category is that of reform or rights groups, perhaps best illustrated by Gisele Halimi's Choisir and its associated feminist party, Parti Feministe Unifee Francaise. Choisir is apparently mistrusted by other members of the MLF, largely because of its participation in mainstream electoral politics. Fourth, the MLF contains various campaign organisations which unite some or all of the component tendencies for occasional political activities. Randall's final category is not a tendency but a group, Politique et Psychoanalyse, called 'Psych et Po' (after its original full name of Psychoanalyse et Politique). Psych et Po was one of the earliest groups to be formed (1970) and has been both influential and widely publicised. Under the influence of wealthy psychoanalyst Antoinette Foque—who rarely used her surname and enjoys an unhealthy influence over the minds of her followers say critics (Randall, 1982, 157),—the group considers other feminist groups to be bourgeois and insufficiently committed to the exploration of women's unconscious and the radical subversion of society. There is no fully articulated statement of Psych et Po's theoretical positions, which are in a permanent state of development and change. The group's preoccupations are often obscure, perhaps because of an important Lacanian influence on its modes of thought. Essentially, it attempts to justify an emphasis on intellectuals and especially on linguistics, arguing in effect that in French culture a dominance on the terrain of words and discourse is a route to dominance of the whole. It is convinced that there can be no revolution without disruption of the symbolic order (in Lacanian terminololology, the order instituted within the individual by language, the carrier of which is the father figure), and that only by dislocating syntax, playing with the signifier, punning, and so on, can the old language (recognisable, evidently, by its comprehensibility and the presence of a coherent subject) and the old order be subverted (Marks and de Courtivron, 1980, 32).

Psych et Po founded Editions des Femmes (a feminist publishing house) and opened bookshops in Paris, Marseilles and Lyons called Libraire des Femmes which became widely known internationally. They are unpopular with the rest of the French movement, who not only appear to be less than reassured by the news that the French language is on the run but are resentful of some of Psych et Po's entrepreneurial activities. Notably, the group usurped and appropriated the name 'Women's Liberation Movement' (originally a press invention, but nevertheless a hallmark) when in October 1979 it officially registered the title 'Women's Liberation Movement' as its name and deposited it as a trademark for commercial exploitation on 30 November 1979. On 15 January 1981, an international dimension was added with the label 'Women's Liberation Movement International'. Other feminist groups and movement affiliates felt betrayed and some considerable controversy ensued. Psych et Po were subject to attack at the Copenhagen Women's Congress in 1980 for its exploitative practices. At home it has been severely criticised for not using what are believed to be substantial resources for general women's movement activities or assistance of any kind (Sauter-Bailliet, 1981, 413). It remains unbowed, however, and appears to exercise a kind of intellectual terrorism over, or at least a morbid fascination for other feminist tendencies. There is little doubt that Psych et Po's activities are interesting and their influence has been widespread and unusual. It is only in France that groups of women 'have come together with the express purpose of criticising and reshaping the official male language and through it, male manners and male power' (Marks and de Courtivron, 1980, 6).

Apart from the distinctiveness of Psych et Po, which itself may be seen as a variant on radical feminism, the categories are not air-tight ones. French feminism has experienced, on at least a temporary basis, the working together of diverse women's groups, notably on the issue of abortion. Various strategies have been used. The Mouvement pour la Liberté et l'Avortement et pour la Contraception first appeared in 1973 and practised abortion (illegally) by the Karman method. The Association Choisir opted for a series of legal battles. Its founder, Gisele Halimi, defended the signatories of the 343 Manifesto and became involved in important court cases involving abortion. A liberalised abortion law was passed in 1975 for a five-year 'trial' period and was passed permanently in 1979, events which involved the participation of thousands of women in campaigns of various kinds. But no similar mobilising issue has since emerged. There are feminist bookshops and coffee shops in Paris and a news service and information agency have also been established, as have various women's studies courses. Throughout the movement, groups have tended to be short-lived and structureless but quickly replaced.

There has never been any sign of a groundswell of feminist opinion in France, which is surprising as at government level a series of major initiatives on women's rights was begun in 1974 when a secretary of state for women's condition was appointed by Giscard. Thus, such initiatives as the Flora Tristan Centre, a Paris battered wives shelter, had government assistance from the outset, which may have inhibited the development of a widespread women's aid network and organisation of the kind found in other countries. Feminist ideas are in the air in France, but they have found no coherent organisational shape and have left no well-established networks on which to base new campaigns. Mossuz-Lavau and Sineau (1981, 122) are particularly dismissive of its impact, arguing that French autonomous feminism's most flagrant deficiencies have been its eschewal of traditional politics and its middle-class intellectual, Paris-centred character, features which prevent it from reaching the majority of French women.

Sweden

If French feminism has reflected the generally elitist nature of French society, then the Swedish movement has mirrored that country's statism. One of more surprising features of contemporary Swedish social and political life is the absence of a second-wave feminist movement of any size. Sweden is a group-conscious nation with what is considered to be a highly developed system of interest groups. Most of the political parties have strong and active affiliated women's groups and women make up one-third of the members of Parliament. In addition, Sweden boasts a far-reaching sex-equality policy and is often cited as a model of equal opportunity provision. But examples of new feminism are few and far between. The feminist Group 8, with a relatively mild platform, arouses hostility and suspicion amongst Swedes. (Adams and Winston, 1980, 136). Founded in 1968, it had about 1,000 members in 1980, mainly in the Stockholm area. Socialist feminist in its orientations, it is relatively tame by continental standards. Its programme and organisation are very little different from those of establishment rights groups, but its confrontationist stances and radical flavour bar it from the mainstream of Swedish political life.

Reformist, or rights, feminism is well entrenched in the form of the Fredrika Bremer Association, a rights organisation dating back to 1894. With over 9,000 members, the Frederika Bremer Association is seen to be representative of the aspirations of such worthy advanced women's thinking as there is. Scott (1982, 159–60) refers to a new spirit in the association which had led it to campaign for more women in public office since 1976, and to turn its attention to changing individual attitudes, using, amongst others, consciousness-raising techniques borrowed from radical feminism. During the 1970s Swedish women's groups had little truck with such personalised politics but focused their attention on people-changing activities at the level of public opinion. Adams and Winston (1980, 136) cite as an example of this the travelling exhibit shown in the late 1960s entitled 'Stop Helping Mother With the Housework'. The exhibition was a widely publicised government and women's party group sponsored initiative which

portrayed the ideal family as one in which household responsibility was shared so that family members no longer saw their task
as helping mother but as assuming a rightful share of household
duties. Scott (1982, 158) points to high levels of hostility to
'feminism', but not to 'women's liberation' in Sweden and indicates that feminist cultural and theory construction activities
found elsewhere in Europe are rare in Sweden.

One explanation of the paradox of advanced policies on
women's rights but a weak feminist movement in Sweden attributes it to cultural factors. In this view the Swedish collectivist
culture is seen as not being readily attuned to individual solutions
to what it tends to view as social problems. What good does it do to
raise an individual's consciousness when she can't get a job
because of failings in the labour market or inadequate support
services? Better, says collectivist reason, to work on improving the
support services rather than disguising their inadequacies through
a focus on the individual. In such a view, self-help measures are
seen as short-term stop-gap measures which may actually be
counter-productive in that they relieve pressure on government to
seek community solutions. Indeed, one Swedish feminist who
supported this argument pointed out that avoiding consciousness
raising techniques also avoided the hostility of those contented
women who did not wish to be reconstructed, something she saw
as the source of the anti-feminist backlash in the USA (Adams and
Winston, 1980, 137).

Most other explanations point to the role of the women's party
groups, especially in the Social Democratic Party. Randall (1982,
158) argues that Moberg's *Women and Human Beings*, published
in Sweden in 1962 and advocating role sharing in the home, broke
the hold that the conservative view that childbearing and employment could not be combined had on the opinions of organised
Swedish women. Adams and Winston (1980, 138–40) remind us
that most components of second-wave feminist ideology are under
dicussion or have actually found policy expression in Sweden.
New feminism has, as it were, been preempted. In their view the
initiative for this has come from the long-standing tradition of
women's groups in the parties, unions and other organisations.
Citing the women's party groups as specific sources of rights
policies, Adams and Winston assert that a strategy of integrating
with men to ensure that women's interests are promoted in the
workforce has been highly successful and resulted in a kind of
social feminism. The continuing existence of women's groups has
meant that there has been a permanent debate on women's rights.

There may be something in this view, and certainly Sweden's women's movement did not experience the interrupted development that war, fascism and occupation brought to other countries. It is difficult to see, however, how the lessons of Swedish rights feminism may be translated to countries which have not had long periods of uninterrupted social democratic rule, which do not have labour shortages, or widely held collectivist attitudes and which are not particularly prosperous—which, in short, do not share the characteristics of the Swedish political landscape.

It should also be pointed out that not all observers of Swedish women's rights policies are as impressed as Adams and Winston. Scott (1982, 158) is particularly critical and asserts that the women's rights programme in Sweden is defined according to male notions of equality. The apparent attitude of Swedish men is that women there are relatively well-off by comparison to women in other countries and have no right to ask for more of what are seen to be favours but which feminists would describe as demands for basic rights.

The absence of second-wave feminism in Sweden is in fact the absence of a strong radical wing to a women's movement which has found continuous expression in rights groups of various kinds. The rights groups have had notable success in affecting public policies, but the lack of a radial initiative and a utopian vision of a feminist future in the movement has meant that many of the most successful people-changing activites generated by the movement elsewhere have either not taken place or were late to arrive. Attitude change at the individual level has not been a priority, with a consequence that a feminist frame of reference does not appear to have developed. Given the strength of the feminist movement in the other Nordic countries, the Swedish example is a surprising one, explainable only by reference to the fact that the timing of second-wave feminism post-dated the enactment of many of the rights policies there. Hence, no extra-organisational groundswell of women's dissatisfaction out of which a radical social movement could grow ever developed.

West Germany

The women's movement in Germany has been affected both by its interrupted history and the division of the state at the end of the Second World War. As described in the preceding chapter, a strong feminist tradition dating to the nineteenth century, with socialist, liberal and radical roots was eradicated by Nazism, which left as a residue a generation of apolitical women.

Under Nazism, women had been cut off from higher education and their emancipation was sacrificed to make way for the glorification of motherhood roles. Their organisations were smashed and their general social progress was halted (see Stephenson, 1975). In the immediate post-war years skyrocketing church attendance marked a religious revival dating from 1945 onwards and was arguably an indicator of a society in which men and women alike shied away from political commitments. Important matters of national survival had particular consequences for German women, a disproportionate number of whom were widows. The returning demobilised soldiers did not arrive home until 1948 and 1949, by which time patterns of family life had been interrupted for at least a generation. A return to 'normal' patterns of life was a priority for most Germans in 1950. During the West German Adenauer years socialist and feminist ideals were out of the foreground, perhaps because they were too closely linked with communist values in the Cold War era (Schlaeger, 1978, 62). Rights groups and prototypes of traditional women's organisations were established early on in the new state, which soon had a wide variety of women's organisations, including professional and religious groups as well as housewives associations. Some became active over questions of sex equality and their umbrella organisation, the German Council of Women, based in Bonn and having over 100 federated women's organisations, with a total membership of over 10 million, adopted a declared goal of 'focussing public attention on the situation of women as a social and political problem—of awakening the consciousness of politicians as well as of individuals to this problem' (Shaffer, 1981, 153). Three of the four main political parties have women's divisions, all of which make demands on party policy from time to time. Only the SPD women's division has a specific sex-equality orientation, however, and it is not as influential as its Swedish counterpart.

Recognisably feminist groups are relatively small, both in numbers and in memberships, but they have been active and creative and are perhaps better recognised abroad than they are at home. German second-wave feminism evolved directly from the student movement at a time when student politics were becoming increasingly socialist. Radical feminism has not been all that successful in moving away from its base in the universities, and the new women's movement has been prone to the same splits as have been prevalent elsewhere, leading to a splintering of what has been a relatively weak movement. Radical feminists tended to be negative to leftist politics, suspecting 'every leftist woman of harbouring a male comrade within herself' (Schlager, 1978, 63). The result was a lack of coalition building and a growing predominance of apolitical modes of thought and depolitisation rather than the mobilisation of women new to political activity. When the campaign to liberalise abortion provision began with the self-denunciation of women who had had illegal abortions, mass-media attention was caught but political institutions remained unresponsive, illustrating a classic dilemma of a weak Left. A profound distrust of the authorities led feminists to concentrate on grass-roots activism, and local campaigns with, apart from *Aktion* 218[6], few nationwide initiatives or attempts to use conventional channels of pressure were in evidence. In contrast to the widespread mobilisation generated by the abortion campaign in Italy, participation in Germany remained limited, even at the peak of the campaign. Alliances were formed mainly with activist Liberal and Social Democratic women, thus not altering the homogenous middle-class character of the social background of the actors. Support was mobilised from those strata engaged in the educational and cultural process, from public administration and the service sector of the state. The abortion movement did not in the end gain and maintain the attention of the general public, and the issue remained a marginal one. The significant feminist bargaining counter of the ability to mobilise those who had previously been apolitical was not a factor in West Germany, and possibly as a result newly formed alliances did not survive the abortion campaign (Marten, 1984).

Nevertheless, the movement persists, with independent local women's groups in most cities and universities undertaking a variety of feminist work. For example, rape crisis centres, battered wives shelters and publishing and film cooperatives exist in many major cities. Groups tend to be self-help orientated or involved in various kinds of support (Shaffer, 1981, 153–4). There are also women's groups in the various professions, including the Association of Female Academicians, which encourages research on women's problems and organises conferences dealing with relevant scientific themes. Self-promotion groups include the German Women Physicians Association and the League of Women Jurists, which also direct some energy to using their skills to help overcome women's problems. Such groups of newly confident women have been one of the by-products of second-wave feminism in many countries and their presence and activism in West Germany may eventually be part of the basis for a more widespread feminist network.

At least some of the relatively uninspired history of West German second-wave feminism must be attributed to the rather unresponsive environment in which it was operating. However, account should be taken of the fact that the major parties and institutions, perhaps in response to European Communities initiatives, have taken up women's questions in various forms, and there is an apparent interest by policy-makers in issues of women's rights.

In addition, the widely publicised electoral success of the Greens from 1980 onwards may be of considerable significance for West German feminism. The Greens, with an 'anti-party' party ethos, have been particularly receptive to women, who are 50 per cent of its membership and over 30 per cent of its parliamentarians (Kolinsky, 1984a, 436). The party has avoided entrenched hierarchies and has preferred a task-sharing style of organisation. Its chief concerns are environmental and life-style issues. Thus, the Greens are both organisationally and philosophically compatible with feminism. They have been instrumental in generating discussions on feminist issues, and their success has given a fillip to the women's liberation movement.

Some stimulus was certainly needed. Most commentaries suggest that West German feminists have been particularly insensitive to the realities of political life and have also tended to overstate the degree of resistance to feminism amongst opinion leaders. There is and has been sympathy for their ideas amongst leading Social Democratic and Liberal women, manifesting itself both in parliamentary discussions during the 1970s and in state funding for women's aid centres and the like. That support has been made more manifest in response to challenges from the Greens. The resistance which proponents of new-wave feminism have expressed towards male-constructed power centres has been understandable, but it does appear that rather less energy was put into campaigning in West Germany than elsewhere. As a result, opportunities for coalition building and alliance formation which might have helped see the movement through leaner times were lost. With the advent of the Greens has come a change in the political environment which provides new opportunities for the West German women's movement. Whether these will be used to advantage remains to be seen.

Feminism and Political change: Greece, Spain and Portugal

Signs of second-wave feminist influences also appeared in Greece, Portugal and Spain, but developments were restricted first by authoritarian regimes and later by the exigencies of constructing new democratic orders in less than auspicious circumstances. Women's emancipation in these countries has been impeded by the entrenched resistance of organised Catholicism in Spain and Portugal and by difficulties in obtaining prioritisation for women's issues in countries characterised by extremes of poverty and relatively low levels of industrial development. The order of the problems faced by women in these countries has been rather different to that prevalent in the rest of Europe. In Greece, for example, the Joint Platform of Women's Associations signified its concern over women's rights in the early 1980s by calling for the abolition of the dowry system. The Democratic Women's Movement, founded in 1974, with the aim of bringing together progressive women had as its aims the promotion of equal opportunities for women, the liberation of women as individuals and the abolition of laws and institutions impeding such a transformation. More recently it has become active over the issue of the official treatment of rape victims. A traditional rights group, its aims are a long way from being met and it has proceeded via normal pressure group methods, drafting model laws on issues of concern and running various campaigns, occasionally in alliance with other women's associations who may also be members of the Coordinating Committee of Representatives of Women's Organisations, a Greek equivalent of the German Council of Women or the British Women's National Commission. Since the fall of the colonels, a great many women's organisations have emerged in Greece, where the number of organised women had risen by 50 per cent in 1984, An autonomous women's movement appeared in the early 1980s, but with so much of the rights agenda still unfulfilled, it has remained rather small (PE 86. 199/fin/C 1984).

Portuguese women were particularly poorly situated during the period of Salazar's rule. No women's organisation was allowed to exist in the secular arena. Only associations run by the Catholic Church for the purpose of upholding the family were legal. But during the last years of the Salazar regime (1969–74) women increasingly were to be found in the labour market, partly because of the absence of large numbers of men fighting in colonial wars and partly because of progressive industrialisation of the country and the search by multinational companies for sources of inexpensive labour. A comprehensive series of laws upheld discrimination against women. Family law in effect gave the husband ownership of his wife and his children. Women could not leave the country with their children without their husband's permission, domestic work was compulsory after marriage, and the penalty for murdering an adulterous wife was only three months imprisonment. A feminist movement became visible after the trial of the women writers known as the Three Marias in May 1974. It was heterogeneous, Lisbon-centred and rights orientated. The Lisbon groups organised a 1975 International Women's Year demonstration, and together with women in the political parties campaigned successfully to get equal rights for women and men written into the 1976 constitution. Additional successes included the passage of a family code which gave women and men equal status within the family and the outlawing of wage discrimination in 1979. Women's rights campaigners have made considerable formal progress, but the situation shows little substantive improvement. In 1981, 80 per cent of all illiterates in Portugal were women, and the Catholic Church remains intransigent over issues such as contraception and abortion. Women's groups within the Communist Party and the Democratic Popular Union have little autonomy, with spokespersons tending to stress that they are not feminist and that their struggle is alongside the men's. Independent liberation organisations are few, concentrated mainly in the urban centres of Lisbon, Porto and Coimbra. Under constant attack, their scope for action is limited. The groups are centred around a publishing collective known as IDM (Informacao Documentacao Mulheres). There is also a National Abortion and Contraceptive Campaign, employing only women and which became a main front of women's struggle at the beginning of the 1980s (Barbosa, 1981, 478–80). Abortion provision was liberalised in 1984.

Spain had had an active women's rights movement during the nineteenth century and women were involved in the Civil War, but the years of Franco rule prevented any continuous development of democratic women's organisations. Tentative women's movement beginnings were apparent in 1970 when the Movimento Democratico de Mujeres (MDM) was formed out of the Communist Party and Communist women began to organise as feminists. Despite legality problems some ninety new feminist organisations came into being, mainly in urban centres (Threlfall, 1985), by the time of Franco's death. Other women formed groups within HOAC[7] groups. These sympathies were kept relatively quiet however, and signs of active radical feminism did not appear until after Franco's death in 1975 (Rague-Arias, 1981, 471).

International Women's Year in 1975 gave Spanish feminism an

impetus by providing an opportunity for the organisation of meetings at which women's problems were discussed. State-wide women's days were held in December of that year at which it was decided that men were not to be present at meetings to discuss women's concerns. 1976 saw a quantum jump in the number of organisations and groups being formed, with consciousness raising groups appearing in many cities and movement-wide demands being formulated. Various organisations had differing theoretical perspectives but were willing to unite for urgent reform campaigns, such as the rescinding of the anti-contraceptive law and the abolition of punishment for adultery. A limited divorce bill was approved in 1981. Both Gallego (1983) and Rague-Arias (1981) agree that before very long the movement was divided between socialist and radical feminists but that it had a relatively coherent national presence from 1975 to 1980, when radical, socialist and rights feminists cooperated on a number of joint activities. Discussion of dual or double militancy was commonplace in those years as Spanish feminists agonised over whether it was possible to be a member of both a political and a feminist organisation. Once reform of divorce and family law was achieved, it became difficult to keep the movement together, despite the fact that abortion law reform had not yet been obtained. From 1980 to 1982 fragmentation of the movement was evident, but women in the trades unions, the political parties and the universities remained active. Theoretical divisions and a multiplicity of practices keep the feminist movement divided, although since 1982 various new organisations in favour of abortion rights have begun to merge (Gallego, 1983, 13), but these face an extremely well-articulated opposition.

Clearly, the Spanish movement is better developed than its Portuguese and Greek counterparts and features many of the characteristics of feminism in the better-established liberal democracies. Accounts of the movement in Spain tend to stress the role of a few individuals and it may be that Spanish feminism has been given a boost by the presence of a few particularly talented women. It is more likely, however, that experience in illegal organisations during the Franco era gave women's movement members a set of skills and resources which enabled them to make maximum use of the opportunities of organisation which occurred during liberalisation. Thus rights groups were quickly re-established and the possibilities of cooperative work existed from the time that new feminist ideas first began to be discussed.

State Socialist Women's Movements

Whilst organisational variety, autonomy and spontaneity characterise the women's movement of Western Europe, in Eastern Europe and the Soviet Union women's organisations are well-regulated agencies of the state. Indeed, the women's movement is non-existent there in the feminist sense of organisational independence from male-dominated political groups.

Under state socialism the prevailing conception of organisation precludes the establishment of feminist structures such as consciousness-raising groups. In such countries all institutions have as one of their stated purposes the execution of party policy and the mobilisation of constituencies for the fulfilment of party goals. Thus, women's organisations are technically mass organisations, distinct from, but closely affiliated to the ruling Communist Party. Many have in fact been dissolved. The absence of a separate official women's organisation in the Soviet Union is justified by the assertion that sexual inequalities no longer exist there, a claim that is belied not only by the publication of the illegal and arguably feminist *Almanach* in 1979 but also by a considerable body of official evidence (Lapidus, 1978).

Most of the mass organisations of women which still operate act as a form of pressure group with fairly modest power and tend to be social and educational institutions of a traditional women's kind, albeit with an especial focus on employment. Molyneaux (1981, 28–9) suggests that these organisations are quite hostile to Western feminist movements and that they do not encourage radical feminist thinking or action. Moreover, they are not particularly sophisticated in their analysis of women's problems, generally missing out the more subtle discriminatory practices and structures, except where these are deemed to have survived from the pre-revolutionary period. Their role is not entirely negative, and they have acted as mobilising agents which have organised women to act against the structures of oppression. However, where such struggles are deemed to have been successfully completed, their role is conservative. Molyneaux's view is that in their very fostering of the belief that women are already emancipated, by diffusing a mystified ideology of motherhood and by promoting gender-typed training programmes, the state socialist women's organisations help to propogate forms of gender inequality. Their roles may divert women from making the further demands needed to complete their emancipation by creating the supposition that the relevant preconditions have already been secured.

Early Soviet policies on the political organisation of women set a pattern which was later followed by other state socialist regimes. Politically, an independent women's movement was inadmissible and feminism was seen as being divisive. Women's organisations were therefore created in the standard image of the mass organisations which have prevailed under Communist Party rule. Over the years, however, some variations in format have occurred. In Albania, Czechoslovakia, East Germany and Yugoslavia a mass women's association is structured along territorial lines and closely supervised by party cadres. Memberships of these organisations number in the millions. In the USSR, Poland, Hungary, Bulgaria and Rumania the mass women's associations were disbanded in the 1950s and replaced by national committees comprised of prominent women who are called on to give advice on women's questions. The activities of these committees tend to be orientated outwards (abroad), although they do organise the publication of national women's journals and compile data on women for presentation to the party leadership. Basic research on women is, however, conducted in the universities and research institutes which have representation on the national committees (Jancar, 1978, 160).

East Germany is the only European state socialist country to have a women's party organisation, thus there is no effective political grouping which is orientated to women's needs in Poland, Yugoslavia, Albania, Czechoslovakia, Hungary, Bulgaria, Rumania or the Soviet Union. However, Jancar records some indicators that as the woman question began to be taken more seriously, committees were being upgraded. For example, Bulgarian and Rumanian chairpersons were appointed to the politbureaux during the 1970s, and the East German chairperson achieved Central Committee Secretary status. But only the Bulgarian Committee seemed able to take any initiatives. Jancar's view is that the mass organisational form is intrinsically ill suited to women's issues as women are not organised along hierarchical, territorial lines. There are women's committees attached to the trade unions at factory and enterprise levels, but the allegiance of these is to the union rather than to women's associations, and their primary function is normally to see to it that laws on women's rights are observed. Thus, national women's committees or organisations have no real roots or support from local units and have little bargaining power (Jancar 1978, 160).

Other scholars are less negative in their assessments than Jancar, although they too point to women's lack of substantive power under state socialism. Heitlinger (1979, 203) reminds us that prior to its seizure of power after the Second World War the Czech Communist Party had a strong women's section, which was abolished once the party was established in power. Women's gradual entry into social production was accompanied by a transfer of responsibility for women's political activites to the trade unions. Problems accumulated and by the mid-1960s the situation was being reappraised. A separate women's association, the Czechoslovak Union of Women, was established, but except for a brief period during the upheavals of the 'Prague Spring' of 1968, it has been under control of the party. Today the Union runs advice centres and performs service functions for Czech women in ways which do not tend to challenge existing stereotypes. The dual burden, for example, is recognised but seen as inevitable. Heitlinger's argument is that Czech and Soviet experiences suggest that there is a need for an autonomous Marxist feminist power base before a revolution which can also play a part in policy priority allocation after the revolution. The East European experience indicates that a male-led state socialist transformation is insufficient to bring about the liberation of women.

Einhorn (1981, 436–9) makes similar points about East Germany. She writes that state socialist countries on the whole see emancipation as something that is given to women without taking anything away from men. It was never envisaged that men would have to change if women were to become emancipated. Thus, whilst East Germany is exceptional in recognising the woman question via both a party section and a separate organisation in the Women's Democratic League of Germany (DFD), its aims have been confined to the encouragement of more women into employment. There is little apparent awareness of gender-defined behaviour patterns as they affect social relations, especially at personal and domestic levels. The concept that the personal is the political is virtually unknown and would find no place in the state ideology if it were known. Western feminism, except perhaps in its peace movement forms, does not get a good press.

The position of women under state socialism provides evidence that the economic emancipation of women in the form of a mass entry into the labour force is insufficient to ensure liberation. Political emancipation is needed as well, and whilst participation in social production does give women more bargaining power and status than they might otherwise have, more is needed. As Heitlinger (1978, 203) writes, the liberation of women in any society will be a dual process involving not only greater participation in the workforce (which has taken place under state socialism) but also a relative withdrawal from the domestic economy (which has not).

Second-Wave Feminism and the Political Mobilisation of Women

Second-wave feminism as a social movement arose out of the turbulence of the 1960s. Although recent contributions to the study of women's history indicate that feminism never completely disappeared (Banks, 1981; Spender, 1983), there is no doubt that the resurgence in the 1970s was the result of a significant new recruitment of women into a sustained social movement.

What were the causes of this resurgence? Why did feminism seem suddenly to gain large numbers of new adherents? There is no one explanation which fully answers such questions. Ergas (1982) refers us to the links between the development of women's autonomous political movements and the politics of the Left. She points out that women's mobilisations have tended to emerge in the wake of sweeping mass mobilisations and at moments of general social crisis. Hence, women's rights arose in the wake of the French Revolution, the American abolition movement, the Bolshevik Revolution, the Italian anti-fascist struggle and the civil rights and student movements of the 1960s. Three distinct but interrelated processes bring this about. First, revolutionary movements may provide particular incentives which bring women into active roles and lead to significant increases in normally low participation rates. Second, recruitment into revolutionary movements stimulates processes of political socialisation and furnishes access to the political resources of theory, organisational and communications networks and leadership skills. Finally, such movements provide a wedge into conventional politics for actors who are otherwise excluded from its arenas.

Such an explanation accounts for the early recruits to the movement and describes well what became of the autonomous feminism once it began, but it does not account for the widespread mobilisation of previously apolitical women as the movement progressed. Randall (1982, 146), approaching the problem from a rather different angle, distinguishes three levels of causality which must be included in a comprehensive explanation of feminist recrudescence. These are the aspects of women's situation which predisposed them to recognise their oppression, ideological and institutional factors facilitating a feminist revival and specific triggering events. Predisposing factors included the increased numbers of educated women in the population, the presence of more divorced and separated women, a tendency to smaller families, an awareness of new contraceptive technology, a greater experience of employment outside the home and a growing sense of relative deprivation. Facilitating factors included, in some countries, the coming of age of the first generation of women to have grown up with the full array of citizen rights and duties and an increase in women's access to political skills gained often during the 1960s New Left movements. From here, says Randall, came the necessary political catalyst in the form of the New Left's stress on equality, on liberatory goals and on unmasking well-concealed oppression by the capitalist state. Both goals and skills could easily be translated for use in an analogous exposure of male dominance (Randall 1982, 147–8), and most accounts of the movement internationally suggest that once the feminist balloon went up in one country, it was inevitable that it would be launched elsewhere.

The commonality of themes of the second-wave feminist movement has been one of its outstanding features. Despite an almost complete absence of formal international organisations, the same campaigns and preoccupations appeared throughout the industrialised liberal democracies. Abortion rights campaigns were critical to the movement's development in most countries. Each movement came sooner or later to the point where decisions had to be made about whether to have a formal structure and hierarchy and whether and to what extent to cooperate with male-dominated socialist parties. It seemed that women everywhere became aware of the double shift, the problem of male violence against women and the one-sidedness of rape laws. Each discussed political lesbianism, attempted to reassess motherhood and exercised itself over problems about leadership and structures (Bradshaw, 1981).

Organisationally, two common concerns were apparent: feminists wished to avoid hierarchy in their structures and saw separatism as an essential precondition of women's activism. At different stages in the movement these preoccupations led to different results. Most women, including liberal feminists content to work in traditional institutions, were prepared to accept separatism for tactical reasons. The argument that women needed an arena exclusively designed for their needs in order better to understand oppression and better to plan the means of ending it was and remains a persuasive one. This was particularly important during the consciousness-raising phases when the processes of small group discussions required a great deal of trust between members. The small group structures which were suited to consciousness-raising served the movements anti-hierarchical goals as well, and for a time combinations of separatism and small autonomous groups seemed to be the only compelling organisational requirements. Consciousness-raising was a particularly useful mobilising technique, which greatly enhanced the self-esteem of those who practised it. However, problems came when the technique was exhausted and a transfer of energies to campaigns or other means of gaining concessions from political institutions was needed. At this stage, inspiration was often taken from rights groups used to working with the political institutions and influenced by the movement to seek feminist goals. During national campaigns, the hierarchies which produce official representatives, leaders and spokespersons and are favoured by rights groups exhibit a better fit between structure and strategy. The equation which states an equivalence between rights groups and policy effectiveness and small autonomous liberation groups and mobilisation is an appealing one, provided it is remembered that a characteristic of the women's movement is that both have been continuous processes. Whilst consciousness-raising groups were relatively rare by the middle of the 1980s, small groups were still common and were the preferred form for study groups, theory groups and various other projects which often enhanced the work of increasingly radicalised rights groups. The vitality of the small-group structure has been convincingly demonstrated by autonomous feminism, which has proved capable of sustaining a leaderless, decentralised movement which avoided hierarchy and bureaucracy for a decade and a half.

Traditional women's organisations were much affected by second-wave feminism. Changes in the perspectives and practices of many rights groups were apparent by the end of the 1970s, as many European feminists transferred their activities to unions and political parties. Feminists infiltrated these institutions rather than were coopted by them. Processes of compromise and bargaining had taken place whereby traditional structures of representation altered their policies on women towards more liberatory proposals at the same time as feminists had to sacrifice some of their early unwillingness to work in male-dominated structures.

New conceptions of appropriate political goals by established institutions are one of the many indications of the impact of feminism on European politics. The redefinition of many private and domestic matters transforming them into public issues has been a phenomenon in many countries. In this sense feminist ideology follows directly from the growth of the welfare state and its expansion into the realm of the family, suggesting that well-established welfare policies may be a precondition of effective new feminist politics.

Paradoxically, the strength of feminism has been in its diversity and in its core of radical ideas, as well as in its constantly changing nature. New preoccupations appear as older issues become resolved and the women's movement continues to change its shape and form. In France and Germany issues of ecology have become important as feminists identify an analogy between the rape of the earth and the rape of women. Economic goals recede for some feminist groups as they come to question the importance of work and the priority it is given in societies which cannot provide full employment. In the UK an important part of feminists energies have been channelled into the peace movement. The widely publicised peace camp at Greenham Common, which began in the early 1980s, came to be seen as much as a feminist as a pacifist initiative (McKenzie, 1984).

The diffusion of ideas across national boundaries has been unmistakable, but few formal international organisations have appeared. The United National Status of Women Commissions' International Women's Decade Congresses (1975 Mexico City, 1980 Copenhagen, 1985 Nigeria) provided focuses for many women but tended to be comprised of national delegations which were rarely selected with feminist cooperation (Randall, 1982, 158). Alternative congresses were generated which were attended by many women, but the United Nations' strong Third World bias prevented these gatherings from becoming a forum for European women. Some cooperation between European women occurs within EEC institutions and at least one network organisation operates within the EEC (ENOW—The European Network of Women), but organisations which link East and West Europe have not emerged, and in general women's movement inter-nationalism takes place via informal contacts, occasional special conferences and the various widely marketed publications.

At the time of writing the issue of women's liberation remains a controversial one in most countries, with the popular press and the other media often showing hostility to feminist causes. Established churches, especially the Catholic Church, often remain hostile, but the greatest potential source of backlash in Europe, as it has been in the USA, comes from women themselves. Like any important social change, the process of the emancipation of women has created both 'ascending' and 'descending' groups. Many women have been made to feel that feminism threatens their status and that a lifetime of investment in domestic pursuits has suddenly been devalued. Ignoring their own economic vulnerability and dependence, they stress old-fashioned (and male-constructed) feminine values and wish to see the preservation of the traditional family. Such responses are understandable, as is the resentment felt by women who have seen their values attacked and their life-styles threatened. The bewilderment felt by many older women who were dismissed as wasted and beyond hope by many feminists was made particularly apparent by one Irish woman who asked what she must have regarded as a group of her tormentors, 'Didn't we rear you, for a start?' (Levine, 1982, 254).

Backlash did not become such a problem in Europe as it did in the USA, however, perhaps because the policy successes of European feminism were fewer and further between and were predicated on a more advanced welfare state basis than in the USA. When threats to women's status came in European countries they tended to take the form of attacks on the welfare state itself, and accordingly were resisted by coalitions of men and women often united in rights or defensive organisations of various kinds. Thus, although the women's movement was on the defensive by the beginning of the 1980s, it was under no threat of dissolution. The indicators are that wherever a strategic unity can be preserved, the movement will persist.

Although perceptible changes in official attitudes may be detected, in the state socialist countries there has been no real second-wave of feminism. There, it is the party leaders who must be enlisted if women's liberation is to become a reality. Whilst they have often been in advance of their liberal democratic counterparts in recognising that economic emancipation is a precondition of liberation, the importance of domestic labour has escaped the attention of East European policy-makers. Women's self-organisation has not been permitted. Given that state socialist countries possess both the ideological wherewithal and the degree of state penetration necessary to promote the cultural changes which are required if women are to be emancipated, there is every reason to suspect that considerations of preserving male power have prevented the necessary policies from being developed.

In the European liberal democracies, processes are more diffuse and explanations are often necessarily more complex. Each of the countries discussed above provides evidence that second-wave feminism had a more insistent presence when both rights and liberation wings were present and where liberal, socialist and radical wings were able to cooperate in a variety of political campaigns. Such a configuration provided the maximum scope for the political development of individual women and allowed for the greatest variety of organisational forms and political practices. Where the movement has been strong it has been strong in all of its components, where one element has been weak, so have the others. An implicit division of labour was possible whereby issues could be raised by the radical branch of the movement, formulated into effective demands by socialist feminists and followed through the political system by liberal feminists. Whilst such a schema exaggerates the clarity with which the relevant processes may be analysed, it nonetheless closely resembles what actually happened whenever the movement was involved in the processes of policy-making.

Although the process of becoming a feminist is in part a process of forging a political identity, the experience of second-wave feminism has had contradictory implications for the political role of women. On the one hand, its mobilising capacity has involved numerous women in political activity. On the other hand, the movement's anti-hierarchical ethos and the separatism advocated by some feminists made many women extremely suspicious of highly structured, male-dominated political institutions. But like other disadvantaged groups before them, women's self-organisation has had a politicising effect. Women mobilised by autonomous feminism have increasingly joined affiliated women and other rights feminists in a quest for political power and influence, seeking membership of political and governmental elites. The widespread changes in the political behaviour and attitudes of women which have occurred since enfranchisement have resulted in a formidable challenge to traditional political institutions. It is to an account of that challenge and the response it has received that we now turn.

Notes

1. The TUC's *Aims for Women at Work* was revised in 1975 and again in 1978. The child-care campaign also found TUC expression in the *Charter for the Under Fives* in 1978 (*see* Coote and Campbell, 1982).
2. Erin Pizzey stormed out of the 1975 conference after a row and has gone her own way ever since (*Ibid.*, 41).

3. The Corrie Bill was an amendment to the 1967 Abortion Act proposed under the Private Members Ballot scheme in 1979. Had it been passed it would have severely restricted access to legal abortion by reducing the upper limit and narrowing severely the grounds on which abortions could be legally obtained.
4. *Dolle Mina* literally means 'Mad Mina'. The group took its name from Wilhelmina Drucker, an early pioneer of the Dutch women's emancipation movement.
5. Apart from laws on divorce (1973) and abortion (1978), these included: in 1975, reform of family law; in 1976, law on consultori; in 1977, equal opportunities at work.
6. *Aktion 218* is the name of a group established to reform Clause 218 of the legal code, the clause which prohibited abortion.
7. HOAC groups were illegal trade unions which operated during the Franco regime and which adopted strange names to disguise their purposes.

4   Patterns of Women's Political Behaviour

If the experience of second-wave feminism and its legal, social and psychological achievements by and on behalf of women are to have a lasting effect, we would expect in its wake to observe a colonisation and transformation by women of significant channels of access to power. This would lead eventually to the penetration by women of important governmental institutions, the processes and policies of which would also be transformed. Assessment of the extent to which such penetration and transformation has taken place is the subject of the remainder of this volume. Our concern is to outline, compare and assess the quantity, quality and impact of the political participation and representation of contemporary European women.

Such assessments are not new in political science which has in the past, however, given only occasional consideration to women's political roles. More recently, a considerable body of research and publications has been produced in the general area of women and politics. The picture which had traditionally been painted of women's political behaviour was, as Evans (1980) has remarked, a 'sombre' one. A standard view had emerged which held that women were more conservative, less active, less interested, less knowledgeable and more readily influenced than men. The overall evaluation was that women were less competent as citizens than men. Such judgments have been taken to task by a number of critics (Bourque and Grossholtz, 1974; Goot and Reid, 1975; Evans, 1980; Lovenduski, 1981b; Siltanen and Stanworth, 1984b), but there remains nevertheless a pejorative thrust in work on women and politics which exaggerates differences in men's and women's political behaviour and sees women's behaviour as falling short of that of men.

The negative bias results almost entirely from the way in which the topic has been approached rather than from the results of empirical or analytical investigations. The problem is a difficult one, stemming from the fact that when women's political behaviour is discussed, it is described first in terms of how men and women differ, and only afterwards in terms of how women differ from each other. This is not unreasonable, and given that politics has been for so long a male-defined and occupied area, it is also inevitable. In accounting for the role and progress of an oppressed group we have no option other than to measure its position by comparison to the dominant group. When we describe women's political status we are outlining a structure of oppression. The bias of such descriptions will alter only as the situation of the oppressed group alters. Only as women come to exercise an influence on how politics is constructed will the political science of women exorcise its inbuilt male bias.

Acceptance of the fact that the dominant group sets the terms of reference is not, however, acceptance of sexism in the discipline. Indeed, a considerable corpus of scholarship and research has been produced by feminist scholars to identify and discredit examples of sexist bias. A good example of such debunking is to be found in Judith Evans' (1980) reappraisal of studies on women and politics, which takes into account both traditional views of political women and the feminist critique of such views. Pointing out that accusations of conservatism and traditionalism are not in themselves offensive in that they merely postulate gender-based differences in political attitudes, she regards other charges against women as being more damaging. Six areas in which women are said to differ from men are identified in the literature, assessed against empirical evidence and scrutinised for explanatory bias. These are voter turnout, levels of citizen activity, unjustifiable influence of spouse (husband), right-wing voting propensity, traditionalist and right-wing views and lower levels of interest and knowledge. She finds that differences between the sexes in voter turnout have been the product of particular conditions affecting specific groups of women, and concludes that these are conditions which are likely to pass. Citizen-activism differences are found to be small, affected by measures of education and employment and are also becoming eroded. That husbands' opinions and voting influence wives' opinions and voting is apparently the case, as is women's right-wing voting. But right-wing voting is issue influenced and not immutable; that is, it is certainly not a gender-determined characteristic. A greater incidence amongst women of traditionalist and right-wing attitudes is a more difficult claim to test as people's belief systems are known to be neither logically constrained nor temporally stable. Such relevant empirical work as existed by the end of the 1970s suggests but does not confirm that women are consistently more right-wing than men. But the question is one which poses considerable methodological difficulties and is, Evans warns, unlikely to be resolvable in a satisfactory manner. Finally, there is a *prima facie* case that women are both less interested in and less knowledgeable about politics than men. In short, men and women do differ politically, but in neither the manner nor for the reasons suggested by traditional studies. Evans' account, which concludes with an important caution against substituting assumptions of identicality for sexist bias, was based largely on British and American data available during the 1960s and 1970s, much of which was compiled from various studies of political participation. However, European evidence supports similar contentions (see Lovenduski and Hills, 1981).

Political Participation

Assessments of gender differences in politics, like class and educational differences, turn on different rates and kinds of political participation, an activity traditionally equated with the formal rights of citizens in the nation state and their exercise of these rights. Accordingly, political participation is normally measured by counting or otherwise weighing the performance or non-performance of civic responsibilities. In such a view, politics was defined in a legal (and juridical) manner. But formal citizen rights, whilst important tools for oppressed groups, are limited in their usefulness for women by the sexual division of labour in society and within the family (Batiot, 1979). This is a systematic limitation on women's political roles which must be taken into account if we are to understand their gendered basis.

Fortunately, the concept of political participation is flexible and wide-ranging enough to provide a framework which takes account of structural inequality. Robert Salisbury identifies at least three kinds of meaning which political participation has had. In the sense that citizens take part in government, they give their consent to its decisions; such acts therefore *legitimise* the regime. Seen in *instrumental* terms, political participation is a necessary means of obtaining political power and is a means for enhancing the position of one's self or one's sector. In its third manifestation, political participation is 'a solvent of political conflicts'. It is a *learning process* whereby citizens come to understand the common good and thus to agree with other participators. Both Mill and Rousseau took this view, placing their arguments in the context of smaller communities, which, along with substantive equality, were essential to the production of consensus by means of increased participation. All three definitions play a part in the understanding of the political role and status of particular groups, as does the analytical level on which participatory activity is assessed. Theorists have stressed the importance of active participation in the political community to the achievement of human potential. In short, political participation is good both for the individual and the society.

But of course at the level of practice, things are less straightforward than that. There are a variety of statuses, kinds and sizes of political community, of participatory acts and of political arena. A relatively easy political act such as voting is of a different order than that of seeking candidacy, and the meaning of both acts may vary considerably according to the kind of political community in which they are situated. Political participations may have both different costs and differing purchasing power depending upon its circumstances. A vote in national politics, a seemingly easy act, may have more influence than the relatively more difficult act of office-holding at local level. Indeed, Salisbury indicates that attempts to rank-order participatory acts by cost or difficulty have generally proved to be unsuccessful and have demonstrated that different modes of participation have represented different dimensions and different participants (Salisbury, 1975, 326–9, 331). Thus, if we are to identify properly differences in men's and women's political participation, we must do so in terms of specific organisations and institutions. That these may be generalised across institutional boundaries should not be taken for granted.

Political Interest

As well as institutional and structural considerations, attitudes must also be taken into account if we are to describe accurately women's political behaviour. Perhaps the most fundamental difference in attitudes to politics is the distinction between those who are and who are not interested. In Europe, women have been found to be consistently less interested. In France in 1953, when 28 per cent of men declared themselves to be uninterested in politics, 60 per cent of women made the same assertion. By 1969, 34 per cent of men but only 47 per cent of women declared a lack of interest, indicating a narrowing gap. Surveys revealed that French women became increasingly more willing to answer complex questions on politics throughout the 1970s, suggesting greater levels of both confidence and knowledge. Rising proportions of women amongst newspaper readers may be regarded as evidence of the same trend (Mossuz-Lavau and Sineau, 1981, 126). Differences between men and women in France were particularly affected by the continuing influence of the Catholic Church in politics, an influence which was maintained in part at least through the habit of giving girls a religious education, a practice which for many years apparently socialised women into a greater conservatism and traditionalism (Inglehart, 1981, 318). The attitudes of French women are not uniform, however. Other scholars have found that the vital factor distinguishing their political attitudes is whether they are employed outside the home. The major polarity is between those who work in full-time paid employment and those who do not leave the home for paid work. The latter are the least likely to be politically involved or knowledgeable about politics. A third category of women, the ex-actives or former wage earners who have returned to the home, occupy an intermediate position (Mossuz-Lavau and Sineau, 1983).

Even more than in France, Italian culture differentiates sharply between masculine and feminine role and encourages feminine indifference to politics. There, too, some of the explanation is the strong influence of the Catholic Church. Religious influences have borne heavily upon the preferences of Italian women who have shown particularly strong preferences for the conservative, confessional Christian Democrats (Weber, 1981, 202–3). Whilst the continuing crisis of Italian politics has produced high levels of political interest amongst its men, no similar effect has been discerned amongst Italian women, although their levels of interest, as measured by whether they discuss politics, have risen, nearing the 50-per-cent mark at the end of the 1970s (Inglehart, 1981, 320). In Austria, another country in which Catholic influence has been strong, a 1973 survey found that 36 per cent of women reported occasional interest in political matters and a further 7 per cent reported active interest. As many as 43 per cent were not at all interested in politics. Respondents expressed general doubts about women's ability to succeed in politics despite a belief that they had the same capabilities as men (Nowotny, 1981, 155).

Data on Great Britain indicate that there are only minor differences in men's and women's levels of interest in politics but that women were less likely to be politically knowledgeable. Amongst respondents to a November 1979 MORI poll, 46 per cent of women but only 27 per cent of men felt that they were not very well informed about world affairs.[1] In the same poll British women were significantly less likely to identify various widely used acronyms of political organisations (e.g. UN, NATO, EEC, IRA, etc.) than were men. A poll earlier that year had shown that only in the case of American and British leaders did women score as high as men in identification tests.[2] Whilst such exercises are probably poor indicators of knowledge, they do suggest lower levels of interest in international affairs amongst women than men as well as a greater parochialism.

It is in West Germany that the most persistent gap between levels of men's and women's political interest is to be found. Drawing on data from a number of surveys, Margaret Inglehart found that in 1959 only 49 per cent of German women were interested in politics and that a sex difference of 31 per cent was evident. By the 1970s interest amongst German women had increased to a mean of 67 per cent (across eight surveys). Indeed, German women with more than fifteen years of schooling were more politicised on this measure than women of any other nation. But male dominance persisted and a gender gap of 20 per cent failed to diminish throughout the decade. This was the widest gap in the EEC, excepting only Italy, where the difference was showing signs of being reduced. Male dominance shows up clearly in West German survey data. In 1977 it was found that 25 per cent of women would prefer to be men and that 54 per cent of both sexes felt that men were better at political judgment than their wives. Reporting a rather wider gap in men's and women's levels of political interest than Inglehart, Jane Hall concurs with the view that West German men have been particularly slow to relinquish their dominant status (Hall, 1981, 158–9). West German women clearly do not feel equal to men in politics, despite their high absolute levels of political interest.

How may such a seeming contradiction be explained? Margaret Inglehart refers to historical factors citing both the long experience of political authoritarianism and the evidence of Protestant emphasis on duty and responsibility, which are still present and which have filtered the persisting crises of political division as well as episodic crises such as outbreaks of terrorism and the tension created by increasing stature of West Germany as a European power. High and rising levels of political interest in politics in West Germany could be simply a reflection of the fact that those politics have been both fraught and dramatic (1981, 319). Hence, the phenomenon to be explained is not women's high level of interest in politics by comparison to women in other West European countries but their relatively low levels of interest by comparison to men's. Indeed, Ingelhart argues that the single most important variable which explains a person's interest in politics is nationality, followed closely by education. All other social factors were found to be of marginal importance. In each of the eight European countries she investigated (West Germany, Denmark, France, Italy, Ireland, Belgium, Great Britain and the Netherlands) women were less politicised than men, but differences in levels of political interest were greater between women of different nationalities than between men and women of the same country. A significant positive correlation did exist between the length of time women had been enfranchised and their levels of political interest but this could be seen to have more to do with the factors responsible for an early rather than a late enfranchisement. Essentially cultural, her argument is that it is historical factors which explain variations in women's politicisation by country. The franchise was awarded latest to women in the countries which had powerful institutions of an authoritarian and hierarchical character, notably the Roman Catholic Church and a strong national army, both of which have tended to retard the advance of political equality. Authoritarian attitudes had to be overcome before political participation by the masses could occur and as both institutions were anti-feminist, initial inroads were made by men alone. In six of the countries in her sample a clear-cut distinction could be found between those with a predominant Protestant tradition (England, Denmark and the Netherlands) and an anti-feminist Catholic tradition (Italy, Ireland and Belgium). Of the two 'exceptions', France was the site of a unique combination of a strong revolutionary tradition and a strong Catholic Church, whilst in Germany a northern Protestantism was influenced by militarism whilst the south was Catholic. Women's levels of political interest were found to be consistently higher in countries with Protestant backgrounds, lower in those of Catholic backgrounds, a difference which was often as high as 10 per cent even as late as the 1970s (Inglehart, 1981, *passim*).

Data on women's interest in and attitudes to politics in the state socialist countries of Europe are rather more sparse. White cites evidence that USSR women read newspapers and political literature rather less than men, that they attend political education classes less frequently and that they are less interested in the political content of the newspapers and magazines that they do read than men. These are differences which hold over time and when controlled for urban as opposed to rural residence and education, leading him to conclude that women in the Soviet Union constitute 'a distinctive political sub-culture characterised by lower levels of political interest and involvement than the national population as a whole' (White, 1979, 156). Similar findings have been produced by Bulgarian and Yugoslav surveys, which reveal low levels of political interest amongst women even at the level of community affairs (Jancar, 1978), indicating that even in cultures giving primacy to the political sphere there exist constraints on women's political involvement.

Throughout Europe, then, survey evidence confirms that women's levels of interest in politics are lower than men's. There is some evidence that when politics is more broadly defined—that is, when respondents are asked about their interest in 'important social problems'—differences between men and women are reduced (see *European Women and Men in 1983*, 130). The capacity of sample surveys to tap anything more than an interest in a very narrowly defined political world is therefore open to dispute. However, the consistency of the available evidence is undeniable. Measurable levels of political interest are greater amongst men than amongst women. And women have been found to be less knowledgeable about politics than men, less psychologically involved and less ideological in their thinking. In an analysis of data on five countries (West Germany, Austria, Britain, the Netherlands and the USA) Jennings and Farah found that women were less likely than men to understand, employ or utilise concepts associated with the political Left and Right. The conclusion that a strong association existed between ideological awareness and participation propensity suggests that their relatively low level of ideological awareness is a further constraint on women's political involvement (Jennings and Farah, 1980, 232).

Political Ideology: Women's 'Conservatism'

An apparent inability to conceptualise left–right distinctions has not prevented women from engaging in political activity and expressing political preferences which have resulted in their being consistently regarded as more conservative than men. Ronald Inglehart has found that West European women have been more likely to be conservative in their political views and voting behaviour than men, a trend which was more marked in the strongly religious countries of France, Belgium and Italy (1977, 88–92). Vicky Randall also refers to the long-standing conservative preference revealed by the votes of European women as a pattern which has been strongly associated with religious leanings and particularly with the Catholic Church. The association has been so strong that women comprised an important basis for conservative support in every West European country for which evidence was available from the end of the Second World War up until the 1970s when the pattern finally began to alter. There is, however, an important analytical problem with most discussions of women's conservatism. As Randall (1982, 50) points out, the concept of conservatism is too broad to have much classificatory use. If, she argues, the assertion of women's conservatism is taken simply to mean the presence of right-wing attitudes, then the evidence that women are more conservative than men is sparse and weak at best. If it is taken to mean a greater traditionalism on the part of women, a greater adherence to the established order, then it should be remembered that the established order itself need not necessarily be a conservative one (e.g. the state socialist societies). Neither does data underlining women's greater protest potential and willingness to engage in direct action (Barnes and Kaase, 1979, *passim*) bear out a conclusion of greater conservatism. In short, what is supposed to be evidence that women are more conservative than men is in fact evidence that women in some countries used to be more likely to vote for parties of the centre Right, but not the extreme Right, than men (Duverger, 1955; Lovenduski and Hills, 1981; Randall, 1982).

Such propensity as women have had to vote for the Right has begun to disappear. Britain is the European country in which women's conservative voting has perhaps been best researched. Women's greater conservatism there had achieved the status of an assumption before the feminism of the 1970s generated a new interest in this area of study (Baxter and Lansing, 1980, 155). The theme was a part of British general election analysis, reported in most undergraduate textbooks and well substantiated by survey data on voting behaviour. Women's Conservative Party voting was higher than men's in British general elections until 1979 when no gender gap was apparent. In 1983 the pattern reversed itself when men proved more likely than women to vote for the Conservatives. A similar reversal had taken place in Scandinavia during the 1970s (Crewe, 1983), and Mossuz-Lavau and Sineau (1981) reported a narrowing of the ideological gap between French men and women during the 1970s, its eradication having been accomplished by 1984 (*Women of Europe*, No. 34, 28). Throughout Western Europe, the smallest differences between the sexes in voting preferences have been found to be in the youngest age groups, suggesting that remaining gender gaps in voting choice are declining over time (Inglehart, 1977, 228–9).

Political Activism

Although differences in turnout have disappeared or nearly disappeared between men and women in most European countries, the gender gap appears to be more persistent in other forms of political activism. Thus, Lafferty (1978, 25) has declared that sex is the most important structural determinant of political activity in Norway. Nie, Verba and Kim (1978) have reported that except in the United States, men have a higher rate of affiliation to institutions of all kinds and are consistently more likely than women to be members of, or otherwise affiliated to, political organisations. EEC data collected in 1983 confirm this pattern for residents of member states (*European Women and Men in 1983*, 145–50). But Helga Hernes cites scattered evidence that data on gender differences in organisational affiliation may not take into account small locally-organised groups without national networks. Hence such data may consistently underestimate women's affiliations (Council of Europe, 1984, Part 3). Similar differences are apparent in the state socialist societies where women's political involvement and activism falls off sharply as the hierarchy of conventional politics is ascended (Hough, 1978; Hough and Fainsod, 1979; Wolchik, 1981; Vasileva undated). In the conventional political arena, men are more likely to be present than women. However, women have been more attracted to less conventional political arenas. Randall uses Hernes and Voje's notion of *ad hoc* politics to describe activity intended to influence public policy which is not formally integrated into normal political processes or which has not been institutionalised. *Ad hoc* participation is participation in political campaigns which may be short-lived, throwing up makeshift organisations and relying on (often spontaneous) direct action. Women's political action groups are most frequently based in neighbourhoods. There it is possible to combine political work, paid part-time work and home responsibilities (Council of Europe, 1984, Part 3). In Britain women have been heavily involved in the community action movement, particularly in housing campaigns, claimants activities and child-care projects (Randall, 1982, 41) as well as in the peace movement. A further example is the organisation of 'Women Against Pit Closures' during the 1984–5 British miners' strike. *Ad hoc* activity such as this is essentially urban, self-help orientated and largely unstructured. It has been an element of the political repertoire of women in Norway (Hernes and Voje, 1980, 177) and has everywhere been an important part of women's movement politics (see above Ch. 3). Barnes and Kaase's (1979) study indicates that such activities are problem-solving rather than institution-building, but Helga Hernes stresses the importance of organisational infrastructures created by women's groups, especially the voluntary associations (Council of Europe, 1984, Part 3).

Ad hoc politics overlap with protest politics, an arena in which we know women have been engaged for at least a century. European history provides repeated examples of women's readiness to engage in revolutionary movements. Terrorist activities too have involved unexpectedly large numbers of women. By 1978 women were 60 per cent of the terrorists sought by the Federal German police. Pridham (1981, 28) and Kolinski (1984b, 238) note the disproportionate presence of women amongst West German terrorist groups, and Randall (1982, 44) indicates that women have been prominent participants in terrorist groups elsewhere. But none of these commentators can offer an explanation of this phenomenon. Important contemporary evidence on women's propensity for less extreme forms of protest appears in Barnes and Kaase's study of five countries and indicates that in the four European countries covered (Austria, Britain, West Germany and the Netherlands) protest potential is associated with being a woman. European Communities' data also indicate a slightly higher propensity to engage in public demonstrations amongst women than amongst men (*European Women and Men in 1983*, 143–5). Whilst such data are measures of declared intentions rather than observed activities, they nonetheless reflect a readiness to be mobilised in political protest, at the same time eschewing the 'male dominated world of "politics"' (Barnes and Kaase, 1978, 184). Such evidence is far from conclusive, but it alerts us to the possibility that women may be less reluctant to engage in the more informal political world of movements, campaigns and direct action of various kinds than in the formal political arenas of parties, elections and legislatures.

Explaining Gender Differences in Political Activism

Explanations offered for differences in men's and women's political activism have been of several kinds. Such phenomena as differential socialisation of boys and girls and the idea of a separate women's culture are said to account for differences between men and women. Attempts to account for differences between women have included reference to variations in family structures, to the effects of different stages in a woman's life-cycle and to the impact of urbanism, which has been found in some countries to have a bearing on women's political participation. Such ideas have obvious explanatory value and are important in coming to an understanding of women's political roles. It is well known that agents of socialisation, notably the family and the school, channel individuals into expectations about occupational and other roles which are class and gender related. Women are particularly victims of this process, having long been assigned roles which are low in prestige and status in most societies. This has had a spill-over effect into politics, producing feelings of low efficacy amongst women, which impede an active interest in an area normally portrayed as male defined and clearly male occupied. Thus, a 1983 survey of men and women in the EEC countries found that women felt themselves to be competent to discuss 'important social problems' in similar proportions to men but were significantly less likely than men to discuss 'politics' (*European Men and Women 1983*, 130).

An additional impediment is the fact that women's life-cycles are more segmented than are men's, with domestic responsibilities—most importantly, childrearing—looming rather larger. Becoming a mother involves important changes of status and outlook and immediate constraints of some considerable duration. Whilst there is no reason why fatherhood should not involve the same life-style alteration, historically changes for men have been less far reaching. In practical terms it must be conceded that motherhood is likely to engage the free time an individual would have had to be active in politics. More tenuous is the idea that a separate women's culture exists which socialises them away from political involvement. Whilst intuitively appealing, there has been little empirical research available to validate such a hypothesis (but see Lafferty, 1978, note 9). Other comparisons stress the connections between types of family structure and politics. Michel (1977) differentiates between traditional, transitional and modern nations in terms of their prevailing family structures and women's roles. In this typology France and Germany are seen as mainly traditional, Britain as transitional and Scandinavia as modern. Essentially, the differences between the three categories are ordered along a parameter which ranges from those cultures which define women in accordance with their domestic roles at one pole to those which see women as individuals at the other. Lovenduski and Hills (1981, 321) have found that variations in family structure are apparently related to variations in political activism, but the effect was mixed. Extended families provided both additional responsibilities and additional assistance, whilst the dual career and single-parent families becoming common in many countries combined a relative freedom from the inhibitions of traditional roles with the additional constraint of extra and sometimes extensive responsibilities. The still-common nuclear family, with its high levels of privatisation, has not been conducive to the entry of women into the political arena.

But the two most important and comprehensive explanations of women's disadvantaged political position are the structural and resource accounts put forward by social scientists and the various dual burden/domestic constraints theories preferred by many feminists. Whilst they often overlap, the two accounts represent rather different approaches to the question of women's political activism.

Structural explanations—that is, explanations which are based upon a group's place in the social structure—come in a number of forms, but their common element is that they emphasise differential access to political resources. The persistence of women's relatively small repertoire of conventional participatory behaviour despite the removal of legal barriers to activism is seen as a predictable outcome of the ways in which advantages are distributed in society. Whilst it is not denied that women fare badly in access to political resources, this is seen to be a result of factors *other than sex*.

Verba, Nie and Kim (1978, 235–65) present what is perhaps the most carefully constructed argument in the category of resource explanations. In a study of political activism in seven countries (Austria, India, Japan, the Netherlands, Nigeria, the USA and Yugoslavia) they found that women scored lower than men on both voting and political activity scales, with the smallest gaps to be found in the USA and the Netherlands. Their data confirmed a ubiquitous gender-based participation gap but also showed substantial variations in its magnitude by country. The gender gap in voting turnout in the five developed countries was insubstantial, but the participation gap was rather greater except in the United States. Interestingly, no sex-related differences were found in participatory patterns for 'medium level' campaign and communal activities, so their data on gender differences distinguish only

between the relatively easy act of voting and more difficult acts on
an overall activity scale. Two possible explanations for women's
abstention from politics were suggested: apathy and/or inhibition; either women abstain because they do not care about
political matters or they do care but are inhibited from participation because of either external- or self-restraint. Levels of educational attainment (a useful indicator of access to socio-economic
resources in a society) were used to differentiate between men's
and women's resources, an exercise which revealed men to be
advantaged in terms of maximum levels of educational attainment, except in the USA. Hence, men in their sample are likely to
have more social resources. But when Verba *et al.* controlled their
data for levels of education, differences between men and women
still remained. In Yugoslavia a larger increase in male than in
female activity was found as the educational hierarchy was
ascended, with the result that there the gap between men's and
women's activity rates was greatest in the best-educated segment
of the sample. Essentially, their finding was that education was
less beneficial to women than to men in terms of its effect on
political activity. To put it another way, men have higher conversion rates of education into political activity than do women.
Although education tended to reduce differences between men
and women in voting, at more demanding levels of activism its
effect was limited. The other resource difference Verba tested was
institutional affiliation. It had been found that institutional affiliations such as party, trade union or other pressure group membership had a capacity to reduce representation differences between
advantaged and disadvantaged groups, pointing to a conclusion
that institutional affiliation was an important political resource.
The team found little evidence that women saw themselves as a
group which might have particular claims on a government. None
of their seven nations featured (at the time of the study) either a
women's political party or a party attempting to mobilise around
women's issues. However, there were no men's parties (as such!)
either, so it was decided to compare the institutional resources
available to men and women by looking at variations in their
memberships and attachments to existing political institutions.
Men were 'more affiliated' in the sense both of being more
strongly attached and more likely to hold memberships of groups
and/or parties all of the nations except the USA. Hence, men in
their study were definitely advantaged in their access to institutional resources. But when the investigators controlled for levels
of institutional resources, they found that differences in activity

rates between the sexes persisted. Men gained more political resources from institutional affiliation than did women.

On at least two counts, then, men convert resources into political capital at a higher rate than women. The participatory disadvantage of women would be only partly reduced if resources were equalised. Verba and his colleagues tried to use their results as a basis for choosing between inhibition and apathy explanations of women's lesser political activism. Their results had shown that women were less psychologically involved in politics than men. Women's relatively good voting turnout records were amenable to an explanation that such behaviour represented mobilised but unconcerned activity. But the very fact women converted resources into activism even though at a lower rate than men's, pointed towards an inhibition explanation. Hence, the conclusion was that the data were not sufficient to determine whether women were less politically engaged because they were apathetic or because something inhibited their involvement.

Further testing was revealing. When factors such as education levels and paid employment were incorporated into the data, differences in levels of psychological involvement between men and women tended to disappear. Analysis by age categories enabled sex-differentiated life-cycle effects to be determined.

The explanatory value of the impact of employment on women's political participation has preoccupied other analysts as well. Carol Christy's analysis of data from nineteen surveys covering eleven nations,[3] indicates that workforce participation in Western Europe has a variable effect on women's political participation which is affected by age, education, occupation, union membership, national culture and the type of political participation concerned. She warns that the assumption that employment stimulates women's political participation is not always or uniformly substantiated by the evidence and that its impact is weak outside the USA. Cross-national variations in the impact of employment on women's political engagement could partly be explained by cross-national variations in the levels of education of those women who were and were not employed. Age, too, had an effect, whereby women's employment most stimulated political participation in the youngest age group, decreasing in its impact amongst the intermediate and older groups.

Paradoxically for younger women, the more difficult the political activity, the greater was the stimulus of employment. A life-cycle effect is apparent here in which younger housewives not in the workforce—that is, those most likely to be responsible for small children—were the most constrained group. Hence, differences between them and their employed counterparts are likely to be great. In the intermediate and older categories of women employment was also a stimulus to political activity but one which was of decreasing strength. As employed women in these age groups were found to have high feelings of psychological involvement in politics, it was perhaps domestic responsibilities, the dual burden, which counteracted their predisposition for involvement. The employment effect was reduced when it was controlled for union membership, which in most countries was found to increase women's levels of political activity at various levels, a result which confirms the Verba, Nie and Kim findings on access to institutional resources (Christy, 1983). Whilst in many respects the resource-focused structural explanations of women's lesser levels of political participation are contradictory, they do agree on the fact that, for whatever reasons, women have lower levels of access to important political resources than men, and this has an apparent political effect. What the studies have not been able to do is provide a basis for determining whether resource explanations explain the same degree of women's political behaviour as men's. Enormous methodological difficulties would attend any such effort, and it is unlikely that an approach to empirical study could ever be designed which would resolve satisfactorily such a question.

But existing work could be considerably improved, not least by building into survey design some basis for assessing independently the differential access women have to important resources. Efforts in this direction have already been made, notably in the important area of differentiating between husband's and wives' occupational status in voting studies. Lafferty (1978, 244–5) accomplished this by assigning housewives to their own category at the low end of his socio-economic status index, distinguishing between those who had no wage-earning employment at all and those who had a part-time job. In such a scheme, when housewives are removed from the analysis, the effect of employment status on both organisational membership and electoral activity all but disappears. In other words, the most important part of the division of labour in its effects on Norwegian political behaviour was that of either holding or not holding a job, a phenomenon which is in practice a gender effect. Empirically, sex turned out to be a better predictor of voting behaviour than class.

A more recent and rather more sophisticated attempt to determine the effect of gender on voting has been made by Patrick

Dunleavy and Christopher Husbands in their study of the 1983 British general election. They found that when women were classified according to their own occupational categories rather than those of their husbands, two different patterns of gender effect on voting were apparent. Amongst 'intermediate non-manual' women (in a four-part scheme of 'upper-non-manual', 'intermediate non-manual', 'skilled manual', 'other manual') women's conservatism was greater than men's, largely at Labour's expense. Amongst 'other manual' women, Labour voting is higher than amongst men. When a social class scheme was used, further differences were revealed. Dunleavy and Husband's (1984; 1985) work is about ideological preference rather than activism as such, but it is nonetheless instructive in that it alerts us to the pitfalls inherent in survey work on women. Most resource explanations of gender differences in political behaviour have been based upon stratification schemes which did not distinguish between husband's and wife's occupational status and may therefore have distorted the effect of occupation on women's political behaviour. Research which takes account of the fact that gender may be both 'logically and empirically prior' to class is a particularly welcome antidote to that which subsumes important aspects of women's political behaviour in her family status rather than scrutinising the differential effects which that status might have.

If political scientists have been reluctant to take account of the explanatory theories of women's oppression produced by feminists, feminist theorists have on the whole been uninterested in explicitly questioning women's political participation and women's access to positions of power in society. Nevertheless, the many discussions of the impact of domestic constraints on all women, of the dual burden on women employed outside the home and of the public-private split on the structure of power in society are important sources of explanations for differences in the political behaviour of men and women.

Margaret Stacey and Marion Price are unusual in producing an account of women and power in Britain which takes account of the impediments to women's political participation consequent upon the separation of public and private life in industrial and post-industrial society. They place considerable emphasis on the impact of industrial and state development in the delineation of a formal, identifiable public sphere of government and administration. The attendant social differentiation relegated women to a private, domestic sphere at the same time as it gradually inhibited the use of private forms of power in public life. Recruitment, even political recruitment, came more and more to be based upon forms of recognised merit. Initially, this impeded women who had little access to the means of qualification. As such access was gained, support grew for the argument that women and men should be judged on the same terms. Such a mode of evaluation could only be of benefit to those women who were not constrained by the demands of domestic roles. Hence, most women would continue to be disadvantaged for as long as family structure and its associated attitudes and (legitimating structures) involved a division of labour between the sexes (Stacey and Price, 1981). Randall too argues that the very location of politics in a non-domestic sphere and women in a domestic one makes participation more difficult for women than for men, and, she notes, the more differentiated the processes of political participation, the greater this relative difficulty becomes. In such a view, women's reported preference for more accessible *ad hoc* politics becomes readily understandable (Randall, 1982, 66).

Other feminist social scientists are less convinced of the utility of the notion of the public/private split in political analysis. Siltanen and Stanworth (1984b, 201–6) are convinced that the 'private women, public man' conception of politics is misleading. The private domain is implicated in political processes and the public domain's boundaries do not coincide with the boundaries of the political. The dichotomous concept turns out, in their view, to be a rather clumsy analytical tool, insensitive to the extent to which the political character of women is publicly determined. Furthermore, it reinforces the tendency to regard masculinity as ideal political behaviour in that it implicitly accepts as political the masculine-defined public sphere. More fundamentally, both men and women have both private and public lives and it would be impossible to produce an accurate account of relations between the sexes which failed to recognise the extent to which men are defined by and define themselves in terms of private commitments. Moreover, much of the activity which takes place in the public domain is routinised and depoliticised. Hence, insistence on the public/private dichotomy represents an essentially conservative posture which plays down important public and private sphere interdependencies and removes ordinary concerns from the conception of what is political.

Siltanen and Stanworth also affirm that gender differences between men's and women's political behaviour are small and that the very act of scrutinising them tends to lead to their exaggeration. But they take Evans' (1980) point that it is important not to overcorrect to the point of injecting equally false assumptions of identicality. Rather, research should also attempt to reveal women's distinctive political contributions. This involves rejections of current masculine-defined norms of ideal political behaviour, the rejection of arbitrary divisions between the moral, social and political spheres so that such phenomena as anti-war movements and community action are more often included and, finally, insistence that rational political assessment may involve abstention as a response. In other words, recognition should be given to women's decision not to engage in a political action which may itself be a self-conscious political act (Siltanen, and Stanworth, 1981, *passim*).

The Political Participation of European Women: Numerical versus Corporate Channels

The majority of theoretical and empirical studies of formal political participation deal with the electoral system, with processes and posts which involve obtaining the sanction of a majority of some sort in order to engage in a political assembly at one or another levels. This avenue of participation and representation has been called the numerical channel. But Hernes and Voje remind us that at least since the Second World War public life has increasingly involved private citizens and voluntary organisations on a large scale in what is often referred to as the 'corporate channel'. In the Nordic countries the corporate channel is particularly well articulated. Highly developed systems of commissions, councils, committees and delegations have been established as channels of communication. These are also apparatuses of mutual support and control for the administration and large-scale interest organisations. They are known to be powerful and important participants in public policy-making and to play a major role in defining the public interest and setting the public agenda (Hernes and Voje, 1980, 163). The phenomenon is widespread and what is often called corporatism or, more accurately, 'concertation' or corporate pluralism, is an acknowledged feature of most European liberal democracies (Smith, 1980; Harrison, 1980). Similarly, corporate forms if not plural practices may be traced in the decision-making structures of the state socialist countries of Eastern and Central Europe (Fejto, 1974).

In practice there are at least four important formal channels of political participation. These are, first, channels of numerical representation on the basis of one person, one vote, manifested for example by the political parties and the various elected legislatures. The second channel is that of agencies of interest representation, and the third is the institutions of administration. These have tended to fuse to form the corporate channel. Finally, there is the judiciary, normally an appointive channel but in important respects different from the institutions of administration. The numerical and corporate channels are not, strictly speaking, separable by reference simply to practices of electoral selection, as there are many important representative posts in the interest organisations which are elected. But these are not elections in which the general public takes part, hence a distinction exists between general and particular representation. All four channels are important arenas of political recruitment and training, and each selects and promotes individuals from amongst a pool of eligibles determined by a number of distinctive criteria. In the numerical channel the primary recruiting organisation is the political party, which, it is important to remember, may also have a say in all of the other channels. In the corporate channel it is the leadership of interest groups and government ministers who are the gatekeepers. It is government ministers who are responsible for making judicial appointments, normally from amongst a pool of individuals who have successfully completed particular forms of legal training.

The distinction between corporate and numerical channels of representation is particularly useful in comparing the access to decision-making arenas of different groups in society. The means of access to both channels are embedded in organisational patterns. But the requirements of electoral systems tend to be less formal in terms of educational and occupational status, thus less likely to exclude women who tend to have lower levels of achievement in these areas. However, political parties are demanding in terms of both personal loyalty and time, tending thus to exclude women responsible for child care. In addition, the political activities of many women take place outside the arena of formal politics and are thereby left unregarded by those responsible for political recruitment. The overall result is that women are better represented in the numerical than in the corporate channels, but well represented in neither. The judiciary, as we shall see, is something of a special case, varying considerably from country to country in its recruitment of women.

Having outlined the terrain of political participation and representation, it is time now to turn our attention to a more detailed account of trends and developments affecting women's presence in the various channels. In the West European liberal democracies as well as in the single-party state socialist systems of Eastern and Central Europe, it is the political parties which have the major say in the recruitment of individuals into the numerical channels. In the corporate channel it is the economic interest groups, most importantly the 'peak' employer and employee organisations, which provide extra access, other appointments being government—and hence often party—determined. Accordingly, the remainder of this chapter will consist of a 'mapping out' of the position of women in a selection of European party systems, whilst Chapter 5 will outline their positions in the corporate channel. In Chapter 6 scrutiny will be made of women's presence in the representative institutions themselves, both electoral and appointive.

Britain

With one of the poorest representations of women in national politics in Europe, the British numerical channel combines a number of characteristics which particularly impede the political promotion of women. Notably, first-past-the-post elections based on single-member constituencies produce a party system in which jealously guarded local prerogatives have overridden central party intentions to increase the numbers of women candidates and MPs.

Amongst the 10 per cent of the adult population who belong to political parties, women are just over 50 per cent of the members of the Conservative Party and approximately 40 per cent of Labour Party members. Accurate figures are not available for the other parties, but the Social Democrats estimate that women are about 40 per cent of their members. Liberal Party women's membership is probably rather higher as is that for the Scottish Nationalist Party. Plaid Cymru (the Welsh Nationalists) and the Northern Ireland parties have never produced a membership breakdown by sex but the extreme paucity of women candidates nominated by them suggests that women may not make up a large proportion of the members of these parties.

Of the four parties which operate on a country-wide basis, the Labour and Conservative parties both have women's sections and both make provision for women's representation at national level. Jill Hills (1981a, 20–1) has found that Labour Party women are poorly represented at conference delegate level but that this is combated to some extent by the reservation on the party's National Executive of five seats for women. Only rarely have women succeeded in gaining election to non-reserved seats. In the Conservative Party, women have places reserved for them throughout the party structure, although in proportions which decrease as the hierarchy is ascended. Conservative women are about 38 per cent of annual conference delegates, about 20 per cent of executive committee members and 18 per cent of members of the important Advisory Committee on Policy at Central Office. In short, both major parties make special provision for women, but both feature a significant underrepresentation of their women members in decision-taking bodies. Amongst the smaller parties, special provision does not exist and only the Social Democrats have regulations which attempt to increase women's chances of candidacy in national elections. Party rules make compulsory the inclusion of at least two women on every short list. At leadership level the Social Democrats have been concerned to be seen to be promoting women, but this often seems to be in spite of their membership. Their Constitutional Congress returned a hung vote on the principle of equal representation of men and women in the leadership (Vallance, 1984).

Neither of the two major parties pay much heed to their annual women's conferences, which have no special access to the agenda of the main annual conferences. Promotion of women within the parties is haphazard and often dependent upon the goodwill of those women who have achieved prominence. Thus, some Labour and Conservative women MPs and Shirley Williams, a prominent Social Democrat, have participated in training schemes for potential women candidates on an *ad hoc* basis. But there is little evidence that the majority of women who have been successful in politics feel an obligation to undertake this sort of work.

Although the proportion of women elected to Parliament has varied since women first voted in 1918, the total has never exceeded 5 per cent of MPs. Whilst legal political emancipation has followed increasing economic activity, women in Britain did not organise themselves to demand better political representation until the late 1970s. After the 1979 general election returned fewer women to Parliament than at any time since the Second World War, Labour women organised within the party to press for better representation. Their efforts were also fuelled by disillusion with the result of the equality legislation of the 1970s (see Ch. 7). Hence, two new groups appeared within the party, the Campaign for Labour Party Democracy—Women's Action Committee

(CLPD-WAC), and Fightback for Women's Rights. It is CLPD-WAC which is concerned with campaigning for changes in the party in order to increase the representation of women, the party and particularly in Parliament. Hence, their demands include equal representation of men and women on party decision-taking bodies, mandatory inclusion of women on constituency short-lists and positive discrimination for women on parliamentary short-lists. Fightback has concentrated on campaigning on general sex equality and women's rights issues. Their presence is permitted by the confederal nature of the Labour Party, which loosely unites unions and sections and thus provides considerable opportunities for internal organisation. The branch-level women's sections within which the CLPD-WAC and Fightback operate are permitted but not required by party rules. Thus, the initial internal struggle for many Labour Party women has been to get local branches to support the establishment of a women's section. Although firmly committed to the Labour Party, both groups are a product of the women's movement and should be seen as an example of the movement by feminists into important political channels which has been characteristic of West European politics in the 1980s.

All four nation-wide political parties put particular effort into encouraging women candidates in the 1983 general election. Whilst the formal constitutional provisions of the Social Democrats were not duplicated in the other parties, concern was evident. Labour's designation of Joan Lestor as Shadow Minister for Women was certainly a signal that the party was prepared to take women's issues seriously (indeed, Labour was the only party to include sex equality issues in its manifesto), and Joyce Gould, the party women's officer, endeavoured to encourage the selection of women candidates. The Conservatives had no policy as such, but vice-presidents in charge of candidates during the run-up to the election (both men) were known to be aiming for women to be at least 10 per cent of party nominees. After the election the Conservatives charged vice-president Emma Nicholson with the task of encouraging more women to enter Parliament (Vallance, 1984).

In the event a total of 276 women were nominated by the various parties, and women were 6.3 per cent of Conservative and 12.3 per cent of Labour candidates. For the first time in British history women were more than 10 per cent of parliamentary candidates (Table 4.1). A percentage increase since 1979 in the number of women candidates was evident in each party.

Table 4.1: *Women party members, 1983 general election candidates and MPs by party (in per cent): Great Britain*

	Membership	1983 general election candidates	Women MP's elected
Conservative	51	6.3	3.3(13/397)
Labour	40	12.3	4.8(10/209)
Liberal	NA	9.9	0(0/17)
Social Democrat	40	14.1	0(0/6)
Scottish Nationalist	NA	12.5	0(0/2)
Plaid Cymru	NA	18.0	0(0/2)

NA = Not Available

However, the actual numbers of women standing for the major parties were low and only in the case of the Social Democrats did their proportion reflect their share of party membership. And women did not get elected in proportion to their candidacy even for the winning party. Amongst the Conservatives, women were 6.3 per cent of candidates but only 3.3 per cent of MPs elected. For Labour the figures were 12.3 and 4.8 per cent, respectively.

It has been known for some time that British voters do not penalise women candidates, that voting is by party and that the impact of any individual candidate on party preference is minimal. Hence, the barriers to women's representation in national politics occur at a stage in the selection process prior to that of electoral competition. Following Hills (1981a) we note that there are three important stages through which a candidate must pass before she is presented to the electorate as an official party nominee. First, she must make herself available as a candidate, then she must be approved by her party and, finally, she must be adopted by a constituency. Working backwards through these stages we find that it is the constituency selection stage which is the most trouble-some. When women lose elections in Britain (and they usually do) it is because they are standing for hopeless or marginal seats in years where the swing is away from their party. Evidence for both 1979 and 1983 (Vallance, 1979, 1984) makes it clear that parties were unwilling to select women for their safe seats. Vallance reports that between 1979 and 1983 all the four largest parties increased the proportions of women on their approved candidate lists: Labour from 10 to 15 per cent, Conservative to 10 per cent, the Liberals to 11 per cent and the new Social Democrats approved a list on which women were 17 per cent of the total. Hence, women were available for selection. But they were most consistently selected for unwinnable seats.

Although there is no doubt that parties at central level would prefer to see more women selected for winnable constituencies, they seem to have little success in prevailing over the constituency parties in this regard. The reasons for this are not altogether clear. Vallance (1981) argues that the selectorate at constituency level tends to be biased against women candidates because of a misconception that women do less well at the polls. Denver (1982) disagrees, stating that in the case of the Labour Party, at least, there is no systematic evidence which indicates the existence either of a bias against women or of a misconception about voting patterns.

Jill Hills (1981a) points out that up until 1979, neither the two major parties nor the Liberal Party fielded more than a token number of women candidates and that in terms of nominating women for winnable seats the Labour party had a slightly, but only slightly, better record than the Conservatives. For the minor and nationalist parties Hills found that the proportion of women nominated was inversely correlated with the chances of success. Whilst increased party competition favoured the number of women candidates, the proportion of women declined as chances of success increased. This is underlined by Vallance's (1984) observation that the majority of women candidates in 1983 were nominated by parties which had no hope of achieving parliamentary representation.

Within the main parties the problem appears to be located mainly at consituency level. Examination of the first two stages of the candidate selection process reveals no evidence that either party is more or less likely to approve the credentials of women who seek approval as candidates or that either party has failed to approve qualified women. Although Randall (1982, 98–9) notes an increased tendency for Labour Party candidates to bypass the central lists and apply directly to the constituency, party centres have been supportive of women's candidacies. However, Labour women candidates are less likely than men to have the trade union backing necessary for placement on the B list (the party keeps an A list of ordinary approved candidates and a B list of candidates sponsored and nominated by the unions). B list candidacy is apparently beneficial. In 1983, 114 of the 153 union-backed Labour candidates were elected, a success rate of 74.5 per cent. Only seven of the 153 were women, five of whom were elected (Vallance, 1984). Hence, union-backed candidates, who are rarely women, fare particularly well in the Labour Party.

It is also widely believed that the British electoral system impedes the political promotion of women. Vernon Bogdanor argues that the British single-member constituency, first-past-the-post system encourages the selection of 'safe' candidates; that is, those who are white, middle-class and male (Bogdanor, 1984, 111). In his view, party-list systems favour the election of women whilst single-member-constituency systems penalise them. Hilary Bryan (1984, Ch. 2) cites a number of studies which show that proportional representation in the form of multi-member, single-transferable-vote systems or party-list systems induce parties to offer voters the widest possible choice of candidates, a constraint which ensures that at least some women will be nominated. British political parties are not so constrained and the relative autonomy of constituency organisations has, in any case, prevented national party leaders from imposing formal or informal requirements about the characteristics of candidates.

When examining the British political parties for the provision of channels for women, two important factors must be borne in mind. First, the parties are significant gatekeepers of the political elite; hence, second, only with party support may a woman embark upon a political career with any hope of success. Whilst in the Labour Party she may be promoted into the party via her trade union, or in all parties gain initial experience in interest groups, a woman must obtain party backing eventually. Women's access to the numerical channel in Britain is party controlled, and whilst nothing in the party's rules specifically impedes their access (Hills, 1978), women have not done well out of the parties in terms of achieving political prominence. Nor have party policies on women been remarkable for their innovation or radicalism. Indeed, at programmatic level there has been little evidence that the British parties recognise the existence of a 'woman question'. Hence, the Liberal Party included equal opportunities as a manifesto component in 1979 and campaigned on the topic. But the Labour and Conservative parties avoided the issue, campaigning for 'the family' instead. In 1983 only the Labour Party included a manifesto pledge on women's rights, although the Liberal-Social-Democratic-Alliance leaders did make verbal commitments to such measures as strengthening the existing sex-equality legislation. The Conservative Party had little to say on the subject, preferring to campaign once again for the family. Opinion data suggest more commitment to women's rights amongst Labour and Alliance than amongst Tory MPs,[4] but this commitment does not appear to have been carried through to the electoral arena. The political promotion of women has yet to become an important party priority in Britain.

Italy

In Italy many of the political characteristics which impede women's promotion in Britain are absent. A multi-party system featuring high levels of political competition is combined with a proportional-representation-based electoral law, which allows voters to take candidates out of order on party lists (preference voting). The system provides numerous means of placing pressure on parties to promote women. Between seven and nine parties have been represented since the Second World War and a further array of fringe parties have appeared in and disappeared from the legislature. General elections in Italy thus cover most of the imaginable political spectrum. The Christian Democrats (DCs) are the largest party and have dominated all post-war Italian governments, whilst the next largest, the Communists (PCI), have never been in government. Other parties clustered around the centre have taken part in various coalitions, notably the Republicans (PRI) and Liberals (PLI) and the Socialists (PSI) and the Social Democrats (PSDI). The tiny neo-fascist MSI has not been regarded as an attractive coalition partner.

Nearly all of the parties have special offices to deal with women and women's issues but only the Christian Democrats and the Republicans have 'autonomous' women's movements, the leaders of which automatically have a seat on the party executive board (*direzione*). The PCI has a women's section the leader of which sits on the executive. For many years strongly associated with the PCI, the UDI (Union Donne Italiane) is Italy's largest women's association. It began as an organisation mainly of the Left with roots in the resistance movement. Founded in Rome in 1944 the UDI was a non-partisan women's organisation which for a long period was a staunch supporter of PCI policy and was dominated by PCI women. It broke away at the beginning of the 1980s, declaring its independence and rejecting continued PCI and PSI financial support in an effort to better its links with the women's movement. The Christian Democrats also have a supporting women's association, the Centro Italiano Feminile (CIF). The Social Democratic Party abolished its women's section and substituted a civil rights section which in practice deals mainly with women's problems. The Socialist Party had a similar policy but reversed it and continues to have a women's section. The Socialists have also an official 15 per cent minimum quota of women for executive board and other internal bodies. The Radical Party (PR) is essentially a federation of movements which emerged in the 1960s as a credible electoral force and which included until the late 1970s the Movimento di Liberazione della Dona (Women's Liberation Movement) amongst its federated organisations. For the duration of their association the Radicals informally had an effective 50 per cent minimum quota of women for both internal committees and electoral candidates.

Party careers in Italy are often made in affiliated organisations, involving movement through these to local and then to central political arenas. Lateral entry career patterns also exist whereby parties recruit people prominent in other areas directly to top-level posts, normally deputyships. However, it is rare for women to have achieved the necessary prominence in Italy's arts, pressure groups, industries, academic life or media, so women's political careers are nearly always party careers (De Santis and Zincone, 1983, 5.21 to 5.23).

The late emergence of the woman question in Italy together with the absence of a strong central state to ameliorate the effects of the Catholic Church on secular society and the early locus of women's rights activists in the workers movements have all combined to place Italian feminism squarely on the left-wing of the political spectrum, whilst more traditional women support the Christian Democrats. Duverger's argument (1955) that parties of the Left are more likely to support women candidates than are conservative or confessional parties has been true of the major (but not necessarily the minor) Italian parties. However, the Christian Democrats, perhaps mindful of the poor record of conservatism on women's issues in Italy, have paid special attention to the women electorate. There have always been DC women in the Italian Chamber of Deputies, although their number has remained more or less constant regardless of the success of the party as a whole (Table 4.2) and bears no relation to women's 40-per-cent share of party membership. The absolute number of DC women deputies has declined since 1948, reaching a low of six in 1983. The party has always nominated some women but has run more all-male lists than the other parties. Nor have women been well represented on DC decision-taking bodies. The one woman on the executive board in 1983 was there as head of the women's movement. There were no women on the more powerful party secretariat. Neither in making nominations to public office nor in

Table 4.2: *Strengths of women in party groups and strengths of party groups in the Italian Chamber of Deputies, 1948–83 in percentages (with numbers of women in parentheses)*

	1948	1953	1958	1963	1968	1972	1976	1979	1983
DC									
Women in party group	5.2 (18)	4.2 (12)	3.7 (11)	4.2 (11)	3.0 (8)	2.6 (8)	3.4 (9)	3.4 (9)	6.0 (6)
Party group by chamber	53.3	44.4	45.8	41.3	42.1	42.3	41.6	38.3	35.7
PCI									
Women in party group	14.5 (21)	11.2 (16)	7.1 (11)	7.8 (15)	4.7 (9)	9.1 (17)	16.7 (39)	18.8 (35)	19.2 (38)
Party group by chamber	22.8	24.2	23.5	26.3	28.1	27.8	35.2	30.4	31.4

Source: Beckwith, 1980; De Santis and Zincone, 1983.

granting women positions in the internal party hierarchy have DC men proved willing to share power with more than a few women.

The PCI has elected more women to the Italian Parliament than all the other parties combined. But before 1976 the party was reluctant to use deputyships to reward or enhance the status of its women activists and was more likely to include well-known figures amongst its women deputies than the other parties. From 1976 onwards, however, the PCI has promoted a large number of unknown women into successful candidacies, and its women have been better distributed throughout the party list (Beckwith, 1980, 246). Women have also been represented better on PCI than DC decision-taking bodies but have not held shares of these posts in proportion to their party membership (about 25 per cent). In 1983 women held one of the nine places on the party executive board and three of thirty-four places on the central committee—9.1 and 14.5 per cent, respectively (de Santis and Zincone, 1983).

Indeed, at the level of internal leadership all of the Italian parties have dismal records if judged according to sex-equality criteria. In 1983 two of the seven board members of the Radical Party were women, making it the only party in which women held more than 25 per cent of leadership posts. Over time the Radical Party has had the best record (in proportionate terms) of electing women to the Italian Parliament. In the 1976 general election the party nominated a woman in all the electoral districts in which it stood and placed a woman first (*capolista*) on each list. Women were 50 per cent of those nominated and 50 per cent of those elected. But in 1979, when the party doubled its parliamentary representation to eighteen, women obtained only four seats and in 1983 women were two of the eleven PR deputies elected.

The PSI, about 19 per cent of whose members are women, has been less responsive to women's issues and to the promotion of women that might be expected from a party of the Left. Despite its 15 per cent quota, the PSI had only three women on its forty-member executive board in 1983. Karen Beckwith believes that their lack of organisational association with the women's movement has made the Socialists unresponsive. Thus, it produces proposals without reference to the demands of, or consultation with, the women it is attempting to represent. In 1983 two of its seventy-three deputies were women, at 2.7 per cent, about an average proportion of women deputies for the party, and an increase on the 1972, 1976 and 1979 proportions, all of which were below 2 per cent.

Amongst the remaining smaller parties, the Republicans have

shown no inclination to promote women, and the Liberals have performed similarly. Surprisingly for an extreme right-wing party, the explicitly anti-feminist MSI has elected more women to the chamber than many more left-wing parties (Beckwith, 1980, 248) and in 1983 had one woman on its twenty-four-member secretariat and four on its ninety-member executive board. On the left-wing of the spectrum the Proletarian Democrats (DP) have nominated women reasonably advantageously but have themselves obtained only a few parliamentary seats. The absence of women DP deputies is not necessarily a sign of failure to accommodate women. The fact that the DPs secretariat contained no women on its six-member secretariat and only two on its thirty-five-member central committee in 1983 is, however, less reassuring.

In policy terms the major parties have all developed positions designed to attract women's support. While the DCs and their associated Catholic Action have treated women consistently in terms of their family role, they have also supported policies for sex equality at work, reasoning that if by some unfortunate chance mothers had to seek employment outside the home, they should do so under reasonably equitable conditions. The party does not, however, call for the equal participation of men and women in political life, but rather favours a joint equality between men and women which recognises and enhances the traditional roles of women. The more controversial issues of abortion and divorce produced negative responses from the DCs which campaigned to have divorce reform abrogated and made considerable efforts to block abortion liberalisation during the 1970s. These postures damaged the party, and many of its leaders prefer to avoid declaring on such issues, a reluctance characteristic of party politicians in most systems. The PCI, after initial hesitation, has gradually become more feminist in its policies. Theses published before the fifteenth party congress dealt specifically with the need to develop female leadership within the party. Communist willingness to meet feminist demands at the policy level have been to some extent constrained by the wish not to offend sections of the Catholic population as the party gradually increased its share of the vote during the 1970s and early 1980s. Hence, considerable ambiguity was apparent in its positions on such issues as abortion reform and rape legislation, which led to a great deal of criticism from the feminist movement. Amongst the minor parties the Radicals have been most supportive of feminist causes. The Liberals, like the PSI, have given some support to women's issues and were active both over the divorce and abortion reforms. The

Social Democrats and the neo-fascists (MSI) have given the least attention to women's issues (Beckwith, 1980, 238).

In 1983 women were 7.9 per cent of Italian Deputies and 4.9 per cent of Senators. The figure for the Chamber of Deputies represented a modest decline from the 1976 high of 8.5 per cent, whilst the Senate figure continued a steady but slow increase of women's presence. Importantly, in both houses the largest delegation of women was from the Communist Party, who in parliamentary terms have promoted women more consistently and successfully than any other party. But for the PCI, the important posts are internal party leadership posts, and deputies are seen as party functionaries put there to implement policy. Hence, the modest proportions of women party officials might be taken as a better indicator of PCI promotion of women. Women fare better in the Italian numerical channel than they do in the British, but not much better. The combination of proportional representation, a thriving Communist Party and a strong women's movement have not been sufficient to push the proportion of Italian women legislators as high as 10 per cent. As in Britain, the presence of women in Italy's numerical channel is disproportionately low and party promotion of women has been in evidence but only to a very limited extent.

France

The rules of entry to the numerical channel in France are about to be altered as plans were announced in 1985 to re-introduce proportional representation. However from 1958 to 1985 they were determined by a multi-party system in combination with a first-past-the-post electoral system operating in two rounds. This combination, which includes elements characteristic of both the Italian and British system, leads to similar patterns of under-representation of women. The French political parties are important areas of political apprenticeship, comprising structures in which power is held overwhelmingly by men.[5] Proportionately, the under-representation of women in party hierarchies is more marked in parties of the Right than in parties of the Left. Thus, in 1983 women were 36 per cent of members of the Communist Party (PCF), 21 per cent of central committee members, 18 per cent of politburo members and 17 per cent of the powerful secretariat. In the ruling Socialist Party (PS) they comprised 27 per cent of members, 19 per cent of management committee members, 15 per cent of executive bureau members and 14 per cent of the secretariat. Amongst parties of the Right, either the disproportion between membership and office holding was greater or the degree of proportionate fall-off increased more sharply as the hierarchy of power was ascended. Hence, women were 40 per cent of republican (Giscardian) UDF members, but held 32 per cent of national council positions, were 20 per cent of the political bureau and only 6 per cent of the secretariat. In the Gaullist RPR the 43 per cent of women members were 8 per cent of the central committee, 6 per cent of the political council and 8 per cent of the executive committee (Mossuz-Lavau and Sineau, 1983, 12).

Because women occupy relatively few positions of responsibility in the parties and unions, they are less likely to be chosen as candidates and to take part in the various informal delegations called for consultation with the government. Typically, women candidates are given poorer positions on party lists with the result that proportionately fewer women are elected than stand as candidates, except in the Communist Party. Overall, women have not had the opportunities to serve the sorts of political apprenticeships required by parties for political promotion and seem ill equipped to deal with competition for positions of power. Throughout the party structure, as within elites (see Ch. 6), a distribution of political labour operates whereby men have charge of high politics and women of welfare and social problems. Hence, women in positions of party responsibility have oversight for such areas as the family, education and women's questions. Such assignments tend to marginalise women, as a result of which periods of political work which ideally would be seen as important training and experience, turn out to be processes of ghettoisation.

France is not unusual in the fact that party leadership selection methods are normally simply processes of confirmation rather than selection. Indirect suffrage is used, often in conjunction with a multi-stage process which dramatically narrows the electorate. This is particularly true of the PCF. In practice opportunities for women have been greatest where there are the greatest number of positions to be filled, and parties wishing to improve women's status might do well to follow the lead of the socialist trade unions, which have increased the number of places on decision-taking bodies and reserved the new positions for women (Moreau-Bourles and Sineau, 1983, 2.43 to 2.45).

French political parties have also responded at policy level to feminist pressure and to the increasing confidence and influence of women generally. Hence, the Giscard government adopted important new legislation on women's rights during the 1970s.

Paradoxically, a right-wing government legalised abortion, reformed divorce law procedures, redefined rape and its penalties and introduced statutes which gave equal rights to father and mother and to husband and wife. The newly formed desire to attract women's support led the Left to bid even higher, with the result that most of the parties were by the end of the 1970s taking initiatives to attract women voters. These included efforts to increase the access of women to positions of responsibility.

The Socialists went so far as to introduce quotas whereby women got at least 20 per cent of places on the various party organs. (This measure was taken in 1979 but had not been fully implemented by 1983). More women were nominated for electoral office and given more favourable positions on party lists. Hence, women were 25 per cent of candidates and 22 per cent of elected MEPs in the European elections of 1979, a major breakthrough. But in the 1981 general election women's presence declined once again. Then women were 2 per cent of RPR candidates (as against 2 per cent in 1978), 3.2 per cent of UDF candidates (4.7 per cent in 1978). The Communist Party proportion was steady at about 13.5 per cent. Only the Socialists nominated more women in 1981 (8 per cent) than they had in 1978 (5.9 per cent) (Moreau-Bourles and Sineau, 1983).

Unusually, the French government has made some effort to come to terms with the problem of increasing the proportions of women candidates in elections, decreeing in 1981 that municipal lists should not contain more than 80 per cent of candidates from either sex. The imposition of a formal political minimum quota had not been tried elsewhere in Europe. Its aim was to get women established at the first rung of the political hierarchy. But the Constitutional Court declared the measure to be unconstitutional in 1983, and it is unlikely that the attempt will be repeated. In 1983 there were twenty-nine women in the French National Assembly (5.9 per cent) and ten in the Senate (3.2 per cent). Women were 53 per cent of the electorate. The results of party efforts to increase women's representation were less than impressive.

West Germany

The West German party and electoral systems are contradictory in their effect on women. Competition, which favours women candidates, increased in the 1980s, when by 1983 the Greens became the first new party to enter the Bundestag for thirty years. The electoral system is half constituency based and half party-list based. Most of the few women who achieve election do so via party lists. Hence, West Germany represents still another variation of the entry rules to the numerical channel. In a society in which attitudinal inhibitions to women's activism are particularly strong (Ingelhart, 1981; Sanzone, 1981), officially all political parties which have representation in the legislature (Bundestag) take the view that the representation of both men and women is a basic criterion of democracy. All agree that a concrete equal rights policy is essential. But West German women are significantly outnumbered by men as party members and men are over-represented on party decision-taking bodies. In 1983 women were 23 per cent of members of the Christian Democrats (CDU), 14 per cent of Christian Socialists (CSU), 25 per cent of Social Democrats (SPD), 24 per cent of Liberals (FDP) and 50 per cent of the newly successful Greens. Women's share of leadership positions ranged from 7 per cent to 12 per cent in the CDU, CSU and FDP, increasing to 15 per cent in the Social Democrats and 50 per cent of the Greens. For a period during 1984/5 women comprised 100 per cent of the Greens' leadership. Shares of parliamentary seats are similarly distributed. 7.3 per cent of Christian Democrats, 5.6 per cent of Christian Socialists, 10.8 per cent of Social Democrats and 37 per cent of the Greens elected to the Bundestag in 1983 were women (Randzio-Plath and Rust, 1983). Neither the explicitly feminist Greens nor the officially gender-blind Liberals have a party women's organisations, but the other three parties do. The SPD is affiliated to the Working Group of Social Democratic Women, the CDU to the Women's Association of the Christian Democratic Union of Germany and the Bavarian CSU to the Women's Union of the CSU. Of these, only the SPD women are specifically orientated to sex equality, and in 1975 they were able to get an equality-for-women commitment added to the SPD programme. The party groups have been established more for the purpose of recruiting than promoting women, but they do, as elsewhere, supply important training for women new to formal political activity. Much has been made by feminists critical of the German parties of their failure to progress beyond the *alibi frau* or token women, but at 9.8 per cent of Bundestag deputies West German women have apparently been better promoted in the numerical channel than their British, Italian or French sisters. Although women's membership has increased since 1980, when it was 8.7 per cent, and indeed increased steadily from a low of 5.8 per cent in 1972, women continued to be assigned to less favourable positions on party lists, condemned, as a result, to electoral insecurity and relatively higher levels of turnover than men (Randzio-Plath and Rust, 1983; Hall, 1981; Shaffer, 1981).

But the promotion of women by the Greens may have galvanised other parties to take more account of women. In the single-list system, which is used for elections to the European Parliament, the SPD was forced in 1984, by the need to compete with the Greens, to place a woman at the head of its list (Katherina Focke). Party electoral propaganda posters placed all the women candidates in the front row, creating an impression that the party was fielding numerous woman candidates. All the West German parties endeavoured to appeal to women in these elections, but the SPD's efforts were more strenuous perhaps because, with the Liberal's left-wing already captured, it had the most to fear from the Greens (Kolinsky, 1984a).

The Nordic States

It is in the multi-party Nordic countries that women have achieved the greatest presence in the numerical channel. As of the end of 1984 women were 26 per cent of the Danish Folketing, 31 per cent of the Finnish Eduskunta, 26 per cent of the Norwegian Storting, 28 per cent of the Swedish Riksdag and 15 per cent of the Icelandic Althingi. All of the Nordic countries have elections based on party lists and some form of proportional representation. But parties themselves have played an important role. In all the countries except Iceland, which has a feminist party, a major increase in women's representation came about through the traditional party system.

In Sweden, for example, the status of women was regarded by the parties as an issue of some importance, and all of the parties except the family-focused Conservative Party supported reforms favourable to women, who are recognised to be a distinctive social group. Eduards (1981) points out that although, in general, supportive of reform, the parties differ in their assessment of correct strategies for improving the position of women. Thus, the Centre Party focuses on the reform of family life, the Liberals concentrate on equal opportunity, the Social Democrats see the equality of women in the context of class equality and the Communists apparently 'regard the liberation of women as both an integrated part of the class struggle and an ideological struggle in its own right' (Eduards, 1981, 213). Proportionately, Swedish women's share of party membership ranges from 26 per cent of the Left Party Communists to 50 per cent of the Conservatives. Each of the parties has a women's section except for the Communists who instead have a standing committee on feminism. The strongest of these sections is in the Centre Party (formerly the Agrarian Party), which has undergone a metamorphosis since the early 1970s. The party polls about 18 per cent of the vote, but it has a women's league membership of 75,000 by comparison to 50,000 women affiliated to the much larger Social Democratic Party. Based in rural areas, the Centre Party's strong attraction for women is in its environmental policy. More than one-third of Centre Party MPs are women and these are a driving force in the anti-nuclear campaign. Since 1973 the Centre Party women's section has engaged in the systematic education of its women members on equality questions and has urged them to join trade unions.

By contrast the Liberal Party sees the future of women's work in *ad hoc* political groups and is officially less exercised over the woman question than either the Centre Party or the Social Democrats. It has, however, succeeded in introducing (in 1972) a quota for women of at least 40 per cent on all party representative bodies and in fact women hold 44 per cent of places on its executive committee (Scott, 1982, 151–2). Women's leagues in the parties are 'rights' groups, orientated towards reformist solutions to the problems facing women. They are an important source of pressure on the parties and are important political training grounds for women, who are nearly as likely as men to be members of a political party. (Eight per cent of women and 9 per cent of men were party members in 1977).

In Finland an early tendency for women to fare better with left-wing parties has also altered as centre parties have become aware of the importance of promoting women. Haavio-Mannila attributes the very great success of women in Finnish politics to the fact that women came onto the political scene at the same time as most men and before deep-seated political traditions amongst men had been established. A system of proportional representation, which provides for preference voting, is also a factor as Finnish women disproportionately support women candidates (Haavio-Mannila, 1979).

Norway is also an 'organised' society containing four major, two minor and several smaller political parties. There a particular effort was made during the late 1960s to increase the political representation of women as a result of which the representation of women in Parliament and in the local councils trebled. All of the political parties and numerous women's associations were involved in urging the electorate to support women candidates as well as otherwise promoting and training women candidates. The campaign was sufficiently successful that it displaced a number of male incumbents and ultimately did not please the male politicians. Cooperation of that top-level kind was not repeated, but at grass-roots level efforts to enhance women's electoral appeal were continued (Skard, 1981). Whilst Danish women have increased their presence in party politics, Icelandic women have met with rather more resistance, resulting finally in the formation of a feminist party which aimed to break the hold of the existing parties over political promotion. So successful was their challenge that women nearly doubled their representation in the 1983 elections, partly as a direct result of the feminist party winning seats and partly as a result of the other parties bowing to pressure to nominate women candidates.

The Nordic political parties have done more to ensure the political promotion of women than other liberal democracies. But women there still do not hold office in proportion either to their presence in the population or to their party memberships. Women in Denmark, Norway and Sweden are still placed at less favourable positions on party lists than men and hold fewer candidacies and fewer positions in party decision-making bodies. However, the advances made in the Scandinavian countries have been considerable and give some indication of what can be done when even a minimum of political will to promote women exists.

Spain, Portugal and Greece

In the three most recently established European liberal democracies, patterns of women's access to the numerical channel have been seriously distorted by the experience of autocracy. Whilst all three countries feature pressure on political parties to take action which would promote women's rights and women's representation, organisation of such pressure and developments in response to it are a long way behind the rest of Europe. In Spain, therefore, parties have taken measures to promote interest in questions of sex equality at work and in society but have done relatively little to promote women into positions of political prominence. Weekend schools for women party members were begun in 1982 by the Centre Democrats (UCD) and the political education secretariat reserves places for women on its courses. In the Socialist Party (PSOE) quotas for women were discussed but not adopted in 1981 and 1982. At regional level, however, the Catalonian PSC-PSOE approved 12 per cent quota for women in all internal and public posts was adopted in 1982. The Communists (PCE), too, have considered both quotas for women and statutory women's representatives on all important party committees, a suggestion which is gradually being put into practice up and down the country. Political education schools were set up for women in the early 1980s at both national and grass-roots levels. The measures have mainly come about as a result of suggestions by the party Women's Commission, which has been seriously exercised over making increasing use of women members. The three major parties (UCD, PSOE, and PCE) all contain women's pressure groups but do not have women's sections as such, apparently because women's divisions are associated in the public mind with the fascist Seccion Feminina of the Franco era, which glorified women's traditional role. The internal pressure groups are not uniformly distributed throughout the country, operating at regional and local levels wherever there happen to be feminists. Reliable detailed statistics of Spanish women's party strength are difficult to obtain, but such data as are available indicate that women in 1982 were 30 per cent of Centre Democrats, 9 per cent of Socialists and 11 per cent of Communists. At leadership level the proportion of women ranges from 3 to 4 per cent of the larger internal assemblies to no representation at all on the powerful executive bodies. As candidates Spanish women fare rather better than women in some other countries, and in the 1979 elections were 7.1 per cent of UCD candidates, 8.7 per cent of PSOE candidates, 10.8 per cent of PCE candidates and up to 9 per cent of regional nationalist candidates (e.g. Basques, Catalan, etc.). In the Communist and Socialist parties, then, but not in the Centre Democrats, women's share of candidacies was in near proportion to their share of party membership (Threlfall, 1982). However, the failure to place women in favourable positions on party lists means that they held only 5.4 per cent of Cortes seats in 1984.

In Portugal and Greece women were 9.2 per cent and 3.7 per cent, respectively, of parliamentary deputies in 1983. But whilst in Portugal women owe their levels of representation largely to the parties of the Left, in Greece support has come from both sides of the ideological spectrum. The parties of the Left have been more willing to nominate women, but the parties of the centre have tended to place the few they have nominated in winnable seats

(PE 86.199/fin/C). Women have been less organised in these societies, and pressure to include women in elites may be more a result of leadership conceptions of democratic norms than of the work of politically motivated women. Whatever its source, the societies have paid more attention to women's rights and issues than scrutiny of their social structures and women's movements would lead us to predict, but rather less than has been true of the better-established liberal democracies.

Women and Parties in State Socialist Systems

In the state socialist systems of the Soviet Union and Eastern Europe the numerical and corporate channels are almost indistinguishable. There, it is the parties—that is, the communist parties—which control all of the available gateways to political power and which set the terms and describe the forms which political activism will take. The whole of the political arena is a formal one in which political aspirants are more dependent upon the parties than in the liberal democracies. There are, it should be said, bases of political power other than in the parties, but these are never more than supplements to party channels.

The fact that sex equality has been, officially at least, a party goal in each of the state socialist systems since its establishment has had an important effect on women's political behaviour. Women's roles have undoubtedly altered since the institution of socialist state forms, but the pattern of role change has been more subject to state direction and has therefore differed from the rather more spontaneous changes which have taken place in Western Europe. In general, East European women have greater access to such resources as education and paid employment but this has not led to concomitantly greater economic or political power (Wolchik, 1981a, 445). Hence, important variations by gender in political participation are apparent.

In the Soviet Union, girls are more conscientious than boys in political activity in schools, as is shown in their share of Komsomol membership and office holding at local level (girls are 53.4 per cent of members and 57 per cent of group secretaries). But the activists tend to be male and women's involvement drops sharply with marriage and more with the appearance of children (Hough and Fainsod, 1979, 313). Women were only about 25 per cent of members of the Communist Party of the Soviet Union in 1984, a figure which represented a long process of increase.

In general, women's participation in state socialist politics has been more visible at local levels but remains less evident in the higher echelon organisations. The impressive levels of representation that they obtain in national legislatures (see Ch. 6) is not backed up by a similar presence in more important party central committees. Their membership of Communist parties was between 20 and 30 per cent during the 1970s. This lower presence in party life impairs progress not only to important government positions but also to many key professional posts for which party membership is deemed essential. Concomitantly with Western women, East European women have been more active in non-partisan groups such as school boards and friendship societies than in political parties. They are also more likely to be members of the Peasant Party in Poland and the Christian Democrats in East Germany than of the Communist parties there. Such trends might be indicative of a greater conservatism on the part of women or they may result from the fact that the 'other' parties have less prestige and are therefore more accessible to women (Wolchik, 1981b, 257).

It may be that women's lower share of party membership is a short-term matter. The proportion of women recruited to the various parties has increased steadily since the early 1950s, although it nowhere reaches women's share of the population (Jancar, 1978, 92). Such increases have not, however, been accompanied by a greater representation of women in party leadership positions at national level. The initial inclusion of prominent women who had been involved in regime establishment (Kollantai, Armand and Krupskaya in the USSR, Ana Pauker in Romania, Marie Svermova in Czechoslovakia) soon gave way to a virtual absence of women at top levels. In 1978, after two women had been selected for politbureau membership in Rumania, women held 8 of a total of 199 full or candidate places. (Wolchik, 1981b, 262; Jancar, 1978, Appendix 1) in the European state socialist systems.

Women hold their greatest share of party leadership posts at local levels, where the rewards of office are less. Thus, in East Germany, women, who in 1981 were one-third of members of the Socialist Unity Party (SED), held 13 per cent of Central Committee places, no politbureau places, but were about 25 per cent of district committee members. Even at local level some positions appear relatively closed to women who held only 5 per cent of the powerful first secretaryships (Shaffer, 1981, 89). A similar pattern was apparent in the Soviet Union in the mid-1970s. Women held significantly more local than national positions in party hierarchies. They were as many as one-third of the secretaries of the primary party organisations in 1982, but their percentage declined sharply to less than 5 per cent of central committee members, and there has been only one women politbureau member since the Second World War.

Clearly, the state socialist ruling parties have not promoted women into politics with as much enthusiasm and rigour as they might have done. However, it is important to remember that women have been consistently better represented in most East European party central committees (except in the USSR) than they have been in the West European legislatures which are their functional equivalents (Wolchik, 1981b, 261). In addition, some allowances should be made for the sheer scale of the problem faced by the promotion of women in less-developed systems. Yugoslavia, for example, features a wide variety of levels of economic and historic development encompassing a range from central European to central Asian types of society. It houses three important religious traditions—Catholic, Orthodox and Muslim— none of which are characterised by enlightened attitudes towards women. The illiteracy rate, about 2 per cent in Slovenia, rises in the south to 21 per cent of men and 42 per cent of women. In such a culture the modernising policies of state and party are often viewed as an attack on cultural or religious prerogatives. Even such policies as secondary education for women in the Moslem areas of Kosovo are resisted as overeducated women are unmar- riageable within the community. How, in an area which is armed to the teeth and has a tradition of guerilla warfare against interfer- ing intruders, is the party to promote women political leaders? (Denitch, 1981, 116).

The political recruitment of women in the state socialist systems has been a policy which has been given considerable, if not sufficient, attention by the various regimes. In an account such as this, which is concerned with comparing women's political roles, assessment may be of two kinds. If we judge the political position of state socialist women by reference to the position of women in liberal democracies, then we are bound to conclude that women fare at least as well in terms of political representation, if not better, under Communist rule. If, however, we judge according to the criteria of sex equality held officially by the regimes them- selves, then women are not present in the political arena in the expected proportions, and explanations for the shortfall should be sought.

Writing about the Soviet Union, Harasymiw (1980, 142) argues that there are three structural features operating at system level which may inhibit the recruitment and advancement of women. First, selection of new party members largely from amongst Komsomol activists (who tend to be male) reduces the chances of recruiting women. Second, recruitment to the party is no assurance of advancement to positions of authority, and third, male personnel managers are the norm in party life. And women's chances of political recruitment have, he reminds us, increased at all but the highest levels of the party. It is important, too, to remember that, to men, women are not equally politically recruitable, a consideration which should be made in assessing liberal democratic systems as well.

Jancar also looks for systemic explanations for the absence of women from the highest echelons of state socialist life. Whilst some of her case is a reflection more of her rather strong antipathy to these systems, other elements of her account are instructive. In particular, she points to party failure to train women in political skills, the ruthless nature of career advancement and the demanding nature of party work. But politics is a ruthless game in every system, and there is nothing especially Soviet about failing to provide special training for women or the demanding nature of party involvement. More telling is her suggestion that the absence of independent organisations for women in the state socialist systems results in the absence of a form of training which in the liberal democracies has proved to be particularly valuable (Jancar, 1978, 112–18).

Political Parties and the Participation of Women

From the 1970s onwards European political parties have been interested in the political promotion of women and in the adoption of policies which would attract support from women. Their efforts to increase women's political representation have often been somewhat desultory but have occasionally included such strong measures as official and unofficial quotas, the enhancement of powers of women's sections and the provision of special training for women activists. Such measures have not appeared unprompted from the imaginations of sensitive egalitarian male politicians but have been enacted in response to demands made by women. And women have taken considerable advantage of the opportunities which have been offered, coming forward in increasing numbers to stand for party posts and carry party banners as candidates in elections.

However, equality between the sexes in political representation, and even parity based on party membership figures, is at
the beginning of 1985 far from having been achieved. Male party
leaders have, to be sure, been placed on the defensive on the
question of women's access to power. Our discussion of how
women fare at national level has in fact been a 'worst case'
analysis. Scrutiny of local party arenas and local candidacy shares
would have revealed a more favourable if far from equal balance
between the sexes. Local patterns, whilst not uniform, do tend to
suggest that there may be more women percolating up through
party hierarchies in the future. But women have always been more
evident at local than national levels of decision-making, and
proportionate fall-off as a hierarchy of power is ascended is not a
mitigating factor—it is the very essence of the problem.

Party standing is of course only one indicator of women's
political clout, albeit an important one. Other forms of activism
are available to politically motivated individuals, and it is known
that women are sometimes more attracted to *ad hoc* politics such
as direct action, community action, protest and movement politics. The women's peace movement with its camps, vigils and
marches has been an important example of such a preference.
With few exceptions, formal political structures have not married
well with the loosely organised networks favoured by feminist
activists and party activists have been given a poor press by
feminists in most countries. Not only the male-dominated apparatuses but also the conflictual, somewhat 'macho' style of party
politics has generated a considerable measure of hostility from
women's movement activists. However, as the second wave of the
women's movement has grown it has more and more come to
involve women who have backgrounds in party politics. Party
political divisions run deep, even amongst feminists and cooperation across party lines is rare. At the same time, many feminists
have found themselves in circumstances in which they have had to
make choices between different parties on policy matters. The
abortion issue in particular generated a realisation that, on occa-
sion, preference for one party over another would have to be
expressed, and that some parties were more amenable to taking
liberatory stands on issues which were especially salient to women
than others. In this regard the abortion issue was a turning point in
many countries, after which feminist entrism into parties on the
European Left became widespread. Hence, questions of how to
play party political games have increasingly become important to
feminists.

The rules of that game have varied considerably, making it difficult to offer generalisations with any confidence. On the whole it has been the parties of the Left which have been most inclined to promote women, except in the Nordic countries, where parties of the Centre have also been particularly active. In France, whilst parties of the Left have offered more, to women it was a process of competitive bidding begun by the Giscardian right which generated specific policies. Similarly, women have apparently fared better as party candidates in systems of proportional representation than in simple plurality systems, but the differences are small and may not be attributable to a simple institutional effect. Parties have less to lose and appear more willing to risk standing women as candidates in winnable positions on multi-member constituency lists. Francis Castles (1981) argues that this is because the existence of a list system enhances the control of party centres, and that national party elites are more likely to promote women than are local selectorates, if only because national elites are more responsive to new intellectual currents. But an argument that party-list systems are a prerequisite to women's greater electoral representation must be predicated upon an assumption that voters penalise women candidates. Evidence for such a penalty is sparse (see, however, Foverskov, 1979). Preference voting too may have an effect in that it allows the electorate to inform the parties of support for women candidates, assuming, of course, that such support exists.

Institutional reforms have a part to play in increasing the proportion of women in politics, but their effect will be mediated by the position of women in a particular society. The experience of the state socialist societies suggest that progress toward equalisation of resources will increase the representation and activism of women, but it will not of itself bring about sex equality in politics. Attitudes based on traditional conceptions of domestic roles inhibit women from seeking political prominence and men from welcoming women's activism. If we define politics differently and consider more informal kinds of activism, we find that the proportions of women participants rise but not to the levels of their presence in the population. The division of labour in the home means ultimately that women are less politically recruitable than men, however politics is defined. Only as attitudes and roles change so that the social implications of gender differences become an array of choices rather than imperatives of behaviour will participatory differences disappear. What is not clear at this stage is whether the increase in women's political activism which began in the 1970s represents the beginning of a process of role change. There is evidence both for and against such a possibility. Supporting evidence is to be found in the increasing penetration by women of both numerical and corporate channels of access to power. Counter evidence lodges in the fact that the aforesaid increase has nowhere led to a colonisation of major citadels of political power, that such toeholds as women have gained have been in the less-certain channels of access. In other words, women, like all political out-groups, are finding that their participation has less purchasing power than that of in-groups; that not only is activism more costly for women than for men but it secures fewer political goods. Evident in the numerical channel of political parties, this disadvantage is particularly apparent in the important economic associations which dominate corporate channels, a factor which has meant that gaining admission to political elites has, for women, been almost entirely dependent upon obtaining party support. Thus, political participation for women is more than a matter of performing citizen duties in a responsible manner, it is the vital component in any strategy to achieve a decisive voice in the construction of emancipation policy.

Notes

1. Included in the *Index to International Public Opinion 1979–1980*, (Oxford: Clio Press, 1981)
2. *Ibid.*, March 1979 Mori Poll.
3. Her data came from the eight Barnes and Kaase studies and eleven national election studies. The countries included are the USA, the UK, Japan, Switzerland, France, Finland, West Germany, the Netherlands, Austria, Italy and Norway.
4. *See* survey of MPs carried out for *Honey* magazine and reported in *The Guardian*, 3 June 1983. The 220 respondents included 22 Alliance, 10 Labour, 80 Tory and 4 other MPs.
5. Attempts by French women to achieve political power independently of the parties have not been successful. Choisir fielded 43 candidates in the 1978 elections and attracted less than 1.5 per cent of the vote.

5 The Corporate Channel: Patterns of Interest Representation

Political influence derives not only from organisations specifically designed for the capture of public office but also from the array of organised interests which are present in modern society. Such groups have been observed by political scientists to have dramatically increased their importance in post-war European politics. Various theories have been constructed to account for their influence in both liberal democratic and state socialist societies. The theories range from an idealised pluralist model at one end of the political spectrum to the somewhat pejorative formulation of corporatism at the other.

Philippe Schmitter (1974, 85) has supplied the most systematic and widely cited definitions of the two terms. He writes that corporatism may be defined as 'a system of interest representation in which the constituent units are organised into a limited number of singular, compulsory, non-competitive hierarchically ordered and functionally differentiated categories, recognised or licensed (if not created) by the state and granted a deliberate representational monopoly within their respective categories in exchange for observing certain controls on their selection of leaders and articulation of demands and supports'. Under pluralism, on the other hand, interests 'are organised into an unspecified number of multiple, voluntary, competitive, non-hierarchically ordered and self-determined categories that are not specifically licensed, recognised, subsidised or otherwise controlled in leadership selection or interest articulation by the state and that do not exercise a monopoly of representational activity within their respective categories'. Pluralism, clearly, is a model designed for application to liberal democracies whilst corporatism derives from the study of authoritarian systems. But both models are ideal types. Reginald Harrison has argued that they are probably most useful in that they raise questions about how to analyse the middle ground (Harrison, 1980, 185). They provide a basis for making normative judgments about practices in the real world.

Harrison, in common with many analysts of contemporary politics, believed that in liberal democracies the pattern of interest intermediation has come more to resemble the corporatist than the pluralist model. This has resulted from the process of 'concertation' or the institutionalisation of consultation between interest organisations and government, largely as a result of government's increasing responsibility for overall economic planning. Concertation has had important and distorting consequences for democracy in many systems. One effect has been that economic associations have been given an important say in political decision-making, over and above that which the numbers they represent would warrant.

A considerable scholarly and polemical literature has been generated by debates on these questions, which, while interesting, are beyond the scope of this study. For our purposes the dominance of corporate forms of interest-representation is important in two respects: first, it is economic organisations which have the major influence in a nation's interest-group structure. Their support (or its lack) over such matters as improving welfare provision or amending equality legislation has been a crucial factor in many women's political campaigns. But, second, as we shall see below, economic organisations have tended to exclude women. Helga Hernes refers to a common pattern of a gendered division of organisational membership across the European liberal democracies, indicating a high degree of gender polarisation in public life. The organisations in which women predominate have mobilising effects but little political clout (Council of Europe, 1984, Part 3).

Women wishing to press demands upon the political system have two interest-group strategies open to them. One strategy is the organisation of a wide-ranging series of mass and elite groups of women organised as are other interests, both to provide services and support for members and to press for members' demands. These might be single-issue groups such as those organised to achieve abortion law reform or multi-purpose associations such as the British Townswomen's Guild or Women's Institute. Such groups exist in most of the liberal democracies of Europe but there has been little in the way of good social science research on them (Randall, 1982, 46). Although we know that traditional women's associations occasionally wage campaigns on matters of importance to women, we have little knowledge of their composition, organisation or political perceptions. What evidence we have suggests that governments tend to be rather cavalier in their treatment of such groups. The British government, for example, actually takes women's interests into account via the Women's National Commission (WNC), which was established in 1969 to ensure that the opinion of informed women is given due weight in government. The WNC is composed of a requisite fifty organisations which must be national organisations with a large membership and must have been in existence for a number of years. These requirements ensure that new feminist groups are excluded, although women's sections of the political parties and unions are members, providing a route for feminist pressure. The Women's National Commission is small, underfunded and rather timid, however, and it is not consulted on major economic or policy issues. The women's interest is narrowly defined officially (see Gelb, 1984), something which may be a consequence of the use of traditional methods in organising women.

The second strategy is for women to take part in the various economic organisations. Ideally, this strategy has several advantages. Their presence in such organisations gives women an opportunity to influence the range of policies which are being pressed upon governments. In addition, the peak employer and union organisations of Western Europe, and to a lesser extent the union organisations of Eastern Europe, are gateways to political elites. Indeed, in Western Europe they nominate individuals to serve on the various tripartite and other bodies of Hernes and Voje's corporate channel (see above, p. 135), and may also be closely linked to political parties. Finally, activity in these organisations is an important arena for training in the more gladiatorial political skills.

Since the first wave of feminism, women have pursued both strategies with varying but never high degrees of success. As much of what is known about women's organisations has been discussed elsewhere in this volume (see Ch. 2 and 3), this chapter will concentrate almost exclusively on the role of women in the economic associations. The most important of these are, in Western Europe, the trade unions and employers associations. In state socialist Eastern Europe the category of 'work' seems to encompass both manager and employee, hence there are only unions to consider.

In Western Europe the role of women in trade unions and employers associations is of considerable importance to their political position. Moreover, rapid and large increases in the numbers of women in paid employment, which have characterised post-war Europe, add another dimension to the significance of the economic associations. We would expect these increases to have had at least four effects on the economic organisations. First, there should have been an influx of women into both unions and employers associations since the war. Second, women's presence in their decision-making bodies should have increased. Third, policies should have been adjusted to accommodate women's demands, and finally, the economic organisations should be using their nominating powers to place women on corporate bodies.

But, as the remainder of this chapter shows, such expectations are not always met. If European unions have varied considerably in their response to growing numbers of women amongst their membership, employers' associations have been more consistent. They have done little either to attract new women members or to assist those few women members they have. Neither side of West European industry has proved particularly willing to accommodate the changing economic roles of women.

Women and Trade Unions in the European Liberal Democracies

The trade unions of Western Europe have both singly and in confederation in their peak organisations tended to go through similar stages of development in their attitudes toward women. Alice Cook (1980, 4) sees the sequence as having three phases: (1) a period of anti-feminism, (2) a period of protection of women and (3) the contemporary period of subscription to programmes of equality. The first two phases are closely linked. Women, who were non-citizens and often legally non-persons, were deemed too frail to do various things. Unions aimed at, for example, legislation to ban night work and the lifting of certain weights, but such bans were readily exempted when they interfered with the demand for women's labour (e.g. for nurses who have always worked at nights and lifted heavy weights). The contemporary period represents more of a departure, inspired as it was by internal union women's groups organised as a response to important changes in the position of women since the 1960s. But although union movements throughout Western Europe have been influenced by demands made by newly organised working women, specific national factors have affected both the form of the demands and the mode of response. Whilst similarities in the experiences of the various countries abound, important differences are also present which arise both from different political traditions and from differences in the position of women.

Unions differ, for example, in the amount of control they have over who is employed and the lengths to which they will go to affect public policy outside their immediate collective bargaining ambit; indeed, such differences will exist between unions within countries as well as between countries. Job regulation may be controlled by the unions themselves (unilateral job regulation), jointly with management (bilateral job regulation) or jointly with mangement and other agencies such as the law and/or the state (trilateral job regulation), in what are often called tripartite organisations or commissions (Ellis, 1980, 30).

Individual unions may be in a position to have a substantial effect on women's job opportunities. Examples are Britain, where Fleet Street print unions virtually control entry to the trade and the allocation of jobs within it, or Italy, where unions together with employers organisations determine which names go at the top of 'numerical' hiring lists and therefore may tell employers who to hire (de Santis and Zincome, 1983, 5.20). Clearly, in such circumstances not only management but also unions must be persuaded of the value of equal opportunities for women. Conversely, a union may have impeccable women's rights policies and credentials but have so little power that this is meaningless. Thus, the distribution of power between union, management and the various mediating institutions will be an important variable (Ellis, 1981, 30). Aspects of power relations may be extended to include pressure-group politics, which are here relevant in two senses. First, a union's willingness to pursue job-regulation policies which favour women or even take into account the needs of women will to some extent depend upon the influence women as a pressure group can bring to bear on the union. Second, a union's willingness to use its muscle with political parties and/or government in support of state-wide sex-equality programmes is likely to be dependent on similar pressure.

Of course, any interest in sex-equality policy or in the recruitment of women members represents quite an 'about-face' in union practice if not in official policies. Historically, male unionists have been hostile to women workers who were often (justifiably) accused of undercutting men's wages and were also perceived to be less militant and less willing to defend workers rights than were men. Whilst there was an element of plausibility in that view, the truth has been rather more complicated.

Generally, unionisation really began amongst skilled workers organising on a trade or craft basis in order to maintain rates of pay via the expedient of controlling the numbers and kinds of individuals who learned the craft or trade. Strategically, the goal was to form a restricted, exclusive group which, by definition, did not include the less skilled and unskilled occupations in which women tended to work. The strategy was only successful for as long as skills were both difficult to learn and in demand, and had to be rethought as technical innovation reduced the levels of expertise required for many occupations. That process was sufficiently advanced in England and Scotland in the 1880s for the 'new unionism' to have begun. 'New unionism' organised general labourers and unskilled workers and was the first phase in union history to include significant numbers of women (Breitenbach, 1982, 69–70), although never in the same proportions as similar (i.e. working) men.

Men were not welcoming of women members, and unions did little to encourage women's participation until well into the twentieth century. Both general cultural attitudes and specific work-place antagonisms were at the root of their reluctance, and women themselves were far from persuaded of the utility of union membership. Their hesitancy could be attributed to the failure of unions to press for the equal pay, which would have overcome many male objections to women's competition in the labour market. But, as Breitenbach (1982, 69–9) points out, the rather appealing argument which says that the problem of lower-paid women undercutting men could have been overcome simply by men taking women's part and standing for equal pay is, alas, far too simple. In the first place, divisions within the workforce were often deliberately exacerbated, resulting in confusions which severely constrain the ability of the relevant groups to act. Second, the argument also assumes that women had the consciousness to demand equal pay when the demand was seldom raised. Third, it contains an implicit assumption that women were well organised and all that was lacking was male solidarity, when in fact women were unorganised. Fourth, such a strategy requires full employment. In early capitalist production, cut-throat competition was common in the labour market and lessons of solidarity and organisation tended to be slowly learned and quickly forgotten. Given that even in the 1980s sectional interests often take precedence over class ones, it is unreasonable to suggest that they could have been easily overcome in the nineteenth century. In addition, the equal-pay issue, where it was considered at all, was often seen as leading to the exclusion of a women from the relevant trade. Although the issue was occasionally in evidence, women were apparently less than impressed. And cultural attitudes too made it difficult for women both to perceive the issue or make the demand. Finally, there existed then a belief which has continued until very recently that it simply cost less to keep a women than a man.

With such an inauspicious start it is perhaps surprising that by the 1970s West European women were a majority of newly organised workers. Indeed, in the West German white collar Deutsche Angestellen Gewerkschaft women were 99.4 per cent of the 1979 membership increase, and British, French, Italian and Swedish unions all reported instances of women comprising unprecedented proportions of new recruits. Thus, at least one of our expectations about women in the unions has been met. Their presence has markedly increased. Increases of women's membership of unions took place for a number of reasons. The first and most obvious cause was, simply, that women everywhere formed an increasing proportion of the employed population. A further reason was that women comprised the vast majority of the low-paid groups, who became a major target for unionisation drives during the 1970s. And in many countries—notably Britain, West Germany and Sweden but also Italy, France, Austria and Finland—some unions, often nudged by peak organisations, made particular efforts to recruit women.

The effect of these factors has been that women's proportion of the unionised workforce has increased in every country for which data are available. But close inspection of these trends reveals that a considerable difference in the likelihood of employed women in different European countries becoming unionised. Table 5.1 data are based mainly on unverified survey returns to the European Trade Union Institute and should be treated with some caution. They do, however, accord with the trends reflected in the most recently available official statistics and are therefore likely to be broadly correct. The patterns indicated in the table are striking. In only two of the fourteen countries included are employed women more likely to be unionised than employed men: Iceland and Eire. In two further countries, Denmark and Sweden, employed men and women are approximately as likely to be unionised, whilst in the remaining ten countries employed women are less likely to be unionised, in some cases (e.g. Luxemburg, West Germany and the Netherlands), dramatically so.

How might such differences be explained? Historical and cultu-

Table 5.1: *Women as a proportion of trade union peak organisation affiliate members and as a proportion of employed persons in selected European countries (1981)*

Country	Union organisation	Women as per cent of employed persons	Women as per cent of union members
Sweden	LO	⎫45.0	40.9
	TCO	⎭	58.1
Denmark	LO	⎫44.0	43.0
	FTF	⎭	56.0
Norway	LO	42.0	33.0
Austria	OGB	40.0	30.2
UK	TUC	40.0	33.3
Iceland	ASI	39.3	46.7
West Germany	DGB	38.0	21.0*
France		34.5	30.0+
Belgium	CSC	34.0	33.0
Switzerland	SGB/USS	⎫34.0	12.0
	CNG/CSC	⎭	11.0
Italy		32.0	30.0+
Luxemburg	LCGB	30.5**	8.0
Netherlands	FNV	30.0	14.7
Eire	ICTU	28.0	32.0

* 1982
** 1979
+ Estimate of per cent. of all union members.

Sources: European Trade Union Institute (1983), 'Info 6: Women's Representation in Trade Unions', Brussels; De Santis and Zincone (1983); Moreau Bourles and Sineau (1983).

ral factors will obviously play a part, as will the presence or absence of union policies on women and union policy content on sex equality, on the recruitment of women and on their promotion or absence once in the union. A further important factor might be the presence of all-woman unions, which exist in France and the Netherlands, or of women's sections of unions which exist in many other countries. Additionally, each West European Trade Union movement has its own unique shape and ethos, which may or may not provide an environment which is congenial to women. Clearly, the interrelationship of all these factors in a particular system will be fully understood only by looking first at the individual union

Table 5.2: *Women as a proportion of trade union peak organisation affiliate members, as a proportion of council members and as a proportion of executive committee members in selected European countries (1981 and most recent congress year prior to 1981)*

Country	Union organi-sation	Women as per cent. of membership	Women as per cent. of congress	Women as per cent. of council members	Women as per cent. of executive committee members
Iceland	ASI	46.7	27.0	18.0	13.0
Denmark	LO	43.0	14.9	23.8	12.0
Sweden	LO	40.9	25.0	12.0	6.7
UK	TUC	33.3	9.8	13.7**[1]	—
Norway	LO	33.0	19.0	12.0 (full members)	6.7 (full members)
				22.0 (alternates)	15.4 (alternates)
Belgium	CSC	33.0	6.4	5.5	0.0
Italy	CGIL	33.0	15.0	15.0	16.7
Austria	OGB	30.2	NA	1.9	14.3[2]
France	CGT	30.0	30.0	24.0	27.0
West Germany	DGB	21.0	7.5	7.9	7.7
Netherlands	FNV	14.7	NA	NA	0.0
Switzerland	CNG/CSC	11.0	6.0	2.0	0.0
Luxemburg	LCGB	8.0	71.0	71.0	4.0

* 1982
** 1983
[1] There are six reserved places for women on the TUC general council of fifty-one.
[2] Statutory minimum of one women on E.C.
NA = Not available

Sources: European Trade Union Institute (1983), 'Info 6: Women's Representation in Trade Unions', Brussels; De Santis and Zincone (1983); Moreau-Bourles and Sineau (1983).

movements, the better to understand ways in which they may or not be comparable. But before turning to such an exercise, it is worth returning to another of our expectations about unionised women, that they should be represented on decision-making bodies. Are women to be found in union executive positions in proportion to their membership or do we find in this arena another manifestation of the law of increasing disproportions? It is difficult to compare individual unions across national boundaries as they reflect variations in economic structures as much as variations in women's positions. But comparisons at peak organisation level are useful as a kind of aggregate data. In addition, such organisations have often given a lead to member unions on the treatment of women, and the position of women unionists in peak organisations may well serve as an example to member unions. As Table 5.2 shows that example is not normally a startlingly positive one. Table 5.2 illustrates how proportions of women members in various national union organisations translate into women's membership on decision-making bodies. Although the various organisations have different structures, most contain councils and executive committees or their equivalents and most hold national delegate congresses. Table 5.2 gives the proportion of women at each important level of the relevant hierarchy for the major peak organisation of thirteen West European countries as at 1981. Where there is some doubt as to which is the major organisation (i.e. France and Italy), the table includes the one in which women fare best.

The pattern which Table 5.2 reveals is a pronounced one and suggests that unions do not adequately promote their women members. In each of the countries except the French CGT (Confederation Generale du Travail) women are underrepresented on the highest union decision-making bodies by a factor of two or more and in most of the countries the factor is nearer to three. At lower levels of the hierarchy the underrepresentation is often less pronounced, but it nonetheless exists everywhere, except in the French CGT, which has a specific policy of ensuring the proportionate representation of women members at all levels of its hierarchy. For the most part, the Table 5.2 data reflect almost a decade of union policies to promote women. Only Luxemburg and Iceland reported no policies directed at improving women's union status (European Trade Union Institute, 1983).

To some extent, our third expectation, that their women members would be accommodated by union policy, is also met.

European trades unions have pursued various kinds of policies to improve the position of women at work and in union hierarchies. These policies have been mainly emancipatory in that they have aimed to remove barriers to women's participation, but some have been liberatory in that they have sought positively to promote women into positions of responsibility. Initiatives for such policies have often been a product of feminist activists within union structures and they have occasionally come from governments or enlightened political leaders. Sometimes the very act of asking for information on the position of women within an organisation has triggered discussion and policy change as sympathetic individuals within union branches and committees have been given the opportunity to raise questions of sex equality. But greater attention to the needs and problems of women members would not have become a union priority without the massive influx of women members during the 1970s at a time when male membership, following male employment, was declining.

The rise of the service sector and new patterns of white collar unionisation served to include more women, as did changes in attitudes amongst women workers and, importantly, new union perceptions of the need to recruit low-paid part-time workers. Such trends were widespread in the 1970s and most union movements experienced a membership growth in their 'white collar' components at the same time as a decline in the numbers of those in the traditional male-dominated manufacturing sectors. Those countries with separate white collar and manual peak organisations experienced different but equivalent trends.

Although it is difficult to generalise, it is likely that the decade also saw a growth in the centralisation of collective bargaining and, indeed, of the role of collective bargaining itself in many economies. Whilst the detail of industrial relations practice are beyond the scope of this book, it should be noted that the general status of collective bargaining may have an important bearing on both the kind and success of the sex-equality policy a nation eventually gets. Union status in the concertation process will depend on numerous variables, including the degree of centralisation, the kind of industry or employment involved, the penetration of the workforce, the level of unemployment, as well as constitutional and legal factors. Political factors, such as party affiliations, will also be important, as will religious, regional and linguistic divisions. All of these factors will have some effect on women's status in the unions.

Activity within the unions has been what Cynthia Cockburn

(1984, 35) has termed the 'paradigm instance of socialist feminist practice' in the 1970s. Although that practice has taken as many forms as there are systems, comparative analysis of the movements reveals common themes. Entrenched male trade unionist opposition to sex-equality policy has been combated by feminists using both entrism and negotiation. Elements of separatist strategies have also been in evidence. Feminists have organised within unions (and their affiliated parties) both to achieve changes in policy and to increase their organisational representation. The discussion which follows traces these developments in detail in Sweden, Italy and Britain. Events in these three countries illustrate the range of feminist intervention in the West European unions during the 1970s as well as the range of union responses to women's increased roles in the economy and the unions themselves. A further dimension is added to our comparison by the fact that the three main types of West European union movement are represented. Sweden provides an example of a union movement divided along functional-occupational lines. The Italian movement is politically fragmented and Britain has an ostensibly unified movement.

Sweden

Sweden has one of the highest women's labour-force participation rates in Europe and, despite the fact that about half of its employed women work part-time, it also has one of the highest women's unionisation rates.[1] Although there are three peak organisations, the LO, the TCO and SACO, the collective bargaining system is centralised and coordinated and Swedish industrial relations are highly organised (Johnston, 1981, 97). The significant peak organisation division is along functional lines between blue collar and white collar workers. Manual workers are organised mainly in the Confederation of Swedish Trade Unions (LO), which dominates Swedish blue collar trade unionism. White collar workers are organised into the Central Organisation of Salaried Employees (TCO) and professionally qualified workers and senior civil servants are members of unions affiliated to the Association of Professional Employees and Civil Servants (SACO/SR). Within the LO, 40.9 per cent of members were women at the beginning of 1982 and 58.1 per cent of TCO members were women (European Trade Union Institute, 1983, 10). Thirty-three per cent of SACO/SR members were women in

1979 (Eduards, 1981, 211). Whilst men's and women's unionisation rates are comparable in Sweden, their activity rates apparently differ substantially. Table 5.2 shows that women represented only 6.7 per cent of LO executive committee members and 12 per cent of council members at the end of 1981. In the TCO, with its majority of women members (58 per cent), no decision-making body contained a majority of women at the end of 1981. Women were 30 per cent of congress delegates, 28 per cent of council members and 20 per cent of executive committee members (Eduards 1981, 42). In 1979, 24 per cent of SACO/SR congressional delegates were women and women comprised only 3 per cent of its managing board membership (Eduards, 1981, 211). Patterns at peak organisation level are reflected in the affiliated unions, which are likely to underrepresent women members on representative bodies, even in unions where women are in the vast majority (Table 5.3). An examination of other indicators of activism reveals a similar gender effect. Maud Eduards (1980) has found that five times as many Swedish men have been union representatives at all levels, an experience differential which is reflected in the fact that relatively few women are nominated by unions to important government commissions. Swedish unions have not contributed significantly to the numbers of women in the corporate channel.

That such underrepresentation of women persists in Swedish trades unions is something of a curiosity in a country where programmatic trade-union backing for sex-equality policies has been a policy feature since the mid-1960s, and where women's political visibility has been high by comparison to other European liberal democracies. Hilda Scott believes that a distinction may be made between the LO and the TCO in that the LO came reluctantly and under pressure to the promotion of women's rights policies, whilst the TCO had been more outspoken. There are clear historical reasons for such differences, which become evident in a brief outline of the history of Swedish women's unionism.

In a similar manner to working women in other countries, Swedish women first formed their own trade unions, and the Women's Trade Union Federation only affiliated to the LO in 1909. Development was slow, however, and women possessed no political voice and were never more than 10 per cent of union members during the entire period before World War One. Nor did unions take much account of women during that time. Instead occasional perfunctory statements in support of equal pay were

Table 5.3: *Percentage of women's membership in some LO and TCO affiliated unions and on their representative bodies (1981)*

	Membership	General Council	Executive Committee
LO			
Swedish Municipal Workers Union	79.0	33.3	38.4
Union of Commercial Employees	74.6	48.6	46.1
Swedish Food Workers Union	39.4	9.1	9.1
Swedish Factory Workers Union	30.3	12.1	18.2
Graphic Industry Workers Union	29.1	8.6	5.9
State Employees Union	27.4	12.0	8.7
Swedish Metal Workers Union	17.3	—	—
Swedish Building Workers Union	1.6	—	—
TCO			
Swedish Union of Municipal Employees	72.0	30.0	38.0
Federation of Civil Servants	66.0	24.0	46.0
Union of Commercial Employees	55.0	40.0	11.0
Swedish Union of Clerical & Technical Employees in Industry	36.0	28.0	39.0

Source: European Trade Union Institute, 1983, 41.43.

accompanied by a studied concentration on the problems of male employees. During the 1930s and 1940s women's share of union memberships increased as did their presence in the labour market. Under the Social Democrats, Sweden in the 1930s entered a period of legislative reform which was considerably to enhance women's opportunities. Legislation was designed to bring about full employment and to obtain greater security for labour and included social benefits such as equal pension rights, paid maternity leave and the prohibition of dismissal on the grounds of marriage or pregnancy. The unions were involved in these programmes but were not particularly militant on behalf of their women members. And the issue of equal pay did not appear in the Social Democrats' programme until 1944.

After the Second World War, however, the newly formed TCO soon found itself reflecting the influx of women in its recruiting market in discussions of equal pay and opportunities. Hilda Scott suggests that TCO women, 89 per cent of whom were middle-class by comparison to the 82 per cent of LO women who were manual workers, were better educationally and socially equipped to articulate and press their particular demands. Thus, she sees the growth of white collar jobs, predominantly filled by women workers, and the increased unionisation of such jobs as an important cause of Sweden's early push for women's employment rights. Moreover, Scott argues that TCO women's rights preoccupations were one source of the pressure which led the LO to create its advisory Women's Council in 1947. At about the same time the LO began to press for equal pay. However, writing separate men's and women's pay scales into contracts was stopped by the LO only in 1960.

Separatism has not been a tactic used by Swedish women unionists. Unusually, in their promotion of sex-equality policy, Swedish unions abandoned their separate women's sections in the belief that change would be best facilitated by creating circumstances in which both men and women discussed women's problems. Hence, the LO Women's Council was transformed into a Council for Family Affairs comprised of six women and five men representing its eleven largest national unions. The 1969 Women's Council report, echoing the 1968 Equality Programme of the Social Democratic Party, became the basis for LO aims in improving the position of women. Targets included the allocation of jobs without regard to gender, relevant child-care service expansion, tax and social security system change and educational efforts to break down sex-role stereotypes.

Scott suggests that the LO, which is linked to the Social Democrats in a similar manner to the TUC and the Labour Party in Britain, was under particular pressure from the Social Democratic women's organisation. This had long attracted the majority of politically committed Swedish women who held left-of-centre political orientations. But feminist pressures from younger women operating outside the established political machinery began to erode the Social Democratic Women's Federation. Before long, feminists, impatient with the slowness of change, began organising separately amongst working women, a process which coincided with a period of steady decline in the membership of the Social Democratic Women's Federation. These two factors, combined with similar events in Norway and Denmark, served to galvanise the LO into taking a more rigorous stance on women's rights at work. The feminism of LO has, however, continued to be noticeably reluctant.

Perhaps reflecting a progression in attitudes, or possibly as a result of its greater proportion of women members, by the time the TCO came to adopt its family-policy reform programme in 1973, it was prepared to be much more outspoken than the LO had

been. The TCO programme demands similar employment opportunities for all adult family members as well as an equal division of
domestic work between men and women. It calls on member
unions to play a part in enforcing these ideals in practice. In 1975
the TCO issued a statement castigating employees in both the
public and private sectors for discriminatory employment practices and for discouraging male employees from taking up their
legal right to paternity leave. All three 'peak' organisations
adopted special action programmes for equality during the 1970s,
which serve as models for local unions at each particular place of
work. Some unions have adopted programmes of positive action,
setting targets for the numbers of women incumbents of official
positions. The TCO affiliated Union of Commercial and Salaried
Employees set itself the goal of 40 per cent women in all union
bodies by 1986 and has a longer-term figure of 55 per cent of such
posts being filled by women. Tactics are cautious, however.
Women are nominated only for posts where the male incumbent is
not seeking re-election. Where men seem reluctant to retire,
committees and boards will be expanded and women elected to
the additional posts. Such procedures have the advantage of not
displacing male unionists whilst promoting larger numbers of
women than would otherwise be possible. Although not unique to
Sweden, they are less common in other countries. Other mechanisms to promote or encourage women include inviting alternates
(usually women) to all meetings and ordering meetings in such a
way that women gain the public-speaking and chairing skills which
are so important in public life.

Given such innovative and comprehensive policies, the
improvements in levels of women's representation in union bodies
seem rather small. The LO found that the ten years following the
abolition of its women's division saw almost no increase in the
number of women representatives except at congress delegate
level (Cook, 1980). Improvement did not, in fact, come to the
other bodies until the end of the 1970s and early 1980s when
women finally obtained representation on the LO executive committee. The abolition of the women's division may well have
exacerbated the slow rate of change, as it does not appear to have
been replaced by any visible women's caucus. Scott could find no
coalition of labour women in Sweden, and she points out that
women must fight directly from the bottom and find it difficult to
obtain places on the ballot in union elections, in contrast to the
political parties where women's representation has steadily
increased.

The absence of a women's division is not the only factor which has accounted for the LO's slow progress in promoting women's union activism. Changing organisational circumstances have also been important. In particular, structural changes in the LO and a policy of amalgamating small units meant that three-quarters of all union branches disappeared between 1969 and 1975. This directly resulted in a decrease in the proportion of women officials, most of whom were at club level. Thus, in 1972 women's representation was lower than it had been in 1959. Occupational sectorialisation is also a significant impediment to union activism, which has both direct and indirect effects. It is systemically impossible for women to have an important role in the industrially based, blue collar LO. Only 18 per cent of women work in industry, and women are less than 18 per cent of the members of the metal workers union, which is the most powerful LO affiliate. The indirect effect is a political one: the one-third of LO members affiliated to the Social Democrats hold high proportions of elected posts. Scott points out that these influential union men, normally skilled workers in traditional industries, do not perceive sex equality as a central issue. Their strategy has been to aim for economic growth and redistribute the extras thus supplied. In such a strategy in Sweden, central issues are union participation in economic management and industrial democracy.

A worker's participation focus has, in the short term at least, its own deleterious effect. The Co-determination Laws passed during the 1970s greatly expanded the areas of union activity and had the effect of raising considerably the levels of skill required by union officials. Shop stewards were now conducting boardroom level negotiations on such matters as work organisation, personnel policy, investments, and so on. Hilda Scott (1982, 57–9) quotes estimates that 50,000 union appointees need to be trained every year. But current family roles leave women little time to obtain the training. And longer-term sex-equality strategies have not found favour in the LO. Member unions have not in practice been prepared to push the six-hour day, which might free women for union and work at the same time as freeing men for domestic labour, as its introduction implies some years without an increase in real wages. But the LO have made it clear from the beginning that work-place equality policy was a union matter. Respect for union prerogatives has meant that at collective bargaining levels many legislative successes have often been symbolic.

Thus, although progress towards sex equality has been notable in Sweden, even there the priorities of unionism have been an impediment. But union prerogatives must be considered in all West European systems. Indeed, however slow women's advancement has been in Swedish unions, it has out-paced progress in many other countries, suggesting that even a half-hearted or partial union commitment to sex equality is better than none at all.

Italy

Italian trade unions are interesting both as an example of a politically and culturally divided unionism and as one which has experienced a very high level of women's movement entrism.[2] At peak level there are three main union associations: the Confederazione Generale Italiana del Lavoro (CGIL), which is close to the Italian Communist Party but has a substantial minority of socialist members; the Confederazione Italiani Sindacati dei Lavoratori (CISL) has been a Catholic association closely associated with the Christian Democrats, but has become more heterogeneous in recent years; and the Unione Italiana del Lavoro (UIL), the Socialist union, which also contains members of some of the minor lay parties. From a position of relative weakness during the 1950s, Italian unions have gradually become more important following the growing significance of collective bargaining as the economy has modernised. They play an increasing role in the running and organisation of some public services and take part in the administration of many state-run social services as well as in most public administration arenas having to do with working conditions. As in other countries, Italian unions act as parliamentary pressure groups and consultation bodies. They also act as consultants to industrial courts. There is no equivalent in Italy to the closed or union shop, hence membership of the union is not a prerequisite for obtaining or remaining in a job. Unionisation rates have risen and declined in fairly dramatic cycles since the Second World War, with best estimates at the beginning of the 1980s suggesting an overall unionisation rate of about 40 per cent. Workers in the building trades, agriculture, pensioners and the unemployed are strongly represented relative to workers in industry and the service sector. De Santis and Zincone believe that official union membership data are likely to be unreliable and that this was especially true for data on women members. At the end of 1982 the CGIL claimed that 35 per cent of its members were women, whilst other unions were either unable to give figures or estimated about 30 per cent. With ISTAT indicating that women were 34.4 per cent of the economically active population and 46.1 per cent of the unemployed,[3] these figures suggest relatively high rates of women's unionisation. But De Santis and Zincone point out that women tend to work in the less well unionised small business and service sector and that union activity tends to be particularly unrewarding for women. They suggest that both these factors are indicators that the official union statistics may be exaggerations. Certainly, women do not hold anything like proportionate positions of responsibility in Italian unions, and this would be true even if membership figures were much lower.

To determine the proportionate share of responsible posts held by women, we need to take account of some organisational complexities of the Italian union structure and to look at unions at factory, productive category, area and confederation level. At factory level, unions have come together in works councils since the 1970s. In 1977 there were about 32,000 of these with some 200,000 members; women's presence at this level is not known. Similarly, there are no reliable 'category-wide' data on the presence of women at the productive category level, general councils and executive committee, the compositions of which are the product of 'guided' delegate congress elections; it is known, however, that women are poorly represented. For area level positions the various categories belonging to the same union come together at local and regional level in decision-making bodies referred to as general councils. These represent, where possible, the various trades but have executive committees and secretariats subject to more open elections. In 1977 the CGIL averaged 19 per cent women on general councils and 16 per cent on executive committees at category level, and 9 per cent on general councils and 10 per cent on executive committees for area groups. Only 4.3 per cent of general secretaries, 1.1 per cent of deputy secretaries and 6.4 per cent of members of secretariats were women.

As elsewhere, Italian unions also both employ and elect officials in administrative and policy capacities. Here, too, women appear to be disadvantaged. In 1980 CISL women held 4.1 per cent of the elected posts, 9.8 per cent of the 'political' non-elected posts and were 78.3 per cent of the technical staff. Data on women's positions on confederation level decision-making bodies simply confirm women's poor representation elsewhere (Table 5.4).

Table 5.4 also confirms the pattern of women's union roles in Italy whereby the Left has apparently been more able to promote women than has the religious Right. De Santis and Zincone (1983,

Table 5.4: *Percentages of women holding decision-making positions at confederation level in Italian trade unions (1981)*

	CGIL	CISL	UIL
General council/general committee	*12.2*	*13.9*	*3.6*
Executive committee	*11.8*	*0*	*0*
Confederal secretariat	*16.7*	*0*	*0*
Total positions	*12.2*	*9.2*	*2.5*

Source: Calculated from De Santis and Zincone (1983), Table 5.5c.

Note: The CGIL proportions differ from European Trade Union Institute data given in Table 5.2. Although the differences are not large enough to suggest that the pattern represented is misleading they nonetheless illustrate the difficulties with using Italian union statistics mentioned above.

5–37) conceptualise this difference in their suggestion that the political and union organisations originally connected to the Catholic Church show a greater *receptive* capacity in relation to women in that they receive more votes from women or have more women members. Organisations of a socialist background, on the other hand, have less receptive capacity but greater *promotional* capacity in that they are more committed to defending the interests of women workers and more willing to promote women in their own ranks and representative bodies. This distinction is less clear-cut than it has been in the past, reflecting a secularisation of Catholic-based organisations which has involved an attendant more favourable attitude to the promotion of women personnel. Concomitantly, socialist-based organisations have become less anti-clerical, and this, combined with the spread of feminist ideas, especially amongst young working women, has made them more receptive than in the past. Indeed, an increased women's presence in the top confederal bodies has been a recent feature of all the mass-based Italian political organisations, a development which may be attributed to the impact of the swell of feminist ideas during the 1970s.

The feminism of the 1970s made itself felt at many levels of the Italian union movement, whose organisations came under considerable pressure to rethink their policies on women. Up until the end of the 1960s trade union women's policies were emancipationist, holding that the main obstacles to feminine emancipation were women's primary responsibility for home and family. Hence, key improvements aimed at facilitating entry into paid employment by increases in child-care and other social service facilities. Such a policy assumed full employment, and its limitations became apparent as women increasingly became unemployed during the recession of the 1970s. At about the same time, the feminist movement brought to the unions' discussions questions about the traditional sexual division of labour and pressed for research uncovering all aspects of the roots of women's oppression (Froggett, 1981, 37).

The feminist groups which emerged in the early 1970s had a particular impact on the unions and gave rise to new forms of internal organisation. Essentially, two kinds of group were formed: those which arose from city-based women's movement groups in Turin, Genoa and Verona, and those which were formed within the union as a result of initiatives from women union officials in Rome, Milan and Bari. In both cases, once established the phenomena tended to spread. The city-based groups led to inter-category groups of women's representatives from the CGIL, the CISL and the UIL coming together and becoming active over issues such as abortion. Known as Intercategoriale and mainly comprised of shop stewards, they cut across confederal lines and may be seen as being part of the same unifying spirit which led to the emergence of the works councils of the 1970s (De Santis and Zincone, 1983, 5.39 to 5.40). Essentially, the feminist invasion of the unions came in the wake of the 1960s, when concern with life-style issues saw numerous examples of demands for pro-grammes of social reform justified by reference to the general goal of improving the quality of life. In the unions this reflected both the rejection of a narrowly economistic trade unionism and the declining contractual power of the Italian working class (Froggett, 1981, 37). Its timing was possibly as important a component of feminism's entry into the unions as its demands. An egalitarian, anti-institutional push (of the 1969 Hot Autumn) had generated new democratic instruments, such as the 150 Hours, the intro-duction of shop stewards and factory-floor meetings, which the women's movement was able to adapt against a background of a growing unification process whereby the blurring of confederal distinctions gave rise to the possibility of a split along gender lines (De Santis and Zincone, 1983, 5.40).

An unusual feature of the feminist penetration of Italian Trade Unions was their use of the 150 Hours, a scheme of paid edu-cational leave negotiated by the metal workers union as part of their work contract in 1973 and afterwards extended to many other categories of worker. The scheme gives 150 hours per year of paid leave to up to 2 per cent of workers from any particular firm to be used attending classes in order to gain the basic middle-school diploma awarded at the end of the period of compulsory schooling. Classes are held during the working day and at first were held in the factory itself. Lesley Caldwell emphasises the significance of such a scheme in a country with an elitist school system and no tradition of adult education. It is a popular innovation with some 320 courses having been organised in Milan and its surrounding province alone in 1982. Significantly, the courses have had a certain political ambiance due to having first been won by a militant union. (Caldwell, 1983, 74–5).

Partly because of a realisation of their political potential and partly because women are often less well-established in other posts, there was an immediate influx of feminists into teaching the 150 Hours. Although tension between feminists and unions over feminist inputs soon became apparent, there was strong union support for the increased attendance of courses on themes of interest to women. Basically, women wanted different things from the course than the unions. Union leaders wanted the growth in women's awareness to be translated into campaigning around union, factory, pay negotiation and political activity. The 150 Hours was another post Hot Autumn opportunity to instil a feminist presence in the unions and became a focal point for arguing a series of connections between feminism and the unions in general. Officially unions have been obliged to be accommodating.

Italian feminists themselves have described their activities in the trade unions in *L'Acqua in Gabbia* (Bacchio and Torchi, 1979), an account which reveals a considerable ambivalence in the unions' response to feminist entrism. Many of the women who became union activists in the 1970s were disillusioned New Left members, some were full-time trade union officials, some were 150 Hours teachers and some were factory committee delegates. These relatively emancipated women often had women's movement experience. They decided to work in the trade unions as a result of a perception that it was important both to confront the problems of work and to relate to a mass movement. They began with intentionally informal meetings for women (*coordinamenti*), held after branch or regional union meetings. As these gatherings were open to any women, membership tended to fluctuate, leading to accusations of unrepresentativeness. Local housewives, homeworkers and unemployed women were included by some groups, a practice which was perceived by the unions as separatism and led to criticism and hostility from male unionists. However, *coordinamenti* proliferated in all the major towns and proved a powerful draw for women (Froggett, 1981, 39). Related to this development was the emergence of 'women only' 150 Hours courses, which often became consciousness-raising groups which continued beyond term. In short, the early to mid-1970s saw the formation of a feminist sub-culture within the unions and were a period of tremendous optimism for those who were involved.

Although such contradictions as arose between the needs of feminism and traditionally perceived unionism tended to be left open, the authors of *L'Acqua* argue that little was achieved in the way of transforming the theoretical understandings that women's oppression is domestically based into strategic demands which could be placed in union platforms. In the face of the enormity of confronting questions of the labour market and its relation to family and social structures, the demands and proposals put forward by the groups were modest. Examples include a fixed proportion of jobs for women in each firm, better training for women and better collection of data on women's employment. More innovative ideas seemed lost at the outset. Proposals that each worker should be entitled to 200 hours paid leave per year to participate in the running of day-care centres, nurseries or other community services and that both parents should be entitled to 40 hours child-sickness leave a year never got beyond the discussion stage (Froggett, 1981, 39).

Outside the immediate economic arena, union responses were more supportive of women's demands. The legalisation of abortion, the establishment of family and health-care centres and the reform of laws on sexual violence all received union backing. Concomitantly, union women have become more assertive in demanding higher health and hygiene standards and a more humane working environment. Union women are better able and more willing to discuss personal problems in relation to home and work and are more confident that the subjective dimension is a vital component of understanding and knowledge. But feminist socialists are dissatisfied with the unions as an arena for political self-realisation (Cockburn 1984, 48–9) and unions continue to be good at neglecting women's interests. Incomes-policy agreements entered into in the 1980s have sacrificed opportunities to increase women's employment by extending nominal hiring provisions without safeguarding potential women employees. Agreements have also been made to proposals of tax relief for single-income families which increase tax for double-income families. And the

unions have assented to projected higher family benefits for
workers who provide for their wives, effectively increasing state
subsidies for families in which the wife has no paid employment
(De Santis and Zincone, 1983, 5.20).

The frustration felt by Italian women unionists and documented
in *L'Acqua* is well grounded, but the pessimism expressed as a
result of that frustration is perhaps less appropriate. A decade of
feminist activism in the unions has established a network of
experienced feminist union activists who have the skills and many
of the resources necessary to advance women's concerns in the
Italian unions. Political fragmentation in the union movement
may in some respects benefit women. Political competition for
recruits has meant and will continue to mean that each of the
union confederations will take account of women's concerns.
Although this may not have an immediate effect in the current
phase of union decline, an improvement in the fortunes of the
union movement may well mean an improvement in the benefits
women will gain from membership.

Britain

Feminist penetration of the union movement was also a feature of
1970s Britain. There, despite many structural differences with the
Italian movement, the impact of the women's movement has been
rather similar in that British unions are more willing to take
account of life-style issues than once they were, but remain prone
to foot-dragging in promoting women's economic concerns. The
British trade union movement appears to be one of Europe's most
centralised, featuring neither functional nor political divisions.
But in practice the limited scope of the TUC is such that British
unionism is in truth amongst the most decentralised. Industrial
relations in the UK operate via a system of voluntary collective
bargaining. There is no standard structure since the parties
involved are independent and fiercely resent any attempt at state
intervention. Agreements are not usually legally enforceable and
are normally of two broad types: substantive agremeents dealing
with terms and conditions and procedural agreements dealing with
the settlement of disputes between employers and workers. Collective bargaining arrangements and customs differ by industry,
locality and tradition. Unions, to which just over 60 per cent of
men and nearly 40 per cent of women in employment belong, are
historically based upon craft/skill groups rather than industry.
Bargaining takes place at all levels—shop floor, branch, regional
and national. Unions also provide members for Joint Industrial

Councils and similar bargaining bodies. There has been a growth during the past decade of single-employer bargaining at company, divisional or plant level, with a consequent decline in the influence of multi-employer or national agreements on wage rates in some sectors of industry.

Membership of a trade union implies agreement to abide by the rules which are usually expressly incorporated into the contract. Such an obligation is not necessarily voluntarily undertaken as about 40 per cent of UK union members are employed in closed shops. Each union operates according to its rule book, which usually may be amended only by the union's annual conference. Typically, unions will employ at least some national, regional and local officials. Within the work-place union representation is by shop steward, the numbers depending upon the size of the work-force. Joint trade union committees are commonly negotiators within many large work-places.

Since the 1960s the trend has been towards amalgamation, and the growth area has been the white collar unions. The peak organisation, the Trades Union Congress (TUC) had 103 unions affiliated to it in 1983, giving it a total membership of 11,05,984. The TUC's powers are mainly advisory and its role tends to be a coordinating one as it has little effective power over member unions. It acts as a pressure group and a channel of communication between unions and the government and the Confederation of British Industry (CBI), the main employers' peak organisation. It is, however, an important corporate channel and is usually consulted by government and the civil service and provides members for working parties on proposed legislation. This may be a requirement of the enabling statute in the case of delegated legislation.

Election to any union office at other than local level involves what may be an inconvenient commitment to attend weekend meetings, familiarity with the rules and taking an active part in union affairs at local level as well as meeting a length of membership qualification. Elected officials must be willing to travel and to take advantage of any training on offer. From the outset, then, acquiring power in the union structure involves a major commitment on the part of the individual involved, as well as an ability to win electoral support. Elections within unions take place at all levels and for all posts, with procedures provided for in the rule books. Often elections are held at poorly attended meetings at which those voting are activists not necessarily representative of the membership as a whole. But change may be on the way here as

Table 5.5: *Proportion of delegates compared with proportion of women members in British unions of over 20,000 members and over 20 per cent women, in order of union size (1982, with 1979 figures in parentheses)*

	Per cent. of members who are women	Per cent. of delegates to TUC annual conference who are women
GMWU	34.3 (33.8)	6.8 (5.4)
NALGO	51.3 (46.3)	23.6 (18.0)
NUPE	66.7 (66.0)	21.9 (22.0)
USDAW	62.0 (60.8)	11.1 (31.7)
SOGAT	31.9 (33.6)	8.3 (11.1)
COHSE	78.1 (76.7)	15.0 (22.2)
NUT+	72.2 (73.5)	8.3 (24.3)
BIFU	48.8 (47.6)	15.0 (11.5)
APEX	55.2 (55.5)	26.7 (23.1)
NAS/UWT+	34.5 (30.1)	11.1 (25.0)
NUTGW	90.4 (89.87)	50.0 (56.3)
NATFHE*	23.8 (—)	21.4 (—)
TSSA+	25.2 (24.5)	7.7 (7.1)
NUHKW	73.0 (71.9)	0 (0)
IRSF	61.8 (61.5)	0 (8.3)
NUFLAT	50.1 (52.0)	0 (7.7)
CSU	34.5 (39.7)	11.1 (10.0)
Dyers, Bleachers and Textile Workers	38.0 (38.8)	37.5 (9.1)
NUJ	25.8 (24.9)	14.3 (16.7)
Equity	47.4 (47.0)	0 (40.0)
AU Textile Workers	44.4 (46.0)	0 (28.6)
Tobacco Workers' Union**	59.7 (62.4)	0 (0)

+ Percentage of women members in 1982 supplied by union
* NATFHE has 68,483 members 1982
** Tobacco Workers' Union has fallen below the 20,000 members level in 1982.

Source: TUC statistical statement.

the Conservative government aims to impose a system of compulsory secret postal ballots designed to remove power from activists who have long been the main beneficiaries of rules, customs and practices designed to empower those best able to bear the social costs of electoral manoeuvring.

In addition to managing internal elections, each union affiliated to the TUC sends delegates to the TUC annual conference in an

Table 5.6: *Representation of women in certain British unions (1980, with 1976 figures in parentheses)*

Union	Membership who are women	Full-time officials		Executive committee members who are women	
	(%)	(No.)	(%)	(No.)	(%)
APEX	51 (55)	2 (1)	3.6	1 (4)	7.0
ASTMS	17 (18)	6 (5)	9.5	2 (1)	8.3
BIFU	49 (46)	6 (3)	14.6	3 (3)	11.1
GMWU	34 (33)	13 (10)	5.3	0 (0)	0.0
NALGO	50 (43)	11 (17)	6.7	14 (5)	20.0
NUPE	67 (65)	7 (2)	4.7	8 (6)	30.7
NUT	66 (75)	17 (2)	15.5	4 (7)	9.1
NUTGW	92 (88)	9 (6)	19.1	5 (5)	33.3
TGWU	16 (16)	6 (3)	1.0	0 (0)	0 (0)
USDAW	63 (59)	13 (4)	8.0	3 (1)	18.7

Source: Coote and Kellner *op. cit.*, p. 11; Corcoran and Lovenduski, 1983, 4.61.

agreed proportion to its number of members. Those delegates, who are often mandated, elect the fifty-one-member TUC general council, which is the executive of the TUC and which therefore is at the forefront of the union, government and employer consultations on major aspects of employment policy.

In 1983 women were 31 per cent of union members and about 40 per cent of employed women are union members. Scrutiny of data on women's membership and activity rates reveals that women's union density is lower than that of men's and the bulk of women are concentrated into a small number of unions, a syndrome which reflects women's work patterns. Until 1981, women's union membership and density increased relative to men's, and as data indicate that the recession-induced loss of membership was lower for women than for men this may have continued to be the case. No data are available on the proportion of women participating in particular negotiations, but the percentage of women unionists who have been shop stewards, 4 per cent, is likely to be a good indicator of such activity at local level. Activism data (Tables 5.5 and 5.6) indicate quite clearly that women are less active in their unions than are men, often by a very large amount, particularly where activity is measured by holding an official union position. There were only two women general secretaries of national unions in mid-1984 and only in September 1983 was a woman (Lil Stevens) elected to a non-reserved seat on the TUC general council, the first to be so elected for 40 years. Regional variations are difficult to assess as union structures tend to mean that memberships overlap, making counts difficult. But Breitenbach (1982, 41) has found that women in Scotland are more likely to be unionised than women in the rest of Britain, although this does not appear to have a measurable effect on their participation at levels of activity above membership.

In general, women are much less likely to be represented in their unions' official posts than are men, and women's representation is more likely to occur at local level (particularly in unions where negotiations are conducted nationally) (Table 5.6). Women union officials are more likely to be branch secretaries (doing clerical duties) than convenors (negotiators); they are also more likely to hold unpaid than paid positions. Women are also much less likely than men to have participated in industrial action or to intervene once at a union meeting. The pattern does vary significantly from union to union, however, and, particularly in the white collar unions at local level, women's participation may be quite high.

In 1979 about half of all British women trade unionists were in five unions—NUPE, NALGO, TGWU, GMWU, and USDAW. But most unions have at least a few members, such as the NUM's organisation of women canteen workers in the mining industry but whose interests have not been protected by the union. Nevertheless, the pattern of women's unionisation is similar to that of men's in that they are concentrated in large numbers in quite a small number of unions. In 1979 women were 28.4 per cent of all TUC-affiliated union members, and 38.9 per cent of women workers were in unions by comparison to 65.6 per cent of male workers. Full-time women workers were more likely to be unionised, suggesting that the prevalence of part-time employment for women inhibits their organisation by unions. High labour turnover, small work places and homeworking are other characteristics of women's work which are known to inhibit unionisation. In addition, women are often concentrated in industries, such as the clothing industry, which are poorly unionised generally. Service industry employment also tends to be poorly unionised, concentrated as it is in small establishments, particularly in catering. Hence, women's industrial distribution does not favour high levels of unionisation. Unions have been aware of the need to recruit more women and to organise in women's places of work for some years and a number of special programmes of recruitment have been devised, one result of which was a 35 per cent increase in women's union density between 1948 and 1983.

Trade union policies which assist women workers are of two kinds: those which are specifically designed to improve women's conditions at work and those designed to improve women's position as trade unionists (Breitenbach 1982, 54). Policies of the first kind include those which have negotiated conditions for women which go beyond the statutory minima enshrined in the employment provisions of sex equality legislation, such as the Sex Discrimination Act, the Equal Pay Act and the Employment Protection (Consolidation) Act. Unions vary widely in their attention to such policies, and some of the variation is due to differences in size, structure and type of work done by members. There is, for example, no need for a union which negotiates at national level for all members to provide model agreements for membership. Such models are useful, however, for unions where negotiations over pay and/or conditions take place at a variety of levels and across a wide range of industries.

Policies of the second type are usually carried out at the national level. The TUC has a standing committee on equal rights with responsibility for both sex equality rights and the rights of ethnic minorities. The report of this committee to the 1981 Annual Congress contained nothing relating to women (TUC, 1981). There is also a women's advisory committee. The TUC womens' conference meets annually, and in 1972 a motion proposing that it should be wound up was defeated. In 1979 the TUC produced a charter on equality for women in the trade unions which the general council recommended to all affiliated unions' executives. Included were a series of ten special measures which unions should undertake in order to increase women's representation at all levels of union hierarchies. Thus, each union executive was exhorted to set up advisory committees within their constitutional structure at national, regional and local level to ensure that the interests of its women members were protected. In November 1980 a conference of constituent unions was called to discuss a programme of positive action both in the employment of women and in sex equality in the trade unions. Proposals were approved in 1981, but it must be remembered that it is activity on equal opportunity in the constituent unions themselves which is likely to make a difference to women's opportunities.

Most unions have their own women's regional conferences which select delegates to attend the national conference and a number have women's advisory committees and women's officers. Legal provision allowing the reservation of seats on governing bodies for women finds expression in the increase in such reserved seats from two to five on the TUC general council in 1980. Some unions have, accordingly, set aside seats on union committees for women or have exercised positive discrimination in other ways, particularly in training activities.

However, the extent to which unions have responded to women's issues should not be overestimated. Few unions employ officers or research staff solely concerned with women's issues, an exception being Judith Hunt of TASS. Marie Patterson of the TGWU spends about a third of her time on women's issues. And some union women's posts (e.g. TGWU and GMWU) have existed since the early 1920s. Also, at least one union, COHSE, used to have a women's officer but no longer does so. Internal conferences for women remain rare outside the major 'women's' unions and two unions, BIFU and APEX, have phased out reserved executive seats for women. Crèche facilities began to appear regularly at annual or biannual delegate conferences in the 1970s but remain rare at regional or local level. The most common approach to helping women appears to be special educational facilities or working parties which may exist at regional as well as national level. Different union policies often stem from disagreement over the principal of special women's sections as well as from differing levels of commitment to the promotion of women. Generalisation is difficult given the variety of practices (Breitenbach, 1982, *passim*).

But women are still regarded, and many regard themselves, as primarily responsible for home and children. Active participation in a trade union is seen neither as an attractive option nor an obligation, but as a separate, additional job. Whilst many women complain that unions do not put issues of interest on the agenda, others think that these issues concern men as well. The TUC has responded to such attitudes, and to a large increase in women's union membership, by issuing reports on educational and training facilities for women in 1972 and on child-care facilities in 1978. Some individual unions have special membership drives for women and have established women-only branches as a way of increasing union density amongst women (e.g. NUPE), but others have made less effort, being reluctant to campaign around such mobilising issues as women's equal pay and opportunities. Many of the traditional unions regard the sex-equality issue as one which potentially may divide the movement and see employment equality law as an infringement of their collective bargaining roles.

But the general trend since 1970 has been towards a greater recognition of the role women unionists might play. Always rather slow, rates of progress vary between unions, often according to whether the union is traditional, craft, mass or white collar, and according to whether women members are amongst the more skilled or higher status grades of employee. Education here as elsewhere is a key variable, but its importance is probably superceded by that of family position. Mindful both of organisational and domestic constraints, the TUC resolution on positive action in 1981 concluded:

Finally, it must be recognised that implementing all the existing TUC policies and pursuing all the steps to positive action ... will still not change the position of women to one of complete equality, unless it is recognised that family responsibility should be jointly shared and all collective bargaining agreements, work practices and legislation ... aimed at enabling this to happen, and unless trade unionists work with determination towards this end.

The relatively extensive data available on women's unionisation in Britain enable us to make a number of observations about women's work-place politics. The questions of positive discrimination, the reservation of special seats on governing bodies for women and the retention of separate women's organisations divide both the union and the women's movement, but opposition to such measures has become much less vociferous as women's difficulties in making significant progress in the absence of such structures have become more apparent (Breitenbach, 1981, 82). Notable in the development of British women's unionism is the syndrome whereby organisational forms which in the 1950s and 1960s were little more than women's auxiliaries, gained organisational strength and political muscle as the women's movement grew. Women's advisory committees became arenas which prepared and trained women to take the struggle for women's liberation into the union movement as a whole. Their advisory status has been a constraint, but union men have become increasingly willing to listen to them at TUC level and their impact has grown apace (Breitenbach, 1981, 82).

The British case also points up the importance of variation in union sizes and structures. It would appear that a small, centralised union such as AUEW (TASS) or ASTMS may move more quickly and effectively to implement measures to encourage women than may a sprawling giant such as the T&GWU (Britain's largest union). The democratic structure of which the T&GWU has been so proud incorporates an inability to impose measures from the top. Hence, when its 1979 biennial delegate conference voted to set up regional equal rights committees, the T&GWU could not instruct the regions on how or when to do so. So the union with the third largest number of women members continues to be controlled by men at virtually every point of its hierarchy, and the few individual officials who are committed to sex-equality find it difficult to have more than a local effect. Organisational unwieldiness presents a considerable obstacle to change. By contrast, NALGO, which is the fourth largest British union and has the second largest women membership, does not face the same difficulties. NALGO women are more vocal, benefiting from the fact that organisation around large bargaining centres makes communication (which is a major and expensive problem in the T&GWU) easier.

In general, the events of the 1970s have made many UK unions responsive to certain kinds of feminist demands. Union support for the National Abortion Campaign was widespread (Lovenduski, 1984), and the TUC has taken stands on such issues as sexual harassment at work. Unions have provided special women-only courses for shop stewards and have come out in favour of paternity leave. There is considerable evidence of a growing sensitivity to the special needs of women unionists. But bread-and-butter issues of equal pay and opportunity at work have not had such a good union response. The problem of union jealousy of prerogatives is here evident and sex-equality legislation applying to collective bargaining agreements has proved difficult to digest.

Thus, in Britain, Sweden and Italy similar patterns are evident. Women's membership of trade unions has increased as their employment rates have risen. Their presence in decision-making bodies has increased at a somewhat lower rate and has only increased significantly where positive action has been taken. In all three countries, programmatic trade union support for women's rights became available during the 1970s or earlier, but political support continued to depend on which area of women's rights was in question.

West European Unions

Scrutiny of other West European trade union systems suggests similar patterns. Except for Iceland and Luxemburg,[4] by the end of 1981 the union movements of all the European liberal democracies had policies to promote sex equality. Women's unionism and union activism appeared everywhere to be on the increase, although activism beyond membership had not, by 1984, begun to approach the level of men's.

Variables at the level of the individual and the system have an impact on women's unionisation and activity. Breitenbach (1981, 71) suggests that an important contributory factor to the greater degree of unionisation amongst women workers in Scotland by comparison to England and Wales arises from a greater preponderance of women full-time workers in Scotland. But domestic roles may mean that part-time work is the only option for many women and unions must therefore accommodate themselves to the representation of the needs of part-time workers if they are to accommodate their women members. Work-place size and occupational sector also have an impact on union membership, on militancy and on union policies. Large work-places tend to be more unionised, strike prone and male. White collar unions tend to be more willing to press for issues like equal pay, reflecting perhaps their longer experience of organising women and their greater numbers of women members. Union organisation generally has never been of uniform strength in any of the countries under consideration, and really strong organisation has always been limited to certain sectors. Strength is known to depend upon such factors as character of the job, level of skill involved, growth or decline of the industry, local and historical factors, the solidarity created by the working conditions in question as well as the factors already mentioned. Such conditions are independent of gender and affect women similarly to men. It is occupational segregation which accounts for a significant part of the differences between men and women.

Sex differences in domestic roles, life-styles and life-cycle may also play a part in differing propensities of union men and women to be active. Italian studies have found that as many as 74 per cent of men working full-time for the union have children whilst only 31 per cent of women do. This suggests that family bonds may be an advantage for men but not for women (De Santis and Zincone, 1983, 5.36). Similarly, amongst delegates to the 1982 Metz Congress of the French CFDT, men were more likely to be married than women and 57 per cent of the women but only 28 per cent of the men were childless; moreover, 60 per cent of the married women were married to union activists (Moreau-Bourles and Sineau, 1983, 2.74). In Britain, Coote and Kellner (1980, 29–30) found that gender-differentiated life cycles were important. The largest discrepancies between men's and women's unionisation rates were amongst 25 to 34 year old full-time workers. Attitudes have a similar effect. The idea that men have a right to earn a 'family wage' is an important idea in British trade union bargaining and has been influential in Germany and Italy.

At system level, such factors as the level of industrial development will have an effect. In Spain, Portugal, and Greece women are less unionised than men (PE1-1129/83/C) but in Spain and Portugal are often more likely to appear in union leadership roles than in other European countries (see *Women in Spain*, 1981, 36–8; *Women in Portugal*, 1981, 46–50), exhibiting the inconsistent pattern which is also apparent in some West German unions (Randzio-Plath and Rust, 1983) and may be accounted for either by reference to tokenism or by determined efforts by leaders to appear to conform with newly perceived national sex-equality norms.

The effect of the presence or absence of separate women's organisations in union structures is not a clear cut one. A 1978 International Labour Organisation (ILO) conference on women's unionism concluded that on balance the most useful means of integrating women into the unions was the most common, that of the updated version of the historical women's division which guaranteed at least a feminist face, voice and vote (Cook, 1980, 20). This observation was backed up by reference to the very small change in women's representation in Swedish unions in the ten years following the abolition of its women's division, when improvement was limited to congress delegate level. Separate women's divisions are not without problems, however. The most notable of these are tokenism, the isolation of women and women's issues from the mainstream of union affairs. Career-minded women unionists have therefore tended to avoid positions in women's sections, preferring to involve themselves in collective bargaining, grievance handling and executive administration; that is, those areas of skill which are known to be important for career advancement.

Of course, if union leaderships are sufficiently determined, a 'feminine face, voice and vote' may be ensured in other ways. In France it has been found that women's opportunities are greatest where there are a large number of positions to be filled. Thus, the 250-member executive committee of the CGT has provided (relative) ease of entry for women and the 1983 expansion of the CFDT national office also served to increase the number (and proportion) of women representatives as most of the new positions were filled by women (Moreau-Bourles and Sineau, 1983). In common with other countries, French unions featured a slow circulation of elites, with four or five consecutive spells in office being usual. This practice makes life difficult for the elite aspirant as does the custom of simultaneous political and union office-holding. Moreover, the relatively aged character of union elites implied by consecutive office-holding may make them less responsive to those women's demands not based on traditional role conceptions.

Reports given at the 1978 ILO conference mentioned above suggest that women's issues and women themselves may be better integrated into unions where bargaining takes place at central levels. Decentralised bargaining may bring issues of special interest to women to a level at which men might see possible competition and confrontation between men and women (Caudart and Greve, 1980, 25).

It is essential when considering women's trade union roles to remember that, for the most part, unions, like all important political institutions, are male inventions. Occasional historical and contemporary examples of women-only unions aside, women have come into the unions in any numbers only after their structures, customs and habits have been well established, and women unionists have therefore had to fight a considerable battle simply to alert their male colleagues to the fact that there are such things as women's issues which are relevant to union policy. Latent sexism is undoubtedly one of the obstacles to women becoming trades unionists on the same terms as men. Whilst men may not have actively conspired to keep women down, male-constructed machinery to improve wages and conditions has repeatedly failed to accommodate the needs of women. The need to recruit newly employed women and the presence of women trade union officials committed to women's rights programmes combined with an influx of feminists into many nations' union movements during the 1970s has meant that many male unionists became willing to raise and discuss sex-equality issues and union environments have become more congenial to women.

But progress has not necessarily been smooth. In France the once-encouraged feminist voice of *Antoinette*, the CGT women's magazine, was chastised in the summer of 1982 for what male leaders regarded as excessive criticisms of sexism. Men have been exhorted to lead the 'fight for women's dignity', feminist self-organisation has been firmly prevented and the CGT women's sector was effectively purged. Cockburn (1984) provides evidence that many of the women who were active in the 'feminisation' of the unions were, by 1984, politically exhausted, both because of their isolation and the tactics they had to use. On such evidence, not only has the task of transforming of union structures only just begun, it is by no means certain that it will ever be completed.

Women and Trade Unions under State Socialism

Whilst many of the variables which affect women's unionisation and activism are present in both state socialist and liberal democratic systems, their importance and effect must be assessed in the light of the rather different meaning of unionism in Eastern Europe. As in the Soviet Union, the unions in the East European state socialist systems do not represent the interests of any particular group of workers against the 'employer', since the employer, constitutionally, is the workers' state. State socialist union systems may initiate labour legislation, may express views on laws which directly affect labour and may represent workers in valid disputes with a manager who may also belong to the same union. In charge of an array of national social welfare measures and institutions, unions also pay an important role in superintending central-plan implementation at enterprise level.

East European unions do have specific capacities to defend women's interests but these do not arise from an independent collective bargaining role. They are rather capacities specifically designed by the state to enable unions to carry out responsibilities for ensuring the implementation of sex equality at work. Thus, a union there would, for example, defend a woman worker if she had been discriminated against by an enterprise director in violation of the law.

Labour shortage in some countries and official ideological commitment to women's rights have meant that some attention has been given to women's trade union role by policy-makers, a preoccupation which is reflected in the fact that women's share of official union positions tends to be high by Western standards, although not proportionate to membership. In the Soviet Union in 1982, for example, women were 59.5 per cent of the 131.2 million union members and were 44.2 per cent of members of central committees of sectoral unions, 47.2 per cent of trade union council members and 51 per cent of representatives on republican, territorial and regional union committees. The proportion of women falls off at the top level of the union hierarchy, where women are only 34.6 per cent of members of the All-Union Central Council of Trade Unions (Srirajyam, 1983). In East Germany between 95 and 96.5 per cent of all working women (and similar proportions of men) belong to the Freier Deutscher Gewerkschaftsbund (FDGB or Free German Labour Union Federation), slightly over 50 per cent of whose members are women. In 1972 women were 49.2 per cent of trade union functionaries. At the eighth FDGB congress 113 women were elected to the executive committee, making the composition of the executive 47 per cent women in 1976. By 1975 women held over 50 per cent of all leadership positions in the labour union structure, including 53.9 per cent at enterprise level and 48.2 per cent, 47.8 per cent and 47.0 per cent of members of governing bodies at country, district and federal levels, respectively (Shaffer, 1981, 95).

In Czechoslovakia, unions took over responsibility for employed women from the women's movement section of the Communist Party, which was abolished shortly after the socialist regime was established. In 1957 the Presidium of the Central Council of Trades Unions passed a resolution laying down the principles of trade union activities amongst women. The resolution ensured the establishment of an auxiliary body, a women's commission of the works committee in areas which employed a low proportion of women with the responsibility of ensuring that women's needs were considered. Such a body was thought to be unnecessary in areas where high proportions of women were employed. By 1959 specific women's demands began to appear on the list of trade union priorities, by which time women's employment rates had increased from 38 to 43 per cent. Unions raised emancipatory issues such as the extension of domestic-related services to relieve the domestic burden and the need for improvements in women's access to training, but there was no evidence of any liberatory demands being pushed even during the heady days of the Prague Spring. Women's representation on union bodies continued to rise however and by the mid-1970s women were 44 per cent of the members of union governing bodies and commissions. The proportion of women holding leading union jobs greatly increased after the eighth all-union congress in 1972, and women were 37 per cent of the members of the Central Council of Trades Unions by the end of the 1970s (Heitlinger, 1979, 75–6). However, as in other East European countries, these positions are all paralleled by party posts and are not regarded as powerful positions. Similar patterns are evident in other state socialist countries. Hungarian sources indicate that women's share of trade union functionary posts is higher than their membership and in all East European countries for which data are available women's unionisation rates are closely in line with employment rates.[5]

When assessing the general pattern of women's high visibility in East European unions it should be remembered that the unions there rarely, if ever, involve themselves in autonomous action: They are concerned with conditions of work, with plan fulfilment, and so on, and women's involvement and activity should be seen in that context. On any reading, state socialist trade unions are less powerful than their liberal democratic counterparts. Hence, a seemingly greater commitment to women's rights must be balanced by the perception of a relatively narrower range of action. Ideologically constrained as they are, East European unions will play little role in discussions over altering women's traditional domestic role, although they might as administrative agents of states with official commitments to sex equality provide some assistance in enabling women to carry domestic burdens. Whilst it is not impossible that state socialist unions may follow their Western counterparts in incorporating more feminist demands, that process is unlikely to involve the sort of direct and overt feminist infiltration which has been characteristic of the West. The other side of this coin is, of course, that Western unions in the liberal democratic states are unlikely to go to the same lengths as their East German or Hungarian counterparts in promoting women into positions of responsibility.

Business Associations

The numerous problems of access and data availability which impede the assessment of women's union politics pale into insignificance when compared to the difficulties of obtaining information on women's role in business associations. German, British, French and Italian researchers have all reported significant gaps in the information available in this arena (Zincone, 1983). Yet the extent to which such organisations are willing to take women's views into account, often measurable only by reference to their proportions of women members and officers, may be a critical factor in the development and implementation of sex-equality policy. This is true not only for employment policy but also in such areas as advertising, product development and credit availability. And, like trade unions, employers associations often control nominations to important official bodies. They are an important part of the corporate channel. The rise of the role of peak organisations in the post-war West European economies, although not always consistent, has everywhere been present (Gunter, 1975, 95). As discussed above, what may have begun as a process of bargaining between workers' and employers' organisations gradually became bargaining between both such organisations and their governments in the growing number of tripartite corporate bodies active in most areas of domestic policy at virtually all stages of the policy-making and implementation processes. It is an inescapable fact, therefore, that such associations take part in the making of decisions which may be of vital importance to women. The specific form of their involvement may vary, but the general pattern is similar for most countries and the exclusion of women is universal as the following examples show.

Britain

In Britain employers associations commonly negotiate with trades unions at industry level, often through a joint industrial council with simliar procedures operating at other levels. They represent the views of their employer members, give advice and provide services. Many are also trade associations. The business associations are normally governed by elected committees with an element of cooption to ensure interest representation, but little is known of the composition of these committees. The main peak organisation is the Confederation of British Industry (CBI), which acts as spokesperson for both industry and commerce. Over 12 million people were employed by CBI affiliated companies in 1983. Membership is corporate, including invidual firms, most of the nationalised industries and trade and employers associations. The CBI is structured along regional lines, with thirteen regional councils elected by local employers and associations. These councils elect 200 of the 400-member general council, which is the CBI governing body. The council also includes representatives of the nationalised industries and the industry-sector federations. The extensive committee structure involves twenty-five standing committees, the general purposes committee and about eighty other committees, sub-committees and working parties.

In Britain, as elsewhere, access to the CBI (or other employer/business Association membership) depends upon being an employer (or a member of senior management). But British firms are not legally required to disclose details of their establishment or of their personnel policies under equal opportunity law or for any other purposes unless they are subject to an Equal Opportunities Commission formal investigation or unless the courts demand such details for a particular case. As a result, very little is known of the status of women amongst employers, even in those few establishments (normally in the public sector) who proudly assert that they are 'equal opportunity' employers. Apart from being an employer, access involves attending the local meetings, paying a membership fee and socialising. Membership of the committees both at local, regional and national level is determined by election. Cooption is common in order to achieve a body which is representative of the particular industry or trade group. CBI meetings are held in London. Those attending are likely, therefore, to be senior members of their organisation who are able to spare the time.

The paucity of the data available on women's presence in employers' associations is itself an indication of the masculine domination of this arena. Two women are on the 400-member CBI General Council and 65 women serve on various CBI committees (which have a total membership of 3,025). Amongst the 660 employers' associations listed by the Department of Employment in 1983, between 2 per cent and 9 per cent had women secretaries. Such data reflect the relative absence of women in senior management posts from which such positions are normally filled.

Although the CBI issued a model equal-opportunity programme to all its members in 1979, no monitoring of its implementation had taken place by the end of 1984 and the CBI had no plans to encourage women in management. Nor has the CBI a special committee or paid official dealing with the promotion of women's rights. Indeed, much of employers' association involvement over this issue has been of a negative kind. The CBI and other pressure groups representing small employers have been instrumental in gaining exemptions for small employers from provisions of the various pieces of legislation protecting employed women.[6] With British women more likely than men to be employed in small work-places, a significant number of women workers have been left without benefit of employment protection legislation. The CBI has numerous statutory rights to nominate representatives to public bodies in Britain, one of which is the Equal Opportunities Commission, the agency which has oversight responsibility for sex-equality legislation. CBI representatives there have been known to block anti-discrimination measures which might cause inconvenience to their members (Byrne and Lovenduski, 1978).

Not all business initiatives are negative, however. Some industry groups have taken steps to improve the recruitment of women in male-dominated occupations; for example, the engineering employers have sponsored special apprenticeships for girls through their industrial training board. Generalisations about this area are difficult to make, but it is safe to say that women's access is hampered at all the three stages of qualification, recruitment and promotion, and that their poor representation is a product of the same factors which account for the horizontal and vertical occupational sectorialisation of women in employment.

Indeed, 'first remove' explanation for women's absence from employers' associations is obvious. Women are neither employers nor members of senior management in significant numbers. Whilst educational changes mean that more women are now entering managerial employment, the failure of the associations, particularly the CBI, to recognise the low presence of women as a problem worthy of concern does not augur well for women's prospects in this arena.

Italy

Italy has a range of employers' organisations, the best known of which are Confindustria (Confederazione Generale dell'Industria Italiana), which represents about 53 per cent of Italian companies, and Confapi (Confederazione Italiana della Picolla e Media Industria), which organises a further 15 per cent. Basically, Confindustria represents the larger firms whilst Confapi looks after small and medium-sized industries. Various industries with state participation are organised into Intersind, and commercial, agricultural and craft industries have their own organisations. These are organised along regional and industrial lines and at various levels are major actors in the collective bargaining process. Empirical data on the composition of their committees and boards are scarce, but those which exist indicate that few women hold positions at this level. Of the 600 board, council and commission members of Confindustria, there were in 1983 only 2 women, neither of whom were members of the 11-person board or 23-person executive committee. One women was a member of the 64-strong consultative committee for external affairs and 1 of the 104-member national commission for small industries. There were no women presidents of area associations and only a few women directors of less important associations. Neither Confagricultura nor Confcommucio had any women on their top bodies (De Santis and Zincone, 1983, 5.42).

Absent from the governing bodies of the organisations of either side of industry, Italian women are, in consequence, absent from delegations for collective bargaining, which takes place mainly above company level and is relatively rare at that level or below.

France and Elsewhere

The three main French employers' federations feature a similar absence of women. In the CNPF (Conseil National du Patronat Français) women were 5 (0.8 per cent) of the 556-person general assembly; 4 (1.8 per cent) of the 216-member permanent committee and 1 (1.8 per cent) of the 34-person management team in 1983. The overall representation of women in positions of responsibility in national associations and federations did not appear to go above 3 per cent. Much of that 3 per cent was accounted for by women deputies, secretaries or activists who were given the task of studying women or social problems (Moreau-Bourles and Sineau, 1983, 2.30 to 2.31). In France, as in Britain and Italy, women's underrepresentation in employers' associations may be largely accounted for by the small number who are directors, which in turn reflects structural, cultural and professional obstacles to woman's advancement which are compounded at the point of entry into representative organisations. The pattern is repeated in West Germany, where women are hardly to be found in upper-level business positions and where they comprised 1 per cent of the BDA (board of directors) in 1983. Sweden numbered no women amongst the 460 directors of associations in the Confederation of Swedish Employers in 1982 (Scott, 1982) and women were similarly absent from Finnish Employers' associations throughout the 1970s (Finnish Council for Equality).

The consistency of the pattern of women's absence from employers' associations is not surprising and explanation is not particularly difficult. Qualification for membership is in each case the ability to dispose of a certain amount of industrial power. Channels of access to that position have been closed to women from the outset, and even in the mid-1980s there are few indications that women are beginning to gain entry.

The Absence of Women from the Corporate Channel

Corporate dominance of interest representation has not, apparently, been beneficial to women. Although women are well represented in union hierarchies in the state socialist systems, the power of such associations to influence or affect the composition of political elites is extremely limited. Women there have not colonised a significant channel of access to political power.

In Western Europe the system is differently structured but has the same effect. The evidence presented in this chapter suggests that the process of concertation has compounded the underrepresentation of women in European political elites. The absence of women from important positions in the hierarchies of the economic interest organisations has had consequences in other parts of the political system. Women are underrepresented on the committees and councils which construct union and employers' association policy. Moreover, they are absent from an important pool of eligibles for nomination to state decision-making or advisory bodies. The economic organisations often control the largest number of positions on such bodies and are arguably the most important components of the corporate channel. Their failure to recruit and promote women internally results in an inability to promote them to external bodies. Thus, in creating gateways to governing elites through which men are vastly more likely to be qualified to pass than women, the growth of concertation impedes women's acquisition of political influence.[7] In short, women have not normally benefited from the enhanced position of the organisations of economic interests which increasing corporatism implies.

Notes

1. Unless otherwise indicated, information on the struggle for policy change in Swedish trade unions comes from the account by Hilda Scott (1982) entitled *Sweden's Right to be Human*.
2. Guiseppina De Santis and Giovanna Zincone (1983) are the main source (in English) of information on women in Italian trade unions and unless otherwise indicated are the source for the Italian section of this chapter.
3. Instituto Centrale di Statistica (Central Statistics Institute).
4. By the end of 1982 Luxemburg's OGB-L began to indicate concern, and its women's section issued a memo calling for a greater involvement of women in the working world.
5. Statements based on information supplied to the author by the various London embassies during 1984.
6. Employers of five or fewer in the case of the Sex Discrimination Act of 1975, twenty or fewer in the case of the Employment Act 1980 maternity provisions and twenty or fewer in the case of the unfair dismissal provisions of the Employment Protection (Consolidation) Act have obtained exemptions from certain legal obligations to women employees.
7. A recent study has argued that in countries where corporatism has become legitimate steps are more likely to be taken to correct the problem of women's disadvantageous position in the corporate channel. The example of Norway is cited where a quota system for women on national bodies was introduced to impel nominating organisations to put forward more women, leading to a rise of women's presence on public bodies of from 12 per cent in 1975 to 26.7 per cent in 1981 (Council of Europe, 1984, Part 3).

6 The Political Representation of Women

The immediate consequence of women's low presence in the leadership of political parties and the most important interest organisations is underrepresentation in governing elites. An inverse power pyramid characterises women's standing in the political hierarchies of Europe, where, as elsewhere, Putnam's Law of Increasing Disproportions is in unmistakable evidence. Putnam's Law refers to the disproportionate advantage of male, educated, high status, elite recruits whose presence increases as the political hierarchy is ascended (Putnam, 1976). European political elites are overwhelmingly male. When it comes to representation in government, even small differences between men's and women's political behaviour are transformed into enormous discrepancies. That those discrepancies represent real differences in political power between men and women, that they demonstrate, *inter alia*, the failure of political systems to honour obligations to represent women politically, has been an important issue amongst politically engaged women since the early 1970s.

Do Women Constitute an Interest?

The argument has perhaps been best put by Virginia Sapiro in an essay published in 1981 entitled 'When Are Interests Interesting? The Problem of the Political Representation of Women'. She begins by pointing out that women's political representation was not at issue so long as it was felt that women were represented via male heads of household. Such a view saw women's interests as coincident with a family interest, which was best expressed by the family ruler and head. The realisation of political personhood by women involved the rejection of such arguments. Political rights were achieved by means of a long process of recognition of separate individualities for men and women, however related. The first breakthrough often came in the form of the granting to women of the right to own property, after which it was but a small step to demand credibly, a political equality based on the franchise (Sapiro, 1981, 701). Once it was established that women had a case for demanding political equality, the possibility that they were a group entitled to representation was raised, but not automatically confirmed.

For women to comprise a group which might be represented politically, they must have a particular interest or interests which are capable of being described. More explicitly, writes Sapiro, it is necessary to determine whether women as a group have 'unique politically relevant characteristics, whether they have special interests to which a representative could or should respond'. (1981, 703). Studies of women and other oppressed groups have shown that denial of the means with which to form themselves into an interest organisation is often characteristic of the oppressed state. An array of research provides evidence that women share a distinct social position and set of problems which may be described as a special interest and that this interest has been and continues to be located in the family. The family is now legally comprised of political individuals. These individuals perform gender-differentiated roles based on a division of labour within the family. That division of labour may be deemed to be a basis for defining interests in political life if public policy plays a role in its determination or if it affects objects of public policy and policy debate.

Gender roles and family stratification systems meet such tests – it can be shown that law and public policy both create and reinforce gender differences in matters of property, contract, personal defence, fertility control, civil rights, child-care control and employment and educational opportunities. Social and individual goods are unevenly divided between the sexes. Women have less education, employment and often health. Women are disproportionately numerous in low status positions and disproportionately few in those with high status. In cataloguing these inequalities Sapiro is underlining her point that, whether consciously or not, women have, objectively, interests to be represented.

Representing Women

But who should represent those interests? Is there any reason to suppose that only women may express or respond to women's concerns? There is certainly no guarantee that such concerns will be pressed simply because women are present in the relevant decision-taking bodies. Women's interests are complex and women are often divided over their nature. Men too are divided over political concerns, a phenomenon which is reflected in their numerous presence in deliberative bodies. The diversity of women's concerns would, in fairness, warrant a similarly numerous presence. But it is the gendered division of labour which is crucial to the argument at this point. No one would argue that business, by being engaged in the same process as labour, adequately could represent labour's interests (Sapiro, 1981, 705). Neither will an argument hold that either side of the sexual division of labour is able adequately to represent the other. The core of women's interests is comprised of their disadvantaged position in the division of labour within the family, and for as long as that division persists it is sufficient reason for insisting that women's interests may be represented only by women.

Women in Political Elites

Interest representation takes place in a number of arenas. At national level the most numerous are the legislative assemblies, which, whilst having latterly experienced an undoubted decline in influence, remain important decision-making centres in the liberal democracies and important symbolic arenas in the state socialist systems. At local level, analogous councils, soviets and assemblies perform similar functions. The most important decision-making bodies in contemporary constitutional terms are the national governments at the apex of legislative and administrative institutions. The administrative institutions themselves, in theory only implementors of policy, in practice employ senior civil servants who exercise considerable if discreet influence on public policy and who comprise an important part of a country's ruling elite. It is the administrative institutions in conjunction with the major interest organisations which comprise the corporate channel of elite access. Increasingly, representatives from economic interests and administrative departments meet to advise on and often to make policy decisions. Finally, the judiciary has a considerable discretion in its enforcement of decisions made in the other arenas and must therefore also be included in any discussion of women's role in political elites.

In the European liberal democracies women were less than 10 per cent and often less than 5 per cent of holders of government office by the mid-1980s. In the 10 EEC countries in January 1984, women held 16 of 187 available ministerial posts, but there was only one woman head of government. Each country had at least one woman minister, but none had more than four. Throughout the European liberal democracies, in the national parliaments women's shares of seats ranged from as low as 3.5 per cent in Britain to 31 per cent in Finland but, except in the Scandinavian countries, was below 15 per cent. Amongst the EEC states, all except Ireland returned higher proportions of women in their delegations to the European Parliament at Strasbourg than were present in their national parliaments, reflecting the relatively lesser powers of the European than the national assemblies rather than any manifestation of a link between internationalism and the promotion of women. Trends in the presence of women in civil services varied, but a gender-based disadvantage was present in all of the countries for which data were available, and a similar pattern was apparent in the judiciary. Trends in both civil service and judicial employment suggest that the underrepresentation of women in these arenas may decrease somewhat in some countries, but nowhere is the dominance of men under any real threat.

In the state socialist systems (in which politics and administration are fused) women are better represented in the symbolic governmental elites than in the effective or Communist Party elites. Although present in higher proportions in governing elites than in the liberal democracies, women have rarely been heads of state or government, or ministers. But women are usually more than 20 per cent of members of the legislature and, indeed, are often more than 30 per cent of deputies (Wolchik, 1981, 258). In both types of system women are more frequently found in the deliberative than in the executive bodies and play a greater role in leadership at the local than at the national level.

To explain women's absence from political elites we must first draw upon the same body of research we used to account for gender-based participation differences in Chapter 4. Participatory differences, themselves related to the sexual division of labour, must inevitably be reflected in gender-differentiated elite access. But the known participatory differences between the sexes cannot alone account for what are enormous disparities in elite membership. Other factors must be coming into play at this point, and additional explanations must therefore be sought.

A concept particularly useful to the explanation of women's virtual absence from positions of political power is that of 'social capital'. 'Social capital' is a term which has been used to mean social knowledge, contacts, privileged access to culturally valued qualifications and social skills which are of value in the various winning strategies used by competitors in a particular social field. Networks of power relations are characterised by their own rules of competition, conflicts, strategies, interests and profits. Social capital is the crucial ingredient in the continuing struggle for success and rewards in which elite aspirants must engage. It is used for the purchase of status, authority and power of various kinds and is both expandable and convertible. As conceptualised by Helga Nowotny (who borrows the term from Pierre Bordieu), the rules for the conversion of social capital differ for men and women. Women, she argues, have been limited both in being able to accumulate only certain types of social capital, which are in turn convertible only into certain other types. Stretching her point a little, she asserts that the private sphere into which women have been relegated offers them only emotional capital. Emotional capital consists of knowledge, skills, contacts and relations which obtain in networks partly held by affective ties. Women have been able to accumulate emotional capital and build up positions of dominance, but their reach has not normally extended beyond the private sphere. Emotional capital is not normally convertible into economic capital and tends therefore to be invested in other members of the family. On the rare occasions that women do accumulate social capital, they lack the networks which enable its conversion into power. Only when women move out of the private sphere can they convert social capital (Nowotny, 1981, 147–8). The kind of social capital necessary for access to a decision-making elite at national level is available only to a very few individuals. Those who accumulate sufficient of that capital will be those with background characteristics which are common amongst elite decision-makers. Elites tend if at all possible to reproduce themselves, to recruit in their own image (Putnam, 1976, *passim*). Hence, a history of male-dominated elites has been more than enough to ensure a future of male-dominated elites.

At a less abstract level, Epstein (1981, 3–5) lists seven views on why women are so rarely members of political elites. (1) Women are inherently incapable of being assertive and dominant, a view held by relatively few individuals of either sex. (2) Social imperatives direct women from the public sphere towards family-centered priorities. (3) Women's gender-associated duties create time and role strains which impede participation in public life. (4) Women's differential early socialisation militates against their assumption of the sorts of demanding and rewarding careers assumed by men. (5) Women have, and indeed may be locked into, a separate culture which excludes the economic, political and professional worlds, which are the focus of male culture. (6) The existence of a few sex-stereotyped opportunity structures account for women's acquisition of some decision-making roles but delimit the areas in which these are held, thus restricting their transferability. (7) Prejudice and discrimination limit women's participation in elites. The first five of these are variations on the theme of differential socialisation in accordance with the division of labour within the family and its concomitant sex roles. The sixth and the seventh views might be regarded as elucidations of the precise form of that differential socialisation. Epstein's own view is that women's poor showing in elites is to be explained in social structure terms, in particular by women's lesser access to the resources of education, opportunity and finance. As a result, those few women who do obtain elite entry are less qualified than men and less of a threat to power-holders, and are, incidentally, not in a good position to pave the way for other women. They possess insufficient social capital.

The lack of formal status prerequisites is a significant disadvantage to women elite aspirants. Randall (1982, 88–90) writes that elite entry normally requires that criteria of eligibility, selectability and functional usefulness be met. Recruitment is a protracted process which involves passing through stages of certification, selection and role assignment. Certification involves gaining entry to the pool of eligibles; that is, achieving recognition of one's qualifications. Eligibility criteria are institution-specific and may include an element of demand for women as well as various formal and informal criteria. Role assignment is self-explanatory; however, it may have a feedback effect whereby women assigned to less prestigious elite positions are accumulating concomitantly less social capital, hence perpetuating patterns of relative disadvantage and marginalisation.

Another constraint on women's elite entry arising from more formal barriers is their lack of access to important established informal networks which are known to play important parts in career establishment. There is a direct relationship between the acquisition of formal power and participation in informal networks. Where women have been excluded from the various educational channels and contact-making milieu, they have been unable to form or to take part in such networks to the same extent as men (Epstein, 1981, 11).

In Europe virtually all of the obstacles barring women from elite positions are informal or structural rather than legal. The obsta-

cles which persist are those of vested interest and the obstruction
implicit in patriarchy and male dominance. Vicky Randall (1982,
92) is particularly trenchant on this point. Listing impediments to
women in increasing order of their dependence upon male chauvinism she reports:

> first and by no means least important . . . is the way that at each level, political
> advancement requires appropriate political or institutional experience. To get
> to the top you have to begin climbing early enough to leave yourself time.
> More clearly related to male chauvinist assumptions are the ethos and organi-
> sation of political activity at each level which reflect the styles and convenience
> of men . . . Finally, the direct expression of male prejudice and power is
> outright discrimination.

Expositions such as Nowotny's, Epstein's and Randall's so vividly
describe the impediments to positions of political power that it
becomes surprising that any women manage to jump all of the
hurdles. Yet some do. Whilst there are no European states in
which women appear in elites in proportion to their share of the
population, there are none in which there are no women at all in
positions of power.

Each country boasts at least a few women senior politicians.
What kind of women are they? Nowotny, writing about Austrian
women, asserts that such inroads as women have been able to
make in the public sphere have been the result of what she calls the
publicisation of the private sphere; that is, the transfer of more
and more functions to public institutions and to professionals.
Moving in harness with this trend, women have carried norms and
values as well as patterns of behaviour developed for the private
sphere into public arenas.

Randall is more straighforward, offering a three-part typology
of successful women politicians. There are, first, male equivalents,
women who have often obtained political office through relationship with politically prominent men and who have traditional
assumptions about women's roles. Second, there are the women
who have come to politics after raising children and who have no
background in the 'eligibility enhancing' professions. Often
women's rights advocates, they are seldom politically ambitious
and in any case severely disadvantaged by comparison to often
younger and better-qualified male colleagues. Third, there are the
new women professional politicians who may well share feminist
values and who will seek a political career rather than just a
political role (Randall, 1982, 105). Each of these types is identifiable in the European politics of the 1980s.

Receptivity to women's elite membership varies considerably by national culture with such factors as ideology, religious tradition and family structure playing an important part. Economic and social differences are also important variables. Levels of employment, economic and demographic goals and class structures all have a bearing on the extent to, and manner in which women are rewarded by inclusion in elites. Each of the accounts which follows is an account of overwhelming male dominance, but each is also a description of distinctive and unique methods of establishing and maintaining that dominance. When all is said and done, if women's political subordination is the result primarily of one cause, the division of labour within the family, it has nonetheless appeared in an astonishing variety of guises and forms.

Britain

The British political culture, entwined as it is with an unwritten constitution, encourages acceptance of a considerable degree of government secrecy, which compounds a tradition of covert rules of elite entry. These, combined with the prevalence of implied criteria of 'soundness', particularly enable elites to recruit in their own image and discourage access to high positions by new categories of aspirants simply by virtue of the fact that they are new category of aspirants. Women are in this view, simply the largest of the groups to be so denied.

The inclusion of women is in fact greater in the numerical channel than in the corporate or various appointive arenas. But the post-suffrage electoral history of women in the UK has not, on the indicator of successful parliamentary candidacy, been a particularly bright one. Women have never been as much as 5 per cent of the membership of the House of Commons, and women MPs have suffered higher rates of turnover, lower levels of education and have been older than their male colleagues upon first entering the house. Admitted to the House of Lords only in 1958, women have been a small fraction of the membership of around 1,200 (between 5 and 6 per cent; see Drewry and Brock, 1983). As we have seen, political parties at constituency level are reluctant to select women candidates for winnable seats. That reluctance reflects local cultural factors and is subject to considerable regional variation. Women are more likely to be candidates in England and Scotland, their proportions falling sharply in Wales and more sharply still for Northern Ireland. Women are more

likely to be nominated for winnable seats in the English constituencies. The process of selection is a private one, with the relative
independence of constituency parties in nominating meaning that
there is no way of estimating how many women who initially put
themselves forward fail to be selected. Nor do we have data on
their backgrounds and qualifications. Vallance (1979) reports that
some women MPs have felt that constituency selection committees were biased against women candidates, but her data are
inconclusive.

In 1979, the general election in which Margaret Thatcher
became the UK's first woman Prime Minister returned fewer
women to Parliament than at any election since 1951. Yet at 8 per
cent of the total, more women had been candidates than at any
previous election. In all 8 Conservative and 11 Labour women
were elected, less than 3 per cent of 635 MPs. Apart from the
Prime Minister, only one woman was included in her cabinet
during her first term of office, Baroness Young, promoted in
September 1981. In the general election four years later in June
1983, women were more than 10 per cent of candidates but only
3.5 per cent of elected MPs. Thirteen Conservative women and
ten Labour women were elected in a landslide Conservative
victory. Three prominent women parliamentarians (Shirley Williams, SDP; Joan Lestor, Labour; Shirley Summerskill, Labour)
lost their seats. The Prime Minister, not an enthusiastic promoter
of women, appointed three women to her government, but none
to her cabinet. By the first cabinet reshuffle of her second term,
Mrs Thatcher's cabinet of twenty-two members contained no
women apart from herself. Her record in this respect has been
completely consistent. When women have been in the cabinet it
has been in the predictable positions of education, health and
consumer affairs. Apart from Mrs Thatcher herself, only two
women, Barbera Castle and Margaret Bondfield, have ever
broken that pattern. Both were Ministers of Labour and Barbara
Castle also served as Minister of Transport. Within Parliament,
women have been better distributed through the committee
system than their cabinet positions would suggest, and whilst
cooperation across party lines on women's issues has been non-
existent, Labour women have organised to promote and protect
women's rights (Vallance, 1979; Hills, 1981a).

At the level of local government it is also normally the political
parties which control the nominations for winnable seats. Few are
won by independents. In contrast to many European countries,
there is no integrated regional tier of government in the UK, nor is

there anything which resembles such a tier in its component parts. Political control and administration are highly centralised, with local finance closely controlled by a centre increasingly concerned to extend its powers. Nevertheless, local and county councillors dispose of measurable power and seats are often sought after, both as valuable political training grounds and as posts attractive in their own right. Comprehensive data on nominations at this level are not available, but scattered evidence suggests that women are nominated in approximately the same proportions as they are elected. Bristow (1978) found that for the 1976–7 county council elections women were 17 per cent of candidates and 16 per cent of councillors. In Scotland, however, in the 1982 regional council elections 25 per cent of women but 41 per cent of men who were nominated were elected (Bochel and Denver, 1982).

The requirement for geographical mobility is undoubtedly a constraint upon the participation of most women in national political office. One would expect, therefore, to find a higher proportion of women in local-elected office, and this is in fact the case. In the local government structure which existed in 1983,[1] women were 14.4 per cent of county councillors in England and Wales, 11.1 per cent of regional councillors in Scotland and 7.9 per cent of Northern Ireland district councillors (Corcoran and Lovenduski, 1983). In each case women were better represented at local than at national level, but in no case was that representation in proportion either to their presence in the population or to their known membership of political parties. And strong regional variations become more apparent when the data for England and Wales are disaggregated. In England in 1983 women were 19 per cent of councillors in the Shire counties, 13.5 per cent in the Metropolitan counties and 14.1 per cent in the Greater London Council (GLC). Women were only 11 per cent of councillors in Wales. The expected inverse power pyramid is also apparent at local level. The proportion of women councillors declines as each level of the hierarchy is ascended. In 1976–77 only 10 per cent of county council committee chairs in England and Wales were held by women and women were only 3 per cent of council chairpersons, vice-chairpersons and convenors or leaders. In 1977–78 the figures were 11 per cent and 5 per cent, respectively (Bristow, 1980). In 1983 in the Shire counties women were 12.2 per cent of committee chairpersons and 13.3 per cent of council chairpersons, vice-chairpersons and leaders. In the Metropolitan councils women were 5.7 per cent of committee chairpersons but held no leadership posts. In Wales women were 2.8 per cent of committee

Table 6.1: *UK non-industrial Home civil service: staff in post in open structure, administration group and all non-industrial grades, by sex*

	Men	Women	Total	Per cent of women
Open-structure levels:	*663*	*31*	*694*	*4.5*
Permanent secretary	37	–	37	—
Deputy secretary	129	5	134	3.7
Under secretary	497	26	523	3.7
General Category				
Administration Group:	*99,830*	*131,232*	*230,462*	*56.9*
Assistant secretary	977	66	1,043	6.3
Senior principal	623	12	635	1.9
Principal	3,705	409	4,114	9.9
Senior executive officer	6,820	536	7,356	7.3
Higher executive officer D	215	8	303	29.0
Higher executive officer	18,087	4,150	22,237	18.7
Administration trainee	118	58	176	33.0
Executive officer	26,514	17,807	44,321	40.2
Clerical officer	27,640	57,901	85,505	67.7
Clerical assistant	14,567	50,205	64,772	77.5
All Non-industrial grades	*272,133*	*241,928*	*514,061*	*47.1*

Source: Civil service statistics, 1983.

chairpersons and 2 per cent of leaders. No women were leaders of the GLC and only one woman (6.3 per cent) chaired a GLC standing committee. A gendered subject-specialisation was evident at this level, with women committee chairpersons concentrated in education and the social services and only a few chairing the powerful policy committees.

In the appointed public administration institutions women are the vast majority of holders of the routine clerical posts but are rare at the highest levels. At the beginning of 1983, when women were 47.1 per cent of 'non-industrial' Home civil servants, there were no women permanent secretaries and only 5 (of 134) deputy secretaries and 26 (of 523) under-secretaries were women (Table 6.1). Thus, women were less than 5 per cent of senior civil servants. Recruitment patterns in the British civil service are known to be non-discriminatory in that they have employed women in the higher grades (i.e. those which lead to senior levels) in proportion to their numbers in the qualified population since the beginning of the 1970s (Brimelow, 1981). But women do not appear to make the same progress as men and are dogged by the employment problems associated with domestic constraints and male-defined measures of career progress (Corcoran and Lovenduski, 1983).

If it is employment conditions which impede the promotion of women civil servants, it is political factors which explain their low presence in the British corporate bodies. Most of the 'corporate' or 'public' bodies in Britain as elsewhere reflect tripartite or modified bipartite arrangements whereby the commission or council of each contains trade union and employer association nominees, independent members appointed by the relevant minister and government representative supplied by the civil service in the form of servicing functionaries. Women's share of such bodies in 1982 ranged from 2 per cent of Department of Industry associated committees to 30 per cent of those connected to the Home Office. Normally, women are ministerial nominees as so few are available in the upper echelons of labour and employer associations. They are dependent, as it were, on the numerical channel for access to the corporate channel. 'Independent' members of such bodies are usually selected by ministers from a 'great and good' list compiled by the civil service (although self-nomination does occur). Appointment is a rather covert procedure. Qualifications are not easy to identify but expertise or a reputation for expertise in a particular area is important. Those with relevant work, union, legal academic or business experience tend to be men, however, and the kinds of experience which women possess have not been valued by those making appointments.

Entry to the judiciary in Britain is normally via the attainment of qualifications and experience in the legal profession, which is divided into two branches, each with its own professional body and system of certification. Progression within each branch differs. Barristers are qualified for all levels of the judiciary whilst solicitors may only rise to the position of circuit court judge. The gateway to the judiciary is thus the Bar. Although women qualified as barristers and solicitors in increasing numbers throughout the 1970s, comparatively few had become queens counsels (QCs) – the group of barristers from whom judges in the High Court and above are chosen – by 1983. In England and Wales women were 11 per cent of barristers but only 3 per cent of QCs; in Northern Ireland they were 12.4 per cent of barristers but none were QCs, and in Scotland women were 6.7 per cent of advocates (the

Table 6.2 *Women in the judiciary in England and Wales (1977 and 1983)*

	1977 Total	Women	Per cent	1983 Total	Women	Per cent
Lords of appeal in ordinary	9	0	0	9	0	0
Lords justices of appeal	16	0	0	18	0	0
High Court judges	72	2	2.8	77 (74)	3 (3)	3.9 (4.1)
Circuit judges	285	7	2.5	344 (332)	12 (12)	3.5 (3.6)
Recorders	370	8	2.2	466 (454)	12 (20)	2.6 (4.4)
County court registrars	133	1	3.0	163 (161)	2 (2)	1.2 (1.2)
Stipendiary magistrates, Metropolitan	41	1	2.4	46	4	8.7
Stipendiary magistrates, provincial	11	0	0	10	0	0
Chairmen of industrial tribunals	72	2	2.8	175	12	6.9
Employment appeal tribunal (lay members)	32	4	12.5	41	8	19.5

Source: Bar list, 1982; lord chancellor's office, May 1983   lord chancellor's figures in parentheses (see Corcoran and Lovenduski, 1983).

Scottish equivalent of barristers). Hence, women are a rather small proportion of the pool of juridical eligibles. Table 6.2 shows that they comprise a still smaller proportion of those who obtain senior appointments, a maximum of 4.1 per cent of High Court judges in 1983. Although increases in the proportions of women judges, magistrates and tribunal chairs are apparent in the five-year period from 1977 to 1983, these increases were very small at the senior levels.

QCs and judges are appointed by the lord chancellor, a cabinet member and therefore a political appointee. Nominations take place through a series of undisclosed channels and it is likely that the lord chancellor consults colleagues and senior judges and for certain appointments, the prime minister. All judges except lay magistrates must be lawyers, and High Court judges must have had ten or more years of experience at the bar. Industrial tribunal chairs must have had seven or more years of experience as either barristers or solicitors. No other training is required. Application for some judicial posts is permissible but unusual. The application form requires the provision of the name of a judge as a referee. Lay magistrates may be the nominees of political parties or they may be self-nominated, and it is at this level that women are most evident in the judiciary, at about 10,000 of 26,000 in 1984. At the higher, paid, full-time qualified levels of stipendary magistrate and above, they are rarely to be found.

The important characteristics of access to the judiciary are the general absence of criteria for entry and the secrecy of nomination and appointment processes, neither of which appear to favour women. In Britain, to varying degrees the senior civil service, the corporate bodies and the judiciary exhibit the characteristics of closed oligarchic groups. Their procedures of appointment and promotion are based upon imperfectly understood implicit qualifications enabling them to recruit in their own image. They have been relatively resistent to reform, a product not of malevolence but of British tradition in such matters, which has been characterised by a reluctance to adopt formal criteria of training and certification for membership of many of its most powerful bodies. Such a tradition has served the male establishment well.

France

The French elite has been more receptive to women than the British in recent years.[2] There, a rather different set of institutional arrangements has tended to place more women in political office at national level but fewer at local level. The general elections to the Chamber of Deputies in June 1981 returned a legislature 5.9 per cent of whose members were women. The Senate, elected by indirect suffrage contained 3.2 per cent women. At departmental level the Conseils Generaux were comprised of 3.8 per cent women members following the 1982 elections, whilst at communal level Conseils Municipaux elected in March 1983 consisted of 14 per cent of women and were the electoral assemblies in which women's representation was highest. As at this level in Britain, women's presence diminished as the hierarchy was ascended. Hence, women were less than 4 per cent of maires. But the result of 1983 municipal elections amounted to an overall increase of 66 per cent for women councillors. The percentage increase was greatest in the small towns and villages and in towns of under 3,500 (from 6.8 per cent to 12.9 per cent) and in towns of from 3,500 to 9,000 (from 13.2 per cent to 21.1 per cent) (Sineau, 1983). Improvements such as these are recent, however, and French women have been a perpetual minority in the numerical channel, a status which has impeded their assumption of leadership roles and channelled them into the least prestigious of available posts. In Parliament the presidency (i.e. speakership) as well as *questeurs*, chairs of political groups and permanent committees all tend to be given to men. In 1983 women were three of twenty-two members of the Chamber of Deputies' president's office. They were one of six vice-presidents and two of twelve secretaries. Of the six permanent committees women held one vice-chairpersonship of twenty and four secretaryships of twenty. The office of the Senate president was staffed by sixteen men. The proportion of women senators declined after the autumn 1983 elections after which they held 9 of 318 seats (previously 10 of 305). Women hold only two official positions on Senate committees, both in the stereotyped areas of cultural or social affairs (*Women of Europe*, No. 33). The same subject specialisation is present at parliamentary level, where women's committee assignments are mainly in the committee on cultural, family and social affairs.

The 1974 creation by Giscard of a secretary of state level post on women's affairs increased the number of positions at government level which might be deemed suitable for women. This post was later promoted to a delegacy and then a junior ministry and for a time upgraded by the Socialists to a full cabinet ministry. On the whole the women who are appointed to positions of government have been appointed in posts such as social or cultural affairs.

Under the Socialists that pattern has begun to change. The three Mauroy governments between 1981 and 1984 contained up to six women, two of whom headed departments directly concerned with women's affairs. Exceptionally, Mme Edith Cresson was Minister of Agriculture from May 1981 to March 1983, a ministry considered to be a masculine one in France. In the 1984 cabinet reshuffle which followed the ascent of M Laurent Fabius as prime minister all six women who served in the third Mauroy government were retained and one, Mme Edwige Avice, was appointed secretary of state for defence, the first women to hold such a position. Of the other five, three were given ministries: Edith Cresson became minister for industrial redeployment and foreign trade, Georgina Dufoix became minister of social affairs and national solidarity, and Huguette Bouchardeau became minister for the environment. Yvette Roudy retained her post as minister delegate with responsibility for women's rights and Catherine Lalumiere became secretary of state for consumer affairs. Hence, three years into the Socialist government women were three of sixteen ministers of state, one of six ministers delegate and two of twenty secretaries of state. Women were just over 14 per cent of members of the government, a share unprecedented outside of the Nordic countries, Austria and the Netherlands (Ambassade de France à Londres, Dec./Lon./IX/84).

With the ascent of the Socalists women have also become more present in minsters private offices (*cabinets*). Posts in these offices are particularly important to those making political or administrative careers in France. Since 1981 women have increased their presence in these pivotal institutions which share in the daily business of government, have superior access to information and considerable influence on policy-making. Ministerial *cabinets* are unusual in that neither public competition nor seniority play any formal part in recruitment, which is entirely at the discretion of the minister. Informal qualifications tend to favour men, however. In June 1981, women were 15 per cent of members of ministers' private offices. Normally, they were not to be found in the most senior positions. In mid-1982 only four women headed the private offices of their minister, the rest were concentrated amongst parliamentary liaison officers, attaches and so on. Predictably the most feminised *cabinet* at that time was at the ministry of women's rights, four of whose six members were women, although the *directeur* was a man. Women were four of eight members of the office of the minister of consumer affairs, three of six members of the leisure ministry, three of ten members of the health ministry, three of nine members of the professional education ministry and two of ten members of the labour ministry (abolished by the third Mauroy government). The private offices of the Ministers of the interior, defence, education and agriculture remained male bastions, with their rare women members normally on the lowest rung of the career ladder. The most senior women in such positions in 1984 were concentrated in the social ministries, a pattern which is also true of the assignments of the private staff of the president, five of whose forty-five private office members were women in 1983.

Although the principle of sex equality has been officially asserted in the French civil service since 1946 and residual legal discrimination was removed by statute in May 1982, a wide gap between formal and substantive opportunities is apparent. Overall, women account for 50 per cent of civil service personnel but are mainly concentrated in the clerical and routine grades. At only 19 per cent of employees in administrative posts, women are mostly to be found at the lower ends of their scale. At senior civil service level, and particularly in the prestigious Grand Corps de l'Etat, Cours des Comptes and Inspecteurs des Finances, women fare rather worse. They were, in 1983, 11.5 per cent of civil administrators and 5.4 per cent of the Grands Corps. The financial inspectorate had only been opened to women in 1975. At Higher Central Administrative level women hold only 17 per cent of 'positions of responsibility' and 2.4 per cent of government appointed posts. Hence, there were six women at permanent under-secretary or similar level, three were rectors (regional heads of education), three were ambassadors and one was a prefect. Gendered subject-specialisation is characteristic and women are to be found mainly in the predictable specialisms of cultural and social areas, and largely absent from technical posts. Government discretion over senior appointments has not been used to benefit women and norms of length of service and mobility for senior appointments tend to favour men. Recruitment to the higher civil service via the Grandes Écoles has virtually guaranteed an imbalance between the sexes. The École Nationale d'Administration (ENA), coeducational since its establishment in 1945, remained until the 1970s an enclave, 90 per cent of whose students were men. As late as 1983 men were 75 per cent of its students. At the Polytechnique, the most prestigious of the Grandes Écoles from which students automatically enter the military, the situation is worse, even more imbalanced. The coming to power of the Left in 1981 marked the beginning of attempts to break the hold of such training and career requirements, and some effort has been made to enhance the career prospects of women civil servants. It will be some time, however, before the effects of such programmes becomes apparent at senior level.

The coexistence of two parallel systems of higher education in France is an important factor in the determination of elite memberships. Those who hold power come, not out of the universities, but out of the Grandes Écoles. A system of state selection of elites operates, in which a competitive ethos and long periods of preparation for examinations tends to disadvantage women, who have poorer access than men to the best preparation classes. Where access to preparation has been equalised, as for the entrance examination for the École Nationale de la Magistrature (ENM), women fare at least as well as men in the examination. Recruitment which favours women is, in such a system, recruitment which is based on the typical university syllabus.

By comparison to Britain, the presence of women in the French judiciary is high. In the administrative legal system, judges in the administrative courts and the Conseil d'Etat are recruited essentially via ENA, which reflects the prevailing gender bias in the civil service. But in the ordinary legal system, on average, their presence is 30 per cent, albeit with the expected proportionate fall-off as the hierarchy is ascended (Table 6.3). Judges are civil servants in France and recruited upon qualification into a recognisable career structure based largely upon competitive examinations. In 1983 at the lower levels the proportion of women was as high as 42 per cent in Paris, reflecting the great increase in women's entry into the École Nationale de la Magistrature over the ten previous years. Similar proportions of women are to be found in the Tribunaux de Grande Instance (the basic unit of French justice, similar to the British crown courts) in Paris. Women were 12 per cent of judges in the courts of appeal and 11.7 per cent of those in the Cour de Cassation, where Simone Rozes became the first woman presiding judge in 1983. Smaller numbers at the higher levels maybe explained by the late opening of the judiciary to women and the fact that women have not yet percolated through to the top. The feminisation of the French judiciary has been a phenomenon of the 1970s and 1980s and represents a remarkable achievement for French women. Their progress has not, however, been uniformly welcomed by the male legal establishment and barriers to promotion remain. For example, the prestigious constitutional council of nine judges has yet to number a woman among its members. Guardian of the Fifth Republic constitution, this was

Table 6.3: *Women in the French judiciary (1983)*

	Men	Women	Per cent Women
Cassation	136	18*	11.7
Courts of appeal	581	79	11.9
Tribunaux de Grande Instance, Paris	243	180	42.9
All judiciary	3,846	1,685	30.5

Source: Moreau-Bourles and Sineau, 1983, Table 2.15.
*Plus Simone Rozes, who became presiding judge in late 1983.

the court which declared unconstitutional the statute ordering that not more than 80 per cent of candidates in communal elections should be of one sex in April 1982 and in effect put a stop to government efforts to establish quotas for women in the numerical channel. Widespread suggestions that the time had clearly come to break the male stronghold in this council were ignored in its triennial renewal in February 1983.

The Economic and Social Council (ESC), the appointment procedures of which are representative of French corporate bodies, contained 14 women amongst its 200 members in 1983. ESC members are nominated by various professional, economic and social bodies and the government. Of the fourteen women serving in 1983, six had been nominated as part of the forty-five-member trade union delegation and five by the government. Women were one of twenty-seven of the private industry nominees, a pattern which more or less reflects the presence of women in senior positions in the major economic associations. By contrast 85 per cent of the membership of the rather more marginal and woman-centred Comité du travail feminin were women.

The pattern in France then has been one in which progress made by women in the numerical channel has been increasingly overshadowed by very substantial gains in the administration, the judiciary and the government. Whilst women have not held the most powerful positions in any of these arenas, their proportionate sphere of appointments by 1984 was substantially higher than any scrutiny of the electoral channel would have enabled us to predict. Given the relative weakness of its feminist movement, the promotion of women by French governing elites is not easy to understand. It is difficult to find evidence of the mass pressure for women's political equality which would explain what appears to be a competitive bidding by party leaders for women's support. Despite its revolutionary image, French political traditions have been inhospitable to genuine mass movements, and its political leadership has been notably elitist. The political climate is, however one in which intellectual considerations carry some weight. It may therefore be the case that the intellectual force of its feminist movement has been sufficient to alter practices of elite recruitment. This raises the question of why, in a country in which women's access to elite positions has increased steadily in appointive arenas, has their progress been so slow in the numerical channel. Moreau-Burles and Sineau believe that the French electoral system has been particularly unfavourable to women and find a strict correlation between the reintroduction of the first-past-the-post system in 1958 and a decline in the proportion of women National Assembly candidates. They argue that the method of election which takes place in small constituencies encourages the establishment of direct links between representative and elector. Through the practice of *cumul des mandats*, widely sanctioned by French law, electoral fiefdoms are created whereby individuals gain a monopoly of positions. This is especially evident in the simultaneous holding of the post of mayor and deputy for a town. In the Senate a system of indirect elections giving particular weight to local office-holders in an electoral college aggravates this effect as does the long (nine-year) period of office holding. In both the Senate and the National Assembly increasing the presence of women must proceed through a feminisation of local elites. Hence, a legal limitation on the political *cumul des mandats* might, as one of its effects, produce an increase in the number of women in elected office in France, simply by virtue of the fact that the number of available places would be increased.

Italy

It is party politics which provide much of the explanation for the relative absence of Italian women from political elites.[3] As most women legislators have been PCI delegates, the proportions of women in inevitably Christian Democrat dominated governments has had to be drawn from a small pool by a ruling elite which has not prioritised the political promotion of women.

Parliamentary election is probably the most significant opportunity for lateral entry into Italian political careers and is also probably the most meaningful political career gateway. In 1983 women were 66 of the 952 members of both houses of the Italian Parliament, 4.1 per cent of senators and 7.9 per cent of deputies. As in France and Britain, the trend of parliamentary represen-tation has fluctuated: in 1948 women were 7.7 per cent of *deputate*, in 1968, 2.8 per cent and in 1976, 8.5 per cent. In the Senate a trend of slow steady growth from a proportion of 0.9 per cent in 1948 has been apparent. The first woman to become a vice-chairperson of the chamber was elected to that post in 1963 and Nilde Jotte became the first woman to chair the assembly in 1978, a post in which she was reconfirmed in 1983. No woman has ever chaired the Senate. Women legislators hold relatively few com-mittee positions, but these are comparatively well distributed by subject area. Significant is the fact that the majority of women deputies are PCI members a party which takes a delegate view of its MPs and therefore normally rotates its representatives in office so that no parliamentarian may gain a position independent of the party. This practice ensures that the maximum number of members may gain parliamentary experience (Wertman, 1977). The sensitivity to women's issues shown by the party from the 1970s onwards has meant that women became less subject to the rotation policy than they had been. The PCI background of women legislators also means that most are professional poli-ticians with a background of party and UDI work, and, especially in the early years of the republic, many of the women had achieved a notoriety of their own as a result of their resistance activities.

The fact that the PCI has never been a party of government in Italy is probably part of the reason why so few women have held government positions. The other parties provide significantly fewer eligible women. Hence, even where the will to promote women exists, there are relatively few suitable candidates avail-able. Only five women held ministerial posts in the more than forty Italian governments formed between 1945 and 1984. Although from 1951 onwards several held positions at secretary of state level, usually at least one and perhaps two per government, it was not until 1976 that the first woman minister was appointed. Tina Anselmi (Christian Democrat) was appointed employment minister after three years as under-secretary in the same ministry. Other ministries held by women have been education and health. Women ministers have been sufficiently rare that it could not be said that the habit of including one woman in each cabinet has been established. Almost all of the women who have held office at government level by 1984 were Christian Democrats with an occasional Socialist and one Republican. All of the women who have become ministers have been particularly competent in their area of expertise. Careers in Italian government normally follow a fixed pattern whereby one does not achieve ministerial status before having been an under-secretary and under-secretaryships normally come only after a second term of office has been won. In addition, ministerial appointment is linked to preference votes which may be achieved as a result of the enhancement of electability an under-secretaryship brings. Ministerial eligibility then depends upon reaching the position of under-secretary. Whilst men occasionally have alternative power bases, normally evident in lateral entry, women are dependent upon party promotion to join the pool of eligibles. Rarely are women more than 3 to 4 per cent of under-secretaries and rare too is their presence in ministerial secretariats. In 1983, the Craxi government appointed one woman minister (of thirty) and two women under-secretaries (of fifty-eight). Franca Fallucci became education minister and Susanna Agnelli and Paola Cavigliasso became secretaries of state in the foreign affairs and health ministries.

In contrast to many countries, the presence of Italian women in local and regional government is often less than at central level. The average proportion elected to the regional councils by 1983 was 5.5 per cent, at which time women held about 3.8 per cent of heads of department positions. Only one regional council is chaired by a woman (Tuscany) and only one regional cabinet is presided over by a woman (Abruzzo). Four women hold vice-presidencies and eight departments were led by women, two of which were in housing and two in social security. In the same year women were 8.3 per cent of councillors of the ten largest cities, and approximately 9.6 per cent of the city heads of department posts were held by women, reflecting perhaps the dominance of the Left in Italian city government.

There were no women in the Italian Constitutional Court by the end of 1983. Constitutional Court members are chosen by judges, including retired judges, university law professors and lawyers with at least twenty years practical experience. Five are appointed by a joint parliamentary sitting, five by the president of the republic and five by the top-level judiciary. Access to the judiciary is via competitive state examination, which is restricted to university law graduates. The 1982 examinations were taken by 2,569 women and 3,469 men; 66 women and 107 men passed it, success rates of 2.7 per cent for women and 3.1 per cent for men. The judicial career was not opened to women until 1963, and this is reflected in the small proportions of women in the Italian magistracy. At the end of 1983 women held 642 of 7,354 positions (8.7 per cent) and were concentrated at the lower levels of the hierarchy. There were three women in the Supreme Court of Cassation, six in the appeal courts and one deputy-general attorney was a woman.

Public administration positions are possibly less meaningful in Italy than in other European countries as an overly hierarchic and schlerotic organisation leads to responsibilities for the same subject being duplicated and dispersed. However, in a nation where government instability is the norm, the civil service is an important locus of continuity. Entry at managerial level takes place after state examinations, which are open to university graduates. The examination favours students who have read law, political science or economics and those with the best results attend the Public Administration High School (Scuola Superiore di Pubblica Amministrazionc), which was established after the 1968 upheavals in the universities and virtually eliminated required components on degree courses, enabling each student to construct an individual study plan.

By the end of the 1970s women were more than 50 per cent of those entering the school and public administration has become more feminised. Excluding school teachers, women were 37.5 per cent of administrators in 1983. In addition, women are taking up increasing shares of the places in university faculties which trained prospective civil servants, and by 1980 were 34.8 per cent of law graduates, 35.4 per cent of political science graduates and 24.2 per cent of economics graduates. However, at the higher levels of the service women were less in evidence. At 39.3 per cent of staff employees in 1983 women held 18.5 per cent of management posts and only 5.8 per cent of the highest executive posts.

In the corporate bodies women's presence reflected their holdings of positions in the relative interest organisations and in the parties. Hence, only two of the eighty members of the important National Council for Economy and Labour were women in 1983. In the various committees, councils and commissions established in conjunction with the ministry of employment and social security, women's share of positions averaged 8.2 per cent, ranging from no positions on the committee for the defence of workers dismissed for political reasons to 46 per cent of the central commission for cottage industries and 33.3 per cent of the commission for the handicapped.

The dependence of Italian women on the numerical channel to

achieve elite membership is at least as great and perhaps greater than that of British women. Party influence is enhanced by a system of proportional representation and parties could, if they wished, promote women. But although some of the smaller parties and the PCI have undertaken such promotion, the Christian Democrats, who have dominated every government since the present republic was established and led all but one, had by 1983 shown little inclination to admit women into the nation's ruling elite.

West Germany

Except in 1957, when women were 10.7 per cent of candidates returned to the *Bundestag*, women have always been less than 10 per cent of West German legislators.[4] In 1983 an electorate consisting of 23.4 million women and 19.8 million men elected a legislature 90.3 per cent of whose members were men. At government level only one woman, Dorothea Wilms, was given a ministry, that of education and science. Amongst the parliamentary state secretaries, only one of twenty-five was a woman, Irmgard Karwatzi, in the ministry of faith and family affairs. The first woman minister in West Germany was appointed in 1961 only after sustained lobbying by CDU and CSU women pressurised Adenauer into naming Elisabeth Schwartzhaupt as minister for health. Since that time governments have normally contained one and occasionally two women ministers, usually in the family, education or health ministries. The exception to the pattern of subject stereotyping in women's appointments was Maria Schlei, who was appointed minister for economic cooperation in 1976. The hostile media reaction to a woman in such a post forced her to resign in 1978 (Hall, 1981, 173).

In the Landtage (state parliaments) women's representation in 1983 ranged from less than 6.5 per cent in the larger states of Baden Wurtemburg, Lower Saxony, Saar and Schleswig Holstein to more than 15 per cent of those in Berlin and the city states of Bremen and Hamburg. Laender cabinets, too, normally contain only one woman but the range of posts is rather more varied than at federal level. Hence, in 1983 Lower Saxony had a woman minister for economic affairs; Schleswig Holstein, a woman minister of justice; and Hesse and Baden Wurtemburg had women ministers to the Bundestag. The record number of four women ministers (of fourteen) in Hamburg were ministers of health, justice, federal affairs and culture.

At local government level in the same year women were 13 per cent of councillors overall, and over 16 per cent of those in cities with populations in excess of one million. In a few cities women held 25 per cent of council seats. But their toe-hold in local leadership was rather more tenuous, at less than 5 per cent of holders of leadership positions such as mayor and head town-clerk.

In the administrative institutions women in senior positions are around 5 per cent of the total at federal level, whilst their share of senior positions in the Laender bureaucracies is almost 20 per cent. This discrepancy is partly due to the fact that most positions in social work and education are at Land level and these are the areas of civil service employment in which women are most commonly found. At the very highest level of the civil service, the *beamtete Staatssekretaere*, there were no women at all in 1983.

Only one woman has ever served on the Constitutional Court at any one time (i.e. one more than in France and Italy), and the proportion of women in senior judicial posts is small. The major reason is that women only began to undertake the necessary training in large numbers at the end of the 1970s. In the social courts women were 2 of 41 professional judges at federal level in 1981 and 176 of 1,490 at local and state levels. In the labour courts, one of 25 federal judges was a woman in 1981 and 84 of 604 state and local judges were women. Women were, at most, 5 per cent of the West German senior judiciary.

Britain, France, Italy and West Germany Compared

Of the four most populous states in the European Community in 1983, women comprised less than 10 per cent of holders of legislative office, less than 6 per cent of senior civil servants and, except in France, were less than 5 per cent of holders of government positions (Table 6.4). Despite the election of a woman prime minister in 1979 and 1983, in the two appointive areas of the civil service and the judiciary, Britain lagged behind in the appointment of women, suggesting a certain lack of will to promote women on the part of successive British governments. In 1963 two women were permanent secretaries in the British civil service, in 1983 there were none. Of the four countries under consideration, only in France, and there only recently, has any government commitment to the promotion of women into elite positions been apparent. There it has been particularly at government level and in the judiciary that improvements have been made.

Table 6.4: *Women in government elites in Great Britain, France, Italy and West Germany (in per cent)*

	Cabinet/ government	Legislature	Judiciary	Senior civil service
UK	4.5	3.5	4.1	4.5
France	14.0	5.9	12.0	5.4
Italy	3.3	7.9	8.7*	5.8
West Germany	5.9	9.3	5.0	5.0

Source: calculated from Zincone (ed.) 1983, *passim*
*all judiciary

The Nordic Countries

Whilst recent developments in France give some idea of what can be done when a government gives even passing priority to improving the presence of women in elites, it is in the Nordic countries that the most sustained efforts in liberal democratic Europe have been made. In Sweden, Norway and Finland women have been encouraged to seek responsible positions in the numerical channel since the early 1970s. And the results have been remarkable.

In Sweden in 1984, women comprised 28 per cent of the members of the government, 28 per cent of legislators and were 29 per cent of local councillors. A similar pattern was apparent in Norway, where women were 22 per cent, 26 per cent and 23 per cent, respectively, of holders of such positions (Table 6.5). In Finland and Denmark women were also well represented, if not to the same extent, at government level as in the other two countries. Only in Iceland were women's shares of elected posts below 20 per cent and of government posts as low as 10 per cent.

The proportions of women legislators in Norway, Sweden, Denmark and Finland rose sharply in the 1970s, since which time slower increases have meant that it is in these countries that women have the greatest share of places in the numerical channel. The increases in the numbers of women in elected office came abouit as a result of party responses to pressure from (often party) women for more say in political life. Proportional representation in each of the countries means that party leaderships have the power to increase the number of women candidates standing in favourable positions on party lists and a tendency in some of the countries (e.g. Finland, see Haavio-Mannila, 1980; and Norway,

Table 6.5: *Women in government, Parliament, local councils and corporate bodies in the five Nordic countries, 1984 (in per cent)*

	Government	Parliament	Local councils	Public bodies and committees
Sweden	28	28	29	16
Norway	22	26	23	27
Finland	18	31	22	10
Denmark	15	26	21	9
Iceland	10	15	12	7

Source: *Newsletter of the Research Committee on Sex Roles and Politics*, IPSA, July 1984; Advance Report on Haavio-Mannila, *et al.*, *The Unfinished Democracy: Women in Politics in the Nordic Countries* (Pergammon, 1985)

see Skard, 1981) for women voters to favour women candidates in preference voting has encouraged parties to continue with such policies. Whilst shares of between 20 and 30 per cent of legislative and government seats do not reflect women's share in the population, or their shares of party membership, they are nonetheless significant improvements on the position which obtains elsewhere in the European liberal democracies. There are also measurable improvements over the shares of seats held by Nordic women during the 1960s. Hence, Nordic women, except perhaps in Iceland, may be reasonably pleased if not altogether satisfied with their progress in the numerical channel.

In the corporate channel, however, improvement has been less consistent. Only in Norway was women's share of seats on public bodies in 1984 of the same order as their numerical channel representation (Table 6.5). Hernes and Voje (1980) report that at the end of the 1970s, Norwegian women were largely dependent upon the numerical channel for their presence in elites. The large industrial organisations which controlled up to 70 per cent of nominations for corporate body membership contained relatively few full-time women officers (7.5 per cent), thus the pool of women who could be nominated was small. But efforts at the end of the 1970s to increase the proportions of women nominated were made especially by the government (which normally controls the other 30 per cent of nominations) and also by interest organisations, resulting in a steady improvement in women's share of places. A predictable stereotyping of subject specialisation is present in the sorts of committees to which women have tended to be appointed (Hernes and Voje, 1980, 173), but this should be seen against the situation in the other Nordic countries were equivalent efforts have either not been made or have been unsuccessful and thus men hold most of the stereotypical women's positions.

In the Nordic countries an increased presence of women in elected office has not led to an aglutination process whereby women automatically enter other elite arenas in equivalent proportions. The evidence there suggests that important corporate channels only become accessible to women if particular and significant efforts are made to make them so. As corporate bodies everywhere become more important women will increasingly have to address the problem of gaining admission to them. Here, too, it would appear that pressure must begin first in the numerical channel both in the political parties (which often have nominating rights) and through pressure on elected positions in the interest organisations, particularly the economic associations.

Elsewhere in Western Europe the pattern of women's political representation is mixed; Austria, with six women ministers of a total of twenty-three has the highest presence of women in government, but women were less than 10 per cent of deputies in 1982. In Holland women were over 19 per cent of the lower chamber of the States General elected in 1984 and were two of sixteen government ministers and three of seventeen secretaries of state. At national level in the Netherlands, women's share of elected posts has steadily increased since the beginning of the 1970s. That trend is repeated at local level, where women's share of provincial deputyships and local council memberships is a little lower that their national representation. Women are just over 5 per cent of Dutch Civil Servants and about 10 per cent of the judiciary.

In other countries women have not made such progress. In Switzerland, where enfranchisement came only in 1971, women were 10.5 per cent of Nationalrat deputies in 1984, a proportion which had steadily increased. Irish women held fourteen of 166 Dail seats (8 per cent) in 1984 and were 7.4 per cent of councillors, corporation representatives and town commissioners. In Belgium, women were 16 per cent of the twenty-five member Marten government in 1983 but were only 7.5 per cent of MPs, while in Luxemburg in the same year women were 14.6 per cent of legislators.

In the more recently re-established liberal democracies of Greece, Spain and Portugal, a similar diversity of pattern is apparent. In 1984 Greek women held thirteen of the 300 parliamentary seats but were only four of 276 mayors and held only twenty-two of 5761 council chairs (PE 86.199/fin/C). In Spain women were 4.6 per cent of all Cortes members (both houses) in 1984, less than 8 per cent of local councillors, and less than 0.5 per cent of mayors. No women were mayors of the fifty-two provincial capitals and only one woman was in the cabinet, the minister of culture (Threlfall, 1982). In Portugal, in the general election of 25 April 1983, 18 women of a total of 250 deputies were elected, a proportion of 7.2 per cent. Substitutions in July of that year raised the proportion to 8 per cent. Portugese women are less than 2 per cent of mayors.

There is no single explanation for variations in the pattern of representation of women at local, regional and national level. Power-pyramid hypotheses would lead us to expect that women would invariably be better represented in assemblies at local than at national level. Clearly, however, this is not always the case. Other explanations might lie with the persistence of traditional attitudes in local communities in some states which might be associated with variations in party power such that control over national electoral lists does not extend to a similar control at regional and local level. It is only in a minority of countries that women are less present at local than national level, and often discrepancies are small. Where a regional tier of government exists, however, such data as are available indicate that women are often less present in assemblies than either local councils or national legislatures. There has been no research published on this discrepancy which, until more is known, will remain a puzzle.

State Socialist Elites

In East Europe, as elsewhere, the part played by women in governing elites will be a function of both their party and state positions. But these will be rather more closely intertwined than in comepetitive party systems, and no corporate channels which are free from party control exist. In these systems, with their long-standing official commitment to sex equality and their experience of social engineering to bring about political equality, one would expect to find high proportions of women in elected assemblies. And on the whole that expectation is met. However, a concomitant presence of women in national executives does not exist. Moreover, legislatures in state socialist systems are normally symbolic bodies at best. They are legitimising systems in which real power is disposed of by the ruling Communist Party. Thus, party central committees are the significant deliberative assemblies and party executives level of government (normally the council of ministers) and party politbureaux or their equivalent, that it is safe to assume that it is success in the party and not the state organs which ensures the assumption of positions of political leadership. But even if inseparable from party positions, state power is itself important. Most important party figures in most state socialist systems hold government positions as well. The parties themselves have constitutional status as the political manifestation of the proletariat, a precaution taken to enhance regime legitimacy and also a genuine reflection of the ideology of socialist rule. In studying the position of women in the elite apparatuses of such countries, account must therefore be taken of both state and party positions.

As we saw in Chapter 4, women's position in the ruling Communist parties is easily described by reference to the Law of Increasing Disproportions. A pattern of steadily increasing party membership has not been reflected in the assumption of leadership positions by women, who comprise less than 20 per cent and normally less than 10 per cent of central committee members and who hold just over 5 per cent of politbureau seats. But women fare considerably better in the national legislatures, where their share of seats has increased steadily since the Second World War, and by 1981 their presence ranged from 17 to 34 per cent. Women were just over 32 per cent of deputies elected to the USSR Supreme Soviet in 1979. At union republic (state) level they were almost 36 per cent of deputies elected to autonomous republic Supreme Soviets and almost 40 per cent of those for autonomous republics in 1980. At the various local levels (territory, region, area, district, city, village) women comprised over 50 per cent of members of the soviets elected in 1982. But many studies have shown that women soviet deputies are less likely to dispose of such power as is available at that level than are their male colleagues. Women deputies are less likely to be party members, they are subject to higher rates of turnover, and they come from less favoured occupations than male deputies (Lapidus, 1975b, 1976; Lennon, 1971; Hill, 1972; Moses, 1976). Indeed, Maher (1980, 190–208) has found that women and men were differently recruited for all types of elective political roles in the Soviet Union. Relative to men, women deputies are younger, they have less formal education and they are less frequently engaged in non-manual occupations.

It is likely, therefore, that many of the women who achieve such positions were recruited as symbolic or token representatives of their gender. Their poorer qualifications relative to men's are in this view no more than indicators of the population they represent. Maher points out that in the instances where women are well qualified, recruitment policy is not gender differentiated. The political role of well-qualified women at this level has been one which, similarly to that of men, is increasingly professionalised. Gaps between the qualifications of men and women have steadily decreased in Soviet society, and trends in republican Supreme Soviets investigated by Maher indicate that both the qualitative gaps in their political representation in assemblies will also decrease. At governmental level, however, it is difficult to make any case that women's share of power is improving. There were no women in the seventy-five positions which constituted the Soviet government in 1981 and no women in the party politbureau. Only two women have been members of the Council of Ministers in the entire post-war period, Ekaterina Furtseva as minister of culture under Khruschev and Mariia Kovrigina as minister of health during the 1950s. At deputy-ministerial level, seven positions have been held by women in the same period, including posts in the ministries of health, light industry, the building material industry, finance (education, health and culture finance) and education. Stereotyped assignments appear to dog the careers of Soviet women in the same way as they do their West European counterparts.

More women are to be found in the governments of the other East European countries, where 20 of 419 posts were held by women in 1976 (4.7 per cent). But these tend to be concentrated in a few countries, notably East Germany, Bulgaria and Rumania. At legislative level women were 106 of the 352 members of the Hungarian parliament elected in 1980 (30.1 per cent), 168 of the 500 members of the East German Volkskammer deputies in 1981 (33.6 per cent) but only about 17 per cent of the delegates in Yugoslavia's indirectly elected federal chambers in 1981. (18.8 per cent of the Chamber of Associated Labour; 11.5 per cent of the Chamber of Local Communities; 22.6 per cent of the Socio-Political Chamber.) 1974 reforms in the Yugoslav constitution militated against increases in women's representation in the federal assembly, access to which became dependent on membership in various male dominated organisations (Jancar, 1978). As in the Soviet Union the overall pattern is one of a steadily increasing presence of women in national legislatures, and substantial efforts have been made in each country to increase the presence of women in political life. An exception is Czechoslovakia, where a pattern of increase in the 1960s appears to have been reversed by the 'Prague Spring' of 1968 and had not fully been re-established by 1980.

Common, too, is a higher proportion of women at local than at national levels of office. Women were over 35 per cent of local soviet members in Bulgaria and Albania and over 40 per cent in East Germany by the beginning of the 1980s. In Czechoslovakia, women's share of local offices followed the same pattern as at national level, rising during the 1960s but declining by the 1970s, at the end of which improvements in women's representation began once again to take place (Heitlinger, 1979, 160). Another exception is Yugoslavia, where women in 1978 were only 7.2 per cent of the self-management organs of local communities, a figure which varied from 16.7 per cent in urban areas to 3.4 per cent in rural areas. Yugoslav women in general fare better the further they are from the countryside (Denitch, 1981).

Women's position in the judiciary in the Soviet Union is roughly commensurate with their presence in the legal profession. In 1975 women were 30 per cent of lawyers and 32 per cent of people's judges. There were twenty-seven women on the Supreme Court and fourteen of its forty-five people's assessors were women. In Moscow, women were 43 per cent of prosecutors and investigators in the procuracy. Aggregate data such as these give no real indication of women's standing in the judiciary other than demonstrating that men remain in the majority. In the institutions of state administration women are known to predominate in the routine and clerical posts. However, the fusion of politics and administration is almost total in the state socialist societies, where there are no ideological requirements for maintaining political neutrality amongst bureaucrats. Indeed, a strong commitment to party goals is an essential qualification for senior position. Women's share of such positions is not known but is unlikely to be any greater than their share of party membership.

As in the liberal democracies, state socialist women politicians tend to have responsibilities in areas traditionally viewed as women's concerns. Women ministers are most often responsible for areas such as health, culture, education and social welfare, a tendency which perhaps narrows the career paths which have been defined for women (Jancar, 1978). The sort of *cursus honorum* which has been preferred for male leadership aspirants has involved party work in a number of geographical areas, with experience in a number of areas of administration and industry. Women tend to be considerably less geographically mobile than men and are confined to a few specialisms, notably those which follow from training in the humanities or education (Moses, 1976; Lapidus, 1978). Those women who have been successful have avoided narrow specialisation and have served in a variety of administrative, political, agricultural and industrial positions.

Throughout the histories of the state socialist societies there has been little evidence of a correlation between levels of political participation by women and their share of top political leadership posts. And women's party roles have not kept pace with their economic and social roles. Part of the explanation for such discrepancies undoubtedly rests with the impact of the double burden in societies which are characterised by high levels of paid employment for women. But where elites have considerable experience of attitude transformation and where parties have considerable propaganda wherewithal, the failure to admit women into the political leadership must be seen as deliberate. If state socialist regimes officially support the politcal equality of women, they have failed to give this goal the kind of priority which has been given to improving women's economic status or, indeed, to many other regime aims. Yet, as Batiot (1979) reminds us, the struggle of women for emancipation is aimed at the socialisation of power as well as of the means of production. State socialism historically has altered the relationship of women to the means of producion but has done so by replacing control by what was largely male private ownership with control by largely male-populated party power.

Legacies of popular attitudes and traditional cultures undoubtedly shape attitudes towards women's access to power in East Europe. However, both Lapidus (1976) and Wolchik (1981b) believe that the best explanation for women's failure to enter elites since the establishment ' of Communist Party rule is elite-determined demand. State socialist elites pursue recruitment policies which leave nothing to chance. Gender is one of the central norms governing the selection of candidates for party and government office and recent increases in women's visibility have been the direct result of explicit policies. If women fail to hold even modest shares of government posts it is because the parties have decided deliberately and expressly that they should not. In this regard at least, the position will change only when the parties decide that it should.

International Organisations

In the international arena women's position is largely a product of their place in the nations which feed into the international forum. In the European Parliament women were 17 per cent of the MEPs elected in 1983 and all of the member states but Ireland returned delegations with higher proportions of women than their domestic parliaments. A similar pattern occurred in the 1979 elections. No ready explanation has been found for this discrepancy but the relatively few powers disposed of by the European Parliament may provide a clue. Women are not present in the more important posts at commission level. European Community administration too resembles national administration in its concentration of women at the routine levels of occupation whilst men predominated in the senior posts (PE 86.199/Fin/C, 296–312). A similar pattern is apparent in the various organisations of the United Nations where women have been less than 10 per cent of General Assembly members since its foundation. In administrative positions women are clustered in the expected way. And whilst neither the European Community nor the UN may, as an organisation, be held responsible for assembly, parliamentary or commission compositions imposed upon them by member states, employment policies are partly within their control (Thorn, 1981). Both organisations have made gestures in the direction of sex-equality and these gestures at national level have often translated into important sources of support for women. The UN sponsored International Women's Decade has given women opportunities to organise at national level which might not otherwise have occurred and has led to the collection and dissemination of information about the situation of women by most national governments. Initiatives taken within the European Community have been more substantial leading to major changes in the structure of opportunities for women (see Ch 7 below). Feminisation in that particular elite has made a measurable difference for many women (Vallance, 1985).

The Absence of Women from European Political Elites

That ruling elites have recruitment mechanisms enabling them as far as possible to maintain their group characteristics is a truism of modern elite studies. Such mechanisms have not been designed expressly for the purpose of exluding women, but they serve male elites well enough in this respect. If we distinguish between formal and substantive arenas of political power in Europe, we find that, except in the Nordic and state socialist legislatures, women are not present. In Britain the rules of entry to the establishment are covert, enabling in-groups to recruit at will. In France the existence of two parallel educational systems and the practice of *cumul des mandats* helps to preserve male domains. There, Socialists aim to break the hold that the Grandes Écoles have over the gateways to administrative elites as well aiming to promote women. In Italy major barriers are found within the party system whilst in West Germany the persistence of traditional attitudes about sex roles make elite aspirations by women rare, and difficult to satisfy when they occur. A cynic might explain the presence of women in legislative arenas in the Nordic countries by reference to the fact that power in those systems had come to rest elsewhere long before women gained admission in significant numbers. In the state socialist systems the friction between traditional attitudes to women and the Marxist ideology of equality appears to have been resolved in favour of the former when it comes to questions of political power-sharing.

There is explicit male resistance within elites to increasing the presence of women. At this the top level of the system, new entrants displace existing power holders and it is therefore not to be expected that doors will simply be opened on request. But elite strategies may vary quite substantially. The efforts made by the French government have resulted in very little transfer of power from men to women, but they have undoubtedly served to forestall criticism and protest by many women. Elites may point to the absence of evidence that women wish to increase their political involvement or proudly draw attention to the inevitable token woman in their midst. Special women's posts may be created. But the sort of concession which involves a woman taking a post in one of the powerful ministries is rare and where, as in the case of Margaret Thatcher's ascent to power in Britain, the occasional woman does succeed, she is most often a surrogate male.

The question of the attractiveness of elite entry to women is an important one. Essentially, women who succeed in the world of men are exceptions when compared to women at large. Male leaders are statistically more representative of male non-leaders than are their few women colleagues. Women politicians sacrifice more for their position. They are less often married, have fewer children and are better trained than other women. They also differ in important respects from male leaders. More often recruited by parties of the left, they tend to be more liberal than male colleagues. Marriage is apparently a positive resource for male politicians, whilst being unattached increases a woman's chances of success in terms of career and public life. Data from country after country confirm such patterns (Vallance, 1979; Lovenduski and Hills, 1981; Randall, 1982; Mossuz-Lavau and Sineau, 1983; Zincone, ed., 1983).

The stereotyping of women's political assignments is also important. Increasingly rare as a feature in parliamentary committee assignments, stereotyping of posts continues to occur at top level. Women leaders tend still to be assigned to posts in the 'soft' ministries of family, welfare, culture and, except where this is considered to be an important post, education. Such posts tend not to lead to further promotion in that they do not provide the experience of high-level management of economic or foreign affairs considered to be important in top leadership selection. On the other hand, they provide important channels of promotion for women. The same may be said of the proliferation of women's departments. If a preponderance of women in cultural, social or women's departments or ministries is not ideal, it is a major advance on a preponderance of men in such posts. And whilst they may be faulted for not being identifiable paths to premierships, such posts are nonetheless concerned with important subjects. It is only measurement based solely upon criteria of political clout which renders them 'unimportant'. The problem is not how to get women out of cultural and social ministries, it is rather how to keep them there whilst at the same time getting other women appointed to other positions.

If quotas, socialisation and social controls have been used to keep women out of elites, they might just as easily be constructed to bring them in. Positive discrimination and the implementation of legal requirements for equality can be used to improve women's status. But, as Epstein reminds us, such policies are temporal. Gatekeepers in the past have maintained hierarchies by sifting out unwanted groups in what appeared to be natural processes. But system maintenance is normally less conspicuous than system alteration. When gatekeepers are forced to admit women, they may still manage to keep them at the bottom of hierarchies once admitted. This, it appears, is what has often happened in Europe. A generally higher proportion of women in legislatures which has failed to be reproduced in executive bodies is an indicator of such a pattern (Epstein, 1981, 6).

Political systems have been reluctant to undertake gratuitous political representation. They have rarely represented a group's interest until and unless the group developed a sense of its own interest and placed demands upon the system. Activism and consciousness are key ingredients of such development, and these often arise in precisely the sort of protest activities and social movements we described in Chapters 2 and 3. The organisation which has been undertaken by women has built networks, affected opinion and generally constructed a reservoir of skill and ability which could lead to the projection of more women into politics. Until the beginning of the 1980s, resources were largely directed into *ad hoc* political activities. *Ad hoc* activities tend to be attempts to circumvent formal organisational patterns in order to articulate and perhaps later aggregate new demands. But the corporate and numerical channels must sooner or later be confronted. Skills learned from *ad hoc* activities (in which, incidentally, elites participate as well) are transferable to the numerical channel from which some access to the corporate channel might be gained. Full entry to the corporate channel is the product of participation in the full array of economic organisations, suggesting once again our two strategies for women. Concerted efforts might be made to penetrate and colonise interest organisations, and women's networks must be given the organisational weight to compete with the established organisations. Only when efforts of both kinds are well advanced will women gain the necessary powers to alter the rules of the political game.

Although there are in each system women who are dissatisfied with their political representation, a groundswell of opinion demanding equal say in government has yet to emerge. European Community surveys indicate that women favour increased access to power, but scrutiny of the political terrain has only recently begun to reveal instances of women organising politically for increased political visibility. It is likely that the most successful of these activities will be those which aim to influence policy in established parties. By the end of 1984 the European liberal democracies were still reluctant to legislate to increase women's access to government. Indeed, in France the imposition of a quota for municipal electoral lists was invalidated by the Constitutional Court. It is widely believed that populations will not accept government manipulation of candidate lists or the establishment of quotas at other points in the electoral system. But within political parties themselves, acceptance is likely to be more easily won. Many parties already have policies to promote women, and almost all political parties have substantial numbers of women members. The basis for well-directed political pressure exists. In competitive party systems a policy initiative from one party may lead to competitive bidding for women's support from others. In the single party systems such pressure is unlikely to be feasible and improvement in the political clout of women is likely to progress at much the same rates as it has done since the 1950s, the glare of international scrutiny providing an occasional boost.

Discussion of ways to improve women's elite access raises the fundamental question of why we would wish to do so. Whilst there is a strong moral argument to be made for the inclusion of women, and there is a system legitimacy case as well, what of its impact on women? An essential *a priori* assumption for some feminists is that only the presence of women within decision-making bodies will allow the improvement of women's position as work. In the course of research on this topic in France, Val Lorwin (1978, 10) found that 'all women in positions of responsibility both in politics and in trade unions have confirmed with us that the only real guarantee of the taking into account of women's interests in a structure, whatever it is, is the presence of women in positions of responsibility'.

But the presence of women so far has not always guaranteed the taking into account of women's interests. The evidence is that many women politicians are surrogate men, that they have no interest in pursuing women's rights or questions of particular concern to their women electors. And even where such an interest is present, it may not be possible to make any appreciable difference to policy. A dilemma for a woman who has started to rise through the political hierarchy is that of having to choose whether or not to take up women's questions. If she does, she risks being prey to the syndrome whereby someone specifically appointed to deal with women's issues is considered to be lacking in the capacity to carve out a normal career. If she does not, she risks contributing to the charge that the presence of women makes no difference to women. Such decisions do not have to be made by men.

The whole question of the effect of increasing women's representation is a difficult one in that there have been so few women to be observed in such positions. The Scandinavian and European Parliament experiences suggest that the number of women must increase greatly if a difference is to be apparent. A certain 'critical mass' of women must exist to enable the development of a group identity and the resistance of socialisation into established male norms of elite behaviour. In such circumstances women build networks and the potential for their incorporation is decreased

(Hernes and Voje, 1981; Vallance, 1985). That 'critical mass' has yet to be reached at elite levels in Europe or elsewhere. Hence, the questions of why women should support the increase of their members in political office, of what difference it will make to women, remains, so far, unanswered.

Notes

1. Both the Greater London Council and the six Metropolitan Councils were scheduled for abolition in 1985.
2. Data for the section on France is based on the report by Moreau-Bourles and Sineau, 1983, unless otherwise indicated.
3. Data for the section on Italy is based on the report by de Santis and Zincone, 1983, unless otherwise indicated.
4. Data for the section on West Germany is based on the report by Randzio-Plath and Rust, 1983, unless otherwise indicated.

7 The Political Management of Women: Public Policy, the State and Sex Equality

As the preceding chapters have shown, it cannot be proved that increasing the presence of women in elites will lead to changes in the content and styles which have long characterised political decision-making. Until many more women come to take part in government deliberations, we will not have the evidence with which to support such a view. However, it is possible to demonstrate the very great extent to which the results of such deliberations in the form of public policy have affected women. In their family and economic roles women are important targets of public policy in all European states. Specific goals of social welfare via family support, pro-natalism and employment equality are common to many European countries which have employed a variety of mechanisms, with varying degrees of success, to ensure their implementation. Similarities within the two main groups of European states have, along with normal processes of diffusion of innovation, led to often very similar packages of policies being adopted by a number of states. But cultural as well as political differences have also played a role, and in some policy areas (e.g. abortion and reproductive rights) differences obtain both within and between blocs. Differences are apparent too in the manner and extent that which woman have played a role in demanding, formulating and modifying gender-specific policies, although everywhere women were more active in such roles in the 1980s than they had been in the previous decade.

Amongst the many obstacles to achieving policy change or even policy recognition of women's issues has been the assumption by decision-makers of gender blindness in many areas of policy-making. This has been possible not because the concept that a policy may affect men and women differently is difficult to grasp but because political structures and processes reflect conflict dimensions other than gender. A recurring motif of women's movement history has been efforts to make women's position an issue in its own right. Despite this, however, the status of women, although given some attention by the East European state socialist regimes, has never been a major political issue in West European politics. Indeed, the component issues of various women's rights policies have only a toe-hold on the political agenda. The two waves of feminism were instrumental in achieving agenda status for the suffrage and emancipation acts of the early part of the twentieth century, followed by the equality and anti-discrimination initiatives of the 1970s and early 1980s. However, many other areas of policy are important to women (Dahlerup and Gulli, 1983) but have not been assessed in terms of their impact on sex equality policy. The differing social positions of men and women have become self-perpetuating as legislation has been enacted and implemented without taking such differences into account. Equality measures themselves have often been opposed, falling foul of such structural impediments as occupational sectoralisation, the customs and practices of collective bargaining and the primacy of better-organised interests.

Not only institutional but also ideological factors have been important in shaping the impact of public policy on women. Whilst the results of ideological differences within, say, a party spectrum may not be all that apparent, strong differences such as those between state socialist and liberal democratic systems may generate important differences between the position of women in these countries. Similarly Communist parties in the predominantly Catholic countries of France and Italy have been forces for improvement in the position of women. Religious factors too have played an important role. Catholic nations have lagged behind in the granting of rights to women and the interaction of religious/ secular conflicts with Right/Left divisions has structured a complex series of political obstacles for those desiring to introduce new modes of assessing and developing policy.

As Randall reminds us, most areas of women's lives are affected by public policy of one kind or another. Such things as power within marriage, control of sexuality and fertility, rights and duties as mothers, the control of wealth and income, employment and education are all the subject of legislation, regulation and other forms of state control (Randall, 1982, 107). Laws directed at sustaining the family as well as those which are specific to women are important. Much of the law which defines women as dependants is marriage law. In turn, from the beginning, assumptions of women's economic dependency have pervaded systems of social security provision. Women are, for example, difficult to fit into pension schemes because of low pay, part-time work and interrupted career patterns. The expansion of women's presence in the workforce since the beginning of the 1950s has been largely an expansion in the number of low-paid, low-status and part-time workers. This circumstance is the result of family patterns which are supported by social policy and the welfare state (Lewis 1983b). Not only are these patterns without benefit for women, they are also often irrelevant. Rising divorce rates, changes in fertility patterns, new employment trends and alterations in family structures have progressed to the point at which it is often simply unrealistic to define women as dependants. Yet policies which treat women as autonomous individuals or regard couples as consisting of equal partners have been slow to develop. And whilst government and political parties may often appear interested in women's issues and problems, they tend to depoliticise them in the interests of the prevailing social order. Women's issues often fit between what are officially dichotomised as public and private interests, falling foul of contemporary definitions of appropriate areas for state intervention (Sapiro, 1981, 710).

But the state is, when all is said and done, an abstraction. It is nothing more or less than the set of institutions through which political processes of policy-making and policy implementation and adjustment take place – a set of power relationships. To the extent that its structures are delineated by a hierarchy of individual office-holders, the state has a capacity to appear to be more than the sum of its parts and hence have a dynamic of its own. This should not be taken too far, however. Whilst there are identifiable imperatives which arise from an organisational need to survive and function, these do not justify the reification of the state. The subordination of women to the requirements of the state is a political process, and the sensitivity of state structures to male need is, in the same way as its sensitivity to dominant economic groups, a product of, in each particular case, its specific historical development. Whilst it is possible to argue that all states oppress all women, it is specific states which are the setting for particular policies. It is important therefore to remember when we discuss women and the state that we are not relating two simple and unproblematic entities (Caldwell, 1982). Rather, we are concerning ourselves with two complex abstractions which have a multiplicity of relationships. Thus, we must bear in mind that not all policies which have reinforced women's traditional familial roles were concerned to ensure male dominance (Randall, 1982, 130) and that neither is the family particularly suited to many of its functions in contemporary industrial society (McIntosh, 1978; Barrett, 1980). The idea of the male-dominated system of capitalist, or state socialist, oppression is a powerful one, but its reflection in state forms is imperfect, an impressionistic image which provides us only with broadest of frameworks within which to assess public policy.

Policy towards women is in many respects shaped by the same forces which affect it in other areas. The process of policy formulation and implementation is determined by a social fabric in which hierarchies based on class, gender, religion, region, race and ideology are intertwined (Diamond and Hartsock, 1981). Its analysis requires understanding of the environment in which it is enacted, its visibility, degree of controversiality and scope as well as the type of policy under consideration.

Those who wish to reform the status of women via the political system face a pre-structured policy process in which gaining agenda status for issues is the first of many difficult steps. At this and later stages, the environmental variables of social, economic and political climate will have an important bearing on whether issues gain consideration. For example, the changes in the social climate of the 1960s which generated the emergence of the New Left and the student movement and included greater educational access, greater economic prosperity and freedom-enhancing technological change contributed to the development of anti-discrimination policies in the 1970s. The economic expansion and growth of the early 1970s was also important. Both of these factors influenced the organisation of women themselves, which in turn influenced the political climate in the sense that attitudes towards women and views of the appropriate role of the state altered. In some states important women's policy networks began to develop which would become able to exercise a significant leverage on political elites. An indicator of the extent of these changes is to be found in the ways in which issues came to be posed. Such phrases as 'a woman's right to choose' were not part of the discourse in the early 1970s, but by the end of the decade described part of the legislative agenda in some states.

The possibilities for influencing policy will also depend upon such systemic variables as the degree of centralisation of government and the scope for different kinds of policy processes. European governments tend to be extremely centralised, which reduces but, as we shall see, does not eliminate the possibility for incremental policy-making. Political variables such as the lobbying strength of women are also important, as are political coalitions, in particular the alliances between women's movement organisations and unions and/or political parties. Leadership considerations are rather less important in the area of women's policy, although the benefit to be gained from more women leaders prepared to take up relevant issues is illustrated by the degree of overload suffered by those few already in position. In many respects women's policies are no different from policies in other areas. If a policy has a low visibility, fits in with prevailing values and involves narrow concerns, its chances of adoption are greater than if it is controversial, wide ranging and conspicuous. Low visibility goals such as the removal of formal quotas from educational access have been accomplished with apparent ease by women's rights campaigners whilst high visibility issues such as the radical amendment of rape and abortion statutes have proved much more difficult to resolve (Bonaparth, 1982b).

The type of policy which is under consideration is also held to be important. Here the most commonly used typology is that produced by Lowi in a study of American business and public policy written in the early 1960s. Lowi identified three types of policy: distributive, regulatory and redistributive. Distributive policies involve the distribution of benefits to individuals or groups, normally in the form of a government subsidy. Redistributive policies involve the transfer of benefit from one group to another, and regulatory policies involve governmental regulation of practices by individuals or groups. Lowi argued that the amount of controversy and resistance a policy generates is predictable from its type: distributive policies are likely to meet little resistance whilst regulatory policies can expect to meet moderate but not insurmountable levels of resistance. Redistributive policies, on the other hand, will be highly controversial and will face high levels of resistance (Lowi, 1964). Widely cited and adapted, Lowi's typology has been criticised particularly for the fact that the boundaries between his categories are not altogether clear, as a policy might in the short run be regulatory but have redistributive implications in the long run, and the perceptions of political actors might allocate issues into them differently. But his scheme does illuminate many of the differences between the kinds of policies which are important to women and supplies us with a vocabulary with which to discuss them.

The various policy areas which are important to women are numerous and discussion of the interrelationships between their strands is impossible in a text of this scope and length. But second-wave feminism has highlighted certain issues which have come to be regarded as of particular contemporary importance, notably abortion, equal rights, rape, domestic violence and equal opportunity. From these may be selected policy areas which are representative of the relationships between women and the state in the 1980s. Between the late 1960s and the mid-1980s most West European states both enacted equal opportunities legislation and liberalised their abortion policies. Change was not always made in response to women's movement pressure, but women's representatives often became involved at some stage and had some influence on the policy process. In the state socialist systems of East Europe, too, attention was given to policy on women during the same period. There, however, the state imperatives of economic development and population replacement were much more in evidence as policy sources.

In the short term, equal rights and opportunities policies are mainly redistributive whilst abortion policy is regulatory; but in the longer term both policies have redistributive implications. However, the disposition of political forces active on each of the two issues may differ substantially in different cultures. In general, established structures of political bargaining have proved better able to cope with the impact of equal rights policy (the full implementation of which they have successfully avoided) than with the lines of division which are brought into play by abortion law reform. Both issues, however, have presented special difficulties for most political systems.

Equal rights law poses problems to do with its nature and with its appropriateness. The concept of discrimination itself is both complex and difficult, raising a number of peculiar legal problems. Discrimination is essentially the overt expression of prejudice, which is irrational. Prohibiting in legislative terms acts which arise from emotions and providing adequate mechanisms presents special problems to legislators. In particular, the substantive law will be likely to be difficult to express in legislative terms and open to wide variations in interpretation. Proof is likely to be a difficult matter, with much of the evidence circumstantial and in the hands of the discriminator. This has implications for procedural law, suggesting that attending equality law are concepts and processes which are not easily digestible by court systems accustomed to dealing with other sorts of issues (Corcoran and Donnelly, 1984, 3).

At the level of statute the major focus of most sex equality policy in Europe has been the labour force, and its prime incentive has been the increasing numbers of women in employment through the 1960s and 1970s and the increasing pressure on government from their representative organisations. Although other areas have been included, it is equal pay and equal employment opportunities which have most exercised legislators. This, of course, raises the question of how far action on one issue has the power to change the totality of women's experience. When equal opportunities are extended to individuals who, because of the nature of their social position – in this case their responsibility for family servicing – are not in an equal starting position, the rights gained are likely to be formal rather than substantive. Concomitantly, the equal treatment of men and women as autonomous individuals in the family (e.g. in regard to their claims for state benefit), with no corresponding commitment to encourage an equal division of work within the family, may well result in disbenefits to women (Lewis, 1983b, 2 and *passim*). To be effective, equal rights policy must also be wide ranging.

The series of Acts which came into force in the 1970s and in the early 1980s in Western Europe were partly inspired by the pressure for the development of a European Community law on women aimed at stimulating a common pattern of law on women's employment opportunities amongst ECC member states. In accordance with provisions and prevailing interpretations of the Treaty of Rome, this pressure was limited to matters of employment, training and certain associated aspects of the social security system. Some states within the EEC and many of the non-member states had policies which recognised the sources of the disadvantaged position of women in the labour market as being lodged in domestic and family constraints. But in each case the regulation of employment was a central strategy.

Essentially, two models of law on equal opportunity of women were evident: the negative model, which concentrated its focus on banning sex discrimination, and an active model in which the discrimination ban was to be complemented by positive action and, in some countries (e.g. Sweden) a duty on the part of the employer to work actively for equality. Most countries also set up policy-making institutions with a brief to promote equality for women, and sometimes with enforcement or other quasi-judicial functions. In most cases these bodies had also to monitor the impact of legislation and make recommendations for change (Nielsen, 1982, 269–70). The institutional and political environment had particular effects on the new policies, with variations in structures of labour law and systems of justice accounting for differing provisions and types of structures.

Diffusion of innovation was also apparent, and not just within Europe. The British Equal Opportunities Commission (EOC) is based to some extent on the Equal Employment Opportunities Commission of the United States. Ireland and the Netherlands also established administrative bodies through which legal redress could be obtained. Agencies to superintend the implementation of equality policy were often accompanied by other institutions with advisory roles. In some countries the preferred solution was a department within the labour or employment ministry responsible for women's employment policy, whilst others, notably France, opted for a full-scale ministry of women's rights. In each case the policies evolved from more modest beginnings, but the real point of take-off was, except in pioneering Sweden, the statutory changes made in the wake of pressures for increased women's rights. These came from international organisations and internal women's rights and liberation movements as well as from women organised within parties and unions.

The experience of the various kinds of anti-discrimination laws has proved to be remarkably similar. In each country the number of recorded grievances has tended to be small, with women proving very reluctant to pursue claims. There is evidence that many women fear victimisation if they use the statutes (Corcoran and Donnelly, 1984) and that women do not get support from their unions. The reluctance to upset traditional collective bargaining procedures has been an impediment to sex equality policy, both in the effect of representatives of industry on legislation itself and in the way in which statutes have been used. The results of legislation have everywhere been disappointing. During the 1980s, therefore, stress has been placed on the importance of positive action to accompany discrimination bans which are recognised as necessary but not sufficient prerequisites to sex equality in employment opportunities. A French law of 1983 makes express provision for plans for occupational equality schemes to be made by employers. Types of action elsewhere vary considerably, often consisting simply of preliminary investigations to determine the extent and nature of a particular arena of discrimination. Binding measures have also been adopted, however, and efforts have been made in such areas as eliminating sexist bias from primary school texts (Ireland), equalising the school curriculum (Sweden, the Netherlands, Ireland), special apprenticeship schemes for girls (Britain, West Germany) and various kinds of special training for advisors have been brought in in most of the countries of Western Europe (Com. [83] 781, final).

Interest has been expressed, too, in the adoption of another American innovation, affirmative action. Affirmative action, which has often been misunderstood, is essentially a requirement placed on United States government contractors to conform with equal opportunity policies and promote the employment of protected groups. Essentially, the affirmative action programmes aim to alter the composition of particular workforces, but they are not, as is commonly believed, quota systems, which would be illegal in the United States. Rather, plans are directed at expanding the pool of eligibles through, for example, statistical analyses of suitable recruitment populations and publicity to encourage application by absent groups. Goals and timetables for change are established and meeting these becomes a condition of retaining government contracts (Meehan, 1983). By mid-1984 European policy-makers were not philosophically reconciled to the adoption of affirmative action programmes, seeing them (often mistakenly) as requiring 'reverse' or 'positive discrimination'. Certain forms of positive discrimination (e.g. in training in Britain) were permitted, but it was felt that such provision in other areas would have the unacceptable effect of redressing the disadvantages caused by past sex discrimination at the expense of those who themselves had not been discriminators. It is believed, too, that women themselves would be unwilling to support policies which promoted them at the expense of more deserving male competitors. Finally, it is feared that 'backlash' would result from such practices and that existing male support for equality programmes would disappear if affirmative action were adopted.

Thus, the special offices, commissions, committees, departments and ministries on women are all by and large committed to programmes which envisage piecemeal change, chipping away at the most blatant manifestations of inequality but unwilling as yet to strike hard and fast at its centre. The pre-established structures, particularly those involved in the collective bargaining process have managed successfully to withstand any diminution of their prerogatives which might be caused by sex equality concerns. Such obstacles have been present in every country on which information is available, suggesting that a major alteration in forms of labour-market regulation is likely to be a prerequisite of meeting goals of equal opportunities for women.

Abortion, too, has been a watershed issue for women, its regulation illustrating many of the disadvantages for them of male-constructed political systems. Here too, however, the specificity of women's experience has varied considerably by country.

Most Western democracies liberalised their abortion policies during the 1960s and 1970s. But the processes which were involved, the political circumstances in which new policies emerged and the content of new laws often differed considerably by country. And women themselves were considerably divided on the issue, with many seeing abortion restriction as a form of chattel law, whilst others took up strong 'right to life' positions rejecting any grounds for the termination of pregnancies. Other political actors regarded abortion as a secularisation issue, symbolising a long overdue rejection of Church influence in civil matters. The lines of dispute over abortion issues often coincided neither with gender nor class nor party positions, and debate over its liberalisation involved actors from all segments of society. The examples of Britain, France, Italy, Belgium, Ireland and the Netherlands all indicate that abortion reform brings about social turmoil and political indecision. It characteristically activates the Catholic Church to the express use of such political power as it might have (Tatalovich and Daynes, 1981) and has been remarkable for its capacity to unite various factions of the feminist movement.

The contests which have taken place over abortion are peculiar ones as the arguments made by competing groups are essentially arguments about competing rights. They are arguments which are inevitably at cross purposes. The conflict potential of the issue is high (see Cobb and Elder, 1972, 110–22) and it is one which policy-makers would prefer to avoid. Historically, abortion policy in Europe dates from restrictive nineteenth-century laws largely introduced to protect women from unscrupulous practitioners but also as part of the process of professionalising (and masculinising) the practice of medicine. By the middle of the twentieth century some reform had taken place in many countries with abortion already accepted by popular opinion as a result of a long process of gradually increasing the grounds for its practice, effecting a slow reconciliation to its provision. This was what happened in Sweden, where virtual provision of abortion on demand in 1975 met with almost no resistance. Elsewhere, however, public debate has been wide ranging and often acrimonious. Liberalisation in some states must be seen in the context of restricted provision in others. In Ireland, for example, the electorate in 1983 voted overwhelmingly for a constitutional amendment banning abortion law, thus placing the most extensive legal obstacles to abortion provision to be found in any European state. Belgium, too, continues to resist abortion liberalisation, whilst a Netherlands law passed in 1981

lagged so far behind abortion practice in that country that politicians were reluctant to allow it out of the legislature for a further
three years.

Abortion rights are seen by feminists as part of reproductive
rights generally and are thus conceptualised as crucial to women's
sexuality. Important to women, the issue is an unusual one for the
political system. It habitually cuts across the dominant socio-
economic cleavage expressed in left/right party politics, a characteristic which makes abortion conflicts particularly difficult for
political systems to resolve. Pressure-group activity tends to be
extensive in such an area and a major achievement of groups has
been to keep abortion on the policy agenda for considerable
periods of time, despite the reluctance of politicians. It is at this
point in the political process that feminists have been most consistently engaged over abortion rights, either combating groups
aiming to restrict its provision or in placing the issue before
politicians in efforts to achieve reform. Other activity has taken
place over the implementation of abortion policy, particularly in
the provision of facilities and state funding. Abortion is a mobilising issue at most stages of the policy process.

In general, the major obstacle to the implementation of sex
equality policy is its necessary locus in the labour market. There,
the political power of the collective bargaining partners is sufficient to obstruct any alteration in existing balances of power. The
problem which the political system must confront is that of convincing powerful economic groups of the utility of the provision of
equal rights for women. The solution of such problems is traditionally difficult but not impossible. Abortion liberalisation raises
rather different problems. Such policies trigger cultural and historical mechanisms which upset the very foundations of political
bargaining processes, leaving policy-makers without the accustomed structures for reconciling opposed interests. In each system
accommodations and adjustments are made over both issues, with
those affording compromise over equal opportunity policy rather
more predictable than those which result from the reform of
abortion statutes. The capacities of political systems to deal with
such accommodations and adjustments varies considerably and
numerous solutions to the problems raised by both issues having
been tried. In each country which has attempted to legislate in
these two areas, the political system has had to accommodate new
social forces. Adjustments have taken place in particular environments and are perhaps best understood primarily as local solutions
to general difficulties. Sex equality and abortion policy, like other

policy, is made in particular cultural, social and economic milieux, and understanding of its general nature proceeds from consideration of its particular development and application. We turn therefore to accounts of such developments in a number of European states.

Britain

Britain is perhaps the country in which institutions and structures have altered least to accommodate women's demands. There, early efforts on policies of equality between the sexes were focused on the removal of various impediments to women's employment. Despite regular proposals from women in the labour movement, it was only at the end of the 1960s that the government turned its attention to the enactment of sex equality legislation in the passage of the Equal Pay Act of 1970. Designed to take effect by 1975, the Act was passed with support from both major parties, and its few critics were those who believed it did not go far enough. In the wake of support from the TUC, Women in the Media and the main political parties, its logical corollary, the Sex Discrimination Act was announced in 1974 and became law at the end of 1975. The Sex Discrimination Act was more radical than previous discussion had envisaged, but it nonetheless passed with little opposition. Its two innovations were the introduction of a ban on indirect discrimination and provision for an agency of implementation and enforcement which was given wide powers (The Equal Opportunities Commission, EOC). The easy passage of both Acts is attributed by Randall (1982, 185) to the climate of social reformism which existed in the 1970s, the role of pressure groups (on these see Meehan, 1985) and of individual committed women MPs, as well as to various external factors; in particular, pressures to comply with provisions of the Treaty of Rome, the Equal Pay and Equal Treatment Directives of the European Commission and with various International Labour Organisation (ILO) conventions. And experience gained in the shaping of race relations legislation as well as plans for changes therein had an important influence on the shape of the Act. Diffusion of innovation was at work too. Although the passage of the Equal Pay Act revealed no conscious emulation of the equivalent American measures, one of the most important concepts of the Sex Discrimination Act, that of indirect discrimination, had no British equivalent or precedent. It was borrowed from the

United States (Meehan, 1983, 171; Corcoran, 1984), where it had been developed by the courts.

At the time of passage the British legislation appeared to be radical and wide ranging, and many of its designers believed that it would lead to a considerable alteration in women's position. The Equal Pay Act initially covered a fairly limited concept of equal work, but in conjunction with the Sex Discrimination Act its effect could have been powerful. And maternity rights first granted in the Employment Protection Act of 1976 would, it was felt, complete a well-conceived policy of equal opportunities for working women. In addition, recognising that a rather haphazard and piecemeal approach to implementation would be the result of leaving action to be initiated as and when individuals chose, Parliament had given to the Equal Opportunities Commission an important strategic role. Its powers of enforcement and investigation were intended to enable the EOC to design a coherent strategy for the advancement of sex equality in employment, education and training, and of access to goods, facilities and services (Corcoran, 1984).

But the impact of the legislation was disappointing. After an initial period of adjustment, women's pay as a proportion of men's appeared to settle at around the three-quarters mark and further movement seemed unlikely until long-standing patterns of occupational sectoralisation were altered. The EOC was strangled by its tripartite structure and its failure to generate a women's policy network at grass roots level (Gelb, 1984). Very early on the EOC decided to concentrate on research and on the use of persuasion rather than vigorous law enforcement. Its powers were increased by provisions in the 1976 Race Relations Act, which charged the EOC with issuing codes of practice as a result of its research findings, thus giving significance to the informal investigations it conducted. Formal investigations were to be more judicial and involve the possible subpoena of witnesses leading eventually to the issue of legally enforceable non-discrimination notices. Codes of practice were to be admissible in courts of law (Meehan, 1983; Corcoran, 1984). But by 1984 there had been only eight formal investigations and no codes of practice had been issued.

The inertia of the Commission in utilising its enforcement powers led the more pragmatic British managers to the conclusion that other legislation posed problems of more immediate concern. Trade unions too were less than cooperative. In the first year after the laws came into effect only about 20 per cent of tribunal applicants under equal pay legislation had union representation at their hearings. The early working of the two Acts suggested strongly that the formula chosen for sex equality policy was not right. This was of course partly due to the implications of policy goals of altering deeply rooted beliefs and opinions, but it also had more specific causes. Tripartism impeded the Commission's work considerably. The reservation of six posts for CBI and TUC (three each) nominees has meant that the majority of the commissioners have been in favour of the industrial status quo. In many matters to do with employment policy the views of unions and employers coincide. Commissioners nominated by the peak organisations have seen themselves as delegates from their organisations rather than as individuals with a responsibility for the promotion of sex equality (Byrne and Lovenduski, 1978b). Thus, over the years since it was established the EOC has used its capacity to fund and to generate research and has assisted complainants in bringing strategic cases but has been reluctant to use its wider powers of enforcement. Its view has always been that if discrimination and inequalities are to be eroded, concerted efforts by all departments and agencies of government were required. The Commission has established and maintained good contacts with other government bodies and ministries with varying outcomes, many of which have been disappointing. Its early eschewal of work with feminist groups and organisations had been dropped by the beginning of the 1980s, as had its almost embarrasingly timid low-key style.

Meehan (1982, 18) argues that the passage of legislation conferring rights or benefits on a particular rising group may be intended to preempt major demands without actually effecting redistribution. Symbolic rights such as those granted in preemptive equality legislation become tangible only when the protected group learns to bargain for implementation with politicians and administrators. The policy network which thus emerges consists of strategically placed individuals in the administration, the equality agencies and the legislature. In the USA, a previously organised but by no means extensive women's movement was encouraged to participate in such a network by equality agency officials. The result enhanced both agency and movement. In Britain no such encouragement was forthcoming from the EOC, and the policy network which formed was elite orientated with almost no basis in grass roots women's movement activities. Gradually, commissioners came to realise that it would be necessary to work more closely with women's organisations and the EOC has implicitly accepted the need for the development of some form of women's policy network. But its role continues to be limited. Tripartism is an impediment to radical initiatives in areas which might impinge upon collective bargaining customs. The British bureaucratic style, which emphasises the neutrality of officials, has provided a setting in which commissioners guard jealously their policy-making prerogatives. Delegation to staff is limited, and infrequent (monthly) Commission meetings make the decision process a slow one. In addition, the strategic placement of feminist staff members in policy networks is discouraged by the lack of delegation. Finally, executive dominance in Britain means that a cluster of interested legislators to which the Commission might be account-able and which would push it towards fulfilling its intended pur-poses does not exist. As Meehan (1983b) points out, sex equality gets low executive priority, and in Britain that goes a long way toward killing the policy. Indeed, from 1979 onwards the EOC has had to look to EEC law for sources of change rather than to the British executive, which has shown no interest in tightening equal pay and equal opportunities legislation. Thus, when the Equal Pay Act was amended to include work of equal value in 1983, this was the result of a finding by the European Court of Justice that the British legislation did not meet the requirements of European Community law. The grudging and minimalist compliance of the Thatcher government to the Court's rulings caused considerable press comment and offended the EOC and many women's organi-sations (Corcoran and Lovenduski, 1983).

British equality policy in the employment arena has been based upon legislation which assumes that the struggle for equality is an individual one waged by women who are abstracted from their family responsibilities. Both the Equal Pay Act and the Sex Discrimination Act rely on the ability of an individual to perceive discrimination and bring a charge. But in a society in which dependency and secondary status are often taken for granted, recognising discrimination may be almost as difficult as proving it (Corcoran and Donnelly, 1984; Lewis, 193b). More importantly, a sex equality policy which does not recognise that family and welfare concerns are important components of women's opportu-nities is doomed to eventual failure, a fact which is widely recog-nised by policy-makers as well as feminists. Converting that recog-nition into practice has been a slow and uneven process, however. The most encouraging developments have been those in the Greater London Council (GLC) in which a women's committee at decision-taking level has been developed and funded. This com-mittee underwrites a variety of women's projects as well as supporting a range of London women's groups and publications. It has proposed and seen established such innovations as equality officers to ensure sex equality in GLC employment policy and keeps a watching brief on possible projects to promote sex equality in London as well as on the gender implications of GLC policy. It has taken initiatives in the areas of health, lesbian rights, transportation, child-care provision as well as in areas directly concerned with employment. The ambit of the GLC women's committee is local and the proposed dissolution of the council will mean that it is likely that the women's committee will have ceased to function by the time this book appears in print. Its experience is instructive, however. The committee has been able to take radical initiatives not simply because of the powers it has been given (which are rather loosely defined) but because the political will to achieve its goals exists. The current, somewhat radical leadership of the GLC has a manifest commitment to equality between the sexes which shows up in sharp relief the absence of such a commitment amongst national politicians. The GLC model has been adopted by a number of Labour-controlled local boroughs, usually as a result of pressure from Labour women, and its ideas are being put into practice in a number of other areas. Employment initiatives taken by a number of local authorities have also been widely copied, with various councils declaring themselves to be 'equal opportunity employers' and taking appropriate steps to give those declarations meaning. Initial agreements are negotiated with unions, but the diffusion of innovation is encouraged by such institutions as the Royal Institute of Public Administration, which has run a series of seminars on the implementation of equal opportunity (Crowe, 1984; Crowe and Matthews, 1981; Campbell, 1984).

Employment policies designed to promote women have been controversial and have been resisted strongly at the point of implementation. Seeming accord as legislation was being developed concealed a well-entrenched collective bargaining hierarchy with the power to gain its objectives. Such syndromes are not unusual in matters to do with the British labour market, and most system responses have been predictable. To win sex equality at work, women will have to play by the rules of a long-established political game.

Policy-making in areas to do with sexuality has proceeded along rather less well-trodden paths, however. Issues such as birth control, rape and abortion have brought a much wider range of forces into play, involving what are normally quiescent social groups and raising difficult questions for legislators, often throwing the normal structures of decision-making into disarray.

Birth control policy was the first of these issues to reach the political agenda after women obtained the suffrage. The provision of contraception had engaged feminists and other women reformers throughout the 1920s and 1930s. Only in the 1930s was government prepared to accept the legality of supplying contraceptive information, a decision which was extended to all married women in 1949. In 1967 the National Health Services (Family Planning) Act instructed local authorities to provide free family planning advice and appliances. But the issue remained controversial, with a considerable debate taking place in the early 1980s over whether doctors have rights to prescribe birth control for minors without parental permission.

Rape law, too, has been controversial, with both the relevant laws and the procedures involved in prosecutions generating considerable discussion. Judicial attitudes were notoriously backward on issues of violence towards women, and it was eventually a series of judicial clangers which caused the law to be changed in 1976. The 1976 Sexual Offences Act guaranteed anonymity to both victim and accused and made it clear that rape could take place without overt violence. But feminists were dissatisfied with the law, not least because it does not acknowledge the existence of rape within marriage, and further changes were under discussion in 1984 (Benn, *et al.*, 1983).

It is the abortion issue which has engaged the British women's movement and political system in its most sustained interaction. The apparent early resolution of the issue of abortion regulation in Britain did not lead to the development of a lasting consensus. In 1967 on a 'free' vote Parliament gave its assent to a private member's bill proposed by Liberal MP David Steel. Essentially, the 1967 Abortion Act legalised abortion on therapeutic grounds on mental and physical indicators, where there was risk to the physical or mental health of a woman's existing children and where there was a substantial risk of the birth of a seriously mentally or physically handicapped child. Medical practitioners were able to take into account the woman's actual or foreseeable environment, the consent of two doctors was required and an upper time limit of twenty-eight weeks was implied.

The fact that Parliament was prepared to reform abortion law was due in a large measure to the activities of a well organised pressure group facing little in the way of organised opposition, the Abortion Law Reform Association (ALRA). By the end of 1967 it seemed that the issue had been settled once and for all. But important amendments came before Parliament on ten occasions between 1967 and the end of 1983, and eight of those occasions were attempts to restrict the availability of legal abortion. Such levels of activity over an issue are unusual in Britain, and in many respects the continued controversial status of British abortion policy is puzzling. Reform occurred at the beginning of a world-wide movement toward liberalisation (Francome, 1978; Tietze, 1981) and in a parliamentary era which saw the abolition of capital punishment, the decriminalisation of adult male homosexuality and the easing of divorce laws. No similar activity has been apparent on those issues. In the USA, which is the only liberalising country to have experienced comparable backlash, the Roe-v-Wade decision legalising abortion on request proved with hindsight to have been far too great a leap for American public opinion to absorb (see Tatalovich and Daynes, 1981). But in Britain liberalisation went nowhere near as far as it did in the USA. Those who had supported the 1967 Act had argued the case not for a woman's right to control her fertility but only for the extension of the number of categories of women for whom abortion should be made available. At its enactment, parliamentarians were specifically concerned *not* to legislate abortion on demand, for which little public, parliamentary or professional medical support could be found.

The continuing prominence of the abortion issue in Britain is due neither to its status as a 'moral' issue nor to an ill-judged initial 'overliberalisation'. Rather, abortion remains controversial because of the activities of the pressure groups formed in opposition to the 1967 Act and because of the countervailing groups largely set up as a reaction to them. The most important of these groups are the Society for the Protection of Unborn Children (SPUC) and LIFE, both of which are opposed to abortion in almost all circumstances, and, since 1975, the National Abortion Campaign (NAC), which supports abortion on demand up to term. SPUC and NAC are promotional groups in that they have been organised especially for the purpose of affecting abortion policy.

SPUC and LIFE chose traditional and direct forms of organisation to mobilise a mass membership in support of their aims and were able to harness Catholic congregations in support of their demands. NAC aimed at generating mass support by linking the energies of the recently emerging feminist movement to the existing structure of the labour movement, a fusion which had not until then been possible. The alliance thus formed was important not only in its effect on the outcome of the parliamentary debates for abortion law amendment (which were important but probably not decisive) but also for the insights it provides on the effect of feminist politics on pre-existing political arrangements (Lovenduski, 1984).

Abortion was a mobilising issue for British feminists. Feminist groups not only engaged in various forms of *ad hoc* political action but also participated in the established structures of British political activity. Lobbies were attended, interventions were made at election meetings, coordinating groups and campaigns were organised and influence was brought to bear by internal party groups of women. Alliances with unions proved important, as did the mobilising capacity of such traditional organisations as the Townswomen's Guild. In Parliament women MPs cooperated using the range of parliamentary skills to protect the 1967 Act. Parties, which had a free vote on the issue, tended to divide along the lines of socio-economic cleavage. However, some Labour MPs favoured restriction and some Conservative MPs did not. Labour Party feminists worked to obtain support for the 1967 Act, an effort which continues.

Whilst, apart from the proliferation of active interest groups, institutional accommodation over the issue of abortion has been minimal, its discussion has involved policy-makers in new kinds of discourse and in unaccustomed areas of discussion. The issue remains on the political agenda and groups like NAC continue to work in the labour movement to campaign for better facilities and to raise funds for the establishment of day care facilities. Some members have also tried to gain election to community health councils, and other means of influencing various stages of the policy process are being sought.

Although women have gained from the Sex Discrimination and Equal Pay Acts and the 1967 Abortion Act has been preserved, it must be said that policy on women in Britain is far from liberatory in its effects. This is due in part to a lack of a consistent interest on the part of policy-makers and stems from an unwillingness to take a comprehensive overview of the disadvantaged status of women. In particular, the critical importance of women's role in the family to their status relative to men's has been given no serious legislative recognition. The seemingly wide-ranging intentions of the Sex Discrimination Act have been overriden by successive unenthusiastic governments, and the Abortion Act, when all is said and done, expresses medical rather than feminist feeling on how such a law should be designed.

It is arguable that the British political environment is one which is particularly resistant to the sorts of policies on women which are necessary to the goal of sex equality. If family policy is an area which is important, and there are good reasons for believing that it is, then the unfamiliarity with the idea of family policy in Britain is an impediment to change. The official view that the family is an intimate sanctuary in which the state may intervene only for the purposes of sustenance is not conducive to the sorts of comprehensive reforms which take account of the realities of most women's lives. And Thatcherism has done little to assist women. Reductions in social service provision have extended family (i.e. women's caring) responsibilities to an unprecedented degree. This has combined with benefit reduction and the erosion of employment opportunities to reinforce women's traditional domestic roles. The theme of Conservative family policy has been the return of state welfare functions to the domestic arena.

Constraints on the direct influence of newly organised women on policy also characterise the British political environment. The growth of administrative power and the importance of a neutral civil service limits opportunities for influencing appointments to key positions. Policy is difficult to monitor and women have been marginalised by their organisation into separate women's groups of parties and unions which have only advisory powers. Occupants of structures of influence have been willing to respond to women's interests but unwilling to share power. The prevalence of tripartism makes it difficult for all but the best-established non-economic groups to gain a foothold, and historically the outlook for attitudinal groups has been poor in terms of size, finance and the ability to gain benefits (Gelb, 1984). Vallance has shown that of the 110 or so women covered in her study of women in the House of Commons, only a minority have felt a duty and obligation to their sex (Vallance, 1979). They have been limited by executive control of the legislative timetable to the use of such weak parliamentary tools as the filibuster, question time or private members bills in their efforts to promote women's causes. Direct legislative access by women has been too uneven and unreliable to make for hope of change. Such factors combined with the reluctance of traditional women's groups to join forces with new feminism (and vice versa) and the consequent absence of a national women's lobby particularly disadvantages those desiring reform of policy on women in Britain (Gelb, 1984, 38).

Italy

In Italy, reforms of policies on women have coincided with changes in political institutions, notably the growth of authority in the regions, the dispersal of various national functions to regional and local authorities and the enactment of such constitutional provisions as the referendum mechanism. Also important was the acceleration of the secularisation process which characterised the 1970s. Whilst the major obstacles to the implementation of equal rights policies in Italy are located in the disposition and receptiveness of the collective bargaining partners, in issue areas such as rape and abortion, cultural and psychological mechanisms are triggered which make compromise difficult.

Equality between the sexes in Italian life is guaranteed in article 3, clause 1 of the constitution adopted in 1946, a document which has been described as mainly a well-meaning statement of intentions (Caldwell, 1982). Sex equality provision was included in the constitution without discussion, in marked contrast to items covering other forms of discrimination. But ambiguity is introduced by article 29 on marriage, which indicates that an inequality between spouses (in favour of the husband) might be necessary to achieve the higher goal of preserving marriage, confirming the subordination of women to the family (Caldwell, 1981, 12). A signatory to the Treaty of Rome, Italy is bound by the Equal Pay, Treatment and Social Security Directives issued by the European Commission during the 1970s. As a result, legislation has been passed bringing Italian law into line with Community law, including an Equal Pay Act in 1977 and an Equal Opportunity Act in the same year. But much of the implementation of policies of sex equality at work has been left to the collective bargaining partners. A national committee for equal opportunities for men and women workers was formed by the Italian ministry of labour only in 1984, and this too includes union and political party representation as well as 'expert' membership (*Women of Europe*, No. 34, 37).

The process of regional reform provided for in the 1946 Constitution but implemented only during the 1970s involved the delegation of certain powers relating to economic planning and professional training to local bodies. The thirty-ninth article of the constitution provides that collective bargaining under certain conditions will result in legally enforcible contracts. This gives a constitutional-institutional status to the unions and employers. Many Italian social laws result from collective bargaining agreements which were later improved upon and rationalised by legislation. Concomitantly, legislators have devolved particular responsibilities to the unions. The Statute of Labour, 1970, and the Equal Opportunity Act, 1977, delegated the enforcement of relevant articles to the discretionary powers of the unions. For example, unions may make all the decisions over the allocation of women to night shifts or 'dangerous' tasks.

The Andreotti cabinet in 1978 created a specific under-secretariat dealing with women's affairs and a specific work commission, the Commission for Family Problems, was formed in the labour ministry at the same time, but neither were continued beyond the life of the government. At local level initiatives have been more innovative but tend to be patchy. Women's advisory committees (*consulti femminili*, a *latere* of local government) were promoted by the National Advisory Council for Women's Participation in Public Life, which is an association encompassing most of the major women's organisations. These began to be institutionalised in towns and regions in the early 1980s and by 1983 were to be found in fourteen towns and thirteen regions, including Rome and Trento (di Santis and Zincone, 1983, 5.51).

Other laws on women have been more radical, and the cultural acceptance of the concept of family policy as evidenced in the existence of a family code has aided more comprehensive policy-making. But Church dominance and a fascist heritage both play an inhibiting role in this area. Family policy is problematic for a state trying to dissociate itself from an authoritarian past. Until the late 1960s Italy still operated a whole set of laws inherited from the 1930s, including those on marriage, sexual violence, contraception, abortion and divorce. And the role of the Catholic Church has been evident, not simply in its impact upon the attitudes of the population but also in its critical role in welfare provision. In Italy Church and state have shared an area of responsibility which in other countries have been the exclusive domain of the state. The Church has, for example, either been responsible for or had a major influence over private institutions which were responsible for welfare assistance of various kinds. Prior to unification in 1861 it was religious organisations which undertook the responsibility for welfare work. Whilst a law of 1890 grouped all of these foundations together under state control in the IPAB (Instituzioni Publiche di Assistenza e Beneficenza), they remained to all intents and purposes ecclesiastical. Thus, the state in Italy is subject to a complicated series of relationships with the church as well as to various arrangements for the distribution of power between centre and periphery which leave the Catholic Church in control of many areas of family policy with basic support provisions therefore reflecting church priorities (Caldwell, 1982, 3–6).

In such circumstances the various changes in social and family policy of the 1970s and 1980s involved a serious reassessment of Church–state relations, as well as of the appropriate status of women. The first important change was one which did not at first involve any appreciable degree of women's movement activism, the law liberalising divorce. Divorce reform was first introduced into the Italian assembly by Loris Fortuna, a PSI deputy. Support was mobilised by the work of the Italian League for Divorce (LID), a cross-party, single-issue group which was masterminded by Marco Pannella, the secretary of the Italian Radical Party. It was an influential pressure group of middle-class liberal professional membership which had the necessary skills to back its demands, and divorce reform secured Chamber approval in 1969 and Senate ratification in 1970. The new law did not make divorce easy; for the first time it simply made it possible, which outraged the Church. Church desire to abrogate the law was sufficiently strong that the government was placed under pressure to set up the enabling statutes for the referendum provision which had been made in the 1946 constitution but never used. The drafting of the details of calling for a referendum was rapidly completed. The processes so outlined were lengthy and laborious and by the time a referendum was finally held in 1974 Italian society had had several years of experience of divorce (Clark *et al.*, 1974). In the event the national referendum on whether to retain divorce was won by those favouring the law, against concerted Church and Christian Democrat opposition. This event signalled a change in the political orientation of Italian women and paved the way for the legalisation of abortion several years later, which in turn provided the experience enabling feminists to place rape legislation on the political agenda in the early 1980s. Begun as a mainly male initiative without organised women's support, divorce, by the 1974 referendum, had attracted widespread women's support, belying fears that women would follow blindly the lead of the Church.

By contrast, abortion was from the beginning very much an issue of the Italian feminist movement, who were able to use the referendum provisions to bring their demands to the attention of politicians. From as early as 1971 the women's movement had been active on the issue, when the MLD had attempted unsuccessfully to obtain the required number (50,000) of signatures to bring forward a proposed law on the basis of popular initiative. Gradually, support for liberalisation grew and feminist and rights groups were increasingly active over the issue. The establishment of clinics challenged the legitimacy of existing laws. The state reacted at first with repression, arresting 263 Trento women for having had abortions, thereby mobilising the whole of the women's movement. Involvement in winning support for the divorce law engaged the attention of many women activists at that time. As the abortion issue became more pressing, parliamentary attempts were made to diffuse women's demands. Various parties proposed reformed but still fairly restrictive legislation. Indignant feminist activists stepped up the pressure using the referendum to call for the abrogation of existing law. The petition obtained substantially more signatures than necessary. The referendum's success meant that no law on abortion now existed. It created a policy vacuum and convinced the PCI in particular that substantial liberalisation of previous proposals was going to be necessary. The law which was eventually passed went appreciably further than legislators wished to go, but did not meet feminist calls for abortion on demand. Once the issue was before the legislature, the women's movement felt it had lost control and the various compromises which were made as part of the parliamentary process appeared to feminists as treacherous betrayals. Particularly disliked were a lenient 'conscience' clause, which allowed a national rate of refusal to perform abortions on conscience grounds of over 70 per cent and a short legal deadline of 90 days. In addition, no provision was made for facilities and abortions were restricted to certain types of hospitals and clinics which were insufficient in number (Eckman, 1983).

The abortion debate in Italy coincided with the emergence of a strong and radical women's health movement which engaged in what was essentially a struggle for alternative medical care. Medical power was felt to be oppressive to women who opened numerous feminist health centres (*consultori*) which were regarded by participants both as political opposition to the medical establishment and as assertions of autonomy from the state. In 1975 the passage of law N405 further politicised the issue by establishing public *consultori*. Characteristically, Italian feminists demanded a say in the management and scope of these local health clinics. They had numerous objections to the law and particularly opposed the devolution of control over *consultori* to the regions, which meant that the DCs would be able to control those in the south of the country for their own purposes. In the event, regional response varied. The DC-controlled south was extremely slow to establish public clinics, whilst the more left-wing northern regions were relatively conscientious. The point is that *consultori* became an issue in the abortion debate as it was possible for women to obtain the relevant medical consents for abortion at *consultori*. Hence, feminists wanted to be certain that they would have a presence there to provide legal advice to women and to ensure that permission was forthcoming. Also important was a longer-term aim of enabling abortions to be performed in the *consultori* (Eckman, 1979).

Placing the issue of abortion on the public agenda was a major achievement for Italian feminists, who, despite their evident resultant disenchantment with parliamentary politics, gained political experience which was to guide them in future political issues, notably the campaign to alter the law on rape, which followed a similar pattern. Detailed attention to implementation was made possible by the existence of the women's health movement, and there are, in some regions at least, signs of incremental policy-making on the issue of abortion provision. In early 1983 the regional administrative tribunal of Emilia heard a complaint by a doctor who had been replaced by a *consultori* management for being a conscientious objector. The tribunal judgment held that the health service had the right to specify that willingness to perform abortions was a condition for the post (CREW 32), a ruling which tightens considerably the unsatisfactory conscience clause.

The progress of the rape issue, however, indicates that the Italian women's movement and political system have some way to go before they come to terms with each other. Reasoning that loss of control over the abortion law was in part due to leaving it to political parties to bargain over the statute's content, feminist strategy on rape was to bring forward by referendum a model bill; that is, the movement aimed to introduce a bill directly before Parliament. This was done via a national petition drive in 1981 which collected 300,000 signatures, 250,000 more than necessary.

One of the things which most exercised Italian feminists was that fascist law made rape a crime against public morality rather than the person. This meant that a victim was required to report a rape, after which the police investigated the extent to which public morality was offended. This opened the way to prurient questioning of the victim both before and during court cases and, understandably, prevented many cases from being reported. Other feminist objections were to the fact that a rapist was deemed to be able to make restitution to his victim by marrying her, rape victims were required to show that violence had been used and the crime of rape within marriage was not legally recognised.

The unique element of feminist strategy on rape law was the use of a model law intended to force Parliament to confront the issue in feminist terms. But during the time the signatures were being collected, parties were able to preempt feminist strategies by presenting their own formulations of laws on sexual violence. Whilst all were agreed that the existing law was unsatisfactory, there were considerable differences of opinion over what should replace it. In all, the parties put forward seven different proposals, all of which went to the justice committee for compositing. The process of parliamentary bargaining was protracted, lasting from 1981 until at least the end of 1984, elements of the feminist model law seeming set for inclusion at that time. But once again women's movement representatives felt that they had lost control of their issue and disillusion with parliamentary processes was widespread (Beckwith, 1983; Eckman, 1983). Essentially, party strategies of obtaining the best possible bill conflict with understandable femin-ist unwillingness to compromise over issues which surround women's sexuality.

France, Germany and the Netherlands

France, Germany and the Netherlands illustrate further variations on the types of setting in which policies on women are made, but reflect also similarities with Britain and Italy. In France a variety of institutions have been devised to implement sex equality pro-grammes, the most distinctive of which has been the ministry of women's rights. First established by Giscard as a *ministère délégué* responsible for the status of women, the office was continued under Mitterand, when for a time its status was that of a full cabinet ministry. When Yvette Roudy took over the women's ministry in 1981, its budget was increased tenfold, indicating the greater commitment of the Socialist government to women's rights. In 1982 and 1983 a series of new laws was enacted and these were amalgamated with relevant existing work laws to set a framework for a programme of equality in employment for women which became known as the Auroux and Roudy Laws (Auroux was the minister for labour). These included require-ments for employers to produce annual reports on the compara-tive situations of men and women amongst their employees. Companies with more than 300 employees must produce quarterly outlines and are expected to prepare action programmes to ensure improvement where women are found to be at a disadvantage. Policies exist to improve women's membership of the professions and to strengthen women's unionisation and their access to training (Moreau-Bourles and Sineau, 1983). The ministry of women's rights plays a coordinating role and presides over an interministerial committee which aims to stimulate and coordinate the work on women's rights related issues throughout the administration. As well as the ministry, a longer-standing body, the committee on women's employment, was established in the labour ministry as early as 1971. This is comprised of specialists on women's work as well as women's association representatives and has been an effective forum for debate, information and preparation of legislative proposals relating to work done by women. It is as a result of a recommendation by this committee that the women's ministry was first established.

In 1984 France also established an Equal Opportunities Commission (Conseil Supérieur de l'Égalité Professionnelle entre les Hommes et les Femmes), set up to monitor the 1983 Roudy law. As well as making provision for information collection and positive action on a modest scale, the Roudy law abolished all protective legislation. It allows for programmes of positive discrimination to enable women to 'catch up', permitting temporary action designed solely for the benefit of women, and provides also for equal pay for work of equal value in keeping with EEC directives. But, as in the British case, where certain provision for positive action may be made in the area of training, France's law on positive action is permissive. Employers are under no compulsion to take advantage of its provisions. Women's groups would like to see these provisions made compulsory.

The Roudy ministry was extremely energetic between 1981 and 1983, establishing programmes on a range of women's issues, including contraceptive information campaigns, the opening of women's centres, the establishment for women of special training centres and the reservation for women of 60 per cent of the places in some mixed training centres. It became involved in the drafting of legislation on the reorganisation of work time and various other measures which had relevance for working women, and attempted to secure by legislation the establishment of quotas for women on electoral lists (a proposal which, when enacted, was declared unconstitutional by the courts). More arcane activities included the establishment in 1984 of a committee to study ways of feminising the French vocabulary. But Roudy was demoted from cabinet status in March 1983 and the women's ministry subjected to budget cuts in 1984, after which priorities became more circumscribed, a concentration on employment rights becoming paramount.

As in other Catholic countries, opposition to abortion liberalisation in France was very much the domain of the Church in conjunction with the political Right. Abortion was ruled by a 1920 law which until 1967 also banned access to contraception. Contraception was legalised in 1967 and abortion in 1975, under a conservative government. By 1975 the acceptance by the public of the practice of abortion had grown to the point where the judiciary could no longer enforce the law. In response to this the government sought to transfer control from the judiciary to the medical profession, who were reluctant to accept the transfer. Under the liberalised law women gained the right to make their own decisions after mandatory counselling, but only during the first twelve weeks of pregnancy. The law was passed for a 'trial' period of five years, at the end of which it was reviewed and made permanent. As a result of splits in the Centre-Right over the issue, the parliamentary Right was unable to obstruct liberalisation and suffered a further defeat in 1982, when an annually reviewable policy of reimbursement for abortions was introduced into the state health insurance scheme (Mossuz-Lavau, 1984). Abortion was important for the French women's movement and groups like Choisir played a role in gaining agenda status for the issue. But women's movement political engagement at other stages of the process has been difficult to detect. The presence of women in governing elites has been important to the development of equal rights policy, the energies of committed women like Roudy being instrumental in effecting substantial legal change. And the establishment of a range of equality institutions and agencies has meant that professionals, often women, in the area of women's rights are being placed, if not in, then within good access to elites providing vital links for the development of women's policy networks.

The Federal Republic of Germany is similar to Italy in that provision of equal rights for men and women is the subject of a constitutional precept. Article 3, paragraph 2 of the Basic Law decrees that men and women will enjoy equal rights and that all laws in conflict with the precept of equal rights will cease to be effective as of 31 March 1953. But in practice freedom of contract has been held to be of higher value than equal rights for men and women in the labour market. Indeed, the EEC Equal Pay and Treatment directives of 1975 and 1976 at first brought no changes in German law. Formal recognition is given to the view that sex equality should be provided for in collective wage agreements, and the executive has frequently stated that equality between the sexes should be observed in individual employment contracts. In 1973 the Bundestag established a Women and Society Commission to inquire into the status of German women. A wide ranging report was produced which suggested numerous measures and was passed to the relevant parliamentary committees in 1981 (Randzio-Plath and Rust, 1983). But relatively little was done. At the end of the 1970s discussion of the new conceptions of sex discrimination abolition as evidenced in the UK, and USA and Scandinavia led to some pressure from party women and women's groups for a German sex equality policy. Fairly quickly division appeared between those who favoured a comprehensive anti-discrimination law on the British model and those, including SPD women, who favoured a Swedish-style new labour-market policy for women with a politically appointed counselling body at the highest level (see below, p. 278). Demand for anti-discrimination legislation was opposed on three grounds: first, it was argued that outlawing particular forms of discrimination would be a step backwards from the absolute guarantees provided by the constitution; second, it was too slow a process; finally, an anti-discrimination law could not be integrated into the existing legal framework. But the Swedish model was objected to on the grounds that it could be no stronger or more effective than those in power wanted it to be, and would easily lend itself to reduction to mere 'alibi' functions. In the event the result of the call by the SPD women for a council was the establishment of a department for women in the ministry of youth, family and health at federal level, with a few states establishing such councils at Land level (Hohmann-Dennhardt, 1982). To comply with EEC directives, a law on equality for women in the labour market was brought in on 13 August 1980. The law satisfied no one, and unions, women's groups and women's associations argued that it lagged behind EEC requirements.

The equal rights agencies at Land level have met with less resistance. There they have either replaced traditional women's departments or opened new fields of policy responsibility. The first was established in Hamburg in 1979 followed by Bremen, Hesse, Bavaria and North-Rhine Westphalia. They have also been established at municipal level in Cologne and Gelsenkirchen. The tasks of these agencies are to help to create the basis and conditions for bringing about equal rights for women and to advise government in the planning stages of the likely effects of policies on women. They take up questions brought to them by women's groups and are resource centres, research funders and compilers of reports. They differ in status from state to state, with only Hamburg's agency having access to cabinet meetings. Women have made some use of these agencies and their establishment might arguably comprise an alteration of the policy process. Certainly, the equality agencies attracted considerable attention at the time of their establishment, and their very existence undoubtedly ensures at least a modicum of protection against sex discrimination. But they have no sanctions and are not therefore what German women's organisations want (Randzio-Plath and Rust, 1983).

As in many other European countries, abortion policy was controversial in Germany during the 1970s. But in Germany opponents to abortion reform have the immense propaganda advantage of being able to play the 'Third Reich card', hence the state has been particularly cautious in this area of policy-making. Women's movement activists first claimed agenda status for the issue via such devices as self-denunciation with taunts to the state to prosecute. Such actions were followed by the formation of feminist groups all over the country anxious to publicise the case for liberalising abortion laws. Debate was suspended by the 1972 general election. But the substantial victory for the SPD-FDP constituted a watershed for abortion policy. A majority of the newly confident SPD deputies were prepared to support liberalising legislation. As discussion progressed it became apparent that political debate centred around four distinct proposals which cut across party lines. The majority in the governing coalition tended to support abortion on demand in the first three months of pregnancy, whereas the majority of the opposition favoured only medical eugenic grounds for termination. The minority on the government side supported a conditional liberalisation only, whilst a minority of CDU/CSU deputies were prepared to support only the grounds of serious endangerment to a mother's health if the pregnancy continued. These four positions were fairly coherently articulated and reflected in the population by analogous sets of opinion. Women on the Left and feminists were united in a demand for complete decriminalisation. A majority of more moderate opinion and mass-based women's organisation favoured abortion on demand during the first three months of pregnancy. The majority of medical opinion supported a permissive law based on specific indicators and Catholic and conservative opinion favoured only a very restrictive reform (Marten, 1984). The abortion law that Germany eventually got (in 1976) was one which was broadly comparable to the British 1967 Act, and the processes through which it was negotiated were similar to those which had occurred in Italy. Both the SPD and the PCI were inhibited by their leadership's strategies of winning Catholic support and the need, therefore, to make some accommodation to Catholic opinion on policy matters. The original lack of enthusiasm on the part of the PCI for feminist abortion law reform proposals should be seen in the light of its strenuous efforts to win Catholic support during the previous decade. Similarly, the transformation of the SPD from a class-based to a 'people's' party had necessitated accommodation with religious influences in society. But like the PCI, the SPD was mindful of the opinion of party women who largely supported a policy of abortion on demand. As a result, in both cases the parties made concessions to the demands of women but did not go so far as to allow organised women control over the type of policy they eventually got. In Germany a considerable women's involvement was detectable in the discussions and negotiations which took place over both issues, suggesting a pattern in which women's organisations are present and participating in policy-making, but have insufficient clout to prevail over better established structures.

The Dutch equality programme began with an emancipation commission, established in 1974 as an independent advisory body to advise government on the construction of a coherent policy to promote the emancipation of women. It consisted of fourteen independent members chosen for expertise in important problem areas, and eleven government representatives from ten ministries and the Social and Cultural Planning Office in an advisory capacity. At a later stage these representatives became the interministerial committee on emancipation policy, in which all ministries are represented. The first task of the commission was to prepare the memorandum on emancipation policy on which the government's policy came to be based. The programme was aimed at removing sex-role restrictions, to aid either sex to catch up in areas in which they had statistically been left behind and to attach greater value to characteristics generally held to be traditionally women's. At the end of 1977 a state secretary was appointed with a portfolio of coordinating and promoting emancipation policy. The machinery at her disposal included a policy department at her own ministry, a government consultative committee, internal coordination groups at various ministries, an independent advisory commission, the emancipation commission later succeeded by the emancipation council and a special parliamentary committee on emancipation policy. Government funding was made available to support relevant activities in the form of subsidies for projects which promoted women's emancipation. Regional and a national resource centres were also set up. In short a sex equality apparatus was established during the 1970s and early 1980s which is today the most extensive and comprehensive in Europe (see Council of Europe, 1982). But in its early stages the equality programme generated a negative response amongst feminists, who were incensed by the manner in which Mrs Kraaijeveld, the first secretary of state, discharged her responsibilities. In her first year in office the secretary left more than half of her budget unspent, whilst many women's groups had been unable to get funding. She also altered many of the arrangements for financing made between feminist groups and the commission and antagonised many moderate feminists by both her cavalier attitude and the pleasure she apparently took in announcing that she was not, in fact, a feminist (Mossink, 1980). Such behaviour and responses are strongly reminiscent of Betty Lockwood in her early days of chairing the British Equal Opportunities Commission. Indeed, it is likely that for some time to come, criteria of government and feminist suitability for office in the state equality apparatuses will diverge, resulting in the exacerbation of cynicism amongst organised feminists towards state emancipation policy.

The Dutch women's movement had rather more success in its intervention in the abortion debate. In the Netherlands, as in Britain, abortion had agenda status prior to women's movement interest in the issue. Hence, most parties had taken up positions by 1972 and abortion had already been politicised by 1974 when the government began to devise its comprehensive emancipation policy. Joyce Outshoorn (1983) argues that the success of the women's movement was the redefinition of the issue in such a way that all legislative efforts were judged in terms of the extent to which they enabled a woman to choose herself whether or not to have an abortion. In her view the women's movement both changed the definition of abortion and maintained its own new definition over a considerable period of time.

A situation had developed in Holland in which abortion in practice was considerably more widespread than the law permitted. Numerous and accessible clinics practised without fear of prosecution (Outshoorn, 1983). Hence, when a 'liberalising' law was finally agreed it lagged behind social experience of the policy.

The bill passed in 1981 finally came into force in November 1984 when it was widely believed it would have no effect on practice. The problem of a discredited law is a fairly hardy perennial in abortion policy, but it is unusual to find one which has been exposed before its implementation. At the time of writing Belgium, too, was experiencing political deadlock over the abortion issue. Restrictive laws had long been ignored by professionals, who performed numerous abortions, the legal status of which was not always certain. A series of trials caused a public outcry and demonstrated the inability of the courts to enforce laws which were at variance with social experience. But the Belgian legislature proved unable to agree a liberalising statute during the six years after the issue arrived on the parliamentary agenda in 1978 (Pereira, 1984). Both the Belgian and the Dutch experiences illustrate the disarray into which a political system may be thrown when confronted by issues with which it was not constructed to deal. Such experiences do not commend normal political mechanisms to feminists.

The Nordic States

Of all the European liberal democracies it is Sweden which has been credited with the most comprehensive and reasoned policy on women. Sweden was one of the first European nations to sign the United Nations convention on equal pay (1960). Since the 1950s a network of contraceptive advice centres has been available to all women over the age of fifteen, regardless of marital status. Abortion law was first reformed in 1938 after which steady progress was made until the liberal 1975 Act was passed (Sward, 1984). The *de jure* provision for abortion on demand is backed by the full range of public facilities. Sweden is also one of the few countries to recognise the crime of rape within marriage.

It was in the late 1960s that Sweden first began to frame an official sex equality policy. In a declaration to the United Nations to the government stated that all legislation and all social policy would henceforth support a shift from the assumption that men were the breadwinners and women the homemakers to a social goal in which society was a set of independent individuals. A long-term programme was launched which aimed at ensuring that everyone had the same practical opportunities. The immediate source of Sweden's programme was a study group of Social Democratic women which had been formed in 1960 and whose 1964 report became part of the Social Democrats 1969 programme. But socio-economic factors were at least as important. Since the 1950s labour shortages had made it necessary for employers to attract women into the workforce. Between 1960 and 1970 women made up the entire increase in the size of the working population. The LO and TCO became interested in questions of sex equality at work and established the joint female labour council in 1950 in conjunction with the employers federation (SAF). This group identified the division of labour in the home as the most persistent source of women's inequality at work (Scott, 1982, 22). In 1972 the joint council was replaced by prime minister Olof Palme's advisory council on equality between men and women. Directly responsible to the prime minister's office, the council consisted of five Social Democrat women who could consult a larger body of twenty representatives from the unions, employers, government agencies and county and municipal authorities as well as various women's organisations. The advisory council initiated an active labour-force policy to combat sex segregation in the labour market using both positive action and quotas to promote equal opportunities for women. The council resigned in 1976, followed electoral defeat for the Social Democrats, and its functions were assigned to a succeeding equality committee (the committee on equality between men and women) with all-party representation which was attached to the ministry of labour. The new all-party committee had less of a sense of direction than its predecessor which had been characterised by substantial internal agreement on policy direction (Nielsen 1982; Scott, 1982; Council of Europe, 1982).

The Swedish sex role equality programme did not turn to equal pay and opportunity legislation until the 1980s. The preferred style had been to leave matters to do with the work-place to the collective bargaining partners who, in exchange for minimal interference, were expected to get on with the spirit of the programme. And to some extent this was successful. For example, women's average hourly earnings as a percentage of men's rose from 68.8 per cent in 1960 to 80 per cent in 1970 and to 87 per cent in 1977 (Scott, 1982, 24). The programme won concrete gains which had not been achieved in other countries. The official view was that sex equality would be best achieved in a decentralised society which emphasised the participation of individuals in the life of the community. However, the largely privately owned system of production in Sweden had different imperatives. Equality is costly in profit terms. Employer reluctance and union protection of prerogatives led to their agreement that labour-market matters were best settled by union and employer representatives. This view was honoured whilst the Social Democrats continued in power. But when the Centre Party entered government it called on the committee on equality to draft sex equality legislation. After initial failure, a bill (the Act on Equality Between Men and Women at Work) which allowed affirmative action and established an equality ombudsman (sic!) was passed in December 1979 and took effect in 1980. The industrial organisations had, in the hope of demonstrating that legislation was unnecessary, meanwhile negotiated and signed a number of equality agreements which banned discrimination and called for sex equality. But the minimal implementation of these agreements may have actually hastened the final passage of the Act (Scott, 1982, 34). An equal opportunities commission was also set up in 1980 (with membership from both sides of industry) which had enforcement responsibilities for the ombudsman's decisions. Coordination was to be ensured by the establishment of an inter-ministerial body in the cabinet office chaired by a special minister for matters concerning equality between men and women. The 'equality' minister is attached to the ministry of labour and the inter-ministerial committee consists of a senior officer from each ministry. Additionally, the minister for equality has a special advisory council consisting of representatives from the largest women's organisations. Union and employer representation on the equal opportunities commission and the unions' role in assisting members with industrial complaints ensures that the powers of the 'social partners' remain intact.

Sweden's women's rights initiatives have, more than in most countries, been predicated on an understanding of women's family roles and the need for their alteration if significant changes are to be made. Role-sharing in the family is seen as one mechanism for change, and policies have been designed to facilitate this. The widely publicised provision for parental leave which may be taken either by the mother or father is an example of this. Social services, too, have been designed to encourage women's entry into the workforce, by providing support services and benefits to assist with the fulfilment of family roles. But this has given rise to its own problems in the generation of a large public sector with an attendant class of service workers, largely women, who are employed by local authorities to perform services which formerly would have been performed within households. Women dominate the lower-paid echelons of this class of workers. Such a situation raises the question of whether a social service system which gives its low-paid, low-prestige jobs to women is breaking down stereotypes or whether it is merely transporting and reinforcing them (Adams and Winston, 1980, 26).

Sex-equality policy has also been an important feature of women's lives in the other Nordic countries, although it is nowhere as advanced as in Sweden. Norway has similar employment equality machinery to that which exists in Sweden, with councils characteristically including representation from unions and employer associations. Tripartism also characterises the Danish equal status council established in 1975. Finland has had an equal pay policy since its ratification in 1962 of the International Labour Conference equal-pay agreement, although implementation has been uneven (Haavio-Mannila, 1981, 228). Finnish government equality programmes underpin the right to work regardless of sex or marital status and include provisions to safeguard women's re-entry into the labour market after periods of child care at home. But progress to equality has been slow, with no examples of cases being brought under the relevant statutes by 1981 (OECD, 1981).

In Sweden the power of the collective bargaining partners has been an inhibition on progress, although not perhaps to the extent that it has been in Britain or West Germany. Certain policies have been avoided because they meet with opposition in the labour-market organisations. For example, Social Democratic women in Sweden have for some years proposed a thirty-hour working week and six-hour day as a basis for employment androgyny and domestic role-sharing. In an economy in which most women workers are employed part-time and most male workers, full-time, the attractions of such a scheme are evident. But unions see their role as one which must give priority to the protection of the interests and incomes of full-time male workers. Hence, the policy has been given little serious consideration. The economic organisations are, it should be said, the site of negotiation of the redistributive implications of sex equality policy in employment, and it is therefore to be expected that they will be obstructive. Understandable and predictable though it is, however, the problem is one which needs to be solved if progress is ever to be made. It is in the overturning of traditional economic organisation priorities that increasing the access of women to decision-making positions may eventually make an appreciable difference to the effects of emancipation policy.

Abortion policy has generated relatively little controversy in post-war Sweden (Sward, 1984), and its liberalisation has not been effectively opposed in Denmark (Dahlerup and Gulli, 1983). But in Norway the issue generated considerable political conflict. Abortion was on the Norwegian political agenda for about fifty years, but no decision was made for thirty of them. The early Norwegian women's movement was reluctant to take up the struggle for abortion rights, despite recognition that birth control, contraception and abortion form important components of a comprehensive emancipation policy. But after 1935 state pro-natalism as a response to drops in fertility finally brought abortion under discussion. Doctors' demands for legal clarification pro-vided an additional pressure. By the end of that year an abortion law was before the Storting. The major debate was over whether social indicators were to be allowable. The issue was still unresolved at the outbreak of war, after which initiatives from women's organisations for liberal legislation began as early as 1945. The bill which was drafted and accepted in 1960 generated little public debate, however, and the 'women's right to choose' position was not an element in the discussion. Only after 1969 did the terms of the debate change. Then the Labour Party, in response to demands from its women members, forwarded reform proposals in which abortion was defined as both a liber-ation and family issue. In 1974 these proposals failed to win sufficient parliamentary support. However, abortion had been an issue in the 1973 elections, and from that time on the women's movement had the initiative, its definitions of the problem a part of the debate. Abortion law was finally liberalised in 1978 (Wiik, 1984).

Opposition to abortion liberalisation in Norway reflects the important role that religion continues to play in its policies. The Norwegian Christian People's Party is at the centre of political life and its adamant opposition to any legalisation of women's rights over abortion blocked a coalition of bourgeois parties after the defeat of the Labour Party in 1982, forcing the conservative parties to form a minority government (Dahlerup and Gulli, 1983). It is unusual for a women's movement concern to be so important a part of the political agenda and in current structures of politics perhaps possible only over the abortion issue. In Norway three main lines of cleavage could be identified as rele-vant to the issue of abortion rights, gender, class and religion. Whilst party structures divide more or less along the lines of the latter two, divisions along gender lines are not easily expressed. The unity of organised women on the question made resolution difficult as women gradually accumulated party support for their views (Wiik, 1984).

International Actors: Effect of the EEC

The levels of development of its policy-making powers achieved by the European Commission by 1984 offered no scope for intervention in the abortion policies of member states. However, in the area of employment rights the EEC has developed an impressive, if narrowly constructed, set of sex-equality policies. Over a twenty-five year period EEC policy on women has progressively broadened from a narrow concern with equal pay to a wider programme dealing with a range of employment rights issues. The basis of Commission policy is article 119 of the Treaty of Rome, the only provision in the treaty which makes specific mention of women. Article 119 states that men and women should receive equal pay and was originally devised to avoid distorting competition between employers using male or female labour, as part of Community labour-market harmonisation objectives.

Over time, the narrow economic construction of treaty matters gave way to broader interpretations which included areas of social concern and led to a climate in which it was possible to test the status of the equal pay provision in the courts of member states. Popular feeling over the equal pay issue in Belgium inspired lawyer Elaine Vogel-Polsky to seek a test case. Her objective was to determine whether article 119 enabled women to claim over and above what the law in their own country required. With predictable attention to their collective bargaining prerogatives, the Belgian unions would not assist Vogel-Polsky in choosing a case, leaving her eventually to find one via the Association of Airline Staffs. A Sabena Airlines employee, Gabrielle Defrenne, had complained that she was expected to retire at forty when men were not and that the terms of her pension were inferior to theirs. After winding its way through the Belgian judicial system the case was heard by the European Court of Justice in 1971. The judges ruled that, for technical reasons, the particular complaint fell outside the scope of article 119, but implied that in straightforward equal pay cases the article would be interpreted as conferring rights on women (Rights of Women Europe, 1983). The first Defrenne judgment (there were two later cases) publicised the equal pay issue and Community obligations to its achievement. It coincided with a Commission-sponsored report on the position of women in employment in all the member states which made clear the disadvantages women faced in the labour market. Pressure came from women within the Commission's social affairs directorate (DGV) for a stronger equal pay policy at a time when it was felt that assistance for disadvantaged groups was important for political stability and might lead to more popular involvement in EEC activities. Accordingly, a social action programme was initiated in 1974 which was aimed at improving working conditions for disadvantaged social groups. Proposals on women prepared in DGV proved easy to slot into this programme (Hoskyns, 1984; Rights of Women Europe, 1983). In 1975 a Commission memorandum was produced which highlighted a number of areas of women's work for attention. In the same year the second Defrenne case produced a European Court ruling that article 119 was, within certain limits, directly applicable to those forms of discrimination which originated in legislative provisions or in collective labour agreements as well as cases in which men and women received unequal pay for the same work on the same premises.

The immediate result of these events was the development of a Community policy on equal opportunities for women which was expressed first in the three equality directives passed in 1975, 1976 and 1979 (Nielsen, 1982). The directives covered equal pay, equal treatment in employment (including training) and equal treatment in social security matters.[1] The equal pay and treatment directives took effect immediately, whilst member states were given until 1984 to bring the relevant aspects of their social security provisions into line. Issuing a council directive on a matter immediately brings into existence a set of European Commission procedures and structures for implementing, monitoring and reviewing its application. Accordingly, a women's information bureau and a women's employment bureau were established within the Commission and the existing equal pay unit was expanded to include the ubiquitous employer and union representatives as well as a few of the more mainstream women's organisations (Rights of Women Europe, 1983). Cooperation with the national equal status councils and commissions was provided for in the establishment of a permanent advisory commission on equal opportunities. This consisted of representatives of the national agencies and provided observer status for employer and union representatives. The advisory commission drafted a new action programme on equal opportunities which was submitted to the council in 1981. Drawing heavily on Scandinavian and United States experiences, its general thrust is supportive of positive action, indicating that only when positive measures accompany equality programmes will significant change be obtained (Nielsen, 1982, 277).

Many observers believe that the directives were passed in the nick of time as the deepening recession of the late 1970s reduced considerably the social policy impetus of the Commission. Be that as it may, by the beginning of the 1980s the various equality mechanisms were beginning to have an effect with a number of infringement proceedings underway and the establishment of a grass-roots feminist network to scrutinise policy on women (Hoskyns, 1984; Rights of Women Europe, 1983). Added interest was generated when the 1979 elections returned a European Parliament nearly 17 per cent of whose members (MEPs) were women, many of whom turned out to have an interest in women's rights. Parliamentary activity began almost immediately with the establishment of an *ad hoc* committee on women's rights, which met and discussed throughout 1980. This was replaced by the committee of inquiry into the situation of women in Europe, which was established as a permanent committee after the 1984 elections (CREW IV/8/9). As European Parliament resolutions are not binding, the committee's work has depended upon its conclusions being taken up in other community institutions. To this end it has become a powerful and important women's lobby, part of a developing EEC-level women's policy network.

Since issuing the social security directive of 1979, the EEC has been unwilling to extend its sex-equality policies to other areas by means of additional directives. Despite a resolution of the European Parliament in January 1984 calling for a legally binding directive on positive action, the Commission has opted for a recommendation, the weakest legal instrument it can propose. Adopted on 18 April 1984, the recommendation on positive action calls for national plans of action to be formulated which are to be aimed at removing legal barriers to positive action. Plans for encouraging positive action schemes are also to be devised in each country. Recommendation, as such, was undoubtedly chosen because it was felt that a directive would have no chance of success. It envisaged information campaigns, statistical studies, more measures to ease the problems of working parents and more encouragement for women to take up decision-making positions in the corporate channel. Two consultancy firms have been approached to examine how industry might be encouraged to start positive action programmes (CREW IV/5).

The development of legislation for women's rights in the European Community was not in any direct sense the product of the activities of second-wave feminism. It was not, as Catherine Hoskyns remarks (1984), fought for in any direct sense by women.

But organised women have paid increasing attention to Community legislation, which has become an important source of change in national policy. In countries in which governments had been unsympathetic to legislation on women's rights, the EEC has in the absence, often, of an organised women's movement, been the only source of legal reform. Its role has been both formal, in the sense of the impact of particular directives on national law, and informal, in that it has been an important filter for the diffusion of innovation. In Greece, for example, the conjuncture of EEC entry and the election of a Socialist government heralded important changes for women. As well as implementing EEC equality directives, laws on rape, on sexist advertising, on the harmonisation of pensions and the promotion of women's cooperatives were all planned by the new government according to Ms Antonious-Laiou, the prime minister's special counsellor for women's affairs. Speaking to the European Parliament's committee of inquiry into the situation of women in Europe on 23 November 1983, the special counsellor described a series of regional offices and equality committees set up throughout Greece in the summer of 1983 to take complaints and provide advice about incidences of direct or indirect sex discrimination (CREW 111/10). Until membership in the EEC was gained, the Greek government had seen no need for laws on equality. And despite constitutional provision for equal rights, other laws were not brought into line. Similar effects are to be observed in Spain and Portugal, both of whom were aspirant EEC members in 1984. In both countries constitutional provision for equal rights were followed by laws compatible with Community directives on equal pay and opportunities.

Community sex-equality policy has provided tangible benefits for certain women. However, like other EEC initiatives it is ultimately reflective of what member governments will agree to and is therefore a minimalist policy, reflecting, in particular, the effective veto power the collective bargaining partners have over the shaping of legislation which covers employment contracts. The policies are part of a commitment to the harmonisation of collective labour law, which has been difficult to advance without altering the balance of power between the social partners. Although Commission statements have been fairly sharp on the topic of the efforts of labour-market organisations to cooperate (Nielsen, 1982, 283), direct confrontation has been avoided, and it seems likely that here, too, policies of benefit to women will fall foul of the wishes of better-established interests.

State Socialist Societies

In the state socialist systems of East and Central Europe the benefit of the absence of an established powerful structure for collective bargaining is neutralised by the concomitant absence of any independent organisations which might express women's interests. State policy-makers in this respect have a clear field for the formulation and the implementation of measures directed at women. Constraints arise from an ideological commitment to equal rights for women at work, the exigencies of pro-natalist population policies and, in some countries, chronic labour shortages. Public policy in the state socialist societies has promoted women's economic, legal and social emancipation up to the point at which these objectives have coincided with centrally held national goals. The benefits to women have been appreciable. They have, for example, had educational and occupational access for longer than women in other states and have gained considerably from early reforms in marriage laws and family codes. But access to birth control has been variable as both pro-natalism and economic priorities have not favoured the development of safer, more convenient modern forms of contraception. For example, the birth control pill is hardly available in the USSR. Social provision for maternity and child care is often extensive, however, and social policy has for many years been directed at the assimilationist policy goal of enabling women to cope with the dual burdens of domestic and public labour. Assimilation by women rather than role sharing has been the favoured solution to dual burden constraints by East European policy-makers, whose most significant policy models come from the Soviet Union, where experience of massive entry by women in to the workforce dates to the first years after the Bolshevik Revolution of 1917.

In the USSR the high participation rate of women in the economy is the result not only of the regime's commitment to sex equality but also a product of economic and demographic goals. The shortages of male labour caused by civil and world war casualties have made women's employment a vital component of economic strategy. Beginning with Stalin's first five-year plan in 1928, the mobilisation of women into the workforce has been an important regime priority and one which has been implemented with considerable success. Up to 92 per cent of Soviet women of working age are in paid employment outside the home, a proportion of 85 per cent having been achieved by the end of the 1940s. But, despite some inroads into normally male-dominated professions such as medicine and certain kinds of engineering, occupational sectoralisation prevails and women's pay is unlikely on average to be more than 87 per cent of men's (Lovenduski, 1981b). Salary rates are lower in the industries in which women are concentrated. Mary Buckley believes that Soviet women are regarded as unstable labour-force participants who have lower productivity rates than do men. This is reinforced by traditional attitudes. But provision of services has not yet caught up with women's workforce participation. Domestic labour relief, which was originally foreseen as being provided by the collectivisation of various tasks (e.g. by the establishment of public laundries, canteens, etc.) is virtually non-existent. And regime prioritisation of heavy industry at the expense of consumer goods has impeded the production of labour-saving household appliances. Child-care facilities have, however, steadily grown in both number and quality, although their availability varies regionally – more than half of those available are located in the Russian Republic. Regional variation may have cultural rather than political sources. Buckley (1981, 85) cites the example of 25 million roubles provided for child care in Turkmenia which were never touched.

Soviet newspaper articles and letters have for many years suggested that women's policy, or at least some aspects of it, has been very much a topic of debate and interest (Hough, 1978). And pro-natalism has been a recurring theme, at first because of general population shortages, more recently because of fears that the Russians and other Slavic groups will soon be vastly outnumbered by the various non-Slavic nationalities, whose birth rates have been consistently higher. Divorce rates too have soared and housing provision is often poor, none of which encourages the production of large families. The regime has responded by attempting to make fecundity financially interesting via maternity benefits and by measures designed to support the family. The 'woman question' has been given new recognition and no longer do officials claim that it is solved. But Buckley writes that discussions are rarely pitched around women's fulfilment. Rather, they are posed in terms of the needs of the economy or of population replacement. There are clear signs that women are dissatisfied, but few that they are able to put organisational pressure on the Soviet elites (Buckley, 1981; Lapidus, 1978).

Similar patterns are to be found in the East European states of the German Democratic Republic and Czechoslovakia. Women benefit considerably from economic strategies which depend upon their presence in the workforce, but are not the focal point of the·

policies, hence have only indirect bargaining power. In East Germany the constitution and the labour code both stipulate that the state is required to create the institutions and the conditions whereby a woman may combine a full professional life with roles as a wife and mother. Accordingly, 92 per cent of all children between the ages of three and six were cared for in state-supported kindergartens, and over 60 per cent of those between six months and three years old were cared for in state-supported nurseries in 1980. After-school centres exist for the supervision of children up to ten years of age. Pregnancy and maternity leave provisions are generous and increase for each child. There is access to birth control facilities from the age of sixteen (Ecklein and Zollinger, 1981).

Training and employment policy include a number of special measures to encourage women's education, including various provisions assisting the retraining of older women. Equal pay is a problem which is considered to have been solved but a pronounced pattern of occupational sectoralisation which concentrates women in the less well paid occupations indicates that it is unlikely to obtain in practice. Measurable indicators suggest that the state women's policy is a successful one in that about 90 per cent of women of working age were in employment by 1980, although a considerable number of these were in part-time jobs. A notable increase in women's occupational status has also been evident. Concerted skilling programmes have been well subscribed and by 1980 seventy per cent of all working women had completed some form of vocational training. Evidence also exists that women are moving into traditional male occupations. For example, nearly 52 per cent of students newly admitted to study building material technology in 1974 were women. By 1980, 40 per cent of all apprentices for technical occupations were girls. And East German trade unions run extensive affirmative action programmes in which the promotion of women is stipulated and enforced by agreements made with management (Ecklein and Giele, 1981).

The policies on women's employment pursued by the East Germans are particularly comprehensive, but they have not met with unrestrained approval from women there. A highly lopsided age-structure has resulted in great demands on labour productivity of those who are employed. Women's dissatisfaction is expressed in a stubbornly low birth rate and a rising divorce rate and more directly in complaints to unions and newspaper editors in the form of letters. Demographic and economic considerations comprise a considerable amount of the motivation for the assiduous attention which is paid to the encouragement of women to take up employment opportunities. However, the policies have proved effective in many respects and there is little doubt that other nations could benefit considerably from the adoption of some of the East German schemes.

Czechoslovakia, which is the other of the two most prosperous socialist states established after the Second World War, has had rather less success with its emancipation policies. The mobilisation of women into the workforce began almost immediately after the war. Strategies were largely predicated on conceptions of women as economic resources. Constitutional grants of equal rights were made in education, employment, the family and in participation in public and cultural life. Direct efforts were made to recruit and train women party cadres and to encourage women into the workforce. The moral and financial incentives employed by the regime relied heavily upon the women's organisations but did not, in this period, challenge the importance of the family. The ideal woman was one who could easily combine family and employment roles with spare-time political activism. The immediate results of these policies were positive in that women's labour-force participation expanded. But in emancipation terms their success was less evident. Occupational sectoralisation caused unequal pay, the provision of child care was inadequate and the strains on women soon became apparent. For many years they were exhorted to solve such strains by dint of better organisation and greater will power, but by the early 1960s it became apparent that policies would have to be reconsidered. From then on consideration has been given to women's roles as mothers as well as their work obligations. As Wolchik writes (1981c) the ideal unitary socialist superwoman of the propaganda of the early years has been replaced by a more cleverly constructed life-cycle-sensitive model which emphasises reproduction at a certain period in the woman's life and production at others. Women in Czechoslovakia are still expected to fulfil all the roles of wife, mother, worker and political activist, but no longer simultaneously.

Policies on women at work in the rest of Eastern Europe have resembled that of Czechoslovakia. For the most of their existence these regimes have suffered labour shortages which have strengthened elite resolve to mobilise women into the workforce. Conditions of economic scarcity impeded the development of collective solutions to the resultant dual burdens and in all such states women's employment policy has been assimilationist – it has aimed at assisting women to cope with their dual workloads rather than at removing family tasks to some other sphere of responsibility. But such strategies proved to have other consequences, notably dramatic declines in fertility rates, as harassed women sought to limit the size of their families. Throughout Eastern Europe the early 1960s were years of fertility decline whilst the West was having a baby boom. Fertility decline coincided with a wave of abortion liberalisations beginning in the Soviet Union in 1955, after which all but Albania had followed suit (although East Germany waited until 1972 to liberalise its laws). The subsequent surge of legal abortions was perceived as a direct cause of falling birth rates and led to active pro-natalist policies in most of the countries in the bloc. In Rumania, Czechoslovakia, Hungary and Bulgaria abortion provision was once again restricted. In most countries, paid maternity leave was either introduced or increased in both amount and time. Childcare allowances and cheap housing loans were provided which were progressively written off with the birth of each child. Indeed, by the early 1970s in Czechoslovakia 10 per cent of the government's annual budget was being spent on direct payments to potential parents plus various other pro-natalist incentives such as nurseries, school meals, subsidies for children's transport, and so on. By the beginning of the 1980s there were explicit pro-natalist policies in all of the countries except Yugoslavia.[2] (David, 1984, 4). The measures varied in their scope and effect. In Czechoslovakia women seeking abortions must appear with their husbands before so-called interruption committees which have the power to decide whether she may have an abortion. It is believed that when the birthrate is high enough the decisions are more lax, but when it falls, the committees become stricter, a pattern which is occasionally manifested in legal changes to the time limit provisions of the abortion law (Fistejnová, 1983). During the 1970s the results of measures to improve birth rates were promising, but downturns occurred in the early 1980s in Hungary, Bulgaria and Czechoslovakia, and as early as the late 1960s in Rumania. Some demographic analysts believe that the effect of the cash-benefit policies was to produce birth earlier than might otherwise have been the case, but not to generate more births. What the pattern boils down to in families with children is the absence of a third child. Families apparently want only two children whilst pro-natalists' goals require three (David, 1982). The problem for policy-makers is how to increase the birthrate without taking women out of the workforce. The encouragement of role sharing is eschewed because the last thing elites want to do is replace men in employment with women.

The full employment of women has been a policy objective in state socialist societies since their inception, and the problems it presents have been experienced more fully there than elsewhere. Difficulties arise not only because women's needs are not given sufficient expression but also because the regimes operate in conditions of considerable economic scarcity and prioritise goals which exclude resource allocation to collectivist relief of women's domestic work. There is ample evidence that state socialist women are dissatisfied with their circumstances, but few opportunities exist for their grievances to be expressed. In this regard East European elites might learn from Western experience, which indicates that imaginative workable policies are unlikely to be devised in situations in which client groups are not consulted.

Equal Employment Policy in Liberal Democracies

The great variety and range of 'new' policies on women introduced since the 1960s have been almost exclusively designed to achieve a credible form of employment equality. Institutions and structures with a brief for women's emancipation in other areas have been relatively thin on the ground. An important objective in most states, therefore, has been equal opportunity in employment, at first most often found in the simply expressed goal of equal pay. As experience of the difficulties of achieving equal pay for men and women has been gained, more complex anti-discrimination measures have been introduced. These have been conceptualised in a number of ways, ranging from legislation designed to remove barriers to particular kinds of employment, to more controversial policies, including affirmative action.

It will be some years before a full assessment of the impacts of such initiatives may be made, but so far all the evidence indicates that gaps between men and women's employment chances persist. In particular, equal pay has nowhere been achieved and its main obstacle, occupational sectoralisation, continues. Patterns of occupational sectoralisation whereby women are concentrated in particular economic sectors, normally the less prestigious and less well paid, are the nub of the problem in both types of European state. Recognition that differential employment patterns are the central area of concern is widespread, but rectifying them has proved difficult. Restructuring efforts must centre on provision for training, but this is a long-term process, and women are suffering disadvantages now. Experts in the field regularly warn that the process of change will be a lengthy one, involving as it does alterations in attitudes and life-styles. For women in employment, announcements that another two or three generations will have to pass before real equality is achieved is not welcome news. As a result, equality policies often meet with cynicism or indifference, and mindful of the possibilities of victimisation, women have not made very much use of legislation, with few cases being brought in any of the countries under consideration. Thus, one of the problems of equality legislation is its lack of credibility with client groups.

Further problems are caused by the particular content or environments of the laws. The new equality laws are largely focused upon the labour market but have statute law as their major source. All contain bans on sex discrimination in employment, and in most countries new institutions to oversee the laws have been set up. The laws are remarkably similar in content, with the most substantial efforts having been made where labour shortages were most acute. Many of the most serious difficulties have arisen from the placement of equality statutes in legal and institutional environments which were not designed for the purpose of promoting the interests of disadvantaged groups. Legal arrangements have been a particular inhibition to the effectiveness of the legislation. Equal employment law has varied in its usefulness to women by whether it is situated in an adversarial or inquisitorial system of justice, by where it places the burden of proof, by the procedural forms employed, by problems to do with the collection of evidence, by the availability of information on its use, by the kind of administrative agency it has generated and by the extent to which legal professionals actually understand the meaning of discrimination (Corcoran and Donnelly, 1984) as well as by the responses of the collective bargaining partners.

These variables have been studied in some detail by Jennifer Corcoran and Elaine Donnelly, who investigated the application of the three EEC directives in the practice of law in the members states during 1983. Whilst their conclusions are cautious, they do suggest that inquisitorial systems of justice may be more congenial to the application of anti-discrimination law. In an adversarial system (e.g. Denmark, UK, Greece, Ireland, Netherlands) the judge expects parties to produce all the documents and evidence necessary to prove their case. Procedural forms tend to heighten disputes and the complainant is virtually forced to treat her

employer as an opponent, making difficult the conduct of amic-
able relations after the dispute. And in adversarial systems complainants have problems in getting evidence unless a specific
procedure has been designed. In the inquisitorial system (e.g.
France, Italy, Luxembourg, Belgium), on the other hand, the
court has a basic duty to take an active part in litigation. The judge
directs proceedings, requests documents and witnesses, puts questions to the parties and has a duty to apply the law to the facts of
the case. In practice, the differences between adversarial and
inquisitorial systems may not be that sharp as judges do often
intervene in adversarial systems.

The placement of the burden of proof was found to be an
important constraint in all the states, as it tended in the first
instance to be placed on the complainant. Where this is interpreted to mean that a simple *prima facie* case is to be made then
there are few problems. But proving discrimination is difficult,
with necessary data and documentation often not available.
Hence, laws which require employers to keep full records on their
workforce are important. It would facilitate matters considerably
if the burden of proof were to be placed upon the employer, as it is
in unfair dismissal cases in the UK, for example. But Corcoran
and Donnelly found that this was opposed on the rather unlikely
grounds that numerous women would bring frivolous or vexatious
cases, putting innocent employers to considerable unnecessary
expense.

A further and important impediment to effective legislation
against discrimination has been the role of the economic organisations. Indeed, this has been a crucial obstacle in most of the
states of Western Europe. Employers have yet to be convinced
that making arrangements to accommodate women workers on
equal terms to men is good management practice and are therefore predictably reluctant to support change. But trade unions are
traditional defenders of workers, established to protect disadvantaged groups. Their reluctance to support anti-discrimination policies is therefore more surprising. Collective bargaining
arrangements are sacrosanct in many countries and the support of
the major economic groups is therefore essential to the success of
an equal opportunities programme. Investigations of union attitudes have suggested that much of their opposition is sited in a
resistance to state imposition on traditional preserves. Unions
would prefer to negotiate equal pay and opportunity in the normal
bargaining processes. In practice, however, such considerations
have been given low priority. Often where national union leaders

have committed themselves to equality policy, local negotiators have consistently failed to deliver. And when unemployment rises and recession bites, unions retreat to their traditional concerns (Gaudart and Greve, 1980, 25–28).

Unions have, it should be said, also been sources of good practice. Some have been particularly assiduous in negotiating parental leave, equal pay and conditions, and promotion and training packages which have benefited large numbers of women. And wider-ranging union strategies have often been especially beneficial to women workers. An example is to be found in the Swedish solidary wage policy whereby low-wage earners (i.e. those earning less than 96 per cent of the average wage) receive an across-the-board flat-rate increase in addition to the percentage negotiated for everyone. A result of such policies is that Swedish women workers, whilst not in receipt of equal pay are appreciably closer to it (at 88 per cent of male wages) than are women in most other countries (Cook, 1980, 15). And unions have also been active in other areas of concern to women workers. Recent TUC take-up of the sexual harassment at work issue is an important example, as is union support for abortion liberalisation. The solution for women to the collective bargaining impasse is not to bypass unions but to infiltrate and convert them. Unfortunately that, as we saw in Chapter 5, is not so easily done.

Equality legislation is important to the achievement of women's rights in employment, but there seems to be little chance that laws alone will solve the problem. They are rather, as Elizabeth Meehan (1983, 188) writes, an essential precondition to which must be added political will and political organisation. The strategic problem for women is that the movement for emancipation must proceed on all fronts. Real equality of opportunity will depend upon women's activities across the full range of political arenas, achievement of which is likely to be difficult when women are not yet present in many important institutions and only a token presence in most of the others. Such policy attempts as have been made have not all been half-hearted, however. Many show fairly conclusively that men do respond to women's interests. What they don't apparently do is share power.

Integrating Policy on Women

Women's lack of political power reflects a concomitant lack of a strong social and economic position. Thus, strategies to improve the position of women, if they are to be effective, must involve the state in integrated policies across the cultural, social and economic components of men's and women's lives. The extent to which sex equality is contingent not just on social change but on other areas of social policy has been increasingly recognised by researchers in the area of women and public policy. Whilst most national strategies include a range of fairly similar programmes in the areas of training and employment, attention to cultural and social dimensions of equality between the sexes is often patchy and idiosyncratic. The most evident exception is in the area of abortion policy, where debate over women's reproductive rights has exercised a number of European legislators in recent years. The issue of rape, too, raises important questions about women's sexuality and highlights the cultural as well as the physical dimensions of sexual oppression.

By and large, however, it has proved difficult for feminists to get the less manageable cultural and social issues onto the political agenda. Gelb and Palley (1982) have demonstrated that in the United States feminist success over a particular issue will vary according to whether it is perceived as involving role equity or role change. The more narrowly constructed role-equity issues for which incrementalism and compromise are possible are more likely to be taken up by decision-makers. But issues which underline the extent to which equalising opportunities for men and women involves new roles for both sexes are avoided by American elites. The shape of European legislation on sex equality suggests that similar patterns obtain there.

To the extent that it is a pre-condition for sex equality, women have an objective interest in role change. To the extent that policy-makers refuse to consider the relevant issues, they do not represent the interests of women. Indeed, accounts of state policy on women have shown fairly clearly that policies on women have normally been made in response to needs other than those expressed by women. Randall (1982) and Sapiro (1981) both demonstrate how various state imperatives of economic growth, population replacement and political stability have been the source of much of what we might construe as policy on women. It is these imperatives rather than the actual or potential power of women which have determined the shape of state women's programmes. It is this interplay between power and policy which is the site of the problem the women's movement has had in accommodating the rules by which the political game is played. The women's movement response to an almost unbroken experience of powerlessness has been to eschew strategies of attempting to gain more power in existing structures. Many women feel that such activity will simply perpetuate longstanding patterns of oppression. As a result, considerable theoretical energy has been expended over ways of restructuring power relationships so that they are more participatory, democratic and just (see, for example, Hartsock, 1983; Okin, 1979). The problem is, of course, that such restructuring only occurs when those who seek change obtain power.

Policy on employment equality has taxed the imaginations of legislators. It has led to the establishment of new institutions and agencies and to revisions of longstanding administrative practices. It has not, however, led to the sorts of fundamental change which will be necessary if men and women are to be politically and socially equal. European state structures were established on the assumption that women were controlled rather than for the purposes of such control. Gradually, mechanisms were introduced which gave legal recognition to male dominance of women; gradually, as women came to appreciate the significance and implications of such laws, they fought for their abrogation. Nearly a century and a half of struggle has resulted in the dismantling of much of the gender-specific apparatuses of state repression. What is now required is the transformation of the remaining institutions into a structure capable of accommodating both sexes.

Notes

1. Specifically these were: council directive 75/115/EEC of 10 February 1975 on the approximation of the laws of member states relating to the application of the principle of equal pay for men and women; OJL 45 of 19 February 1975; council directive 76/207/EEC of 9 February 1976 on the implementation of the principle of equal treatment for men and women as regards access to employment, vocational training and promotion and working conditions – OJL 39 of 14 February 1976; council directive (79/7/EEC) of 19 December 1978 on the progressive implementation of the principle of equal treatment for men and women in matters of social security – OJL/6/24 of 10 January 1979.
2. Yugoslavia is distinctive for being the first country to incorporate into its constitution the right to decide freely on child birth.

Bibliography

ACAS (1982), *Annual Report*

Adams, Carolyn T. and Katherine T. Winston (1980), *Mothers at Work: Public Policies in the United States, Sweden and China*, New York and London: Longman

(*ALMANACH*) (1979), *Women and Russia*, London: Sheba Feminist Publishers

Ambassade de France à Londres, Doc./Lon./IX/84, 'Composition of the French Government', 19 July 1984

Atkinson, D., A. Dallin and G. Lapidus (1978), *Women in Russia*, Hassocks: Harvester Press

Banks, J. A., and Olive Banks (1964), 'Feminism and Social Change: A Case Study of a Social Movement', in G. K. Zollschan and W. Hirsch, eds. *Explanations in Social Change*, London: Routledge and Kegan Paul.

Banks, Olive (1981), *Faces of Feminism*, Oxford: Martin Robertson

Barbosa, Madelena (1981), 'Women in Portugal', in Bradshaw (ed.)

Barnes, Samuel H., and Max Kaase (1979), *Political Action: Mass Participation in Five Western Democracies*, Beverly Hills and London: Sage Publications

Barrett, Michele (1980), *Women's Oppression Today*, London: Verso

—— and Mary McIntosh (1982), *The Anti-Social Family*, London: Verso

Batiot, Anne (1979), 'Women as Political Subjects: Notes Towards the Theorization of Women's Liberation'; paper presented at the workshop on 'Women's Movement and New Concepts of Politics', European Consortium for Political Research Joint Sessions, Brussels, 17–21 April, 1979

Baxter, Sandra, and Marjorie Lansing (1980), *Women and Politics: The Invisible Majority*, Ann Arbor: The University of Michigan Press

de Beauvoir, Simone (1949), *The Second Sex* Harmondsworth: Penguin Books, 1972

Beckwith, Karen (1980), 'Women and Parliamentary Politics in Italy, 1946–1979', in H. R. Penniman (ed.)

—— (1983), 'Representation in the Italian Parliament: Isomorphic Representation of Women and Policy Responsiveness to Women's Issues', Paper prepared for the Congrip-NSF Workshop on 'Institutional Performance in Italy', Bellagio, June 14–19

Benn, Melissa, Anna Coote and Tess Gill (1983), 'The Rape Controversy', London: NCCL Rights for Women Unit (pamphlet)

Bidelman, Patrick Kay (1976), 'The Politics of French Feminism: Léon

Richer and the Ligue Française pour le Droit des Femmes, 1882–1891', *Historical Reflections*, 3

Billington, Rosamund (1982), 'Ideology and Feminism: Why the Suffragettes Were "Wild Women"', *Women's Studies International Forum*, Vol. 5, No. 6

Blumer, Herbert (1951), 'Social Movements', in A. M. Lee, ed., *New Outline of the Principles of Sociology*, New York: Barnes and Noble

Bocchio, F., and A. Torchi (1979),, *'L'Acqua in Gabbia' voci di donne dentro il sindicato*, Milan: La Salamandra

Bochel, J. M., and D. T. Denver (1982), *Scottish Election Studies*, Dundee University

Bochachevsky-Chomiak, Martha (1980), 'Socialism and Feminism: The First Stages of Women's Organizations in the Eastern Part of the Austrian Empire', in Yedlin (ed.)

Bogdanor, V. (1984), *What Is Proportional Representation?* Oxford: Martin Robertson

Bonaparth, Ellen, ed. (1982a), *Women, Power and Policy*, New York: Pergamon Press

—— (1982b), 'A Framework for Policy Analysis', in Bonaparth (ed.)

Bouchier, David (1979), 'The De-Radicalisation of Feminism Ideology and Utopia in Action', *Sociology*, Vol. 3, No. 3

—— (1983), 'The Feminist Challenge: The Movement for Women's Liberation in Britain and the USA', London: Macmillan

Bourque, S. C., and J. Grossholtz (1974), 'Politics an Unnatural Practice: Political Science Looks at Female Participation', *Politics and Society*, Winter

Boxer, Marilyn J. and Jean H. Quataert, eds. (1978a), *Socialist Women: European Socialist Feminism in the Nineteenth and Early Twentieth Centuries*, New York: Elsevier

——, —— (1978b), 'The Class and Sex Connection: An Introduction', in Boxer and Quataert (eds.)

—— (1978), 'Socialism Faces Feminism: The Failure of Synthesis in France', in Boxer and Quataert (eds.)

—— (1982), '"First Wave" Feminism in Nineteenth-Century France: Class, Family and Religion', *Women's Studies International Forum*, Vol. 5, No. 6

Bradshaw, Jan, ed. (1981), 'Special Issue: The Women's Liberation Movement—Europe and North America', *Women's Studies International Quarterly*, Vol. 4, No. 4

Branca, Patricia (1978), *Women in Europea Since 1750*, London: Croom Helm

Breitenbach, Esther (1981), 'A Comparative Study of the Women's Trade Union Conference and the Scottish Women's Trade Union Conference', *Feminist Review* 7 Spring, pp. 65–86

—— (1982), *Women Workers in Scotland*, Glasgow: Pressgang

Bridenthal, Renate (1977), 'Women Between the Two World Wars', in Bridenthal and Koonz (ed.)

—— and Claudia Koonz, eds. (1977), *Becoming Visible: Women in European History*, Boston: Houghton Mifflin Company

Brimelow, E. (1981), 'Women in the Civil Service', *Public Administration*, Vol. 4 Autumn

Bristow, Steve (1978), 'Women Councillors', *County Council Gazette*, December

—— (1980), 'Women Councillors: An Explanation of the Underrepresentation of Women in Local Government', *Local Government Studies*, Vol. 6, No. 3

Bryan, Hilary (1984), 'Women and Proportional Representation: The Case Examined', MA Dissertation, Colchester: Essex University

Buckley, Mary (1981), 'Women in the Soviet Union', *Feminist Review*, Summer

Byrne, Paul, and Joni Lovenduski (1978a), 'Sex Equality and the Law in Britain', *British Journal of Law and Society*, Vol. 5, No. 2

——, —— (1978b), 'The Equal Opportunities Commission', *Women's Studies International Quarterly*, Vol. 1

Caine, Barbara (1982), 'Feminism, Suffrage and the Nineteenth-Century English Women's Movement', *Women's Studies International Forum*, Vol. 5, No. 6

Caldwell, Lesley (1982), 'Women, the State and Italy', paper presented to the Conference of the PSA Women's Association, October 1

—— (1983), 'Courses for Women: The Example of the 150 Hours in Italy' *Feminist Review* 14, Summer

Cammet, John M. (1981), 'Communist Women and the Fascist Experience', in Slaughter and Kern (eds.)

Campbell, Beatrix (1984), 'Town Hall Feminism', *New Socialist*, No. 21, November

Caplow, T. (1954), *The Sociology of Work*, London: McGraw Hill

Cassell, J. (1977), *A Group Called Women: Sisterhood and Symbolism in the Feminist Movement*, New York: David McKay

Castles, F. G. (1981), 'Female Representation and the Electoral System', *Politics*, Vol. 1, No. 2

Christy, Carol A. (1983), 'Gender, Employment, and Political Participation in Eleven Nations', paper prepared for delivery at the Annual Meeting of the American Political Science Association, Chicago, September 1–4

Clark, Martin, David Hine and R. E. M. Irving (1974), 'Divorce—Italian Style', *Parliamentary Affairs*, Vol. 27

Cobb, Roger, and Charles D. Elder (1972), *Participation in American Politics: The Dynamics of Agenda Building*, Boston: Allyn and Bacon

Cockburn, Cynthia (1984), 'Trade Unions and the Radicalizing of Socialist Feminism', *Feminist Review* 16, Summer

Colombo, Daniela (1981), 'The Italian Feminist Movement', in Bradshaw (ed.)

COM (83) 8781 Final (1984), 'Progress Report on the Implementation of the New Community Action Programme on the Promotion of Equal Opportunities for Women', Brussels, January

Cook, Alice H. (1980), 'Women in Trade Unions', in International Institute for Labour Studies, *Women and Industrial Relations*, research series No. 56

Coote, Anna, and Beatrix Campbell (1982), *Sweet Freedom: The Struggle for Women's Liberation*, London: Picador

—— and Peter Kellner (1980), 'Hear This, Brother', London: *New Statesman*, pamphlet

Council for Equality (1975), *Statistics about the Position of Women in Finland*, Helsinki

Corcoran, Jennifer (1984), 'Law and the Promotion of Women in the UK', *Equal Opportunities for Women in the United Kingdom and Australia*, Occasional Seminar Papers, Australian Studies Centre, June

—— and Elaine R. Donnelly (1984), 'Report of a Comparative Analysis of the Provisions for Logal Redress in Member States of the European Economic Community in Respect of Article 119 of the Treaty of Rome and the Equal Pay, Equal Treatment and Social Security Directives', prepared on behalf of the Equal Opportunities Commission and the Emancipatieraad; EEC Advisory Committee on Equal Opportunities for Women and Men, February

—— and Joni Lovenduski (1983), 'Women in Decisional Arenas in the United Kingdom', in Zincone (ed.)

Council of Europe (1984), 'The Situation of Women in the Political Process in Europe', Council of Europe Human Rights Division, Strasbourg

Council of Europe (1982), *Equality Between Women and Men*, Strasbourg

Culley, Lorraine (1981), 'Women's Organisation in the Labour Party', *Politics and Power* 3

CREW (Centre for Research on European Women), REPORTS (1981 to 1984), Brussels

Crewe, Ivor (1983), 'The Disturbing Truth behind Labour's Rout', *The Guardian*, 13 June

Crowe, Virginia (1984), 'Equal Opportunity: A Landmark on the Road to Good Resource Management', *RIPA Report*, Summer Vol. 5, No. 2

—— and Jane Matthews (1983), 'Equal Opportunities for Women in Public Sector Employment', *RIPA Report*, Autumn

Currell, Melville (1974), *Political Women*, London: Croom Helm

Dahlerup, Drude (1978), 'Women's Entry into Politics: The Experience of the Danish Local and General Elections 1908–20', *Scandinavian Political Studies*, Vol. 1

—— and Brita Gulli (1983), 'The Impact of the Women's Liberation Movement on Public Policy in Denmark and Norway', paper prepared for the ECPR Joint Sessions of Workshops, Freiburg, March

David, Henry P. (1982), 'Eastern Europe: Pronatalist Policies and Private Behavior', *Population Bulletin*, Vol. 36, No. 6, February

Delamont, Sara (1980), *The Sociology of Women*, London: George Allen and Unwin

Denitch, Bette S. (1976), 'Urbanisation and Women's Roles in Yugoslavia', *Anthropological Quarterly*, No. 47

Denitch, Bogdan (1981), 'Women and Political Power in a Revolutionary Society: The Yugoslav Case', in Epstein and Coser (eds.)

Denver, D. T. (1982), 'Are Labour Selectors Prejudiced Against Women Candidates', *Politics*, Vol. 2, No. 1, April

Diamond, Irene, and Nancy Hartsock (1981), 'Beyond Interests in Politics: A comment on Virginia Sapiro's "When are Interests Interesting? The Problem of Political Representation of Women"', *American Political Science Review*, Spring

Drewry, Gavin, and Jenny Brock (1983), *The Impact of Women on the House of Lords*, Glasgow: CSPP

Dunleavy, Patrick, and Christopher T. Husbands (1984), 'The Social Basis of British Political Alignments in 1983', paper presented to the Annual Conference of the Political Studies Association, Southampton, 4 April 1983

Dunleavy, Patrick and Christopher T. Husbands (1985) *British Democracy at the Crossroads*, London: George Allen and Unwin

Duverger, M. (1955), *The Political Role of Women*, UNESCO

Ecklein, Joan Levin, and Janet Zollinger Giele (1981), 'Women's Lives and Social Policy in East Germany and the United States', *Studies in Comparative Communism*, Vol. XIV, Nos. 2 and 3

Eckmann, Eleonore (1978), 'The New Conception of the Politics of the Modern Feminist Movement: With Special Reference to the New Italian Feminist Movement', paper presented for the Joint Sessions of the ECPR Workshops, Grenoble, April 6–12

—— (1979), 'The Feminist Concept of Politics in the Consultori Practice', paper prepared for the Joint Sessions of the ECPR, Brussels, April 17–21

—— (1983), 'The Impact of the New Italian Women's Movement on Politics and Social Change', paper prepared for the Joint Sessions of the ECPR Freiburg, Federal Republic of Germany, March 20–25

Eduards, Maud (1980), 'The Swedish Woman in Political Life', The Swedish Institute, Mimeo

—— (1981), 'Sweden', in Lovenduski and Hills (eds.)

Einhorn, Barbara (1981), 'Socialist Emancipation: The Women's Movement in the German Democratic Republic', in Bradshaw (ed.)

Ellis, Valerie (1981), *The Role of Trade Unions in the Promotion of Equal Opportunities*, Manchester: Equal Opportunities Commission

Elshtain, J. B. (1981), *Public Man, Private Women*, Princeton: Princeton University Press

Engel, Barbara (1979), 'Women as Revolutionaries: The Case of the

Russian Populists', in Bridenthal and Koonz, *Becoming Visible: Women in European History*, Boston: Houghton Miflin
—— (1978), 'From Separatism to Socialism: Women in the Russian Revolutionary Movements of the 1970s', in Boxer and Quataert (eds.)
Epstein, Cynthia Fuchs (1981), 'Women and Elites: A Cross National Perspective', in Epstein and Coser (eds.)
—— and Rose Laub Coser, eds. (1981), *Access to Power: Cross National Studies of Women and Elites*, London: George Allen and Unwin
Ergas, Yasmine (1982), '1968–79—Feminism and the Italian Party System: Women's Politics in a Decade of Turmoil', *Comparative Politics*, April, Vol. 14
European Trade Union Institute (1983), 'Info 6: Women's Representation in Trade Unions', Brussels
European Women and Men in 1983, Commission of the European Communities, Brussels
Evans, Judith (1980), 'Women and Politics: A Re-Appraisal', *Political Studies*, Vol. XXVIII, No. 2
Evans, Richard J. (1979), *The Feminists*, London: Croom Helm
—— (1980), 'Bourgeois Feminists and Women Socialists in Germany 1894–1914: Lost Opportunity or Inevitable Conflict?', *Women's Studies International Quarterly*, Vol. 3
Evans, Robert R. (1973), *Social Movements*, Chicago: Rand McNally College Publishing Company
Farnsworth, Beatrice (1978), 'Bolshevism, the Women Question and Aleksandra Kollantai', in Boxer and Quataert (eds.)
Fëjto, F. (1974), *A History of the People's Democracies: Eastern Europe since Stalin*, Harmondsworth: Penguin Books
Figes, Eva (1972), *Patriarchal Attitudes*, London: Panther
Firestone, Shulamith (1971), *The Dialectic of Sex*, New York: Bantam
Fistrejnová, Věra (1983), 'Women and Abortion in Eastern Europe (with special reference to Czechoslovakia)', *Journal of Area Studies*, No. 7 Spring
Foverskov, Peter (1977), 'Women in Parliaments: The Causes of Under-representation Exemplified by Denmark and Norway in the 1960s', paper presented to the European Consortium for Political Research, Berlin, March
Fox-Genovese, Elizabeth (1982), 'Placing Women's History in History', *New Left Review*, 133
Francis, J. G., and G. Peele (1978), 'Reflections on Generational Analysis: Is There a Shared Political Perspective Between Men and Women?', *Political Studies*, Vol. XXVI, No. 3
Fransella, Fay, and Kay Frost, (1977) *On Being a Woman*, London: Tavistock Publications
Freeman, Jo (1975), *The Politics of Women's Liberation*, New York and London: Longman
—— ,ed. (1983), *Social Movements of the Sixties and Seventies*, New York and London: Longman

—— (1983a), 'A Model for Analysing the Strategic Options of Social Movement Organisations', in Freeman (ed.)

—— (1983b), 'On the Origins of Social Movements', in Freeman (ed.)

Friedan, Betty (1963), *The Feminine Mystique*, New York: Norton

Froggett, Lynn (1981), 'Feminism and the Italian Trade Unions: L'Aqua in Gabbia: A Summary and Discussion', *Feminist Review*, 8, Summer, pp.

Gallego, Maria Teresa (1983), 'Women's Movement and Democracy in Spain', paper prepared for the ECPR Joint Sessions of Workshops, Freiburg, March

Galli, Giorgio, and Alfonso Prandi (1970), *Patterns of Political Participation in Italy*, New Haven and London: Yale University Press

Gaudart, Dorothea, and Rose Marie Greve (1980), 'Women and Industrial Relations: Framework Paper and Analysis of the Discussions of an International Symposium' (Vienna, September 1978), Geneva: International Labour Organisation

Gelb, Joyce (1984), 'Feminism in Britain: The Politics of Isolation', paper prepared for the Annual Meeting of the American Political Science Association, Washington DC, August 30/September 2

—— and Marian Lief Palley (1982), *Women and Public Policies*, Princeton: Princeton University Press

Gerhard, Ute (1982), 'A Hidden and Complex Heritage: Reflections on the History of Germany's Women's Movements', *Women's Studies International Forum*, Vol. 5, No. 6

Glickman, Rose L. (1978), 'The Russian Factory Woman', in D. Atkinson, A. Dallin, G. Lapidus (eds.)

Goot, M., and E. Reid (1975), *Women and Voting Studies: Mindless Matrons or Sexist Scientism?*, Sage Professional Papers in Comparative Political Sociology

Graham, Ruth (1977), 'Women in the French Revolution', in Bridenthal and Koonz (eds.)

Greenwood, Victoria, and Jock Young (1976), *Abortion in Demand*, London: Pluto Press

Greer, Germaine (1970), *The Female Eunuch*, London: McGibbon and Kee

Grozdanić, Stanislav S. (1980), 'Representation of Women and Their Interests under the Workers Self-Management System in Yugoslavia', in International Institute for Labour Studies, *Women and Industrial Relations*, Research Series, No. 56

Guadagnini, Marila (1980), 'Politics Without Women: The Italian Cases', paper presented to the Joint Sessions of the European Consortium for Political Research, Florence, March

Günter, Hans (1975), 'Trade Unions and Industrial Politics in Western Europe', in Warnecke and Suleiman (eds.)

Gusfield, Joseph R., ed. (1970), *Protest, Reform and Revolt: A Reader in Social Movements*, New York: John Wiley and Sons

Haavio-Mannila, Elina (1979), 'How Women Become Political Actors:

Female Candidates in Finnish Elections', *Scandinavian Political Studies*, Vol. 2, New Series, No. 4

—— (1981), 'Finland', in Lovenduski and Hills (eds.)

Hall, Jane (1981), 'West Germany' in Lovenduski and Hills (eds.)

Harasymiw, Bohdan (1980), 'Have Women's Chances for Political Recruitment in the USSR Really Improved?', in Yedlin (ed.)

Harrison, Reginald J. (1980), *Pluralism and Corporatism*, London: George Allen and Unwin

Hartsock, Nancy (1983), *Money, Sex and Power: Toward a Feminist Historical Materialism*, London: Longman

Hayward, J. E. S., and R. N. Berki (1979), *State and Society in Contemporary Europe*, Oxford: Martin Robertson

Hayward, Jack (1979), 'Interest Groups and the Demand for State Action', in Hayward and Berki (eds.)

Heberle, Rudolf (1951), *Social Movements*, New York: Appleton-Century Crofts

Heitlinger, Alena (1979), *Women and State Socialism: Sex Inequality in the Soviet Union and Czechoslovakia*, London: Macmillan

Hernes, Helga Maria, and Kirsten Voje (1980), 'Women in the Corporate Channel: A Process of Natural Exclusion?', *Scandinavian Political Studies*, Vol. 3, New Series, No. 2

Hill, R. J. (1972), 'Continuity and Change in the USSR Supreme Soviet Elections', *British Journal of Political Science*, No. 1, pp. 47–67

Hills, J. (1978), 'Women In the Labour and Conservative Parties', paper presented to the Annual Conference of the Political Studies Association at Warwick

—— (1981a), 'Britain', in Lovenduski and Hills (eds.)

—— (1981b), 'Candidates, the Impact of Gender', *Parliamentary Affairs*, Vol. 34

Hindell, Keith, and Madeleine Simms (1971), *Abortion Law Reformed*, London: Peter Owen

Hohmann-Dennhardt, Christine (1972), 'The Impact of EC Directives on National Equality Legislation', in Hvidtfeldt *et al.* (eds.)

Hollis, Patricia (1979), *Women in Public Life 1850–1900*, London: George Allen and Unwin

Hoskyns, Catherine (1984), 'Women's Equality and the European Community—A Feminist Perspective', paper prepared for the Annual Conference of the Political Studies Association, April 3–5 and *Feminist Review*, 1985 (forthcoming)

Hough, Jerry F. (1978), 'Women and Women's Issues in Soviet Policy Debates', in D. Atkinson, A. Dallin, G. W. Lapidus (eds.)

—— and M. Fainsod (1979), *How the Soviet Union Is Governed*, Cambridge, Mass.: Harvard University Press

Hough, J. R. (1982), *The French Economy*, London: Croom Helm

Hurwitz, Edith F. (1977), 'The International Sisterhood', in Bridenthal and Koonz (eds)

Huws, Ursula (1985), 'Move Over Brother', *New Socialist*, January

Hvidtfeldt, Kirsten, Kirsten Jorgensen and Ruth Nielsen, eds. (1982), 'Strategies for Integrating Women into the Labour Market', *European Women's Studies in Social Science*, No. 1, Copenhagen

Inglehart, Margaret L. (1981), 'Political Interest in West European Women: An Historical and Empirical Comparative Analysis', *Comparative Political Studies*, Vol. 14, No. 3

Ingelhart, Ronald (1977), *The Silent Revolution*, Princeton: Princeton University Press

Jallinoja, Riitta (1983), 'The Women's Movement in Finland and the Problem of the Definition of Private and Public Issues', paper prepared for the ECPR joint sessions of workshops, Freiburg, March

Jancar, Barbara Wolfe (1978), *Women under Communism*, Baltimore: Johns Hopkins University Press

—— (1981), 'Women in the Yugoslav National Liberation Movement: An Overview', *Studies in Comparative Communism*, Vol. XIV, Nos. 2 and 3

Jaquette, J., ed. (1974), *Women in Politics*, New York: John Wiley and Sons

Jayawardena, Kumari (1983a) 'The Feminist Challenge in the 18th Century', in Mies and Jayawardena (eds.)

—— (1983b), 'Liberalism and the Women's Movement', in Mies and Jayawardena (eds.)

Jeffreys, Sheila (1982), 'Free from All Uninvited Touch of Man': *Women's Studies International Forum*, Vol. 5, No. 6

Jennings, M. Kent, and Barbara G. Farah (1980), 'Ideology, Gender and Political Action: A Cross National Survey', *British Journal of Political Science*, 10

Johnston, T. L. (1981), 'Sweden', in Owen-Smith (ed.)

Johnstone, Diana (1982), 'Liberté, Dignité, Fraternité', *New Statesman*, 23 July

Juusola-Halonen, Elina (1981), 'The Women's Liberation Movement in Finland', in Bradshaw (ed.)

Kaplan, Temma (1977), 'Women and Spanish Anarchism', in Bridenthal and Koonz (eds.)

Kawan, Hildegard, and Barbara Weber (1981), 'Reflections on a Theme: The German Women's Movement Then and Now', in Bradshaw (ed.)

Kern, Robert (1918), 'Margarita Nelken: Women and the Crisis of Spanish Politics', in Slaughter and Kern (eds.)

Killian, Lewis M. (1964), 'Social Movements: A Review of the Field', reproduced in Robert R. Evans (ed.) (1973)

King, Wendel (1956), *Social Movements in the United States*, New York: Random House

Kleinbaum, Abby R. (1977), 'Women in the Age of Light', in Bridenthal and Koonz (eds.)

Kolinsky, Eva (1984a), 'The Greens in Germany: Prospects of a Small Party', *Parliamentary Affairs*, Vol. 37, Part 4

—— (1984b), *Parties, Opposition and Society in West Germany*, London: Croom Helm

Koonz, Claudia (1977), 'Mothers in the Fatherland: Women in Nazi Germany', in Bridenthal and Koonz (eds.)

Kuhn, A., and A. M. Wolpe (1978), *Feminism and Materialism*, London: Routledge and Kegan Paul

Lafferty, William M. (1978) 'Social Development and Political Participation: Class, Organizations and Sex', *Scandinavian Political Studies*, Vol. 1, New Series, No. 4

Lafleur, Ingrun (1978), 'Five Socialist Women: Traditional Conflicts and Socialist Visions in Austria, 1893–1934', in Boxer and Quataert (eds.)

Lapidus, G. W. (1975a), 'USSR Women at Work: Changing Patterns', *Industrial Relations*, Vol. 14, No. 2, May

—— (1975b), 'Political Mobilization, Participation and Leadership: Women in Soviet Politics', *Comparative Politics*, Vol. 8, pp. 90–118

—— (1976), 'Changing Women's Role in the USSR', in L. Iglitzin and R. Ross (eds.), *Women in Soviet Society*, London: University of California Press

—— (1978), *Women in Soviet Society: Equality, Development and Social Change*, Berkeley: University of California Press

La Vigna, Claire (1978) 'The Marxist Ambivalence Towards Women: Between Socialism and Feminism in the Italian Socialist Party', in Boxer and Quataert (eds.)

Levine, June (1982), *Sisters: The Personal Story of an Irish Feminist*, Dublin: Ward River Press

Lewenhak, Sheila (1977), *Women and Trade Unions*, London: Ernest Benn

Lewis, Jane, ed. (1983a), *Women's Welfare, Women's Rights*, London and Canberra: Croom Helm

—— (1983b), 'Introduction', in Lewis (ed.)

Lorwin, Val R. (1978), 'Decision-Taking in Unions: the Absence of Women', *Colloque Jean Meynaud*, Brussels

Lovenduski, Joni (1981a), 'The USSR', in Lovenduski and Hills (eds.)

—— (1981b), 'Toward the Emasculation of Political Science', in Dale Spender, ed. *Men's Studies Modified*, Oxford: Pergamon Press

—— (1984), 'A Political Determinant of Abortion Policy', paper presented to the ECPR Joint Sessions of Workshops, Salzburg, April 13–18

—— and Jill Hills, eds. (1981), *The Politics of the Second Electorate: Women and Public Participation*, London: Routledge and Kegan Paul

Lowi, T. J. (1964), 'American Business, Public Policy, Case Studies and Political Theory', *World Politics*, Vol. 16, No. 4

Mackie, L. and T. Pattullo (1977), *Women and Work*, London: Tavistock

Maher, Janet E. (1980), 'The Social Composition of Women Deputies in Soviet Elective Politics: A Preliminary Analysis of Official Biographies', in Yedlin (ed.)

Marks, Elaine, and Isabelle de Courtivron, eds. (1980) *New French Feminism: An Anthology*, Amherst: University of Massachussetts Press

Marsh, David, and Joanna Chambers (1981), *Abortion Politics*, London: Junction Books

Marten, Marianne (1984), 'The New Politics: Political Responsiveness to the Feminist Campaign for Abortion—A Comparative Study of the Italian and West German Abortion Policies', paper prepared for the ECPR Joint Sessions of Workshops, Salzburg, 13–18 April

Matsell, C. (1981), 'Spain', in Lovenduski and Hills (eds.)

Meehan, Elizabeth (1982), 'Implementing Equal Opportunity Policies: Some British American Comparisons', *Politics*, Vol. 2, No. 1, April

—— (1983a), 'Equal Opportunity Policies: Some Implications for Women of Contrasts Between Enforcement Bodies in Britain and the USA', in Lewis (ed.)

—— (1983b), 'The Priorities of the Equal Opportunities Commission', *Political Quarterly*, Jan./Mar.

—— (1985) *Women's Rights at Work: Campaigns and Policy in Britain and the United States*, Basingstoke: Macmillan.

Michel, Andre (1977), 'Family Models of the Future', in Bridenthal and Koonz (eds.)

Mickiewicz, Ellen (1971), 'The Status of Soviet Women' (review article), *Problems of Communism*, pp. 59–62.

Middleton, Lucy, ed. (1977), *Women in the Labour Movement: The British Experience* London: Croom Helm

Mies, Maria (1983), 'Marxist Socialism and Women's Emancipation: The Proletarian Women's Movement in Germany 1860–1919', in Mies and Jayawardena (eds.)

—— and Kumari Jayawardena, eds. (1983), *Feminism in Europe: Liberal and Social Strategies 1789–1919*, The Hague: Institute of Social Studies

Miles, Angela (1981), 'The Integrative Principle in North American Feminist Radicalism: Value Basis of a New Feminism', in Bradshaw (ed.)

Millett, K. (1972), *Sexual Politics*, London: Abaccus

Mitchell, Juliet (1966), 'Women: The Longest Revolution', *New Left Review* 40

—— (1971), *Women's Estate*, Harmondsworth: Penguin Books Ltd

—— (1974), *Psychoanalysis and Feminism*, London: Penguin

Moller, Grethe Fenger (1980), 'Women in Danish Politics', *Danish Journal*, special issue on 'Women in Denmark'

Molyneux, Maxine (1981), 'Socialist Societies Old and New: Progress Toward Women's Emancipation', *Feminist Review* 8, Summer

Moon, S. Joan (1978), 'Feminism and Socialism: The Utopian Synthesis of Flora Tristan' in Boxer and Quataert (eds.)

Moore, Lindy (1982), 'Feminists and Feminity: A Case Study of WPSU Propaganda and Local Response at a Scottish By-Election', *Women's Studies International Forum*, Vol. 5, No. 6

Moreau-Burles, Marie-Ange, and Mariette Sineau (1983), 'Women's Presence in Norm Development Structures in French Labour Law', in Zincone (ed.)

Moses, Joel C. (1976), 'Indoctrination as a Female Political Role in the Soviet Union', *Comparative Politics*, Vol. 8, July

Mossink, Marijke (1980), 'Emancipation or Liberation? Government Emancipation Policy and the Feminist Movement', Joint Sessions of the Euoprean Consortium for Political Research, Florence, 25–30 March

Mossuz-Lavau, Janine (1984), 'Pouvoir de droite, pouvoir de gauche et problèmes de l'avortement en France, 1973–1983', paper prepared for the Joint Sessions of the ECPR, Salzburg, April 13–18

—— and Mariette Sineau (1981), 'France', in Lovenduski and Hills (eds.)

——, —— (1983) *Enquête sur les femmes et la politique en France*, Paris: Presse Universitaires de France, coll. Recherches Politiques

McBride, Theresa M. (1977), 'Women's Work and Industrialisation', in Bridenthal and Koonz (eds.)

McDougall, Mary Lynn (1977), 'Working Class Women during the Industrial Revolution, 1780–1914', in Bridenthal and Koonz (eds.)

McIntosh, Mary (1978), 'The State and the Oppression of Women', in Kuhn and Volpe (eds.)

McKenzie, Diana (1984), 'Bigger Gate', *The Guardian*, May 25

Nielsen, Ruth (1982), 'Transferrability of Equal Opportunities Legislation', in Hvidtfeldt *et al.* (eds.)

Nowotny, Helga (1981), 'Women in Public Life in Austria', in Epstein and Coser (eds.)

O'Brien, Mary (1981), *The Politics of Reproduction*, London: Routledge and Kegan Paul

O'Neill, W. L. (1969), *The Woman's Movement: Feminism in the United States and Britain*, London: George Allen and Unwin

OECD (1981), 'Review of Policies for Equality of Opportunity, National Report of Finland'

Okin, Susan Moller (1979), *Women in Western Political Thought*, Princeton: Princeton University Press

Outshoorn, Joyce (1983), 'The Women's Movement and Abortion Policy in the Netherlands', paper prepared for ECPR Joint Sessions of Workshops, Freiburg

Owen-Smith, E. (1981), *Trade Unions in the Developed Economies*, London: Croom Helm

Pattullo, Polly (1983), *Judging Women*, London: NCCL

Paulson, Ross Evans (1973) *Women's Suffrage and Prohibition: A Comparative Study of Equality and Social Control*, Glenview Illinois: Scott Foresman and Company

PE 86.199/fin/C (1984), 'Report Tabled by the Committee of Enquiry into the Situation of Women in Europe', European Parliament Working Documents 1983–1984. 5 January

Peattie, Lisa, and Martin Rein (1983), *Women's Claims: A Study in Political Economy*, Oxford: Oxford University Press

Penniman, H. R. (1977), *Italy at the Polls 1976*, Washington DC: American Enterprise Institute

——, ed. (1980), *Italy at the Polls 1979*, Washington and London: American Enterprise Institute

Pereira, Berengere Marqus (1984), 'Ideology of the Common Good and the Process of Politicisation of Abortion in Belgium', paper prepared for the Joint Sessions of the ECPR, Salzburg, April 13–18

Pinder, P. (1969), *Women at Work*, PEP Broadsheet N. 512, May, p. 631; quoted in Ellis (1981)

Poggi, Gianfranco, ed. (1968), *L'Organizzazione partitica del PCI e della DC*, Bologna: Il Mulino

Pope, Barbara Corrado (1977), 'Leisured Women in the Nineteenth Century', in Bridenthal and Koonz (eds.)

Pridham, Geoffrey (1981), 'Terrorism and the State in West Germany during the 1970s: A Threat to Stability or a Case of Political Over-Reaction', in Juliet Lodge (ed.), *Terrorism: A Challenge to the State*, Oxford: Martin Robertson

Putnam, R. (1976), *The Comparative Study of Political Elites*, Englewood Cliffs, New Jersey: Prentice-Hall

Quataert, Jean (1978), 'Unequal Partners in an Uneasy Alliance: Women and the Working Class in Imperial Germany', in Boxer and Quataert

Rague-Arias, Maria-Jose (1981), 'Spain: Feminism in Our Time', in Bradshaw (ed.)

Randzio-Plath, Christa, and Ursula Rust (1983), 'Decisional Arenas and Women's Work in the Federal Republic of Germany', in G. Zincone (ed.)

Randall, Vicky (1982), *Women and Politics*, London and Basingstoke: Macmillan

Rasmussen, Janet E. (1982), 'Sisters Across the Sea: Early Norwegian Feminists and Their American Connections', *Women's Studies International Forum*, Vol. 5, No. 6

Register, Cheri (1982), 'Motherhood at Center: Ellen Key's Social Vision', *Women's Studies International Forum*, Vol. 5, No. 6

de Reincourt, Amaury (1974), *Women and Power in History*, Bath: Honeyglen Publishing

Rights of Women Europe (1983), *Women's Rights and the EEC*, London: Rights of Women Europe

Rosenthal, B. G. (1977) 'Love on the Tractor: Women in the Russian Revolution and After', in Bridenthal and Koonz (eds.)

Rowbotham, Sheila (1973), *Women's Consciousness, Man's World*, Harmondsworth: Penguin

—— (1979), 'The Women's Movement and Organising for Socialism', in Rowbotham *et al.* (eds.)

—— , L. Segal and H. Wainwright (1979), *Beyond the Fragments*, London: Merlin Press

Sacks, Michael Paul (1978), 'Women in the Industrial Labour Force', in D. Atkinson, A. Dallin, G. Lapidus (eds.)

Salisbury, Robert H. (1975), 'The Workshop: Research on Political Participation', *American Journal of Political Science*, XIX, 2

De Santis, Guiseppina, and Giovanna Zincone (1983), 'Women at Work in Italy: An Institutional Approach', in G. Zincone (ed.)

Sanzone, Donna S. (1981), 'Women in Politics: A Study of Political Leadership in the United Kingdom, France and the Federal Republic of Germany', in Epstein and Coser (eds.)

Sapiro, Virginia (1981) 'When Are Interests Interesting? The Problem of Political Representation of Women', *American Political Science Review*, Vol. 75

Sauter-Bailliet, Theresia (1981), 'The Feminist Movement in France', in Bradshaw (ed.)

Schlaeger, Hilke (1978), 'The West German Women's Movement', *New German Critique*, Vol. 13

Schmitter, Philippe C. (1974), 'Still the Century of Corporatism', *The Review of Politics*, Vol. 36, No. 1

Scott, Hilda (1982), *Sweden's Right to Be Human*, New York: M. E. Sharpe

Seligman, L., C. Kim and R. Smith (1974), *Patterns of Recruitment*, Chicago: Rand McNally

Shaffer, Harry G. (1981), *Women in the two Germanies: A Comparative Study of a Socialist and a Non-Socialist Society*, New York: Pergamon

Siltanen, Janet, and Michelle Stanworth, eds. (1984a), *Women and the Public Sphere: A Critique of Sociology and Politics*, London: Hutchinson

—— , —— (1984b), 'The Politics of Private Women and Public Man', in Siltanen and Stanworth (eds.)

Sineau, Mariette (1983), 'French Women in Politics: Stagnation or Change?', *Journal of Area Studies*, No. 7. Spring

Skard, Torild (1981), 'Progress for Women: Increased Female Representation in Political Elites in Norway', in Epstein and Coser (eds.)

Slaughter, Jane (181), 'Humanism versus Feminism in the Socialist Movement: The Life of Angelica Balabanoff', in Slaughter and Kern (eds.)

—— and Robert Kern, eds. (1981), *European Women on the Left: Socialism, Feminism and the Problems Faced by Political Women, 1880 to the Present* London: Greenwood Press

Smith, Gordon (1980), *Politics in Western Europe*, London: Heinemann Educational Books. Third Edition

Sowerwine, Charles (1982), *Sisters or Citizens? Women and Socialism in France since 1876*, Cambridge: Cambridge University Press

Spender, Dale (1983), *There's Always Been a Women's Movement this Century*, London: Routledge and Kegan Paul

Springer, Beverley Tanner (1981), 'Anna Kuliscioff: Russian Revolutionist, Italian Feminist', in Slaughter and Kern (eds.)

Srirajyam, Sinha (1983), *A Story about Soviet Women*, Moscow: Novosti Press Agency Publishing House

Sokolowska, Magdelena (1981), 'Women in Decision-Making Elites: The Case of Poland', in Epstein and Coser (eds.)

Stacey, Margaret and Marion Price (1981), *Women, Power and Politics*, London and New York: Tavistock

Stephenson, Jill (1975), *Women and Nazi Society*, London: Croom Helm

Stern, Bernhard J. (1934), 'Women, Position in Society: Historical', in *Encyclopaedia of the Social Sciences*, XV

Stites, Richard (1980), 'The Women's Liberation Issue in Nineteenth-Century Soviet Russia', in Yedlin (ed.)

Sward, Stefan (1984), 'The Moral Dimension of Politics and Abortion on Demand in Sweden', paper prepared for the Joint Sessions of the ECPR, Salzburg, April 13–18

Tatalovich, Raymond, and Byron W. Daynes (1981), 'The Politics of Abortion: A Study of Community Conflict in Public Policy-Making', New York: Praegue

Thom, Betsy (1981), 'Women in International Organisations: Room at the Top. The Situation in some United Nations Organisations', in Epstein and Coser (eds.)

Threlfall, Monica (1982), 'Women in Political Elites in Spain', Council of Europe Study on Women in Political Elites

—— (1985) 'Politics and the Women's Movement in Spain', paper presented to the Annual Conference of the Political Studies Association, 16–18 April

Tilly, Louise A. and Joan W. Scott (1978), *Women, Work and Family*, New York: Holt, Rinehart and Winston

Torchi, Antonia (1981), 'Feminist Responses to the Book', *Feminist Review*, 8, Summer

TUC (1981), *Annual Report* London: TUC

Vallance, Elizabeth (1979), *Women in the House: A Study of Women Members of Parliament*, London: The Athlone Press

—— (1981), 'Women Candidates and Elector Preference', *Politics*, Vol. 1, No. 2, November

—— (1984), 'Women Candidates in the 1983 General Election', *Parliamentary Affairs*, Vol. 37, part 3

—— (1985) 'Do Women Make a Difference in Politics? The European Parliament Examined', paper presented to the Annual Conference of the Political Studies Association, 16–18 April

Vann, Richard T. (1977), 'Women in Pre-Industrial Capitalism', in Bridenthal and Koonz (eds.)

Vasileva, Professor Dr Tsveta (undated), 'The Participation of Women in the Bulgarian Political Life', Mimeo

Vedder-Shults, Nancy (1978), 'Introduction', to Schlaeger

Verba, Sidney, Norman H. Nie, Jae-on Kim (1978), *Participation and*

Political Equality: A Seven Nation Comparison, Cambridge: Cambridge University Press
de Vries, Petra (1981), 'Feminism in the Netherlands', in Bradshaw (ed.)
Warnecke, Steven J. and Ezra N. Suleiman (1975), *Industrial Politics in Western Europe*, New York: Praeger
Weber, M. (1981), 'Italy', in Lovenduski and Hills (eds.)
Weir, Angela, and Mary McIntosh (1982), 'Towards a Wages Strategy for Women', *Feminist Review*, 10
Wertman, Douglas (1977), 'The Italian Electoral Process: The Elections of June 1976', in Penniman (ed.)
White, Stephen (1979), *Political Culture and Soviet Politics*, London: Macmillan
Whittaker, Cynthia H. (1976), 'The Women's Movement during the Reign of Alexander II: A Case Study in Russian Liberalism', *Journal of Modern History*, 48, June
Wikert, Christl, Brigitte Hamburger and Marie Lineau (1982), 'Helene Stöcker and the Bund Für Muttershcutz (The Society for the Protection of Motherhood', *Women's Studies International Forum*, Vol. 5, No. 6
Wiik, Jorum (1984), 'A Feminist Perspective on Abortion Policy in Norway', paper prepared for the Joint Sessions of the ECPR, Salzburg, April 13–18
Willenbacher-Bahlmann, Barbara (1982), 'Social Security by Divorce Law?', in Hvidfeldt, *et al.*, (eds.)
Wilson, Elizabeth (1980), *Only Half-way to Paradise: Women in Post-War Britain 1945–1968*, London: Tavistock
Wolchik, Sharon L. (1981a), 'Ideology and Equality: The Status of Women in Eastern and Western Europe', *Comparative Political Studies*, Vol. 13, No. 4, January
—— (1981b), 'Eastern Europe', in Lovenduski and Hills (eds.)
—— (1981c), 'Elite Strategy toward Women in Czechoslovakia: Liberation or Mobilization?', *Studies in Comparative Communism*, Vol. XIV, Nos. 2 and 3, Summer/Autumn
Women of Europe, (1978–84) Nos. 1–36, Supplements 1–16, Brussels: Commission of the European Communities
Women in Portugal (1981), Supplement No. 11 to Women of Europe, Brussels: Commission of the European Communities
Women in Spain (1981), Supplement No. 8 to *Women of Europe*, Brussels: Commission of the European Communities
Yedlin, Tova, ed. (1980), *Women in Eastern Europe and the Soviet Union*, New York: Praeger
Yemelyanova, Y. D. (1975), 'The Social and Political Activity of Soviet Women', in *Soviet Women: Some Aspects of the Status of Women in the USSR*, Moscow: Progress Publishers
Zald, Mayer N., and Roberta Ash (1966), 'Social Movement Organizations: Growth, Decay and Change', in Joseph R. Gusfield (ed.) (1970)

Zincone, Giovanna, ed. (1983) *Decision-Making Arenas Affecting Women at Work in Four European Countries*, final report to Directorate-General Employment, Social Affairs and Education of the Commission of the European Community

Index

314